Ove Arup   Philosophy of Design

Ove Arup   Philosophy of Design

Essays   1942–1981

Edited by Nigel Tonks

PRESTEL

Munich · London · New York

Contents

6	Foreword, Derek Sugden
8	Introduction, Nigel Tonks
15	Notes on the Text
19	Science and World Planning, 1942
22	Shell Construction, 1947
27	The Practice of Building, 1954
34	Structural 'Honesty', 1954
42	The Integration of Structure and Architecture, 1955
45	Modern Architecture: The Structural Fallacy, 1955
50	Structure in Relation to Architecture, 1957
53	The Education of Engineers, 1958
58	The Architect and the Engineer, 1959
64	An Account of Progress in Reinforced Concrete Design, 1961
68	Coventry Cathedral: How the Plan Took Shape, 1962
70	The Design of Bridges, 1964
82	An Artist in Small Matters, 1964
91	The Problem of Producing Quality in Building, 1965
96	The ABC of Building Design, 1965
99	Art and Architecture, 1966
108	Builder Extraordinary, 1966
116	Aesthetics and the Engineer, 1966
122	Architecture Is Sick: Should It Be Revived?, 1967
127	Advances in Engineering, 1967
130	Teams for Total Design, 1968
133	The World of the Structural Engineer, 1968
147	An Engineer Looks at Architecture, 1969
151	Architects, Engineers and Builders, 1970
161	The Key Speech, 1970
169	The Architect's Human Role, 1970
174	I Am Not a Prophet, 1970
177	Future Problems Facing the Designer, 1971
182	The Built Environment, 1972
197	Institution of Structural Engineers Gold Medal Speech, 1973
200	Co-Operation between Architects and Allied Professions, 1975
202	The Building Centre, 1978
206	The Engineer Looks Back, 1979
216	Thinking and Getting Things Done, 1981
219	What I Believe, undated
221	Index
223	Picture Credits/Permissions for Texts
224	Acknowledgments

Foreword

Dem Kind im Manne:
'Im echten Manne ist ein
Kind versteckt: das will spielen.'

To the child in man:
'In true man a child is hidden:
that wants to play.'

Friedrich Nietzsche

I first met Ove Arup in 1953, when he interviewed me for a job. The experience was quintessentially Arup: 'What shall I ask you?' he began. A somewhat disconcerting question. I was soon to learn that this approach in many ways defined Ove Arup the man and Ove Arup the engineer. I found him intriguing.

I had actually thought of giving up engineering and doing a degree in English. I'd had two or three interviews for jobs not long before, all of which were very depressing, and I couldn't think of anything more different than my interview with Ove. It was extraordinary and refreshing. He was obviously saying what he thought, as he shuffled his papers and asked me embarrassing questions.

To his first question I answered, 'You could ask me what I've done', and then described for him my year on site with a contractor and five years' experience with another consultant. He said, 'Oh, I'm sure that's very important but if you meet an architect, can you *design* things' – and he waved his arms – 'can you *design* a structure?' He shuffled his papers some more, then suddenly looked up and said, 'Are you intelligent? ... Oh, that's a silly question, isn't it?' Then he said, 'Well, I think you've got a nice sort of face and will fit in. How much do you want?'

Joining Arup changed my life entirely. The atmosphere was so different from my previous two firms, absolutely marvellous. It was led by Ove Arup, Ronald Jenkins, Geoffrey Wood and Peter Dunican, and it was only forty-strong. Now it's 10,000.

You were, in many ways, left on your own. Although there was a general direction, and one absorbed very quickly the ethos of the firm, you were left to your own devices. There were checks, of course, but you were given an enormous amount of freedom. I'd been there about a week when an Austrian engineer with some drawing office experience came up to me and said, 'Derek, what are the rules?' I said, 'What do you mean, the rules?' He said, 'What are the drawing office rules?' I said, 'There aren't any, it's not that sort of place.' He told me that at the other firms he'd been with, in Germany and Austria, they gave you a book of rules. He was all at sea without a book of drawing-office rules. I said, 'Well, this isn't the same at all. As long as you draw it properly and make it clear, that's all that matters.'

Ronald Hobbs (one of the original partners of Arup Associates) and I met with another chap who'd been with us some while but wasn't happy. He complained that he wasn't being given proper authority. Hobbs told him: 'In this firm, authority is lying around knee-deep; all you have to do is bend over and pick it up!' That summed up the atmosphere. The idea to create a staff-owning partnership was, in a way, a financial definition of the atmosphere that Ove had created. This was an idea developed together by Peter Dunican and Ronald Hobbs. It was terrific; to feel you're part of a partnership and not working for some shareholders.

The firm had many facets. There was new thinking. Ove was so keen on what he called 'Total Design'. Not just thinking of the engineer making a building conceived by the architect to stay up, but that the structure, the mechanical engineering, the electrical engineering – and every part of it – contributed to the anatomy of the building. His approach was to pursue this joint design where you involved all the professions right from the start.

He developed a very strong relationship with all the architects of the modern movement. They came to Arup for this holistic approach to the work, for the atmosphere of freethinking and for some brilliant people: particularly Ronald Jenkins, who made an enormous contribution to the analysis of shells and indeterminate structures. There were these two sides to the practice: not only a feel for architecture and for the total building but also an extraordinary ability to analyse structures. That combination was something very unusual in consulting and engineering.

Arup Associates was created in 1963. That was an innovation, the idea of an engineering firm having a multi-disciplinary approach. There were other firms, but they had sprung from architectural practices. Some eminent architects were concerned that setting up Arup Associates was in competition with them and so didn't go to Arup for the next job. Ove wrote to them to say: 'Our responsibility is to architecture, not to the architect.'

He could be extraordinarily blunt, but he was very open and honest, said exactly what he thought, which sometimes people found disturbing. He had enormous influence and, to a certain extent, a rather special sort of charm.

Throughout his essays, odd bits of quotations and verse appear, often in German, particularly Kant's 'Das Ding an sich'. This was very characteristic of him. One of his favourite anecdotes was 'Umgekehrt ist auch was wert', or 'the other way around may be equally sound' – a reflective criticism and acknowledgement that his views were by no means absolute. In one essay he describes himself as 'one of those unfortunate people who must see a thing from all sides'. Unsurprisingly, there are within his lectures quite a few instances of him saying, 'on the other hand …'. It was a phrase you heard often when you talked to him. Someone once commented that perhaps Ove 'did not have enough hands'.

Philosophical and practical, conformist and anarchist, complex and uncomplicated, serious and playful, wise and impetuous, a spiritual materialist: these are all descriptions of an exceptional man. Working with him was both a challenge and a delight.

This collection provides an insight into the character and thinking of this philosopher-engineer, whose remarkable contribution to engineering and design continues today.

Derek Sugden, *former associate of Ove Arup & Partners and founding partner of Arup Associates and Arup Acoustics*

Introduction

The best human endeavour: that which produces outstanding quality, delight, the great works of art, the really human and satisfying environment; that which lifts humanity above the soulless efficiency of an ant-heap [...] is rare and cannot be bought. The driving force behind it is passion for perfection, a dream of a better world, an artistic urge [...] mixed in various proportions with ambition, dreams of fame, recognition, applause.

Ove Arup, 'The World of the Structural Engineer'

'A bit of a dreamer' (see 'The World of the Structural Engineer')

This collection gathers together, for the first time, original essays, lectures and interview notes by one of the twentieth century's most celebrated engineers, Ove Nyquist Arup (1895–1988). Ove's name is associated with the Sydney Opera House and with the firm of consulting engineers known as Arup, which continues to realise ground-breaking projects around the world.

Ove pioneered new ways of working and the use of new materials in the built environment, and was a fundamental contributor to the language of modern architecture. He was also a philosopher, who sought to master the art of building and to inspire others through sharing his vision. This collection of material, written between 1942 and 1981, provides engineers, architects, designers and scholars with an insight into his deeply felt concern for quality of design in the built environment.

Ove's career spanned five decades, during a time of great political, social and technological upheaval in the middle of the twentieth century. He designed and built buildings, bridges and civil infrastructure. Towards the end of his career, his influence was widely recognised by the industry: in 1966 the Royal Institution of British Architects awarded him its Gold Medal (see 'Art and Architecture'); in 1971 he was knighted; in 1972 he spoke at the inauguration of the Building Services Engineering Society (see 'The Built Environment'); and the following year the Institution of Structural Engineers awarded him its Gold Medal (see 'Institution of Structural Engineers Gold Medal Speech'). Inscribed on the medal are the words: 'Awarded to Ove Nyquist Arup for his contributions to structural engineering through his rare ability to influence the thoughts of his colleagues, engineers and architects alike in fundamental matters of form, function and structure.'

The broad philosophical sweep played out in these papers and the universality of themes such as quality, unity, delight, value, collaboration and

Ove on Coventry Cathedral Roof, 1962

Ove at the Penguin Pool, London Zoo

the influence of our environment continue to be pertinent in any creative arena. This is remarkable, considering the advances in construction technique that have occurred during the fifty years since much of this material was written. Modular construction methods, systematisation and prefabrication, continually develop. The speed of construction too has increased, and costs have been reduced. Quality control is more precise. Build cost is more closely scrutinised. Analytical techniques, predictive testing and fabrication methods are more advanced. These factors, combined with developments in heating, cooling, electric lighting and façade design, have led to new forms of architecture, enabling us to build almost anything in any environment. The questions that Ove posed are as pressing as ever: with all this increasing capability, what should we build, what type of environment do we want?

Philosophy and engineering

Ove was born to Danish parents in Newcastle upon Tyne, but his family moved to Germany, where he went to school briefly in Hamburg, before being sent to boarding-school in Denmark. He went on to study philosophy at Copenhagen University but became disillusioned with the inward-looking nature of academia and felt compelled to combine thinking with doing: 'to create anything which was good of its kind would give satisfaction' ('An Artist in Small Matters'). His friends were mostly artists, but he doubted he had the artistic ability to become a great artist or architect. With a feeling for mathematics, he turned instead to the applied sciences and graduated in engineering from the Polyteknisk Læreanstalt, Copenhagen, in 1922 – the same year that Le Corbusier published his seminal work *Vers une Architecture*.

Ove joined the civil engineering contractors Christiani and Nielsen, who were pioneers in quay design and marine structures, and after two years working in Hamburg moved to their London office. In 1934 he joined the construction company J. L. Kier & Co. as director and chief designer to work on building projects. Just before the Second World War a number of architectural *émigrés* had arrived in Britain from Europe. Their outlook was inspired by Le Corbusier, the International Style and the teachings of the Bauhaus. They were now enthusiastic to use new materials and to express new forms in building. They were drawn to Ove by his expertise with concrete (at the time still an emerging technology in buildings) and by his desire to experiment with it. However, unusually for an engineer, it was

Original *Times* supplement on Coventry Cathedral: 'How the Plan Took Shape', 25 May 1962

Ove's background in philosophy and interest in the arts which gave him the ability to understand and sympathise with the aims of the architect, breathing life into his technical skills and ambition. These factors mobilised 'intuition, invention, ingenuity' ('The Problem of Producing Quality in Building') to 'arrive at proposals which will further the architect's wishes' ('The Architect and the Engineer').

In 1935 Ove became a member of the executive committee of the Modern Architectural Research group (MARS), which drew him closer to the world of architecture. He visited Le Corbusier's Swiss Pavilion in Paris, which made an impression on him (see 'The World of the Structural Engineer'). His collaboration with Berthold Lubetkin and Tecton during the 1930s resulted in a number of buildings that continue to be celebrated today: the Penguin Pool (1934) and Elephant Enclosure (1935) at London Zoo, Highpoint flats, Highgate (1935), and the Finsbury Health Centre, London (1938). By the mid-twentieth century Ove was collaborating with Ernö Goldfinger, Wells Coates, Maxwell Fry, and Yorke, Rosenberg & Mardall.

After the war Ove felt that the commercial pressures experienced within the contracting industry hampered his freedom to explore new ideas. He moved away from combined contracting-and-consulting into a pure consulting role so that he could experiment more freely, and in 1946 he founded the firm of Ove Arup & Partners, Consulting Engineers. Notable projects included his collaboration with Sir Basil Spence on Coventry Cathedral and with Jørn Utzon on the Sydney Opera House. He personally supervised the design and construction of Durham's Kingsgate Bridge in 1963.

Ove Arup and Partners became the test-bed for Ove's philosophy of 'Total Design'. What began as a firm of structural and civil engineers grew to embrace technical specialists of every kind necessary for building. This approach broke new ground in 1963, when Arup Associates was formed, separately from the engineering practice, as a partnership of architects and engineers working on an equal basis as building designers.

Between 1966 and 1977 ownership was transferred from the company's partners to employee and charitable trusts, in recognition that the firm was defined by shared ideals. During this time, senior colleagues persuaded Ove to set down his ideas about the firm in an explicit statement, which became an address to staff known as 'The Key Speech'. Forty years on, it continues to be a touchstone for future generations of Arup employees.

In 1971, the year before the opening of the Sydney Opera House, the firm won the design competition for the Centre Pompidou in Paris, cementing Arup's place on the international architectural stage. Its central role in the wave of British Hi-Tech design that followed was testimony to the advancing technical virtuosity and escalation of specialist expertise in building design and construction.

Aims and means

It is beyond the scope of this introduction to do justice to the many themes raised in these texts. While Ove's writing is not technically difficult to appreciate, it can be dense. 'The World of the Structural Engineer' is a lecture that would have taken over an hour to deliver (in a pronounced Danish accent), and which contains over 100 provocations worthy of debate. A degree of commonality builds, however, throughout the works (in some cases there is repetition, as successful passages are re-worked into alternative approaches to familiar themes).

Much of Ove's thinking is concerned with two principal areas: the *aims* and the *means* of building. He considered the *aims* to be the most important and most difficult to agree on. He believed that engineers, in particular, should have a greater appreciation of the aims of their work: 'Engineers have a big role to play in this discussion about aims […] it is no good doing things which serve no useful purpose or are harmful to humanity' ('The Built Environment'). He was sensitive to the influence that the built environment has on people, as 'a constant source of happiness or misery' ('The Problem of Producing Quality in Building'). The chief aim of building was to meet the needs of society by building a better environment, efficiently.

Quality was crucial to the whole endeavour and an end in itself. In 'The Key Speech' Ove exhorts: 'for our own sake we need the stimulation produced by excellence.'

The challenge of defining quality, what is *good*, is at the core of much of Ove's thinking. He sought a 'composite quality', one that was 'the best possible compromise between conflicting aims' ('What I Believe'). Revisiting Sir Henry Wotton's interpretation of Vitruvius, Ove held that 'We demand of a good design that it functions well, lasts well, looks well and costs as little as possible' ('Aesthetics and the Engineer'). His vision for comprehensive design necessitated the careful use of scarce resources as well as a consideration

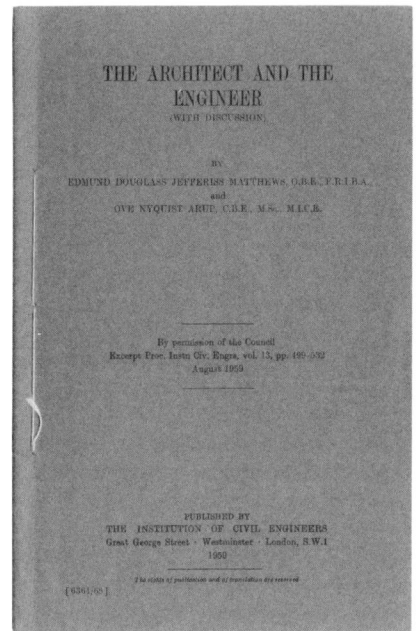

Original publication of 'The Architect and the Engineer', August 1959

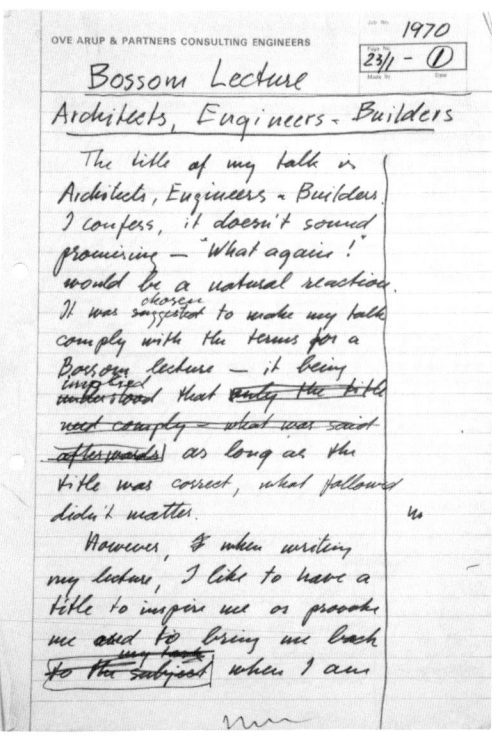

Ove's handwritten draft of 'Architects, Engineers and Builders'

of pollution and of the spoliation of the natural environment. He recognised that, while these could sometimes be conflicting aims, it was their synthesis that constituted the quality of a design. This was the ideal at the heart of what he called 'Total Design'.

The *means* by which these aims are accomplished drew close attention. As early as the 1940s, Ove outlined 'one of the central problems of our time': as technology advances, technique increases in sophistication and specialisation adds greatly to complexity:

> a wealth of new knowledge, new materials, new processes has so widened the field of possibilities, that it cannot be adequately surveyed by a single mind [...] This produces the specialist or expert, and the usual problem arises: how to create the organization, the 'composite mind' so to speak, which can achieve a well-balanced synthesis from the wealth of available detail. ('Science and World Planning')

Forty years ago Ove lamented the problem was becoming even more pressing: 'Jobs are getting larger and more complex and [...] design is split between dozens of other professions, specialists, experts, manufacturers and contractors' ('Future Problems Facing the Designer').

It is a process that continues today, as clients hiring professional teams will be aware. The number of professionals that are necessary to contribute to the planning phase of a project has perhaps tripled. Even a modest undertaking that twenty years ago would have required the services of an architect, a structural engineer and a building services engineer is now likely to include environmental consultants, transport planners, geotechnical engineers, acousticians, IT and security consultants. It is not only the engineering profession that has fragmented in this way: architecture has generated façade consultants, materials specialists, specification writers, construction managers, lighting and interior designers, signage and access consultants.

Ove saw that the difficulty for design was that each professional was 'at best pursuing his own kind of quality'; specialisation, both in further education and in the professional sphere, curtails an individual's ability to judge quality in allied technical fields. This echoes the view expounded by Walter Gropius in the Bauhaus school, during the first half of the twentieth century: 'Only those who have been taught how to grasp the comprehensive coherence of a larger design, and incorporate

Original publication of *A Society for the Built Environment*, 1972 (see 'The Built Environment')

'No theory, no ideology, no set of rules can deal with human complexity, human sensitivity or vulnerability' (see 'What I Believe')

original work of their own as an integral part of it, are ripe for active cooperation in building' (*The New Architecture and the Bauhaus*, London, 1965). The formation of a composite mind 'requires teamwork of a much higher order' ('The Future Problems Facing a Designer'). The crucial distinction Ove makes is that a team in which the bundle of requisite experts is merely gathered together will not be sufficient to achieve design excellence. The ability to extract the best from all collaborators requires a team whose members collectively understand each other's methods and aims, who share an appreciation of the point of view of others, and who share the same desire to create 'Total Design'.

This was to be the basis for the growth of Ove Arup and Partners; as an ever-increasing number of specialist needs emerged, it sought to develop and attract a membership of like-minded individuals, collectively engaged in 'Total Design'.

Fiercely sceptical of ideologies and classifications, Ove considered the distinctions between engineering and architecture divisive and exaggerated: 'the architect should be part engineer and the engineer should be part architect in order to achieve a fruitful collaboration' ('The Architect and the Engineer'). Engineering, he argued, bears a close relationship to art: 'as in art its problems are underdefined, there are many solutions, good, bad and indifferent. The art is, by a synthesis of ends and means, to arrive at a good solution.' This synthesis, Ove believed, was a creative activity involving imagination and intuition, recognising that 'possible solutions often vary in ways that cannot be directly compared by quantitative methods' ('The World of the Structural Engineer').

Ove comes full circle from his decision to move away from philosophy to take up engineering when he acknowledges the role of practice, rather than theory, in properly answering questions of design:

> to study architecture [...] one should study it *in statu nascendi* ['in its original form' or, perhaps, 'in the making']. One should be privy to the working of the minds of the creators. Creating architecture – good or bad – consists of making a great number of choices [...] get to know what these choices were, what was rejected, as well as what was adopted, and why. [...] we instead would witness [...] the exciting battle going on in the designer's mind to find the right answer among scores of possible solutions. ('The Design of Bridges')

In re-reading these papers, it is tempting to think that Ove took up engineering in order to practise philosophy. Peter Rice observed in 'A Celebration of the Life and Work of Ove Arup' (*RSA Journal*, June 1989): 'somehow, you feel there was more, a complete philosophy which might have shed light on a larger part of the human predicament.'

The title of this collection is taken from a short document by Ove entitled 'Milestones', dated 1985. In the closing paragraph he asks:

> Why did I have to study philosophy? Why did I abruptly switch over to engineering? [...] Why did we [the Arup firm] not stick to Civil and Structural Engineering but embark upon 'comprehensive design' embracing architecture as well as all branches of the relevant engineering disciplines?
>
> The answers can perhaps be abstracted from my many papers, published or unpublished, which deal with what could be called my 'philosophy of design' and the crucial role 'design' plays in the affairs of mankind.

Nigel Tonks, *Director, Arup*

Notes on the Text

These thirty-five essays have been selected from over 300 items held in the library at the firm of Arup and in the 'Papers of Sir Ove Arup' collection at the Churchill College Archive, Cambridge, UK. They represent a fraction of Ove's work, estimated by biographer Peter Jones to exceed 3 million words. These papers, as well as other notes, notebooks, professional and private correspondence, may be accessed by prior arrangement with the archive. The index can be accessed at: www.janus.lib.cam.ac.uk.

With the possible exception of the 'Key Speech', these papers are not widely known. Virtually nothing has been reprinted since their original appearance. In 1985, in celebration of Ove's ninetieth birthday, Arup published a small selection of works in a special edition of the *Arup Journal*. David Brown, assistant editor for that collection, recalls that Ove personally selected the articles, which opened with 'The World of the Structural Engineer', from 1968. Brown explains the prominent position given to this essay was at Ove's request.

The original papers exist in a variety of formats: faded newspaper cuttings, institute journals, yellowing type-written manuscripts, handwritten memos and so on. Transcription to a common format has been greatly simplified by digital scanning techniques and is faithful to the original text. No attempt to modernise the language has been made, and some choices of words or phrases may appear ungainly or outdated. Likewise, no attempt has been made to standardise orthography or punctuation. Spelling mistakes have been corrected. In the originals, underscoring and italics for emphasis were interchangeable and have been changed to italics throughout. Editor's notes are indicated by square brackets. Footnotes have been added to help clarify references to people, places and projects; however, it has occasionally not been possible to identify an allusion or reference with absolute certainty. Multiple drafts exist for some of his lectures, indicating a careful re-working. Transcripts of interviews offer insight into Ove's thinking in a less rehearsed atmosphere.

Few of his lecture notes refer to images. If slides accompanied his lectures, there are no detailed records of which images he used. Unless otherwise noted, the photographs included here are for historic interest only and bear no specific relation to the text.

Essays 1942–1981

Science and World Planning

This paper was given at the Conference on Science and World Planning held by the British Association for the Advancement of Science on 27 July 1942.

The development of modern science and technique enables us to construct buildings, which are satisfactory in every respect: warm, soundproof, well ventilated, with all the amenities and labour-saving devices which one could wish for. Modern buildings as actually constructed, however, are not nearly as wonderful. They are often badly planned, badly ventilated, badly heated, etc. In other words, only limited use is made of all the existing technical knowledge. One reason for this is simply that this technical information is not available to the designer of the building. This may be because he has not got the knowledge he ought to have, but even if he were a very able architect with the best possible technical education, he could not hope to be familiar with the complete range of modern technical possibilities. He is, therefore, unable by himself to arrive at the right solution, and is a prey to the various commercial interests advocating their own particular products.

The problem is the same here as in other spheres of human activity – a wealth of new knowledge, new materials, new processes has so widened the field of possibilities, that it cannot be adequately surveyed by a single mind. Corresponding to this increase of means there are increased or entirely new requirements to be satisfied. Our needs increase with the means. Standards are raised, new services introduced.

This produces the specialist or expert, and the usual problem arises, how to create the organization, the 'composite mind' so to speak, which can achieve a well-balanced synthesis from the wealth of available detail. This is, I suppose, one of the central problems of our time. How then can we overcome this difficulty?

Apart from the obvious way of improving the technical education of the architect, which, however desirable, would I am afraid not carry us very far in this connection, there are two main remedies.

1) One is to have the planning carried out by a team of experts whose combined knowledge covers a substantial part of the relevant technical information.

2) Another is to have all the technical information which may have a bearing on the problem checked up, classified, standardized and made easily available.

Both these methods are being employed, but not sufficiently.

The architect does, of course, invoke the assistance of various specialists, but mostly at too late a stage to affect the main conception.

Take for instance the case of the structural engineer; his work has a fundamental bearing on the planning, and architectural harmony can only be achieved if architect and engineer collaborate intimately right from the start. At the moment, there is however no recognized machinery for such collaboration. The appointment of an architect does not as a rule carry with it the appointment of a consulting engineer. The architect must therefore either:

1) confine himself to employing a more or less established structural system of which he has sufficient knowledge himself;

or

2) he must entice a consulting engineer to collaborate with him 'on spec';

or

3) he must seek advice from a firm of structural engineers and contractors who will offer this advice possibly from purely altruistic motives, but possibly also in order to improve their chance of obtaining the contract by putting the architect under some sort of obligation to them.

This sort of semi-collaboration does not produce the best results. Similar remarks apply to the collaboration with other specialists.

One remedy, as mentioned, which is already being applied in some cases, especially in the USA, is the formation of larger planning units consisting of firms or companies who have on their staff experts on the various aspects of the work to be planned. The organization may be on more or less democratic lines, but the importance lies in the fact that the various experts are in constant close co-operation and learn to understand each other's points of view, so that each can see his work as part of a whole plan, and make the adjustments required for smooth dovetailing. The value of such close co-operation can be seen in every sphere of planning.

Of special importance is the close connection between design and execution. A thorough knowledge of building costs and building processes is essential to the designers, and this knowledge is best obtained if he, or his team, directly controls building operations on the site, thus taking over the function here carried out by the general contractor.

Such larger planning groups are also in a better position to cope with the modern trend towards prefabrication in building. Prefabrication obviously means studying factory production, and calls for team work. In fact the spread of prefabrication will in itself tend to eliminate the private architect. His place will be in the factory, or inside the public or private planning group.

The trend towards the formation of larger planning groups on a commercial basis which is already apparent has, however, serious drawbacks. One of the major purposes of each group is to be successful, to make profit. This may fit in with the interests of society as a whole, but often it does not. The group will try to keep its experiences secret, it may be financially interested in certain materials or certain processes, and may want to push them even if this does not make for the best possible scheme. It may even buy up and suppress new inventions, and will tend to turn any gain of efficiency into increased profit rather than benefit to the consumer.

Then again, no group covers a wide enough field. The client therefore still needs expert advice to enable him to choose between the bewildering variety of possibilities, and when large-scale planning is undertaken, the work of the various groups should again be coordinated, for which there exists no machinery.

Team planning of this kind does not solve the difficulty of discriminating between many new materials and patent processes, information about which is only available in the form of biased trade publications.

We therefore turn to the other remedy – the creation of a fund of unbiased information available to all. This would mean the setting up of institutions working for the benefit of society as a whole, which would therefore probably have to be financed by the State. I enumerate at random some of the services which should be rendered. One would be the proper scientific testing of all new, and for that matter old, building materials. No new materials should be generally released without having passed such tests, and the results should be available to the general public. This sounds reasonable and innocent enough, but it would have far-reaching consequences. The authorized testing institutions would require permanently, powers that are contrary to the interests of some commercial firms, which are therefore rarely given, and then only for a limited purpose and period, namely, those of a governmental commission of inquiry. To publish unbiased information, however, should logically be followed by a restriction of production to useful products, and would therefore interfere considerably with the present organization of industry. To have this unbiased testing extended to building processes, tools and plant, would obviously also be very useful and result in enormous savings, but it would call for large research stations with ample staff and resources.

Another would be to eliminate some of the unnecessary repetition of detail planning which goes on in thousands of offices. Everywhere the same or almost the same problems crop up, and are painfully solved over and over again, sometimes reasonably well, often not so well. If the best possible solutions were found to these problems and embodied in a series of standards, the task of the designer dealing with a particular job, and also production generally, would be simplified immensely. Standardization has, of course, been carried out to a great extent already, but the process could be extended much further, provided there was a reasonable choice of alternatives, and the possibility of revision was safe-guarded.

Such a systematic standardization of the elements of industrial planning should logically embrace international agreements on the fundamental standards, such as measurements. To be forced to translate kg/cm^2 into lbs per in^2 etc., is wasteful, and hinders international exchange of ideas.

Hand in hand with the standardization of those units from which planning proceeds, should go the standardization of human needs. Minimum housing standards, workshop standards, etc., should be laid down and applied universally, and from these should spring building regulations, etc., which should safeguard the interest of society as a whole, but should not be drafted so rigidly as to be a drag on progress. The service must be run on democratic lines to allow revisions and additions to penetrate from below, from local to central bodies, to avoid over-centralization, and bureaucracy, and allow for regional differences. But there must somehow be power to direct or influence production. The centre of gravity must be shifted from private enterprise to public service. The best brains should be attracted to this service, and it would be reasonable and profitable to combine these planning and research centres with the technical education of students.

Once the principle is accepted, that the public has a right to expect the elimination of the obstacles which prevent the application of scientific and technical progress, it is not easy to stop half way. Organization of industry and communications, the planning of towns and agriculture, the extension of social services are all problems which, as far as I can see, cannot possibly be left to private initiative, but which everybody now realizes ought to be tackled in the interest of humanity.

To take an example, the proper heating of houses and workshops in the winter, and the supply of hot water on tap, could be made a public service by the introduction of district heating supplied from a number of central heat-electric stations which would combine the generation of electricity with the supply of heat in the form of superheated water. Such a system would considerably reduce the total coal consumption, and would at the same time supply an abundance of electric power which could be used for heating in outlying districts. It would also affect the design, and reduce the cost of new buildings, and would improve housing conditions where improvement is most sorely needed. Again, however, such schemes could only be tackled on a national scale.

Conclusion

It becomes more and more clear, therefore, the more one delves into the question how the benefits of modern technique can be made real, that this is not a technical problem at all. It is not even mainly a problem of organization. The organization could no doubt be worked out if everyone really wanted to benefit humanity. The difficulty is rather one of getting agreement as to what benefit to humanity means, and also of overcoming the fact that people are more concerned with benefiting themselves than humanity. It becomes therefore a moral or social or political problem. It should be obvious to scientists and technicians that the value of their work depends on the solution of this social problem, and they should therefore, as citizens with a social conscience, do everything in their power to contribute to its solution.

Shell Construction

This article first appeared in Architectural Design, *17 November 1947.*

Architecture is concerned with the enclosure or division of space. Space is confined by curved or plane surfaces, just as a surface is confined by curves or lines. A study of surfaces, their arrangement and intersection, is, therefore, of the essence of architecture. This fundamental fact is obscured by the difficulties obstructing the physical embodiment of our ideas. We cannot simply plan according to our fancy, considering only the need of man. We must consider the stability of the structure against the forces of gravity, of wind, and so on. And we can only go so far as our limited knowledge of these materials and their behaviour under load will allow us.

Until recently, the available sheeting or cladding materials could not fulfil their function of dividing space, without being held in position by other purely structural members. Gravity walls, domes and vaults were an exception to this general rule, but their inability to resist tension or bending put a severe limit on the forms which they could assume. We, therefore, think in terms of columns, piers, architraves, beams, trusses, rafters, as the elements of architecture – all members necessitated by structural and not by functional requirements.

But new materials and increased engineering knowledge enable us more and more to free ourselves from the old limitations. The use of steel in building made an enormous change – it largely freed the architectural plan from the tyranny of load-bearing walls and piers – and reinforced concrete, properly used, can take us a step further.

In the beginning, the potentialities of reinforced concrete were only partly realized and, to a large extent, that is still the position today. Reinforced concrete was used as a substitute for timber and steel, and assumed the forms characteristic of these materials. The column, the beam and the slab were thought of as separate members. This attitude does not do justice to the salient feature of reinforced concrete, which is its plastic and monolithic character. It can be moulded and built up to any shape, after which the whole structure forms one jointless unit, and it should rightly be considered and calculated as such.

The calculation of reinforced concrete is thus complicated, but designs are consequently produced which differ essentially from the traditional beam and slab structure.

We have for the first time a material which can be formed into comparatively thin plates or shells for enclosing space – or, in engineering structures, for retaining earth, containing water, coal, grain, and so on – which can at the same time be made to resist the forces acting on the structure with only limited recourse to external structural members.

There are, of course, limitations to our freedom of design, and they are mainly of two kinds. One is imposed by the formwork; the other by difficulties of calculation.

The temporary formwork is responsible for a very large proportion of the cost of reinforced concrete structures. If we were to ask for a double curved shell, needing shuttering on both sides, the cost might far exceed that of the concrete and reinforcement, and such a structure would, in many cases, be ruled out for financial reasons. To reduce costs, forms should be simple and should be re-used often. Further, it is naturally an advantage if the slope of the surface allows concrete to be deposited without top shuttering.

From this point of view, plane surfaces are to be preferred to curved, single curved surfaces to doubly curved, and flat slopes or curves to steep ones. More important still is repetition through standardization of lay-out.

The difficulty of calculating shells of various shapes, subjected to varying loads, is considerable and it is only lately that theories have been developed which enable us to deal with some of the surfaces which can be mathematically defined.

[Gabriel] Lamé and [Emile] Clapeyron laid the foundations for the membrane theory as early as 1825, and a general theory for dealing with shells was arrived at by A.E.H. Love,[*] towards the end of the last century. But it is only since 1910 that these general theories have been further developed and made applicable to large span roofs. Germany led the way in this development, although France also contributed some original work. Lately, however, contributions have come from many different countries. A recent British publication, R.S. Jenkins' *Theory and Design of Cylindrical Shell Structures*,[†] gives the modern elasticity basis of design in a form suitable for practical application.

In order not to make the calculation too difficult, it is still desirable to confine the use of curved shells to spheres, cylinders of different kinds, paraboloids, hyperboloids, cones and other surfaces, which have simple geometric properties. That does not mean that other shapes cannot be attempted. I was told that a team of four engineers worked for over half a year on the calculation of a shell roof with an irregular base, covering the main concert hall of the new Broadcasting House in Copenhagen. Obviously, it is only rarely possible to go to that amount of trouble.

In the new approach to reinforced concrete design, the basic element is the comparatively thin slab, plate or shell, extending in two dimensions. Slabs have, of course, always been a feature of reinforced concrete design, but they have almost exclusively been considered as members resisting forces perpendicular to their own plane and therefore, mainly subject to bending. The fact that a slab is much stronger when resisting forces in its own plane has been surprisingly neglected.

In the British Codes of Practice and Regulations, for instance, there are no design regulations for thin load-bearing walls; a vertical slab is always considered as a panel to be held in position by a frame – a wrong way of looking at it, leading to clumsy and faulty designs. The new approach takes great note of the strength of slabs and shells in their own plane: it can almost be said to be based on it.

Perhaps the most spectacular results of this approach are the concrete shell roofs, where large spans up to 200 feet or more are achieved with shells only a few inches thick. But these are only special examples of a general tendency, permeating modern concrete design, where the structure is conceived as a spatial monolithic whole. It is easy enough to gain a rough idea of how concrete shells act.

Fig. 1 represents a simply supported slab, uniformly loaded. It is subjected to bending only.

Fig. 2 shows the slab replaced by two inclined slabs. Each of the slabs is still subjected to bending, but the span is smaller, and the deflections are therefore smaller. But in addition, the system is subjected to compressive forces in the plane of each slab, transferring the resultant force at the top to the bearings. These forces can, however, easily be taken by the slab, and the total result is a lighter construction, provided the bearings can withstand the outward thrust exerted on them.

In Fig. 3 and Fig. 4, the two slabs are replaced by three or four slabs, resulting in still smaller

---

[*] A.E.H. Love (1863–1940) was a mathematician famous for his work on the theory of elasticity.
[†] R.S. Jenkins, *Theory and Design of Cylindrical Shell Structures*, Ove Arup and Partners, London, 1947.

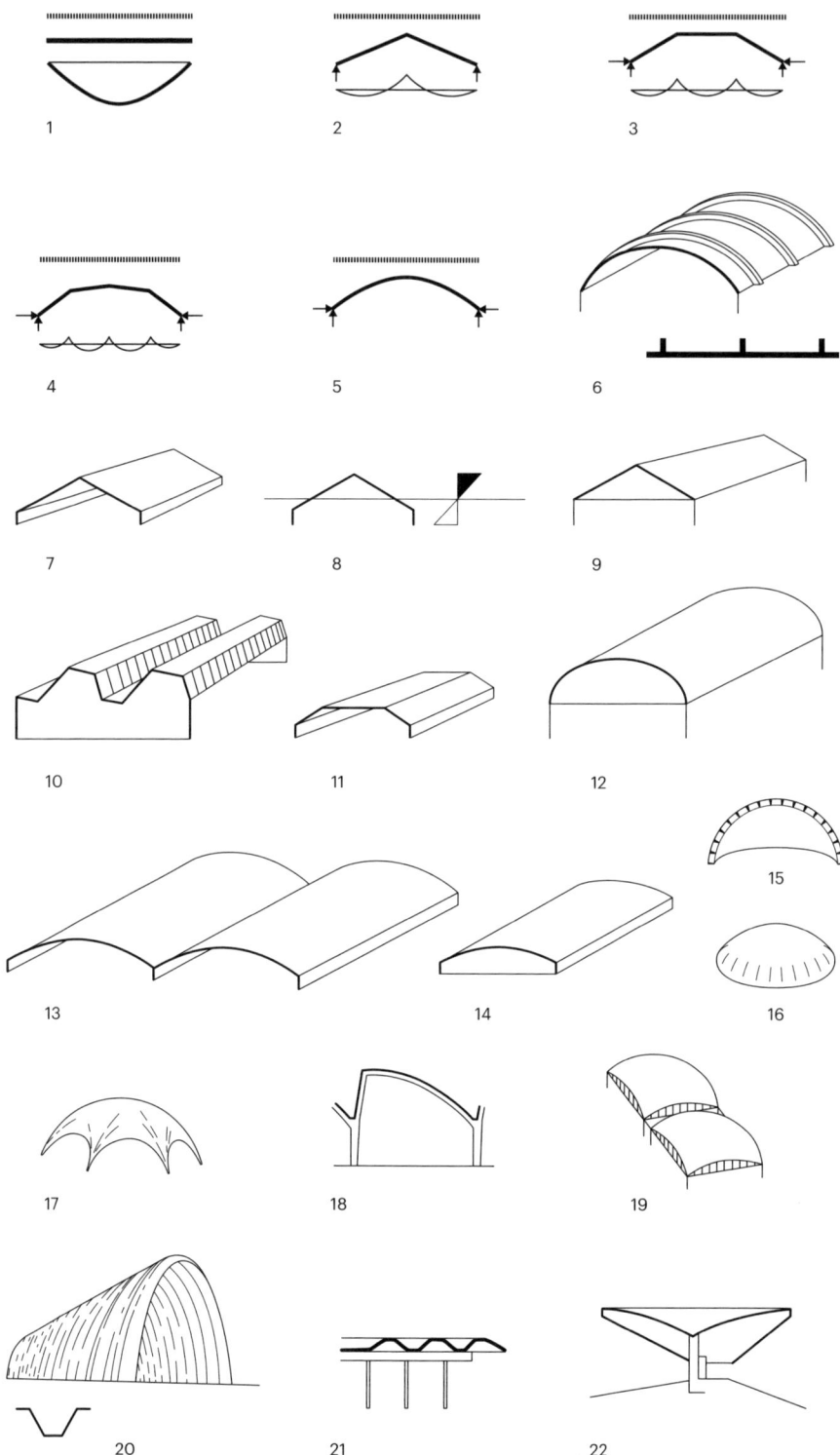

Figs.1–22 Shell structures

Shell Construction

moments, without increasing the thrust, and in Fig. 5, the arched slab, the moments disappear altogether, *provided the thrust-line coincides with the arch*. This can, however, only happen for one particular set of loads – as soon as the load varies, moments are introduced.

The moments, mostly caused by wind and snow, are very much smaller than they would be for a slab of the same span (Fig. 1), where also the dead load contributes to the moments, but for large spans they are nevertheless considerable and the slab must be fairly solid and well-reinforced to withstand them. If the arch slab cannot be taken right down to the foundations at each side, but has to spring from the level of the eaves, it will, in most cases, be necessary to provide frequent ties at this level.

This plain, tied, arch slab has been used frequently in the past for medium spans. It is *not* what is generally understood by a shell construction, because it can only resist unbalanced forces by bending moments in the slab, whereas a proper shell is mainly supposed to be subjected to normal and shear stresses in its own plane. But if we introduce arched ribs, as in Fig. 6, then the singly-curved slab can transfer the unbalanced forces to the ribs through direct stresses in the slab, provided the latter is sufficiently stiff and the curvature is not too small. This means that the arched slab can be constructed as a comparatively thin shell.

Constructions similar to that shown in Fig. 6 have, of course, been used for many years, but before modern analysis showed the way, the orthodox method of treating them was to let the ribs take all the moments – and possibly even the whole of the thrust – and to span the slab between the ribs, disregarding its curvature.

To illustrate the action of the shell, let us look at another set of figures.

Fig. 7 is a cross-section through a structure, consisting of four slabs, joined together as shown. If this structure is supported at the two gable ends by a stiff wall or frame, which prevents any relative movements of the four slabs at these points, then it will be able to span freely between the two gables, if suitably reinforced. Each slab will act in two ways, *as a slab* transferring dead weight, wind loads, etc., crosswise to the corners, and *as a beam*, transferring the resultant forces in their own plane to the gable ends. It is obvious that at the junction line of two slabs, no movement can take place without moving one or both slabs in their own plane, and such movement will be resisted by the slab spanning as a very deep beam from end to end.

The matter does not end here, however. We must take into account that the four slab-beams are joined at the corners and therefore react on each other. In fact, if the structure is mainly subjected to vertical forces, the tension zones of the two inclined slabs are joined to the compression zones of the two lower slabs. Obviously the corner cannot both be in compression and in tension, and this is an example of the absurdities sometimes resulting from the artificial splitting up of the structure into simple elements. The structure acts as a whole, and the various parts act on each other. In order to assess the magnitude of these internal forces, we must resort to rather more complicated calculations, taking into account the elastic deformations of the structure, and as a result, we shall find that the lower part of the combined structure – up to a so-called neutral axis – is in tension, and the upper part in compression, as shown in Fig. 8.

We find, in fact, that the whole structure will act approximately as a beam, but we must ensure against distortion of the cross-section. If, in Figs. 7 or 8, the two lower flanges were left out, as in Fig. 9, the free ends of the two slabs would probably sag in the middle. The shape of the cross-section is therefore important if we want to reduce the moments acting in the plane of the cross-section.

Structures such as the one shown in Fig. 7, consisting of plane slabs joined at the edges, are called *Faltwerke*, in German. We might call them 'slab-frame' structures and various books and papers have been written about their calculation, but the principle is obvious and has been used widely, without giving it a name, for industrial structures. An example is the shed roof in Fig. 10, used by the writer before the war for spans up to 70 ft.

If we increase the number of slabs in Fig. 7, for instance, as shown in Fig. 11, we reduce the transverse moments in each slab element, but we complicate the calculation and are still more dependent on the shape of the cross-section, to avoid distortion. If we go the whole hog and change the section into a smooth curve, as in Fig. 12, we can reduce the bending moments to a minimum.

This form of construction, a barrel vault shell of approximately elliptic cross-section, spanning 'the wrong way' was first developed in the 1920s by the firm of Dyckerhoff and Widmann in Germany, in conjunction with the Zeiss optical concern, and patented under the name of 'Zeiss Dywydag Gewoelbe'. The patents covered the method of calculation as well as the practical application.

An explanation, with calculations, is given in *Handbuch des Eisenbetonbau* by Dr. Franz Dischinger of Dyckerhoff and Widmann. In the beginning, great care was taken to give the shells the correct mathematical shape and to make them very thin, so as to correspond to the theory, which assumed that all forces acted in the plane of the shell and were evenly distributed over the thickness, but later analytical and practical research showed that other forms were possible. Now these shells are mostly given the shape shown in Fig. 13.

This has the advantage that the slope of the curved section is such that no top shuttering is required, only the straight vertical ribs requiring double shuttering. Top lighting can be provided, as shown in Fig. 14.

While it is easy to see that sections such as Figs. 7, 10, 11, 12 and 13, must be able to span some distances, the actual calculations are rather involved, and some simplifying assumptions must be made. One method is to treat the structure according to the usual beam theory, assuming that plane cross-sections remain plane after loading. This is not very exact, and the method used by Dischinger is the so-called membrane theory, which makes the assumption that the membrane is infinitely thin (mathematically speaking), and that all stresses must be parallel to the surface.

The difficulty is to balance the system of forces with the existing boundary conditions, and in any case the assumptions are not correct, as the shells must be given certain thickness and the moments cannot legitimately be disregarded, however thin the shell. This throws us back on the general theory of elasticity, applied to a spatial structure, and to an isotropic material with a certain stress-strain relationship and a certain value for Poisson's ratio. We must consider the equilibrium of each small element and of the system as a whole, and make the boundary conditions conform to the physical facts. In short cylinders of large radius it may be necessary to introduce stiffening ring beams to deal with the bending moments.

When we come to doubly curved shells, it is actually easier and more correct to apply the membrane theory with a correction in regions near the edges. The construction of domes and double-barrelled vaults is possible even in a material which will not resist tension, as has been known for hundreds or thousands of years. Sometimes, the dome was prevented from spreading out by a tension ring or chain at the springing (Fig. 15). Actually, the whole lower zone of the dome is subject to circular tension, and we may, therefore, have cracks in the lower part, as in Fig. 16. In a reinforced concrete shell, the reinforcement can be placed where it is needed, and the dome can be made much flatter and thinner, as we are not dependent on gravity to bring the thrust line down.

We can also make use of many other double-curved or single-curved surfaces. Figs. 17 to 22 illustrate some of the possibilities. Any kind of corrugation can be used to increase the stiffness of a slab – which does not mean that they are all equally effective. In the new bus terminus, now being built at Store Street, Dublin, a canopy made of corrugated reinforced concrete has been designed, cantilevering 20 ft., although the thickness is only 2½ in. (Fig. 21). If a corrugated section is arched at the same time, as in Fig. 20, the effect is further increased.

Shell construction is the most important development in reinforced concrete in recent years and will undoubtedly contribute to the character of the coming architecture. It places at the architect's disposal a new form of construction, which serves the dual role of cladding and structure, and gives him greater freedom of planning and elevational treatment to meet both functional and architectural requirements.

At the same time, it should be noted that its proper design calls for more intricate calculations on the part of the engineer, to deal with a statically indeterminate three-dimensional structure. Early collaboration between architect and engineer becomes very necessary.

Conclusion

Perhaps the future development of shell construction will depend largely on the way in which the contractor approaches the constructional problems involved, as these differ considerably from those encountered in normal construction. Standardization of shuttering and a large number of uses are essential for economy, and this is a point which should be borne in mind when general layouts are being considered. Methods of depositing concrete in large areas of thin slab, while still improving the quality of work, require consideration, and the general planning of sequence of construction, stage by stage, is essential. As these and other problems are mastered, there is little reason to doubt that shell construction will compare favourably with more orthodox forms of construction for covering large uninterrupted spaces.

The Practice of Building

This lecture was delivered in South Africa in 1954.

First I should like to thank the Pre-Stressed Concrete Development Group and the South African Concrete Association for inviting me to talk to you this afternoon. It is a great honour, but I am a little afraid that I may not be able to measure up to whatever expectations you may have.

Normally I take care to talk only to architects. That is much less of a risk, because if I touch on architectural matters, my remarks are obviously those of a layman and need not be taken very seriously, whereas if I talk on structural matters, I have at least the comfortable feeling that I may know a little more about the subject than they do. This comfortable feeling is totally lacking to-day. I am quite aware that South African Engineers compare favourably with those from the larger countries in Europe and America, a view which has been confirmed by what I have seen of your country, and by the fact that the comparatively large number of South African Engineers which are or have been on our staff have without exception been very good – much better in fact, than the average recruit from England.

I don't think, therefore, that I have very much to teach you, but I have lived longer than most of you, and have had occasion to deal with structural problems both from the angle of the contractor, designer and lately even of the client (I am about to have a house built for myself) and this under conditions which vary a good deal from those in this country; and perhaps some of the things I have come across or thought about may be of interest to you.

The difficulty is to decide what to say and where to stop. It is obviously no good to go too much into details; I cannot in our talk discuss the theory and various methods of pre-stressing for example. I will have to generalise, and to show you some slides illustrating various points in my talk or being of interest for other reasons.

What I should like to talk to you about is the enormous change which has taken and is taking place in engineering and building methods, and its impact on the organisation of the whole business of building, and especially on what I call *design* in the widest application of the term. But this subject is far too comprehensive, and I can only give you a few scattered remarks bearing on it.

In every form of human activity, we can distinguish three phases:

1) The aim – an idea with an emotional charge which acts as the motive power.
2) The consideration and choice of ways and means necessary and available to achieve the aim, and
3) The definite action (or actions) by which the aim is attained.

These three phases are not always clearly defined. In primitive, spontaneous or emotional actions, the second phase may be practically non-existent, whereas in an over-developed intellect this phase may be so prolonged as to inhibit completely the will to act. However, as this is not supposed to be a paper on psychology, I had better concentrate on the kind of activity we are considering here, that is the building or construction of an engineering structure.

The three phases in this case correspond to:

1) The aim, or client's brief.
2) The design or scheme.
3) The execution or construction.

The point I want to make here, is (to emphasise the importance of design – or rather of good design – and to show) that the design stage, taking design in its widest sense, really permeates both the briefing and the construction stage.

The word design is used in many different ways, and in fact there are a whole group of words such as design, plan, scheme, project, sketch, proposal, arrangement, structural method, etc., which all have something in common and yet have each their particular shade of meaning, which although not clearly defined, is generally obvious from the context. What they have in common is that they are all, potentially at least, instruction to the Builders, Contractors and workmen who carry out a job, they are all the results of thoughts about how a thing is to be done.

These instructions can be given in words and in the case of a specification or building manual etc., which belong to this group, they are so given, but mostly the instructions are more conveniently expressed in pictorial form, in the form of drawings, sketches etc.

The word design generally implies something which is, or can be put down on a drawing, but the design is really not complete without its specification.

The difference between primitive and more advanced construction or building, is this, that more attention has been paid to the design stage, and more thought has been given to *how* to build before action is taken; and it is in this wide sense that the design stage, as I mentioned before, permeates the other stages.

Take the client's aim or brief for instance. The architectural design or lay-out, can largely be considered as the special interpretation of the client's wishes. *The client does not really know what he wants before the architect has put pencil to paper and has shown the client what could be done.* The process of briefing may go on throughout the development of the design. It is the job of the client or his representative, to make decisions on policy, and it is the job of the designer, be he architect or engineer, to make plans for the execution of this policy. *But policy depends on possibility,* and the possibilities are not known until at least tentative designs have been prepared and costed. At any stage (both) the client (and the designer) may have to be brought in to decide such questions of policy.

This business of briefing is really most important for the success of the job, and I am afraid that (most) clients have a lot to learn in this respect. I think there are two successful ways of doing it. Either the client should interfere as little as possible and leave his technical advisers a free hand to make minor policy decisions, of course, after having acquainted them as fully as possible with the whole purpose of the undertaking. Or the client should take an intelligent interest in the various technical possibilities and work with the engineer or architect to find the best solution. The point is, *that wise decisions must be based on a knowledge of facts, and if the client has no time to absorb the relevant facts, he should leave the decisions to somebody who has, and whom he can trust.*

A wise old lawyer, Mr. Oppenheimer, once said to me: 'Whoever decides to act as his own solicitor, has a fool for a client.' Perhaps the same can be said of clients who refuse to take technical advice before plunging for a solution. Of course, clients don't often act as their own engineers, but they may think that they can dispense with the services of engineers altogether, or they may think that they can get the necessary engineering services for nothing by placing an order for something entirely different – an astonishing naiveté to be found in many a hard-headed business man. And thousands of badly planned factories and housing estates, testify to the disastrous effect of laymen acting as their own architects or planners. The man who 'knows what he wants and means to get it' is often his own worst enemy, unless of course he really *knows* what he wants.

In extenuation it must be admitted that there is a lot of architectural or technical advice which it is not worth paying for, what the client must do, is to choose the right advisers, but how to do this is another question. We all face the same problem when choosing our doctors or dentists.

We have seen that briefing or policy making and design overlap, and must be thoroughly interpreted. The same applies to design and execution. A building operation consists of thousands of separate actions by many different people, and each of them has what we may term its design or planning stage, where possibilities are weighed and decisions taken, and they all have to be co-ordinated by somebody. Where is the mixer going to be placed? Should the concrete be precast or cast in situ? (Where should the order for the steel be placed?) There are thousands of such decisions to be taken on every job, and many of them may involve the making of drawings for site-layout, scaffolding form-work, shop-details, bending schedules; drawings often prepared by the contractor and not in ordinary parlance deemed to be part of the design proper.

A consulting engineer's design, for instance, may mean the whole set of instructions issued by him in the form of letters, specifications and drawings to indicate exactly what he wants the job to be like when it is finished. These instructions may or may not concern themselves with *how* the work is to be carried out, *but if they don't*, then someone else must make these decisions, and the more thought that is given to them, the better.

When I first started work in England with a firm of designers and contractors, the general practice was to leave the method of shuttering to the foreman carpenter on the job. But we soon introduced the practice of designing all our shuttering, and to have it prefabricated in panels to save labour and increase re-use. But we found, of course, that it would be a great help if the method of shuttering had been considered in the design stage. And that applies to all other methods of execution.

It is essential for economy that the design takes into account the method of construction as well as the final structure.

I have been working for over twenty years inside firms combining design and contracting, and I remember well how exasperated we were when we as contractors had to carry out designs by consulting engineers, who did not seem to mind in the least what unnecessary difficulties they put in the way of the contractors. In those days it was not done for a mere contractor to propose modifications to a consulting engineer's design. I think there has been a change for the better since then.

After all, to design should mean to indicate the best way to carry out the job, and the best way is the one which achieves the desired result with the least trouble and expense. It follows that the designer *must know a good deal about the practice of building* and the cost of various alternative methods, and that he must design to facilitate the chosen method. In civil engineering, for instance harbour work, the method of construction often dominates the design. To decide whether to use piling, cylinders, caissons, solid or hollow blocks or construct inside a cofferdam, a knowledge of the economy of these methods is necessary, and the designer must all the time visualise every phase of the work, so that he can fit the design to the execution.

Where a more or less standard of construction has been developed, as was the case in ordinary traditional building, the question does not arise so much – everybody knows how to play their appropriate role. But this situation has changed. Nowadays there is such a bewildering variety of new materials and building methods that we hardly know how to build. The designer can of course go on designing in the way he has been brought up to, but that is hardly fair on the client. If there is a better and cheaper way now, it ought to be adopted, and then this will in most cases have to be reflected in the design.

We see then, that the design-stage really permeates the whole building activity from the first conception of the plan to the last finishing touches on the job. Advanced, as against primitive, technique means more design throughout, more planning of every step, more direction, more organisation, instead of leaving to chance. This again means thorough integration of design and execution.

Does not this mean then, that the designer should be part of the construction team, that designing and contracting should be carried out by the same firm? There is a lot to be said for this. It is the custom in some countries – Germany and Sweden for instance. And in industry – cars, refrigerators, wireless sets – the maker also designs. But there is a lot to be said on the other side. Conditions are rather different in building and construction. It is very valuable for the client to have an independent adviser, who is on his side, and who is not interested in advocating the particular form of construction in which his firm happens to specialize. However, it would take too much time to discuss this question at length.

Design and execution can of course be integrated without necessarily merging the firms concerned. There is such a thing as close collaboration between engineer and contractor, and that is a very necessary and valuable thing. The difficulty is that this collaboration cannot start before the contractor has been appointed, which normally means after the design has been more or less fixed. In most normal cases, that does not matter so much, if the engineer has got the necessary knowledge and experience of contracting methods. But where the case is an unusual one, where new ground has to be covered, it would be better to dispense with ordinary competition and nominate a contractor who could then be part of the design team. This method has been used on several occasions, and even the London County Council have accepted it on a very important job, the experimental buildings at Picton Street in South London. In this case, which involves the building of 600 flats in 11 storey and 4 storey blocks, the L.C.C. have appointed a firm of contractors an a consulting engineer to work together with their own architects and quantity surveyors and various members of building research station on the design team. They are investigating a good many different solutions, and are trying to find one which will mean an advance on previous methods.

At any rate the old fashioned attitude of the omniscient consulting engineer is disappearing. The engineer must realize that he is paid to look after his client's interests, and they are best served by incorporating in the design all the best ideas, whether they originate with engineer or contractor. He should, therefore, be willing to listen to alternative proposals and judge them on their merit. He cannot be expected to get all the brain-waves himself, but he is expected to know a good thing when he sees it.

We have seen that 'design' permeates the whole building operation from the clarification of the underlying purpose to the organisation of operations on site; and the modern tendency, fostered by the need for economy, is to emphasise design or planning, rather than to trust to luck. We will now have a short look at the new building techniques themselves and their influence on design.

New building techniques are developed as the result of progress in many different departments of science and technology. Ours is the age of specialisation, but the most spectacular practical advances generally result from a pooling of specialist knowledge from different spheres.

We have made progress in:

A) The theoretical understanding of structures and their calculation. Purely mathematical techniques such as the use of matrices for solving simultaneous equations have been successfully applied to structural problems. Ultimate load theories have widened our understanding of the factor of safety – or vice-versa – [and] the design of shells has progressed from the first crude membrane theory, soil-mechanics is now a science in itself – etc.

B) Then we have a better understanding of the properties of materials and have improved on entirely new materials at our disposal. There are special steels for a variety of purposes, aluminium alloys, plastics, lightweight concretes etc.

C) Then we have developed new machines, new plant and tools. We have bigger and better cranes, excavators, mixers, pumps, electric tools of all kinds, means of handling materials etc.

D) And side by side with that we have new construction methods. I don't know whether pre-stressed concrete comes under this heading or under new materials, but it is one of the most important developments of recent times. Then there is sitewelding on steel, new methods of piling, boring, tunnelling, of scaffolding and moving large shuttering panels, sliding or climbing forms, the vibration of concrete, vacuum process of concreting steam curing, and hundreds of other innovations.

E) And finally there is the growing application of factory production to the problems of building. This trend towards prefabrication as it is sometimes called, has been the subject of discussion in the technical press for a long time.

If we confine ourselves to a bird's eye view of the trends, which is the only thing possible in a short talk, we can say that they all amount to a better exploitation of our resources – of our own brains and of the materials and the labour at our disposal. The most striking is the saving of labour through mechanisation, factory production and better organisation – all evolved through better designs or better planning – bringing our thoughts to bear on every little stage in the organisation of building processes.

As far as actual building operations are concerned we can divide them into two main categories:

1) Improved site operations involving plant, tools, methods of transport, hoisting and moving of scaffolding, formwork, templates and other labour saving devices.
2) Factory production, where the plant is stationary and the raw material is moved to the factory and finished products aren't transported to the site and form part of the structure.

The *key* to both these trends is the *Exploitation of Repetition*.

To make the construction of a large and expensive piece of plant a paying proposition, it is necessary to have sufficient work for it to do, either on a series of jobs where it can perform the same kind of task, like excavating concrete or mixing it, or on a job which is sufficiently large to write off the cost of the plant; as when we design very large shuttering units or travelling scaffolding which is purposely made for one large job only. The same applies to factory production – it obviously does not pay to start a factory unless we require a great many units of the same kind. Factory production is mass-production, and the necessary corollary is standardisation. If we want to manufacture wall panels for a number of schools, for instance, they should be of the same size, or at least a limited number of sizes, and the schools must be designed on a grid system which takes this into account.

The amount of repetition which is required to make use of a particular building technique, depends entirely on that technique, and varies from case to case. Inversely, the number of repetitions decide which kind of technique we can economically use.

We cannot economically use a tower-crane on a small house, nor can we use pre-cast, pre-stressed and steam cured concrete units in such a case, unless there is a factory nearby which delivers such units to this and a lot of other small sites.

This explains why the most modern and labour saving techniques have not penetrated very far into ordinary small-scale construction.

All the more spectacular techniques require building on a large scale – either very large jobs on one building site, or standard unit jobs spread over a larger area, but controlled by the same design organisation.

This also explains, partly at any rate, why there is a tendency to large-scale building. It is only large scale building which offers an opportunity for rationalisation and mechanisation, or for some sort of modular planning and unit construction.

Another matter is, that this opportunity is rarely fully exploited even when it exists, and this again is partly due to the fact that the whole set-up of the building industry – including its direction by clients and designers – has not yet been adapted to modern methods, and partly because the necessary centralisation of direction is not really desired.

Take the case of the London County Council mentioned earlier, here is a case where one authority spends many millions each year on the building of units, which could very well be standardised to a very high degree, even allowing for variations in finishes and disposition of blocks to avoid monotony. Theoretically, the quantities involved would be sufficient to place large-scale orders for the various parts, or to call into being special factories for the production of standard components of pre-stressed concrete, wall panels, stairs etc. It would also be possible to construct elaborate purpose-made plant – hydraulically operated sliding shutters, portal cranes lifting whole walls or floors into place – or whatever large scale production method could be thought of. The result would undoubtedly be that the first dozen blocks or more would cost more than if traditional methods were used, but there would be a fair chance of bringing down the cost in the long run, if the same construction teams could be kept on the job for years and really acquire speed and efficiency in applying the chosen system, and if large scale orders for years ahead could be placed for all equipment and prefabricated parts. This however, amounts to complete centralisation and would be politically and practically undesirable.

The L.C.C. insist that the execution of future buildings shall be divided into medium sized jobs so as to give all – also the small builders – a chance. All that can be done, therefore, is to experiment on one site, with a chosen contractor on the team, with the proviso that we cannot count on any special plant being re-used on other jobs or repeat orders later on, and the cost of the job must not exceed the cost of similar jobs constructed by familiar methods. Under these conditions no spectacular savings can be expected, although it is hoped that a careful study of all design problems and a comparison between alternatives will produce some benefit. However, it is undoubtedly very difficult both to introduce new methods and also make a saving – unless you have a sufficiently long run.

School-construction is another field where standardisation and prefabrication might yield results. The Hertfordshire C.C. and the Ministry of Education have used this kind of procedure on a large scale.

In Hertfordshire a large scale programme was completed in record time by using a standardised light steel frame – the Hill system, and lately they have also experimented with other systems, for instance the Punt system of plywood construction which follows the same grid as that previously used for the Hill. The Ministry of Education have in conjunction with a firm of designers and contractors developed a pre-stressed concrete system, and the first school in this system has just been completed.

As far as I know, these various prefabricated schools do not show any spectacular advantage from the point of view of cost, but they certainly do facilitate the planning of a large school programme by a single authority. The Hertfordshire school programme could certainly not have been carried out in such a short time by traditional methods.

Ordinary one storey factories are another possible field for large scale standardisation, in this case however, there has not been a single authority in England controlling a large amount of building, and the same applies to South Africa. The development has therefore been controlled by private enterprise. In Sweden, the firm Strengbeten manufactures all the necessary pre-stressed concrete units to put up sheds of any size, delivered off the peg so to speak, and covered with lightweight concrete slabs. This sort of thing is only possible where there is a big demand for more or less standard buildings in the vicinity of the factory. This is of course, not so very much different from the old north-light roofs of structural steel, which even if they could not be ordered off the peg, at least became an almost standard product.

Then there are the factories for pre-cast and pre-stressed concrete which play a role of increasing importance. This is a part of the developments towards prefabrication of building components. There are as yet very few standard components, they have to be especially ordered in sufficiently large quantities to make it pay – but at least the factory layout, plant, stretching beds etc., can be used for a large number of jobs by changing the forms.

This prefabrication of building components, reducing the site-work to an assembly of parties has been a favourite theme for discussion amongst architects for many years. The object is to make full use of modern methods while retaining the freedom to assemble the standard parts into different patterns, thus retaining architectural control. Many people think this can be achieved by modular co-ordination of dimensions – but I am afraid it is not so easy as that. You cannot design the parts without at the same time designing the whole, and modular planning of this kind is only possible where the same design teams controls a large body of building of a repetitious nature. But this could be a lecture on its own.

In civil engineering and industry, where the jobs aren't so amenable to standardisation, the emphasis is more on plant and methods of construction such as post-tensioning. The latter method enables us to make a continuous structure out of pre-cast concrete elements, and I think it has a great future in civil engineering – bridge building, harbour works, water tanks, etc. But it would take too long even to give a bird's eye view of all the many improvements which have taken place, not to mention the new materials – fibre-glass etc. – which are round the corner.

The engineer who is responsible for the design of a particular job has certainly got a great many possibilities to choose from. How can he make sure that his design takes as much advantage as possible of the many new techniques at his disposal?

We must assume that he and his collaborators have kept abreast of developments and are familiar with the technical advances which affect their type of work, otherwise he can obviously not make use of them.

This does not mean however, that he should at once try to apply all the latest techniques just to show how clever he is. New techniques tend to be expensive, the first time they are used.

His job is, to design a factory or bridge or whatever it is, which meets all the client's requirements, and costs as little as possible. To that end, he has to make use of the resources – the materials, the plant, the labour and the contracting experience – which are locally available.

If it is a small job, he can probably do no better than follow local practice in construction while concentrating on the design.

On larger jobs it may be possible to introduce special methods or plant new to the district, but he is then really dependent on the collaboration of contractors, who are willing and keen to try something new. It may in such cases be difficult to obtain realistic competitive tenders. That is in fact one of the major difficulties which face the engineer who wants to introduce a new technique. He must find somebody to build what he designs, and contractors tend to overestimate anything with which they are not familiar.

One way is to work with nominated contractors – which I think is an excellent way if you know and trust the contractors. But the time is not yet ripe for a general application of this principle.

As an illustration, I can tell you what we did in the case of Donny-brook Garage in Dublin, built for the C.I.E., a kind of Irish transport board. The plan was to build 5 or 6 of such garages, which all had a main hall, 110' wide by 400' long. It was just the case for shell-concrete, steel was difficult to get after the war, and by making movable forms for 5 bays – there were 10 40' bays per garage – the timber framework could be used 10 to 12 times. But no Irish contractor had built concrete shells, and they were afraid of it. We persuaded the client to give the job to an Irish firm collaborating with a Danish firm who were familiar with the technique. Their contract provided that a target price should be worked out, and that they should be given cost plus a small percentage of profit plus a large percentage of the saving in relation to the target. This worked very successfully and there was a saving, even on the first job. The others were never built, because there was a change of government and of policy which affected a lot of other jobs too.

The making of thin concrete shells is a technique which most contractors learn, and which does not require elaborate plans – although it can only usefully be employed where the formwork can be re-used a number of times. We have even designed shells for West Africa – in spite of the fact that the local pundits shook their heads, and the University tried to veto it. Here in South Africa you are familiar with this type of construction and some of the largest shell covered areas are to be found here.

There are, however, other techniques which depend on elaborate plant or factory production, and which are the monopoly of certain contractors. That again cuts out competition, and in most cases affects the design profoundly.

In a situation like that, the guide must simply be the client's interest. If the most economical solution is for instance, to buy the factory more or less ready made from a firm having all the facilities for making the units then that is the advice the client should have. In less extreme cases it may be a matter of specifying certain proprietary floor units or similar requirements. The point is, that the engineer should know of the various possibilities before he starts designing, and obtain the quotations he needs to arrive at the right decision.

On jobs where there is an architect in control of the design, and where the purely architectural considerations are of major importance, a further complication is added. It is essential in such cases to produce a tailor-made structure, which exactly fits the architectural intent, so as to create a harmonious and neat job. This calls for a flexible technique. Many of the modern techniques especially those which operate with large pre-fabricated units, but also some which apply rigid shuttering systems – impose a severe restriction on architectural expression, and this is becoming more and more of a problem. The most flexible of all techniques – apart from brickwork, which has a limited application – is reinforced concrete cast in situ. You can do almost anything with reinforced concrete and in some cases it is therefore, the only possible solution. I will show you a few jobs of this kind which are 'tailor-made' to a very high degree, representing an intimate unity of architecture and structure. They can only be satisfactorily produced by hard work and intimate collaboration.

If it is intended to make use of a particular highly mechanised method of production, then a different architectural approach is required. In such cases the Architect must subordinate his design to the requirements of the method of construction.

Other materials have each their particular kind of flexibility and rigidity. Structural steel is limited to particular sections, but site and shop welding has increased flexibility and continuity enormously.

Structural aluminium alloys are flexible in the sense that the extruded section can be designed to fit each particular job. In fact it is economically necessary to do so, the standard sections are much too wasteful in material, and the extra cost of dies is insignificant. The extra effort demanded of the designer is considerable – but that is not a matter which ought to be taken into consideration. You don't get anything worth having for nothing.

Pre-stressed concrete in the form of pre-cast units has not much flexibility, unless the units are swallowed up in a matrix of cast in situ work, but post-tensioned concrete, where the cables are applied in situ, can be as flexible as reinforced concrete.

We certainly live in a very exciting time where each year sees the birth of new techniques and methods of construction. It is increasingly difficult for any single engineer to be familiar and keep abreast of all these new techniques, and only by collaboration between a group of engineers and even calling in specialists is it possible to cover the field.

Structural 'Honesty'

This lecture was delivered to the Architectural Association of Ireland, 1954.

It happens to be my job to design the structure of buildings under the guidance of various architects. A very interesting job, if one happens to be interested both in structure and in architecture.

The guidance I receive from architects on these occasions varies very much in intensity, in quality and in kind. You may not be aware of the fact that architects, and even modern architects, sometimes differ in their outlook on architecture.

This can be puzzling for the engineer.

It is natural that I should be concerned about what might be termed the 'ethics' of structure. I am supposed to find the 'right' solution. But the right structural solution is only part of the right architectural solution. The two are completely mixed up. This is my excuse for poking my nose into your architectural affairs tonight.

I can of course simply take my instructions from you – and I do, I am really a very good boy in that respect. But one would like to understand what one is doing.

To do that, one must first investigate the interrelation between structure and architecture.

Commodity, Firmness, Delight

To start with Architecture, we might define that as the art of making satisfactory buildings.

Satisfactory that is, to human beings, both those who are going to use the building and those who are only looking at it.

Those who are going to use the building – who have to live in it, or work in it or play in it – will be mainly interested in that the building should make their living, working or playing more pleasant, that it has the right spatial arrangement, keeps out the weather, has the right gadgets, is properly lit and heated, and so on. The user is interested in utility, fitness for purpose, amenity; in short, the proper function of the building. That is what old Wotton calls Commodity.*

The onlooker, on the other hand, will consider the building as a piece of sculpture in a landscape or a series of tableaux of interior decoration. He is mainly affected by the aesthetic effect of the building, by its psychological impact on him, which is achieved through its form, style, artistic content, or whatever we like to call it. This is covered by the third of Wotton's conditions for well-building: Delight.

Naturally, the user and the onlooker may be the same person, and commodity and delight may be inextricably entangled. Such distinctions as these can nevertheless be useful – they are the normal tools of methodical thinking – as long as the underlying unity is not forgotten.

What about the second condition, *Firmness*?

To my mind, firmness is on a different plane from Commodity and Delight.

Commodity and Delight are what we *want* of a building. Firmness is merely a condition we have to fulfil in order to get the other two. It is a means to an end. Without firmness the building would collapse, and we would not be able to enjoy the other two for long. Firmness stands for all the qualities in a building which make it permanent, for its structural strength, which enables it to withstand the force of gravity and other forces of nature, and the weathering and wearing qualities of the materials employed. The degree of firmness required is therefore to some extent dependent on the intended life of the building.

In a way firmness is a purely negative quality. We don't notice its existence, only the lack of it.

Economy of Means

There is another condition of Well-building which might have been mentioned with the other three. It is the need for Economy of Means. This is another negative or restricting condition. A building which is very wasteful in its construction can hardly be called good architecture. Cost is the limiting factor which we are always fighting; it might truthfully be said, that the best architect is one who can produce most Commodity and Delight from a given sum of money.

It might be argued that the concern about cost is a modern phenomenon, which has nothing to do with the fundamental principles of architecture. I don't think that would be right. Cost may have nothing to do with the artistic value of the final result, but architecture is not only Art. The architect who can obtain the same amount of Commodity and Delight – assuming that it was possible to measure them – for a lower cost, would be a better architect, and his work would be better architecture.

The criterion

I am therefore tempted to try to improve on Wotton's time-honoured criterion for good architecture. To me, architecture is the result of a struggle to get as much as possible in the way of Commodity and Delight – out of a given expenditure of effort or of money – if I may mention so mundane a matter. It is easy enough to provide more Commodity, if not more Delight, by spending more money. To me, the skill of an architect and the excellence of an architectural solution is measured by the ratio between what is obtained, and what is expended. This criterion is, I think, valid for Architecture, but not necessarily for 'pure' Art. For the latter, the measure of its greatness may be the impact on the recipient, no matter how it is obtained. But in the case of Architecture, economy of means is an essential aim, and must therefore be taken into account in any judgment of merit.

By the way, if Architects took this matter more seriously, their service to the community and their standing in the eyes of the public would be enhanced.

My 'formula' for judging the excellence or the efficiency of an architectural solution is as follows:

$$E = \frac{BC + EC + D}{Cost}$$

BC stands for 'Basic Commodity', which is meant to indicate the basic requirements of the scheme – minimum floorspace, degree of heat insulation, etc., in other words, the minimum standard of performance indicated in the architect's brief.

EC stands for 'Excess Commodities' provided in excess of the basic commodities. They may be commodities of the same kind, or they may consist of desirable features not covered by the specification or brief. Different architectural solutions, which all can be said to satisfy the basic requirements, are bound to differ in respect of 'Excess

---

* Henry Wotton opens his *Elements of Architecture* (1624) with the 'aims for Well Building' being 'commodity, firmness and delight'. The book is a translation of architectural principles from the first-century Roman work *De Architectura*, by Vitruvius.

commodities,' and this difference must in fairness be taken into account, when we compare two schemes.

D stands for 'Delight,' or aesthetic excellence. It could have been included under 'Excess Commodity,' but it may be better to have a special heading for all those intangible forms of 'Commodity' which cannot be measured by a Quantity Surveyor.

'Cost' is the total effort to be expended or sacrifice to be made, to achieve a desired result. Costs are measured in £ s. d., but other considerations such as scarcity of materials or labour, come under this heading.

The trouble with this formula is this, that whereas Cost can be measured in money terms, and Basic Commodities can be reasonably valued at the lowest cost for which they can be produced, it is very difficult to put a money value on Excess Commodity and Delight. If Excess Commodity is considered to be superfluous in a particular case, no great value will be put on it. And as regards Delight, it is not even possible to obtain agreement on what constitutes Delight. Nevertheless, it is generally agreed that 'delight' has a value, and that it is the business of the architect to fight for it.

'Firmness' has not been included in the formula because it is not an end in itself, and it does not come under 'Cost' either. We can divide firmness into two parts, stability and durability. The latter indicates the wearing qualities of the building, its resistance against the ravages of time. It has a money value, for one thing because it decreases the cost of upkeep. It could be counted as Excess Commodity, and may even add to Delight. If we could build in granite, bronze, and teak rather than in concrete, steel and softwood, we would no doubt prefer it.

Stability on the other hand is a necessary condition for the enjoyment of commodity in any form, but we do not enjoy it for its own sake, and we want only so much of it as is required to ensure the safety of the building. Beyond this point, additional stability is valueless, whereas additional commodity, delight and durability as well as a saving in cost, are always welcome.

Safety and Cost

I might try to illustrate the relationship between commodity, delight, firmness and cost by an example from another sphere. In judging between different modes of travel we might set up speed and comfort as the things to aim for, and as the result of that we might give the prize to air-travel.

But two other factors enter into this business, Safety and Cost. Without safety we will not get very far, it is an essential condition for the enjoyment of the other two. On the other hand we only notice it, if it is absent, and we do not want more than approximately 100 per cent of it. As for cost, it plays the same role here as in building. And these are the difficulties which Air-travel has or had to contend with.

If we now turn our mind to the function of structure in building, it is clear that its main function is to ensure stability at as low a cost as possible consistent with the preservation of Commodity and Delight.

A good structure is first and foremost an economical structure. If a structure is sufficiently strong for its task, that is all that we need; if we made it twice as strong, it would hardly add to the value of the building. But if we could make it for half the cost, that would be very welcome indeed.

If this was all, it would be very easy to measure the excellence or otherwise of a structure. There would be no need to talk about elegant structures, ingenious structures, clumsy structures or perhaps honest structures – there would only be economical and expensive structures. But it is the reservation mentioned above which creates the difficulty: 'consistent with the preservation of Commodity and Delight'. We might have added: with the preservation and enhancement ... because the structure of a building is affecting its architectural qualities as well as providing for its stability.

Let us begin by considering a 'pure' structure, if we can imagine such a thing, and try to find out how it can be judged.

Economy of means

Its main job will undoubtedly be to fulfil its structural function, and to do so as economically as possible.

But apart from this, every physical structure is an object in space, and can therefore be judged from an architectural or aesthetic point of view. Its form, the pattern created by its members or parts, the treatment of its joints and connections, all are subject to aesthetic laws, and aesthetic judgment. In this sense we may speak of a beautiful or elegant structure, meaning that it gives us pleasure as a pattern or a piece of sculpture. The criteria we apply then have nothing to do with the structure as such.

We may derive another kind of pleasure from the contemplation of a structure *as a structure*.

We may admire it from a craftsman's point of view. It may represent an elegant mathematical solution, a novel, ingenious or simple way of solving the problem.

This kind of pleasure springs from a true understanding of the economy of means employed. It is the appreciation of an expert, not an expert on aesthetics and plastic art, but an expert on structure. It is the craftsman's pleasure in a job well done. I do not know whether this kind of pleasure would be included in what Wotton calls delight, but there it is.

Of course sometimes a structure is judged 'as a structure' by a layman, perhaps an architect or a client who have their own ideas about what a 'safe' structure should look like. It may be demanded of a structure – at least it has often been demanded of a piece of architecture – that it should give the onlooker a sense of security of balance, even if he is not a structural expert. This sense of security is only produced by the appearance of the structure, it is the psychological effect of the structural pattern on the onlooker. It may have nothing to do with the way the structure really acts, and it may even lead to the unnecessary increase of dimensions or the accentuation of a structurally false pattern. However, this kind of requirement, if it is justified at all, belongs more to the sphere of architectural criticism. I certainly do not think it has any place in the consideration of a structure. The technique of structure is advancing all the time, and the danger of evoking apprehension in the onlooker is not sufficient reason to stop this progress. He will get used to it. An effect of shock and surprise may even be deliberately intended as a part of the architectural effect.

Structure and architecture

It is now time to consider what role structure plays in architecture, or what influence it has on architecture.

First and foremost, structural technique makes building possible by providing stability. In doing so, it imposes a limitation on architecture – it gets in the way, so to speak. Columns and beams occur where they are not wanted, valuable space is lost. These structural limitations are often, perhaps even mostly, of an economic nature. New materials and advances in technique have made it possible to free architecture from structural fetters to an extraordinary degree, but this freedom has still to be paid for. What is structurally possible may not be financially possible, but both these limitations are being reduced all the time by technical progress.

If we view the structure in this light, as a utilitarian necessity, we can say that the best structural design is the one which is most economic and least obstructive. It is not easy to reconcile these two opposed aims, but much can be done by skilful design.

However, we shall probably never reach the stage when we can entirely eliminate all visible structural supports, and in the meantime structural elements are very much in evidence, whether we like it or not. And that brings me to the second way in which they affect architecture – as subject matter for artistic creation. Columns, beams, arches etc., are elements in the architectural pattern just as are windows, walls, chimneys, stairs and the rest, and as such they must be submitted to architectural – or perhaps we should say here – aesthetic discipline. From this point of view they may not be a nuisance at all, they may be a welcome help to artistic articulation. By collaboration between the architect and the engineer it may be possible so to arrange and so to shape the structural members that they positively contribute to Delight.

Structural 'rightness'

Thirdly, structural elements can be felt or considered as structural elements, rather than as mere special patterns. They may give satisfaction, because they are felt to be structurally right or give a pleasing sense of balance or strength. I have already touched on this point, and it is a difficult one. The pleasure felt may require expert structural understanding or may be based on a layman's misunderstanding. But it does not seem right to demand of an architectural critic that he should be a structural expert as well, neither does it seem right to praise or condemn a building on the basis of a fallacy. Perhaps the way to look at it is this, that structural 'Rightness' as such contributes to architectural quality mainly through its beneficial effect on costs, its avoidance of interference with the architectural plan and/or its contribution to the aesthetic pattern, but that the expert's delight in an ingenious structural solution falls outside the sphere of architectural criticism. On the other hand, the impression which the layman receives of structural security, strength or balance may form part of the architectural delight, even if it is not based on a proper understanding of how the forces are transmitted. However, this form of delight, or rather its opposite, caused by a seeming structural insufficiency, is likely to be changed by habit, and is therefore perhaps not fundamental to architectural criticism.

The fourth point I want to consider is the impact of new structural forms and techniques on aesthetic sensibility. Do they in themselves create new architecture?

The artistic climate

It is obvious that modern buildings look different from those built 50 years ago. It is equally obvious that this different look has in many cases been achieved by using techniques which were not available then.

But this does not mean that these techniques have created the new architecture. Such techniques do not become Architecture in the true sense before they have been assimilated by the architect and subjected to architectural control. Architecture results from building technique plus artistic or aesthetic direction, and it is the latter which is the important factor if we consider Architecture as an Art.

Building materials and methods of building are the raw material for the architectural artist. Naturally, the material does influence the final result. Just as the work of a sculptor is affected by whether he works in stone, timber, bronze or clay. But the creative intention is the main thing.

What has happened in the last decades is therefore not so much that we have been forced by new techniques to change our architecture, but that we have changed our ideas about what kind of architecture we want to produce. We build modern buildings because, and if, we want to, not because we must. And we want to, because the aesthetic sensibility of our time has changed. The artistic climate has changed. Visual Art has changed. When Corbusier created his first modern buildings, it was not as a result of necessity. Technically, the buildings were probably not so very good, they were at any rate expensive and difficult to keep in good shape. But his artistic vision demanded the free plan, the piloti, and the rest. Cubism has something to do with it. But I am getting out of my depth. What I wanted to stress is simply that artistic intention counts for more than building techniques in forming the new architecture. If anybody still doubts this, it should be sufficient to point to the difference between the Unilever building in New York and the new official buildings in Moscow.

New technical developments

When this is said, it can be admitted that new technical developments have some share in creating the new aesthetic sensibility. The worlds opened to us by micro-photography, aerial photography and many other technical and scientific developments, have enlarged enormously the reservoir of images from which artists draw their inspiration. And the feats achieved by engineers with the aid of new materials, the new bridges, long span roofs, light and spidery yet strong structures – these have fired the imagination of architects and have taught them to see new beauty in forms and patterns derived from the natural exploitation of the properties of new materials.

As architects experience engineering structures mainly as spatial forms, and less as devices for the transmittance of forces, their enthusiasm for, followed by imitation of, these forms can lead to the creation of structural clichés which gradually lose their structural justification. It is a well-known process in the history of Architecture, and it seems to be repeating itself now.

Aesthetic and human standards

Advance in technique may thus be a source of inspiration to the architect. But it also represents a serious menace to Architecture, and this is my last point.

Advance in technique is governed by economic forces, and the two combined drive us relentlessly towards mass production and standardisation. This tendency may prove very dangerous to Architecture, because Architecture can only thrive when there is freedom of choice. It may change the whole organisation of our building activities, and with it the position of the architect. There are two things we can do about this, and one thing we cannot do.

We cannot stop this development. The social or moral atmosphere of our time urges us to extend the 'good life' – or at least the freedom from want – to everybody, and that can only be done by utilising all advances in technique and production. But we can insist on certain aesthetic and human standards as well as the standards of efficiency. That means two things: first, to consider the aesthetic or architectural angle right from the beginning, whenever it is decided to launch a new building component or a dimensional standard; in other words, to bring the architect or the aesthetically trained industrial designer into industry ground level. Secondly, that we refuse to be guided solely by considerations of material efficiency, but insist on certain human standards even if the cost goes up. When I recently visited the Copper Belt in Northern Rhodesia and saw the Native and European 'compounds' from the air – regular dots in a square grid – then I strongly felt that somebody should say: It may be the simplest and cheapest way of building houses, but it is not what we want, and we won't have it! To sum up, what we have found about the inter-relation between structure and architecture is that:

1) Structure, in providing stability, is a necessary condition for building.
2) It is part of the artistic content of building.
3) The sense of structural 'rightness' can be pleasing to expert or layman.
4) New structural forms may provide inspiration, but
5) New industrial techniques may also be a danger to architecture.

In short, structure is seen:

1) As a means to provide 'commodity.'
2) As an element of design which can be used to create 'delight,' but only if this and all other elements of design are subject to aesthetic control.

Functionalism

Having got so far, I have still not reached the subject of my lecture, which was 'Structural Honesty'.

On the face of it, honesty is a term borrowed from ethics, it is a human attribute, and does not seem to have much application in the sphere of structure or architecture. But it is in fact often used in this sphere. Why? There is amongst some architects the feeling that it is honest to expose the structure, dishonest to conceal it. Brickwork is honest, plaster and stucco dishonest. Beams and columns making a nuisance of themselves are 'honest,' false ceilings are dishonest. Some even like the appearance of pipes and conduits as showing honestly how the services work.

I think that this point of view, with its puritan flavour, is an aftermath of functionalism.

Functionalism was a healthy reaction against the school of Beaux-Arts, against the idea that 'delight' was a result of the application of rather stale clichés in certain accepted patterns.

It was becoming more and more difficult to fit the new building techniques into this pattern, it led to great inconvenience in planning and to unnecessary expense. Architectural delight – and a rather stale form of delight at that – was felt to be the enemy of commodity and economy, and the new social atmosphere required that fitness for purpose and economy of construction should be emphasised.

It was felt that 'delight' should not be an addition but should be immanent in the economical and functional building.

The first result of this very sound view was undoubtedly that the architect, in his new freedom from traditional design discipline, neglected to exert sufficient control over the new elements of design. It was thought that if priority was given to function and the engineer was given a free hand, delight would automatically be created. We know better now, but I think this is the origin of the idea, that there is *eo ipso* [in itself] a virtue in showing the structure, and that it is important to show how everything works.

But there is a mixture here of many different things. There is a love of new structural shapes, applied perhaps from designs for bridges or large-scale engineering structural and applied on a wrong scale. There is simply a wish to be modern, or different. Structural 'honesty' is simply an excuse for doing what the architect wants to do. Just as in the Middle Ages philosophers had to prove the correctness of their logical deduction by interspersing the text with quotations from the Bible, so will certain modern architects rationalise their purely whimsical predilections by reference to function or structural honesty – often purely fictitious.

What in any case would structural honesty be? What is the 'honest' shape of a structure?

There are two different ways of looking at it. There is what I will call the organic structure and there is the economic structure.

Organic shape

The organic structure is economical in the use of materials, the economic structure is economical in means of production. The two may coincide, but mostly they don't.

In an organic structure, the material would be disposed in the most advantageous way to resist the forces acting on it. In Nature we often find shapes, like the structure of a leaf, for instance, which seem to follow this principle. Hence the name 'organic', grown like a tree. But although the structure of a cabbage leaf may be economic in the use of materials, it would certainly not be economic to reproduce it with modern structural materials. Each material made or fashioned by man, or rather by man-invented machinery, has its own characteristic economic shape, and this is generally not an organic shape. Take a steel joist, for instance. The shape is designed to resist the maximum bending moment in the centre of the span. But it is not the right shape for the end of the beams, where the bending moment is reduced and the shear forces prevail. The organic shape would be one which changed section all the time, and it would be an aesthetically attractive shape. But it could not be economically produced. The old 'fish belly' cast-iron beams had a shape which approached the structural or organic ideal, but they were superseded by modern mass-production methods. That is the tendency throughout.

Concrete structures

Reinforced concrete is the modern material which still lends itself to the creation of organic shapes, and that is no doubt the reason why it is so beloved by some modern architects, in spite of its drawbacks in some other respects.

And in large-scale structures, such as bridges, dams, large-span roofs and some industrial structures, the 'organic' shapes may be the economically correct ones, because it is most important to save material and reduce the dead weight of the structure. But in ordinary buildings simplicity of formwork tends to predominate over saving in concrete, from an economic point of view.

Moreover, the 'organic' shape is only correct for a particular set of forces. If the wind blows from the other direction, or the maximum load occurs in the next bay, the shape should really be different to be effective. The right shape is therefore one which 'envelops' all the organic shapes appropriate to the varying conditions, and this is not likely to be nearly so interesting.

In pre-stressed concrete and all factory produced concrete the shapes of the members are governed more by production technique than by the flow of the forces to which the members are eventually subjected. Mass production imposes its own mechanical stamp.

To come back to structural 'honesty'. I suspect that many of those who talk about exposing the structure as a sign of structural honesty, really are animated by a perfectly legitimate desire to use the structure as a means to create 'delight'. That is why they are often tempted to use 'organic' structural shapes which are really uneconomic in this particular context. It may very well be, then, that this talk about honesty – which presumably is meant to convey that none of the client's money is spent on unnecessary frills – really turns out to be dishonesty – not on the part of the structure, which is not capable of such complex behaviour – but on the part of the architect, who deceives himself and his client by giving the wrong reasons for what he is doing.

Knowing what one does

For it is of course true that honesty cannot be found in structures, but can be found in architects and engineers. And honesty, to my mind, consists in knowing yourself what you are doing, and being open about it. It is perfectly honest to use the structure to create architectural unity, strength, interest or what you will, and it is equally honest to try to keep the structure out of the way and of the mind altogether, provided you make no bones about it, and provided you do not pretend to do for economic reasons what you really do for aesthetic reasons.

Whether it is right to expose or conceal the structure depends of course entirely on what type of structure we are dealing with, and how it is done. In the modern multi-cellular building – the block of flats or offices, the structure can never be seen as a whole. Corbusier's idea of a series of slabs supported by a grid of free-standing pillars has aesthetic validity, but in practice it will be messed up by partitions and furniture – which cannot always be made entirely of glass. In such cases, the best way to achieve 'delight' may be to make the structure as inconspicuous as possible.

I come to the conclusion, therefore, that there is no need to add a demand for structural honesty, whatever this may mean, to the criteria already advanced for judging a structural solution. We need only ask ourselves two questions:

1) Is it an economical way of providing the necessary stability?

    and

2) Does it help the architect in providing 'delight' and perhaps additional commodity?

Integration

These two objects are of course often fighting each other. How much weight should be given to each depends on many things, mainly on the type of building we are dealing with. But if we want as far as possible to reconcile the two aims, that is to provide delight without involving the client in much extra cost, it is necessary to spend a good deal of thought and work on two different kinds of 'integration':

1) An integration of the architectural and structural idea, achieved by intimate collaboration between architect and engineer,

   and

2) An integration of the structural idea and the method of construction, achieved by pooling the knowledge of structural design with the knowledge of the economics of contracting and manufacturing processes. This can best be achieved by an early collaboration in the design stage with a nominated contractor.

Much has been said about the first kind of collaboration, for instance by myself, and time does not permit me to add more to it here. But I should like shortly to point out that we are rapidly moving into a situation where collaboration between engineers and contractors will become increasingly important.

I have always maintained that this kind of collaboration, or at least the pooling of the two kinds of knowledge, was essential for the successful design of large engineering structures such as marine structures, bridges, etc. It was of much less, or perhaps even of hardly any, importance in the design of buildings constructed in the orthodox manner which had prevailed for centuries, simply because the architect knew all there was to know about building. But this situation is changing. So many new techniques have been developed, many of them based on mass production in one form or another, that the architect and even the engineer are unable correctly to assess their economic implications. But to develop this theme would require another lecture.

Let me finish by extolling the virtue of simplicity of construction. Structural clarity, leading to simplicity, is often the key both to economy and delight, but how to achieve it is another matter.

The Integration of Structure and Architecture

A footnote to the original states '1955 Lectures in America'. There are gaps in the original denoted by ellipses ([...]), which indicate that it may have been transcribed from a recording or from shorthand where the transcription failed to capture words.

As I am supposed to talk to you about the *integration* of structure with architecture, it would be appropriate to start with a *definition* of these two terms. But that would, I am afraid, involve me in a *lot* of talk, and I suspect that both you and I will be relieved when I come to the point where I start showing you some slides. So I will shortly define architecture as the Art of Building, and point out, that a building must *first of all* satisfy certain functional requirements. *Secondly*, it should give us pleasure to look at it, outside and inside, and *thirdly* it should not cost more than absolutely necessary to achieve these two other aims, which we, with [Henry Wotton] may call commodity and delight.

The emphasis on these three factors varies considerably with the type of building, but generally speaking the architect is always fighting to provide as much commodity and delight as possible for as little money as possible.

The role of the *structure* is to provide *firmness*, to ensure the *stability* of the building under all conditions. We must, of course, have firmness, otherwise we cannot enjoy commodity and delight, but we do not value it for its own sake. We would not be interested in having more of it than necessary under all conditions. We do not even notice it – only the lack of it.

However, to provide the necessary stability under all foreseeable circumstances costs money, *more* or *less* according to the structural means employed. We are always interested in not throwing money away needlessly – at least the engineer, in his professional capacity should, almost by definition be interested in it – and it can therefore be said that a good structure is one which not only provides stability – that is taken for granted – but which does it at as low a cost as possible.

That is the main purpose of the structure, but as the structure necessarily influences the architecture, it will also be judged by whether it furthers the architectural aims of commodity and delight.

Structure affects commodity by occupying space and getting in the way, in the form of [...] columns, protruding ribs, beams and girders. Or it can, with some grandiose sweep, free the architecture from these structural fetters – but generally at a cost. Non-interference with commodity is generally in conflict with the aim of low cost, and the engineer is always challenged by the architect to achieve the impossible in the elimination of structural supports without any increase in the cost.

The same applies to the contribution of structure to delight. It also, as a rule, costs money. The structure forms part of the architectural pattern, just as windows, walls, stairs and the rest, and it must therefore be subjected to architectural discipline. This means that the shape and disposition of structural members should not be determined only by considerations of economy and function. They must also satisfy aesthetic standards.

We can therefore define the purpose of the structure, or the aim of the structural engineer as follows:

To provide the necessary stability of the building at as low a cost as possible consistent with the preservation or creation of commodity and delight.

All things of quality require a certain effort to achieve and the effort in this case is directed towards resolving the natural conflict between what we would like to have and what we can afford. But there is even more in it than that, because even if we could *afford anything*, we cannot buy aesthetic satisfaction – we cannot create beauty solely by brutally piling up expensive structures. Economy of means is just as necessary for its own sake; it is part of beauty.

But I had better leave this subject before I get too involved, and get down to this business of integration. It is obvious, that if the right structural solution depends both on its architectural quality and on its economy, than it can only be achieved by two kinds of integration: 1) that of the structural design with the architectural ideas; and 2) that of the structural design with the available means and possible methods of construction.

This integration can be brought about in various ways. In the old days the builder was also the architect and the engineer, and the integration could take place *inside one brain* – by far the most effective way. In these days of specialization this way is no longer possible, and must be replaced by collaboration between a number of persons. Of these, one may be the architect, who is mainly responsible to the client for the proper functioning of the building and for its aesthetic quality. He would therefore naturally be the representative of the client in the council of specialists. He would be assisted by a structural engineer and other engineering specialists on heating, acoustics, etc. And finally the building or contractor would be able to advise on practical and economic methods of building, which does not necessarily mean the same thing as designers using a minimum of materials. These various experts can be organized in different ways. They may all operate separately or the architect and engineers may be combined in one firm, or the structural design may be carried out by the contractor. It would be interesting to analyze the merits of these different systems, but there is no time for that here. But whatever the systems, two things are required for a successful collaboration: 1) that there exists the necessary machinery for enable their collaboration to take place right from the start; and 2) that the members of the team, besides being experts in their particular field, have a fair knowledge and understanding of what the other fellows are driving at. If each member only sees and understands his own point of view, collaboration is not possible.

Enough has been said about the necessity of infinite collaboration between architect and engineer, and it is obvious, that even the initial concept of a scheme has its structural implications. Architects and engineers should be educated to understand each other's work, and, as professional men, should find it easy to collaborate. But the collaboration, in the design stage, between engineer or architect and the builder, presents greater difficulties.

A generation or more ago this integration of economic building practice and design was easy enough to achieve in ordinary building because the architect – who generally was also the engineer – knew all he needed to know about building practice and building costs. Since then a bewildering variety of new materials and methods of construction have come into being, and it is becoming increasingly difficult to make sure that the best possible method is chosen. Moreover, the builder is rarely brought into the picture before the design is finished. But even if this handicap were overcome, for instance by nominating a contractor from the start on a fee basis and bringing him into the design team, a practice which has much to recommend it, and is being increasingly used – even then, the difficulty very largely remains. This is because one single contractor is not necessarily able to give an un-biased and well-founded opinion on the best way of tackling an unusual job, where new methods are being introduced. One would have to tap the best available contracting experience and imagination

– and how to harness this to the design team is a difficult problem. The only really satisfactory solution is for the designer himself to have the necessary building experience and practical imagination, and to be able to draw on advice from those experts whose knowledge is relevant to the problem in hand. Or to have on the design team a contractor of more than usual ability and broadmindedness, and with a professional interest in finding the right solution. But this simply amounts to saying that the better the team, the better the design – which, I expect you know already.

Anyhow, it is certainly difficult for the designer now-a-days to keep abreast of all the exciting developments which are taking place in the methods of building, and it is especially difficult for him to estimate their effect on costs. Costs are not only a question of the amount of materials and labour required. With the movement towards site mechanization and factory production, which is now gathering momentum, the method employed and therefore the design, depend to a large extent on the size of the job, on the number of repetitious building units or operations, and on distances and traffic facilities between factory and job. The estimator – and the designer must of course be an estimator at the same time – is concerned with running costs and [...] of for instance pre-stressed concrete production yards with assessing the possibility of using them for other jobs or with the possibility of contractors taking undue advantage of a monopoly position created by proprietary rights or the ownership of means of production, thus eliminating competition.

The imaginative designer is also handicapped, if he is not himself a contractor, by his inability to back up his own ideas. He may be convinced, and may be able to prove that a new type of design or method of building involving unusual features may be economical – but he has to convince a contractor of this before the advantage can be realised in practice. And contractors are often conservative and canny. They like to know exactly what they are in for. It is of course also true, that any new departure invariably costs more money the first time it is tried, so that it must possess outstanding merit to overcome this handicap, unless the contractor has sufficient imagination and interest in his job to take a long term point of view.

This trend towards mass-production, standardization and capital investment in means of production may also be a great danger to architectural and imaginative design. The tailor-made job tends to be replaced by the ready-to-wear article. It started with the production of structural steel sections – most structural steel jobs are simply a matter of piling one joint on another, the calculation a matter of looking up tables. The same happens now with prestressed concrete units. That way materials may be wasted, but labour and design are simplified. These developments have come to stay, but it is important not to neglect the tailor-made job where a real effort is made to integrate the structure with the architectural requirements, which has a much greater chance to create architectural delight.

Different materials and methods of construction vary greatly in respect to the freedom, which they allow the designer. Reinforced concrete cast in situ is a wonderful material in this respect, and the development of concrete shells and other continuous structures has great architectural possibilities. Post tensioned concrete, where the stress is produced by cables, can also be used with great freedom and so can extruded aluminium alloys owing to the facility with which new sections can be produced to fit each particular job. Site welding of steel also introduces the possibility of more imaginative structure in this material.

On the other hand, factory production of building units tends to freeze design, and with it architectural freedom. The answer is to apply architectural control at the source. Let the architect interest himself in these processes – or rather, let the sponsors and owners interest themselves in the architect, as at least in the good architectural solution – but this opens up a new chapter on the important question of how to educate the client and we will leave it at that.

Modern Architecture: The Structural Fallacy

This article was published in The Listener,
7 July 1955.

I want to discuss here the rather complicated relationship between the structure of buildings and their architecture. There is now a wide range of new structural possibilities through the use of structural steel, of reinforced concrete, pre-stressed concrete, of aluminium alloys, and other materials in all their varying forms. This, together with the advance in engineering knowledge, has enabled us to create structures of an incredible lightness and strength, compared with the old gravity structures. We can soar into the sky and span if not the oceans at least long distances with the greatest of ease; in fact, we can do most things we want to do, if we want them badly enough.

Side by side with this extension of the range of structural possibilities, a gradual change in the processes of production has taken place. Work on the site has been largely mechanized, and more and more building components are being mass-produced in factories. The former aspect of modern building technique has given the architect greater freedom to do what he likes, the latter tends to restrict this freedom in the interests of standardization. How are architects responding to this twofold new situation? And how does it affect architecture?

Maxwell Fry,[*] in a talk entitled 'The Architect's Dilemma' printed in *The Listener* of February 17, went back to the beginnings of modern architecture. It set out, he said, to be 'entirely freed from subjection to any style; its only criteria being: carefully analyzed function, honestly expressed structure and the demands of applied sociology'.

It is significant that this definition contained no mention of aesthetic principles, or of architecture as an art. Indeed the pioneers of the movement, or some of them, thought that if only they attended

---

[*] Maxwell Fry (1899–1987) was a British architect who became a leading member of the Modern Architecture Research Group (MARS).

to the function of a building, and – to quote again from Maxwell Fry – 'adopted a structure arising from engineering, and clearly expressing, instead of hiding, its structural function', then beauty would automatically arise, and the result would be architecture.

The aesthetic programme of the modern movement is hidden away in an excessive admiration for all things technical, for new structural forms and materials, for making full use of all the latest technical innovations long before they are economically justified, and for the 'honest expression' – whatever that may mean – of the structure. So much enthusiasm for the means of building is suspicious, it shows that there is more in it than meets the eye. And so there is. There has been a revolution – we all know it – in aesthetic sensibility. It started 50 years ago in painting and thereafter permeated all the visual arts; it derived inspiration from primitive art, from the new patterns and images brought to light by scientific investigation and made accessible by modern photography and reproduction techniques; it derived a further impetus from the new structural forms developed by engineers. Through the opening up of these new worlds, we have learnt to see beauty where it did not occur to us to look before.

But modern architecture has still not produced a new architectural language which is universally accepted by our time. Aesthetically we are still in a state of flux, and that is perhaps not a bad thing. We see the romanticism of a Frank Lloyd Wright side by side with the classicism of a Mies van der Rohe. We see the beginnings of a great many different fashions, with *clichés* originated by the great going their round in architectural magazines, and being copied with glee all over the world; but they do not seem to stick, they have not congealed into a new academicism. The nearest approach I can find to a common ideology is the frequently expressed conviction that a regeneration of architecture in our new technical age must come through the truthful expression of structure. This sounds attractive enough – especially to an engineer – but what in fact does it mean?

In an ordinary brick building, the walls have a number of things to do – they enclose space, and keep out the weather, they retain heat, insulate against cold and sound, and they also carry the loads from the floors and roof. But in this latter capacity they are only partially employed, and without opening up the floors and finding out which way the timber joists are spanning it is difficult to see which of the walls or parts of them are structurally active. Expression of structure hardly comes into the picture, and yet some very good architecture – Georgian, for instance – has been produced with brick. When the walls are pierced by large window openings, and when they also have to act as buttresses for vaulting or to ensure stability, as in the case of the Gothic cathedrals, we can begin to talk about structural forms and possibly also of the expression of structure: if structural economy is to be achieved, the enlarged scale and the magnitude of the gravitational forces impose a certain discipline of their own.

Carried to its logical conclusion, Gothic architecture does represent a structural idea: the gravity structure soaring upwards, but pared down to the minimum thickness that will ensure stability. Its forms may approach what I have called the 'organic structure'; in a structure of this type the material is disposed so as to take care of the flow of forces in the most advantageous way. The ideal Gothic forms flow solidly from the ground, where the heaviest loads occur and are attenuated towards the top. The rounded arch, vault, or dome, of masonry or brick, represents a slightly different structural idea, with the emphasis on spanning horizontally rather than soaring upwards. But here we can distinguish between two different approaches. The 'organic structure' of this type would be given the structurally correct form – somewhat approaching a parabola – which would reduce the bending moments and therefore the mass to a minimum, and the thickness of material would at every point be adjusted to the force. Architects have, however, often preferred a simple geometric form; they have turned the arch into a half circle – in former times this was partly due to ignorance, but also because in classical architecture, and in modern architecture with a classical flavour, it is considered an aesthetically more satisfactory form. This kind of disciplined structure we might call 'geometric structure', to indicate that it is modified or purified to fit into a geometric pattern.

Modern structural materials, such as steel and reinforced concrete, have given architects the possibility, with the help of engineers, of creating a number of *new* structural ideas or archetypes, so to speak. There is, for instance, the three-dimensional structural steel grid or frame. Steel, being a purely structural material, cannot be used economically to form floors or walls; in a building it provides only the framework on which the other materials are hung. Being produced by rolling it is available in uniform sections; for this and other reasons it does not lend itself to the creation of an organic structural pattern in the way of a tree, with tapering branches, but it is very suited to the imposition of geometric discipline. Modern architects have seized this opportunity to create the idea of the ideal structural grid – a three-dimensional rectangular system of lines evenly disposed, of even and as small as possible section throughout, and with no disturbing excrescences at the joints, a conception of pure geometry.

Mies van der Rohe especially has struggled hard to give effect to this idea, and that implies of course expressing or showing the structure, otherwise there would be no point in the attempt. In his Lake Shore Apartments in Chicago and some private houses the walls are therefore made of glass, so that the grid itself can be clearly perceived and nothing shall mar the purity of the conception. Then there is reinforced concrete, which can enclose space and – with a little help – keep out the weather, besides providing structural support. The structural carcass of a building in this material may be thought of as a series of horizontal slabs – the floors supported by a regular grid of columns. The box-frame or egg-crate is another very simple geometric idea characteristic of reinforced concrete construction; it consists of a regular system of vertical and horizontal slabs. Reinforced concrete has also given birth to other structural forms – the cantilever, for instance – like a branch of a tree, strong at its base and tapering outwards; and thin concrete shells, which can take on a great number of shapes and now replace gravity vaulting. Then there are all the various forms of frames, arches, trusses, and girders and there are tent-like constructions based on suspension cables, and the so-called space-frames: three-dimensional triangulated grids, which at present have a vogue in architectural schools far in excess of their importance.

These structural forms are mostly developed by engineers for utilitarian or economic reasons, but they exert a strong fascination on architects, who are apt to react to them in an emotional or intuitive way, seeing them as spatial forms or patterns which are capable of being organized artistically. This can be done either with a bias towards organic, so to speak romantic, forms, or on strictly controlled geometrical and classical lines.

Sometimes architects seize on a characteristic structural feature and use it for purely aesthetic ends where it is neither economically nor structurally justified. This has happened throughout the history of architecture, and there is nothing wrong in that, as long as the aesthetic purpose is acknowledged and achieved. Take, for instance, the hinge, which impels all the forces to meet in a single point.

In nature, hinges or joints are used to allow movement, as in the case of an elbow joint. Plants which are stationary have no joints; it would mean an unnecessary weakening of the structure. In structural engineering hinges are introduced for two reasons: to facilitate calculations by making the structural system statically determined, as in the three-hinged arch, and, as in nature, to allow movement – for instance, a settlement of foundations or temperature expansion of a bridge.

But architects love hinges for their own sake.

In the new Coventry Cathedral, Basil Spence* makes the columns carrying the internal canopy taper downwards ending in a kind of ball-bearing; and Saarinen's spectacular, triangular, concrete shell at the Massachusetts Institute of Technology† rests on three points, formed as steel hinges. There is no structural or economic reason for this – it is a purely aesthetic device conveying a feeling of crispness and also of a purified structural idea, which may be aesthetically justified in spite of being slightly bogus. Incidentally, the appeal of the hinge or focal point is strikingly revealed in the architectural drawings of [Saul] Steinberg,‡ when he shows enormous arches and suspension bridges ultimately supported on needle points. As an artist he catches the essence, the aesthetic spirit of engineering structures, and architects have often a similar approach.

The engineer, in accordance with his training and purpose in life, is trying to find the most economical structure. I mean economical in the means of production. He takes into account available resources and the characteristic manner in which each structural material is produced. This does not necessarily imply the most economical use of material as in the concept of an 'organic structure', although in large-scale structures that concept may be approached. It is not always the aesthetically most satisfactory approach either. Nevertheless it is in the quest for economic ways of solving difficult structural problems that the new and exciting structural forms have been evolved. They generally need a little trimming, a deviation from the strictly most economical solution, to bring out their inherent beauty, which may be of an organic or geometric type in accordance with the materials and methods used. But the point is, that whereas in large-scale and difficult

---

* Sir Basil Spence (1907–1976) was one of Britain's most celebrated modern architects of the post-war era.
† Eero Saarinen's Kresge Auditorium was built in 1955, the year this paper was published.
‡ Saul Steinberg (1914–1999) was a Romanian-born cartoonist and illustrator, best known for his work in The New Yorker.

engineering structures, such as bridges, dams, and long spanning roofs, economy and beauty often coincide – or nearly so – if a clear and simple structural idea is logically pursued; it is not at all easy to cash in on this fact in architecture, as architects would dearly love to do.

In our normal multicellular buildings the structure, besides being of an elementary and unexciting kind, is cluttered up with walls, stairs, flues, service-ducts, lift-shafts, and so on, and to submit it to a strict aesthetic discipline and then to expose it sufficiently for it to be understood as a whole, would in most cases require great sacrifices in money and the disregard of other necessary functions. In our climate buildings must have an overcoat and a raincoat, and there is no particular reason why the structure should be left out in the cold. And, internally, we do not want to be reminded of it; it only gets in the way.

Recently, on a tour in the United States of America, I had occasion to show some slides of the new Hallfield Estate in Paddington [London], by Drake and Lasdun. In this scheme the access balconies and other elements of the facade are used to make a formal pattern; this pattern, however, bears no relation – or at least does not truthfully express – the structure behind, which is a simple box-frame of reinforced concrete. At Harvard, Chermayeff* thought that this was by far the best piece of architecture which had come out of England after the war. But others, at the University of Pennsylvania, and especially at the Illinois Institute of Technology where Mies van der Rohe is in charge, were very scathing in their condemnation of this aimless doodling, which they considered dishonest, fortuitous, and futile. They insisted that the box-frame behind the facade should have been expressed on the outside.

It is difficult to analyze this attitude – it is a mixture of sense and nonsense. As so often happens, means become aims; the expression of the structure, which may admittedly be a means of creating architectural unity (although sometimes an expensive and unnatural way of doing it), becomes an end in itself. This moral streak, which was certainly present in Victorian architecture before it pervaded functionalism, leads to the naive assumption that straightforward, unadorned, economic building will somehow display the quality which is so admired in engineering structures. The fact is, of course, that it requires a major *tour de force* to impose this quality on ordinary buildings, as Mies' Lake Shore Apartments show. Ordinary buildings are much more influenced by building technique proper: by standardization, mass-production of building elements, and so on.

The expression of structure makes more sense in buildings providing large spaces – factories, exhibitions halls, and so on. Here the structural members are often bound to be prominent and have to be organized.

But there should be no moral compulsion about it. Acoustic ceilings, water-proofing insulation and service ducts may make it impractical to reveal the structure, especially if it is of the economical but ordinary, rather than the inspiring, variety. The engineer is probably as keen as the architect to evolve an exciting structural solution but it is his duty to point out to the architect that the beautiful structure is rarely the same as the economical structure, although in some inspired solutions the two may almost coincide. Yet, in spite of all this, I would count that there is something valuable and right in this architectural approach to structure, and many engineers might do with a dose of it.

Architecture is concerned with 'organizing the functional elements so as to create something aesthetically coherent and with a personality of its own', as J.M.Richards† put it in a talk entitled 'Architecture Dehumanised' printed in *The Listener* of January 6. It is a matter of giving the proper weight to various conflicting claims and creating harmony and order out of chaos. Organizing the available material in space means imposing on it some easily recognizable pattern or main motif, creating a simple, if subtle, balance of masses and spaces, tying it together with lines and planes, creating unity by consistency, by limiting the means of expression to a chosen few. Subordinate to the main pattern there may be other patterns, elaboration of detail, but they must not obscure the clarity of the main conception, which acts as a frame of reference, making the whole thing intelligible and obvious at a glance. A certain simplicity, a sense of the unavoidable, of essential Rightness is, I think, common to all great art.

A clear, simple and well-proportioned structural system can be eminently suited to the role of providing this general pattern, this orderly frame of reference. The wish to express it is therefore a very natural one, as long as ethics are not mixed up with it and as long as it is realized that this 'organization of the functional elements' can just as well, or just as legitimately, be achieved by other means.

The importance of having a simple guiding idea to help in the solution of an architectural problem was brought home to me when in 1946 Clive Entwistle† was working on his scheme for the Crystal Palace competition in my office. It contained, as a central feature, a very large pyramid covered entirely in glass-bricks.

Le Corbusier, who took a friendly interest in the work of his pupil and worked on the scheme for several days, suggested that the inside of the pyramid should be treated in an organic manner, so to speak, with ceiling heights getting smaller towards the top, and everything else in proportion. He was at the time very full of his modular system of proportions, and he drew a kind of tapering Christmas tree to indicate his conception. Clive disagreed with this: for him this building was a crystal, where every part was like every other part, and floors equidistant throughout, and he stuck, I think rightly, to his conception. The problem could have been approached from a purely functional and structural angle, but both architects felt the need to subordinate this approach to a general principle. This has a bearing on ideologies and theories in general; although it could be argued, as I have done, that they matter less than the amount of artistic effort expended, or the degree of synthesis achieved, they may nevertheless be a help to the creative artist. If so, well and good, but it is the result that matters.

* Serge Chermayeff (1900–1996) was a self-taught, Russian-born, British architect.
† J.M. Richards (1907–1992) was a writer on architecture and editor of *The Architecture Review* from 1937 to 1971.
‡ Clive Entwistle (1916–1976) collaborated with Peter Yates and Ove Arup on the competition for a new Crystal Palace.

Structure in Relation to Architecture

Notes handwritten on the manuscript indicate this lecture was given in Belfast on 17 April 1957 and was 'unpublished'. The language in places is more outline and sketchy than the vast majority of Arup's lecture notes, and the text ends unconventionally with either an introduction to slides or the suggestion of continuation. Together, these suggest the manuscript may have been a draft. It is further distinguished by a focus on technical matters, steering away from a broad philosophic exploration, which suggests it was intended for a singularly technical audience. This pre-dates the lecture he gave the following year in Belfast on 'The Education of Engineers'.

Perhaps I should start with a definition of structure – and of architecture – but I think I will skip it – we know more or less what we are talking about, and this is not a scientific dissertation. And to define architecture is in any case next to impossible.

The main job of the structure of a building is to make it stand up to the forces acting on it – force of gravity, wind etc. This is a *must*, there can be nothing half-hearted about it. On the other hand it need not be stronger than necessary – but unfortunately what is necessary is to some degree arbitrary, because we do not know exactly how big a wind pressure we may expect, whether the soil will give a little, whether the materials or workmanship may be slightly faulty and whether our calculations and assumptions are correct.

So we must give ourselves a margin – the so-called factor of safety – and it would be quite easy to spend hours and days on discussing how that should be fixed.

It is an important question, because stability costs money and the second great demand we must make on our structure is that it should not cost more than necessary.

Stability is necessary, but more stability than necessary is not only unnecessary but a complete waste of money.

The third claim to a satisfactory structure is that it should not obstruct the function of the building more than necessary. Columns, for instance, and deep beams and other structural projections, are nearly always in the way – it would be better not to have them, but if they are necessary – and that happens – then it is important that they should be arranged so as to do the least harm.

And finally, there is the aesthetic effect of the structure. The structure has obviously a strong influence on the architecture of a building, directly or indirectly, and as soon as we begin to talk about architecture we plunge headlong into controversy of the most confused kind, as when stirring up a hornets' nest. What are the demands of architecture on a structure apart from the three uncontroversial points I have already mentioned? Should it be subordinated to a formal pattern? Should it be unobtrusive and unnoticeable? Should it tell a story about how the building is made to stand up, or should it constitute the main architectural interest of the building?

All these views, and more, have been and are being held with great conviction, and it is of course unwise for a mere engineer to meddle in this fray.

After which I will proceed to do so.

Let us first see how far we can get by considering the three uncontroversial points:
Stability, Economy and *Unobtrusiveness*.

1. Stability

We need not waste much time on the first, but I should like to mention two things in this connection, both of which should be considered under the two headings: Stability and Economy.

We have mentioned that a building should not be stronger than necessary – as this would be wasteful.

This also means that it should be evenly strong all over. Most buildings, or structures, are strong in some parts and weak in others. To some degree this is unavoidable, and it can also be unimportant if it does not affect the cost of the structure, but there are far too many cases of mixed extravagance and meanness as regards strength.

A chain is no stronger than its weakest link, – and in a well designed structure all links should be equally strong or weak.

The second point is the question of the durability of the structure – for how long should it be stable. This of course is largely a matter of economy, and also of aesthetics – because the more durable materials and finishes are generally more pleasing as well as more expensive.

It has often been suggested that we should design our buildings for a limited life, because they in any case become outmoded. This of course rests on the assumption that a building which lasts only ten or twenty years will be cheaper than a 'permanent' building – but I am afraid this is wrong. A building which lasts that amount of time will last for ever – more or less – if it is properly maintained. The difference is only in the cost of maintenance. It is therefore largely a question of finishes – but it should be borne in mind, that buildings which need a lot of maintenance will generally not get this service and will soon look shabby. Therefore the Architect and Engineer should always strive for permanency or minimum maintenance.

2. Economy

The first and foremost aim of every Engineer is to strive for economy of building.

3 Aspects of Economy

1) *Detail design.* Even strength to factor of safety. Use of continuity – statical indeterminacy. Organising details in orderly repetitive manner.
2) *Integration of design with method of building.*
   Use materials naturally, suit manufacture and building. Consider local conditions. Wash out *how* the thing is to be erected – plan execution as well as design.
   Use repetition – consider formwork.
3) *Integration of structure with architectural plan.*

We are here moving into the next point – but I mention it here because it is my experience, that the architectural plan has more influence on cost than anything else. If this plan is simply economic in space and permits the adoption of a sensible structure which is easy to build – then half the battle is won. This can only be achieved by close collaboration between Architect and Engineer in the early stages of a job. Give and take –

Sometimes architecture is dominant, sometimes structure.

3. Unobtrusiveness

This point is partly the same as mentioned under 2 – that the plan and the structure should fit together.

The one thing which dominates the whole joint undertaking is that the building must fulfil its function.

The structure is not part of the function, it is only a necessary evil – but it may, very well obstruct the function. Columns in the middle rooms, projecting beams and pilasters and all that are in the way, they impede function and can be disastrous architecturally. Therefore, the structure must be integrated with the plan.

This is not simple – requires hard work.

Fundamental conflict between the desirable and the economic possible. The obvious example columns – large spans.

Also *Flexibility*.

Often costs more than it is worth.

How far have we got?

If we have a building where structure and plan have been integrated, where the structure is sensible, easy to build and economical and does not obstruct, and is permanent without too much upkeep, etc. how far have we got towards creating Architecture with a capital A?

Quite a distance – I should say, assuming that the building also functions well. But we are not there yet. All these things are necessary, but not enough. We have not yet spoken about proportions, for instance, which everybody will agree is very important. And there is spatial relationship, colour, texture and all the other elements of architecture.

They must be organised artistically.

And I am afraid that there is not any recipe which will guarantee a successful outcome.

There have of course been plenty of recipes, plenty of advice about what to do and what not to do. For instance, the early functionalists in the Twenties seemed to imply that function and economy was all that was required. But they soon went further demanding also 'honesty' whatever that may mean, the truthful expression of structure, the rank expression of primary building materials, and of the entrails of buildings, an attitude which seems to be repeated in some of the pronouncement of the New Brutalists – although I am not suggesting that this term or those pronouncements should be taken seriously.

But other attitudes can also be found – there are formalists who would emphasise the purely pictorial or sculptural aspects of a building, and there are all the many instances of an aesthetic choice being camouflaged as based on function, economy or some theory or other.

For instance, there are the many cases of what I have called 'structuresque' architecture, where structural motives are used aesthetically, although pretending to obey some structural necessity. Altogether Architects are often afraid of admitting that they do something because they like it. They think it necessary to invent some functional, structural or economic reason for it.

I do not think that any of these rationalisations should be taken seriously. They may be very important for the architects concerned, of course. They have to impose order and clarity on all the spatial and visual elements of a building, and there are so many ways of doing it. They may find it useful to have an idea to express a theory to guide them. But these theories obviously have no universal application, because there are many conflicting theories, and each of them can produce both good and bad architecture.

The Education of Engineers

The manuscript title is 'Talk Given at Belfast Conference September 1958', and a footnote adds 'Belfast Conference Talk on Postgraduate Education of Civil Engineers 10 September 1958. Conference on the role of the University in the education of civil engineers.'

First of all I should like to make it clear that I am not an expert on education and I have made no special study of it. Having myself received my technical education abroad I have never penetrated what to me looks like the jungle of British technical education. It strikes me with awe, wonderment and admiration, but I am afraid that in spite of my 35 years in England I have not been able to shed certain Continental prejudices which you presently will be able to see in action.

When I have nevertheless been honoured with a request to speak to you today it is presumably because I have had the pleasure of working with a great many British engineers trained in various educational establishments of this country, and indeed, also with many engineers trained in Scandinavia, Poland, Holland, Germany, Switzerland, France, Czechoslovakia, etc. and that I, therefore, should be able to make some pronouncement on the value of their education.

I am afraid that all I can offer you is some rather imprecise impressions, probably biased, but at any rate not supported by any methodical study of the usefulness of engineers in relation to their education. Such a study would in any case be complicated by the impossibility of eliminating intelligence and general character, which in the long run have a much greater influence on the result.

My theme is Postgraduate Education which is education in addition to that given in the standard undergraduate course. It follows that postgraduate education cannot be considered in isolation. What is needed plainly depends on what has been taught before. This is my excuse for talking as much about pre as of postgraduate education.

Secondly, it makes a difference whether we consider postgraduate education as part of the standard equipment of an engineer, whether we are satisfied that the normal undergraduate course is sufficient for the majority of engineers so that only a few need take these extra courses. If we take the latter view – and that seems to be so in practice if not in theory – then it has naturally a bearing on the curriculum for the undergraduate course.

This must then be complete in itself. It must produce graduates who are ready to go out in practice and pick up the additional knowledge they need as best they can. The postgraduate courses will then be for engineers, older or younger, who feel that they need more knowledge in a special branch of engineering and who, either by their own efforts, or with the help of grants, can afford one or more of such courses. If postgraduate courses of this kind are of the right quality they can obviously fill a real need and do a lot of good because a young engineer may easily find that his place of employment does not give him enough opportunity to improve his knowledge, and it is often difficult to know where to find the material for private study.

If, on the other hand, postgraduate courses are part of the standard training then the curriculum must be considered as a whole. It simply means that we have a four or five years' standard course instead of a three years' course, and that it is divided into two parts, Part I being the same for all and Part II allowing for specialisation. This arrangement would make it possible to put in a year or two years' practical employment between Part I and II but that is a secondary question. It may be a very good idea because it will give the student more time to think about what he wants to specialise in; a taste of extra-mural life may give him greater maturity and a sense of responsibility before taking his final degree, and he may be better able to relate the teaching of the practical subjects to his outside experience. On the other hand, he may not. I think I should at present be inclined to vote for a break, but only just. It is a question about which I do not know enough. But if there is an interval it should not be more than two years, if that; otherwise the students get out of the habit of studying.

What is important, however, is what should be taught in Part I, undergraduate level, and what in Part II, postgraduate level. In other words, how much should all civil engineers know and where does specialisation start. This business of specialisation is in some ways the curse of modern civilisation, but it is the only answer to the steady accumulation of technical as of other knowledge. But where to set the limit to specialisation is debatable. Specialisation is an evil because it makes a person narrow-minded and makes communication with others difficult. After all, the various specialists have to get together again to collaborate and that requires a common language and mutual understanding. Imagination and invention – essential for a creative engineer – flourish on cross fertilisation from other fields of knowledge. It would not do, therefore, to teach an engineer only that which he needs for a particular job. In any case he cannot know what he may come up against; he does not know which job he will get and whether he may not want to change it for another. On the other hand, he cannot possibly learn all that any kind of civil engineer may want to know. He must specialise. The question is, how much of practical engineering knowledge can safely be left for the engineer to acquire in practice, how much should be taught only if he chooses the subject in his postgraduate course, and how much should every civil engineer know.

Previous speakers have pointed out that the undergraduate course is already overcrowded, which is bad. Some want to include a lot of additional instruction like taking out quantities or making reports, which makes it worse still. There is, therefore, a great temptation to cut down on the theoretical side, mathematics, etc. in order to relieve the situation. This is Professor Fisher-Cassie's position.[*] He wants to transfer engineering science to an applied scientist's course and to free the energy of the engineers so that it can be applied to creative design, which is his real job. I was much impressed with this part of his argument. I agree absolutely that creative design is the most important of all, although it may be difficult to teach it. But in these days creative design is severely handicapped if not founded on a thorough theoretical training. It may not be the job of the designer to contribute to engineering science, but he should create scientific engineering. In fact, I suggest that there should be much more and not less theoretical training. My experience with undergraduates coming straight from college is that they know far too little solid geometry, theory of structures, etc. and, incidentally, they are often not able to draw, which makes them rather useless in an office to begin with.

This is, of course, a matter of opinion. It is undoubtedly influenced by the fact that I have had my technical education on the Continent where it generally takes five years to get an engineering degree and that I have been mainly engaged on the design of structures and their construction. In this branch of engineering the scientific equipment of the engineer is rather important if one does not wish to be confined to design according to some given set of rules and one has to be prepared to meet all sorts of contingencies in giving effect to the design. In the Danish firm in which I started my career and where I stayed 12 years, they certainly believed in using all the resources of science to make their designs more competitive.

They had a whole library of original reports on interesting jobs, designs, tests, original inventions and various design data, and these were regularly distributed to all their engineers. I think that policy influenced their success all over the world.

Can we really afford to lag behind other nations in this respect? My impression is that Britain is not meeting the challenge of international competition in the field of civil engineering design.

It may be argued that the majority of civil engineers do not later in life require so much theoretical knowledge and that, therefore, the standard at undergraduate level can safely be lowered, provided those who really need more of this kind of knowledge have the opportunity of acquiring it at postgraduate courses.

It is true, of course, that the degree in civil engineering at the moment provides an entrance to widely diverging occupations, the design, construction, maintenance and administration of harbours, railways, roads, sewage and irrigation works, structures of all kinds, contracting, etc. In all these branches the majority of jobs are routine jobs or subordinate jobs where one can get by without initiative and creative imagination. One has the feeling that it is often by historical accident that these occupations are classed together as civil engineering, and that one could usefully review the situation to see whether some of them could be separated out and given a special kind of education. Nevertheless, in their original creation and in the development of their technique they all have something to do with the conquest of Nature by man, and those who advance the boundaries of technical knowledge may need the theoretical tools forged by previous generations in order to advance. The administration of railways may be largely a routine matter, but the improvements of railway technique is something quite different and needs scientific research and all the resources of engineering.

The real distinction, although a gradual one, is, therefore between engineers who are capable of breaking new ground and those who merely assist or follow a given routine. The former can benefit greatly from a thorough training in scientific method and theory no matter what kind of civil engineering they embark on. And although they are a minority they are an important minority because their contribution determines Britain's position in the engineering world with the consequences that follow therefrom.

It may be argued that the pioneers of this calibre will make a break through no matter how they are started in life and that, in fact, the British genius has often manifested itself in self-made men with a genius for invention and perseverance and only a modicum of scientific ballast. But times have changed. Imagination and a genius for invention are as necessary as ever, but it will be more and more difficult to dispense with a solid theoretical foundation.

If we, therefore, make things easier for ourselves by curtailing those studies which, after all, are the foundation for independent thought on technical matters and make those studies the subject of postgraduate courses instead, then we run the risk that the large majority of engineers will never attend them and the general standard of the profession is lowered. For these theoretical studies are exactly those which are best acquired in youth. It is very hard indeed after some years in practice to devote a year or more to purely theoretical studies.

On the other hand, if we taught everybody the amount of science and theory which I think an engineer ought to know there would be hardly any time left within the first three years to study any practical engineering subjects at all. That would mean extending the curriculum to, say, five years by making the postgraduate courses part of the standard education.

Perhaps the solution would be to have two kinds of engineers, one studying three years with the other five years. The five-year students might take a break after three years of mainly general engineering science which should include some work on drawings, the making of perspectives and free hand sketching. This training, besides being of some use in an office or site, would help develop their imagination and further aid the teaching of solid geometry, a subject which I think is too much neglected.

If there were these two kinds of engineering degrees, the higher giving a much more thorough training in theoretical subjects and scientific method, then those who had the ability and could afford the time would certainly go for the higher course. How it should be made possible for the students to attend this longer course economically is a social and political question which I do not propose to discuss here. But obviously there should be a possibility for those taking the shorter course to supplement it with private study or postgraduate courses so that they may take the higher degree.

---

* Professor William Fisher Cassie CBE, Emeritus Professor of Civil Engineering at the University of Newcastle upon Tyne, lectured at the Queen's University of Belfast, University College, Cardiff, and University College, London. He played a significant, pioneering role in broadening civil engineering education.

I should like to make another suggestion. One way of getting a quart into a pint bottle is to increase the concentration of the liquid – in this case to improve the technique of education. We all agree that education is frightfully important and that as a nation we do not spend nearly enough of our resources, energy and thought to improve the scope and quality of our education. But I wonder whether you agree with me when I suggest that the actual method of teaching has not changed much in the last hundred years or more, and that probably much could be done to make teaching more efficient. I will not say much about the application of psychology, animated cartoons and films or subliminal advertising – inaudible sound waves expounding the theory of structure while you sleep – although this might open up promising prospects. What I am mainly thinking of is the provision of adequate, authoritative, readable and up-to-date text books.

I know that nothing can be better than an inspired teacher who is available to his students and can give them some individual attention. But not every teacher is inspired, and in any case in these days of mass production of technicians and engineers – as of everything else – there will simply not be enough teachers to go round. I know I am prejudiced because I have never been able to understand the British system of having next to no text books but making notes at lectures. How can you try to understand an argument if you have to concentrate on getting everything down on paper? And if it has to be done why do not all students at least start learning shorthand, or better still collectively employ a secretary to take down the stuff? I can only explain it as some sort of self-denying ordinance which is supposed to be good for the soul. By putting further obstacles in the way of learning it may engender qualities which might be invaluable in an emergency, teach one to do two things at the same time, or something of that sort. But it strikes me as impractical.

I believe there are people who can much better absorb teaching through the ears rather than through the eyes. But they can still listen. I am not proposing to abolish lectures, only to provide good text books. And those who can read can learn as much from a good text book as from a series of lectures. I must confess – and it is a shocking admission to make in front of an audience like this – that I only attended a few lectures during my time at college because I found it so much easier to read the excellent text books provided, with the added advantage, as I thought then that I could read a book at a stretch.

Think of the economy of the thing. I do not know what a good professor costs the State per year per student, but it is fairly safe to say that it is more than ten times the cost of a text book for each. I know this argument is spurious because the professors will still be needed. But I only mention it to show that, if we really made an effort to provide the best possible text books, then the cost in comparison to the cost of running a school would be small and the beneficial effect, I think, great.

Consider also that not all teachers are equally good, but that text books could all be good if the problem were tackled thoroughly. And a good text book is, I submit, better than a bad teacher. Moreover a text book is available to all, everywhere, students and practising engineers and would enable them all to keep abreast of development even if they could not afford the luxury of a full-time university course. But to achieve this the text books must be good. And by a good text book I have in mind something much more elaborate than the text books we are used to. If a book is well written then what it teaches cannot be explained any better verbally at a lecture, or if it can there is something wrong with the book. It would be a wordy kind of book not so suitable for revision or use as a reference book. Therefore, it should be accompanied by an extract giving all the essential information, formulae and summaries and so on to enable the reader to refresh his memory at a glance.

There should be an authorised version on every subject taught. This should be written by the best people in the profession or by groups of people and it should be subjected to criticism by everybody who has something to contribute in this sphere, and by students who would be asked to say what they found difficult to understand so that it could be improved in the next edition. For, of course, there should be frequent editions to improve the book and bring it up to date. I have in mind something on the lines of the Oxford Dictionary – a national undertaking sponsored by the Government or leading universities, and ample funds should be provided to pay handsomely for contributions asked for, even perhaps those which were not found to be the best and were, therefore, not included. If this task could be performed it would simplify education everywhere. The syllabus to be covered by every kind of examination could be indicated by pages so and so in the official text book.

It is, of course, absolutely essential that there should be free criticism of the authorised version;
it should be a living thing subject to change. Individual professors might well choose to deviate or differ from the book. But it would represent

a rather high minimum standard at least. It would affect the nature of postgraduate courses because, with the book in hand, the teaching could take the form of demonstrations, exercises, discussions, answers to queries – in fact, the students might come to the course partly prepared and get more out of a freer interchange of ideas between students and teachers, spending more time on understanding and less on memorising.

What I propose is certainly Utopian and will be dismissed as crazy, amateurish and perhaps even sinister, inaugurating a totalitarian regime. I am myself a little disturbed about the latter aspect. And I am willing to compromise on the proposal that professors should pay more attention to furnishing their students with text books containing the knowledge they are supposed to absorb. I am aware that I have not made the necessary effort to investigate the implications and the feasibility of this suggestion, but I think it is worth considering.

Note to accompany transcript of talk

It was a very interesting experience to attend this Conference – I think it taught me more about British educational methods than all my years in practice. It made me wish that I could have written my paper after, rather than before, the Conference – I would have known more about the issues at stake.

Perhaps you will allow me to add a few words to my paper.

I make two suggestions:

1) That at least some engineers could do with a good deal more theoretical and fundamental training,

and

2) That an effort should be made to provide good textbooks in all the subjects taught.

My views in both cases are undoubtedly influenced by continental practice, which makes them suspect, perhaps, but not necessarily invalid.

On the first I am adamant. I agree that the essential qualifications for a creative engineer are imagination, structural sense and a flair for design, qualities or aptitudes which, if not innate, are probably best acquired in practice. But knowledge of engineering science, and the basic sciences is the material on which the imagination has to work. And for advanced creative design this theoretical basis must be fairly thorough and up to date.

I agree that the majority of engineers will not need all this theoretical knowledge. But neither is it a good thing if it is only possessed by the few who have the energy and ability to acquire it on their own. It is the kind of knowledge which is best acquired at a University, and I think it would be highly desirable if one University, at least, would provide a five-year University course – divided in two parts, if desired – aimed at producing a body of engineers who possessed the theoretical equipment to tackle advanced design problems.

On the question of textbooks, I am rather shaken by the unanimous opposition of the Professors who have had experience of teaching students which I have not. It seems, therefore, that I have to admit the possibility that some students get on better without textbooks, but I must say that it is inexplicable to me.

The Architect and the Engineer

This lecture was published in ICE Proceedings, *vol.13, August 1959.*

The work of architects and engineers has much in common; in fact it can be said that it is essentially the same kind of work – to prepare drawings and specifications to enable other people to erect certain structures or buildings and to supervise their erection. When it has been decided to build something – whatever it is – they are the people who are called in to do the thinking about what the job should look like and how it should be built, and their labours finally result in *the design* for the job. By 'the design' is meant (in this Paper) all the instructions in the form of drawings or other documents necessary to enable a skilled contractor to erect the structure.

To create such a design is a highly skilled job. It involves satisfying and reconciling the often conflicting claims of function, stability, appearance, practicability, and economy; and thus giving the client the best possible value for his money. To do this, the designer must possess certain technical and other general knowledge and experience; drawing on this knowledge, and understanding the specific circumstances and requirements of the job, he must set his imagination and intuitive processes to work so that he more or less simultaneously can consider its various aspects and arrive at the right compromise solution.

The difficulty which faces designers nowadays is that the knowledge required to design a modern building or structure is far too extensive to be mastered by one mind. This is so because of the enormous technical progress which has taken place in the past 100 years, and because, as a result, the design has become much more important, besides being much more complicated. Old-fashioned building relied on tradition for its guide. In contrast, modern technique is distinguished by the fact that every step taken towards the goal is carefully planned beforehand, and the design is the key to all this planning. It has been proved again and again that it is cheaper to think and plan before building than to build by trial and error. Therefore the design cannot be created without intimate knowledge not only of the exact functional requirements – which again depend on technical possibilities – but also of all the modern structural techniques and labour-saving devices, including production engineering. In addition, of course, everything which is built, whether a building or engineering structure, poses aesthetic problems.

The answer to all these problems, as usual, can only be found by the collaboration of specialists. There is, however, a great danger in this. 'Design by committee' is not practicable. The process of weighing the pros and cons of the innumerable major and minor possibilities cannot be put down on paper or argued out between a number of designers with different technical education: there would be no end to it. It must be largely intuitive, and that means it must take place in one brain with access to all the necessary expert knowledge and advice as required and with authority to make the final decision. It has always been true (and the Author thinks it will always be true) that really outstanding work bears the imprint of a strong personality who has exercised control over the evolution of the design.

For a time this difficulty could be overcome by having two different kinds of designers – architects and civil engineers – with a different basic training, and dividing the work between them accordingly. Architects would take over the jobs where functional requirements were mainly a matter of spatial arrangement, and where the aesthetic aspect was of major importance. And the engineers would deal with jobs where the functional requirements were easily stated, as in the case of a bridge, dam, pier, or water-tower, but where structural and economic problems dominated.

Nowadays, such a complete division of all building activity into two distinct spheres is simply not feasible. In the architectural sphere practically every job needs, at the design stage, the knowledge not only of structural engineers but of electrical, heating, acoustical, and other specialists, as well as of the contractor's methods of building. In the engineering sphere, the need for architectural advice is recognized more and more. Collaboration is therefore necessary. It is a question then of creating the conditions in which this collaboration will give the best results.

Unfortunately the infinite variations in types of jobs, architects, and engineers make it impossible to generalize. But it would seem desirable to adhere to the principle of undisputed leadership. The leader should, in most cases be either an architect or an engineer, because only a technician is qualified to be in charge of a design. Only a technician can really appreciate the viewpoint and arguments of other technicians, whereas a layman often cannot, and that is why it can be very unfortunate if a layman meddles too much with the details of a design, as clients have been known to do.

It is desirable, therefore, to retain the two spheres of building, one where architects are in charge, and one where engineers are in charge, in each case assisted by members of the other profession. Which jobs should go to which profession can of course be a matter of dispute, and some miscasting undoubtedly takes place. Actually it does not matter so much whether in borderline cases an architect or an engineer is in charge. What matters is, that the leader should appreciate his own shortcomings. If an engineer is in charge of a mining camp or a factory, and if he is not himself capable of doing justice to the architectural aspects of the job, then he should insist that the client should appoint a consulting architect – or he himself should obtain the necessary architectural advice. If an architect is in charge, he should likewise make sure of his technical assistance on matters of production technique or structural design before proceeding with the design.

It is, unfortunately, not given to everybody to know his own shortcomings. But to get the best possible result is largely a question of leaving the decisions to those best qualified to make them. And a very necessary part of leadership nowadays is an ability to understand and appreciate the point of view of others, to be able to judge quality also in the allied technical fields so as to extract the best from all collaborators; in short, to be a tactful, understanding and forceful chairman.

An architect in charge of a large and complicated job must make the final decisions on hundreds of different questions and deal with hundreds of people in the process. There are first his own staff – he should be able to guide them easily enough, because he understands all that they are doing – they are, so to speak, extensions of himself. Of course, sometimes in a large organization it may be a member of the staff who really is the architect – but that is a different matter, and one must here consider the firm as a unit and leave them to sort out their own organization.

Then he has to deal with the many suppliers of materials and other sources of facts about local conditions, available resources, and materials – everything which has a bearing on the design. Here he is in the position of buyer or customer. While he can count on a ready response he must be able to distinguish between facts and propaganda.

His relation to his technical advisers – for instance, his structural engineer – is rather different. He cannot guide them in the same way as he guides his own staff. He is dealing with a different independent profession; he is asking for their advice; and he is bound to accept it – if he does not change his adviser, which is very difficult. If the engineer points out that a proposal conflicts with the law of gravity there is not much the architect can do about it. On the other hand he should not always take no for an answer – a structural difficulty need not be a structural impossibility.

The main difficulty about this relation is really that the architect should have his technical advice even before he starts sketching out his first conception of the job. When he starts designing in his head, letting his mind wander over the various possible solutions, rejecting them one by one until an idea is deemed worthy of further investigation, then the possible structural arrangement must be an essential factor – or can be, because there are of course hundreds of different kinds of jobs into which structural considerations hardly enter. But if they do, then the architect should really be an engineer as well – and a good one, too. (This happens, of course, but this is not the right juncture to consider these few ideal exceptions.) If he is not, he should have the engineer at his elbow as soon as he starts sketching. That, however, is rarely feasible. As a rule, the engineer is not even appointed then – which is wrong, of course. As a result it is often the architect who makes all the main structural dispositions, and the engineer is left the task of calculating the sizes of beams, columns, etc. Many architects, and still more clients, assume that to be the job of the structural engineer: even some structural engineers would accept this. But that is a degradation of the role of the structural engineer.

Where structure is a major consideration, the engineer should be a partner in evolving the design, so that the proper integration of structure and architecture can be achieved. It is of course his job to assist the architect to realize his architectural conception, and he must accept his role as an assistant. But he should be a useful assistant, and that means that he must understand and sympathize with the aims of the architect, so that he, in his own intuitive thinking, can arrive at proposals which will further the architect's wishes – just as a pianist in his own right should not deem it beneath his dignity to act as an accompanist, as long as he is not asked to play with one finger.

The conclusion is, then, that the architect should be part engineer and the engineer should be part architect in order to achieve a fruitful collaboration. The architect should have an understanding of the basic structural principles – which can almost be boiled down to a thorough understanding of the force triangle. And the engineer should have a feeling for form and proportion. The best way for both to achieve this is through actual collaboration. The fact that a young man straight from college still has a lot to learn must be accepted. The engineer receives the best architectural education from the architects he is working with – or some of them – and the architect, through the same collaboration, gets to know what a structure can or cannot do. When two persons or firms have worked together for a long time a mutual understanding develops which makes collaboration easy and fruitful. Perhaps a foundation for such collaboration could be laid already at school. The Author believes firmly that civil engineers should learn more solid geometry, freehand sketching, and appreciation of architecture – if that is possible.

It would be tempting to try to describe at some length the various patterns of architect-engineer relation which occur in practice, but there is space for only a few remarks.

There are the great many cases where the architect does not really care very much, and where the job – or at any rate the solution – is of a routine nature. The relation is a business matter, efficiency in delivering the goods is what counts most, and there is really no problem to discuss. It is when the architect or engineer or both really make an effort to think afresh, to find an original solution, that there may be a difference of opinion.

Architecture, being a particular kind of art, suffers from, or glories in, being subject to fashion, changing taste, theories, ideologies, or personal idiosyncrasies, and it can be difficult for the engineer to follow suit. Some architects believe in a sculptural, classical, or formalistic approach to architecture; for them the structure has to do exactly what they want it to do, they are after certain spatial and visual effects, and the engineer must somehow contrive to make them possible, whether it is natural and sensible from a structural point of view or not. This attitude may be perfectly justified – it depends so much on the nature of the job and on how well it is done. But if the engineer is asked to do violence to the structure for no very good reason that he can discover (in other words if he does not see eye to eye with the architect), then the collaboration is not a happy one.

There is another school of architects who consider that architecture should grow out of the structure, and who are anxious to give the engineer a completely free hand. Again, depending on the type of job, it may work or it may not, because it may simply mean that the architect does not in fact exercise architectural control, which is bad.

Of course, the variations are endless. There may be engineers who are much better architects than the architects they are working with. And there are architects who have a much more imaginative grasp of structural possibilities and who have the greatest difficulty in getting their pedestrian engineering colleagues to go along with them. It is a fact that some of the most daring conceptions in shell-design have originated with architects – but they tend in some cases to be somewhat extravagant and not based on very sound structural reasoning. It often becomes the sad duty of engineers to restrain the enthusiasm of architects for new structural forms.

Where the structural problems are dominant, there should as a rule be an engineer in charge and he should preferably be an Eduardo Torroja,* who is a great architect as well as a great engineer. Failing that – and this appears to be common practice – an architect should be appointed consultant. But he should not lay down the law. Some architects have the idea that an architect, if employed at all, must always be in charge. But in the case of a bridge, for instance, the form and main architectural quality arise from the engineering solution – it requires a great understanding on the part of the architect to be really helpful. On the other hand, the engineer, if left alone, even if he has produced a masterly design, is likely to mar the whole effect by unfortunate detailing of abutments, railings, etc. The Author believes that this happened even with some of [Robert] Maillart's bridges.†

Even if the collaboration between architects and engineers can thus assume hundreds of different forms, according to the job and the personalities involved, there is as a rule no difficulty about it. In the overwhelming majority of cases it proceeds smoothly enough, even if it is, of course, rare to find the ideal collaboration where two friends work together in complete understanding and with great enthusiasm for a common aim.

Of course, here as elsewhere the play is spoiled by bad direction and bad acting. The quality of the job depends on the quality of the leadership, and mediocre leadership is the most frequent cause of bad design. But to do anything about this is at best a long-term business.

Apart from that, it is when the conditions for a fruitful collaboration are not present that frustration and difficulties arise. It has been suggested that the main requirements for success are:

1) Clear undisputed high-quality leadership.
2) That the leader should have access to all relevant information and advice.
3) That he should choose or at least approve of his collaborators.
4) That they should be available right from the start.

These requirements are very rarely met, partly because the need for them is not understood, and partly because there are inherent difficulties in the way of meeting them.

Some of the greatest difficulties arise from the interpretation and evolution of the client's wishes and his sometimes enigmatic identity. The fount of all decisions about a job is the client's wish to have something built, coupled with his ability to pay for it. He is the buyer, and is entitled to decide what he wants to buy.

Unfortunately he cannot see what he is buying, he has to buy the 'cat in the bag'. He wants something made for him, and therefore he cannot avoid the obligation of explaining what he wants made. But that is exactly what he cannot do – owing to his lack of technical training. The client does not really know what he wants – or only in a vague general way – until the architect has put pencil to paper and shown him what can be done. Policy depends on possibility. And possibility is technical – a design matter. And not unnaturally, the client will not only want to know how his need can be met, he will also want to know the cost of the offered solutions. This is an inherent difficulty, which it is almost impossible to solve. Before the cost can be estimated, the whole design should really be decided. Naturally the client does not want to spend a lot of money before he knows what he is buying, and this means in practice that the vital decisions are made in a hurry and without proper technical advice, since engineers – structural, mechanical, or electrical – and contractors are not yet appointed. And the harm done by hasty or ill-considered initial decisions may be difficult to undo.

Actually this whole business of establishing the correct brief for a job bristles with difficulties. A full discussion of it is beyond the scope of this Paper, but it would certainly repay closer study, because it is both the most important and the most neglected aspect of building.

---

* Eduardo Torroja y Miret (1899–1961) was a Spanish structural engineer and pioneer in the design of concrete-shell structures.
† Robert Maillart (1872–1940) was a Swiss engineer and entrepreneur known for his early twentieth-century arch bridges.

In an excellent paper Davies has pointed out that the study of building needs has been sadly neglected by modern architects.* They have tried to put the responsibility for the architect's programme on to the client, but really it is a matter of architect-client collaboration, and of scientific research sponsored by the state or private institutions like the Nuffield Foundation's division for architectural studies. Far more harm is done by building the wrong things than by building things wrongly. And it is as often as not the clients who want the wrong things built, because they do not know any better. The architects have a responsibility to the public, to society, or to Architecture with a capital A, and it is often the clients who are the main obstacles to good design. In such cases the architect is in a very difficult position and his only remedy may be to resign.

It can also happen, contrariwise, that it is the client who is the main inspiration, but to be a good client is difficult. There are two roads to success in this matter: either the client should interfere as little as possible and leave his technical advisers a free hand to make minor policy decisions after having acquainted them as fully as possible with the whole purpose of the undertaking; or the client should take an intelligent interest in the various technical possibilities and work with the architect or engineer to find the best solution. The point is that wise decisions must be based on a knowledge of facts, and if the client has no time to absorb the relevant facts, he should leave the decision to someone who has, and whom he can trust. If he interferes like the proverbial bull in a china shop, he is his own worst enemy.

The situation is not much better when there is no easily identifiable client – and this is becoming more and more common. Who, for instance, is the client in the case of a large teaching hospital? The government agency who appoints the architect? The medical staff? The patients? It may be difficult to find anybody who really can take decisions, but there may be many who have power to put spokes in the wheel. In such a case the establishment of the brief may be more important – and more difficult – than the making of the design. It may be the same with a very complicated factory, where processes of production may be the most important factor in the design of the enclosing shell. In such cases the leader of the design team should perhaps be the production engineer, or the clients themselves.

Another set of complications arises from the growing mechanization of site work and the rapidly increasing importance of factory-produced components. Knowledge of these processes and their economic import is also required at the design stage, but the possessors of this knowledge – contractors and manufacturers – are certainly not officially part of the design team. The engineers are appointed somewhat too late – but can perhaps still influence the design. But the contractors are appointed only when the design is finished.

The fact is of course that the technical revolution in the building industry has outstripped the organization which was devised to cope with a much simpler form of building. And so it can be seen that the whole set-up of client, architect, engineer, and contractor – with or without quantity surveyor – is being bypassed or disregarded in so many cases. Large contractors and builders increasingly prepare their own designs – architecture included. These designs are certainly closely integrated with the firms' structural resources and techniques – they are meant to be competitive and are designed with an eye on cost. And it is the failure – or reputed failure – of sections of the architectural and engineering professions to design competitively which encourages this development. But such designs on the other hand tend to disregard functional or architectural requirements – they are just as lop-sided, only in a different direction. It is total integration which is wanted, but how is it to be achieved?

The Author can offer only a few tentative suggestions which will certainly not cover the whole complex field, and which may be impracticable – but which he hopes will offer points for discussion.

Somehow clients – and there ought to be a recognizable client or client's representative – should be made to understand the over-riding importance to themselves of establishing the right brief and getting the best possible design, and they ought to be prepared to spend effort, time, and money on it.

The first step is to choose an architect or engineer to be in charge of the design. This step is fraught with consequences, good or bad. It is like choosing a doctor in an unknown town, he might kill or cure. Doctors, of course, have their patients completely under the thumb. It would not be fair, and at any rate would be very difficult, to treat clients in the same way. The Author thinks – and to some this will be heresy – that the client should be allowed to have a little peep at not only one 'cat in the bag', but at several, before making a final decision. He should be allowed to approach several architects or engineers and ask them to submit sketch designs to enable him to see, how they would tackle the job. Such designs should be paid for of course, and moreover it should be understood that the designer should be entitled and expected to obtain advice from allied technologists as required and pay for that too. The practice whereby architects put themselves under obligation to contractors and others who are prepared to work on a design for nothing should not be encouraged. But the fee to be paid should be much less than the present RIBA scale. The Author thinks it would be a very good thing if there could be an element of competition in design – that is sadly missing in the present arrangement. And designers might be prepared to make some effort towards obtaining a job and pit their wits against others on a basis more or less of getting their costs paid. But there are pitfalls!

Anyhow, even if only one designer is approached, he should assemble his team of consultants in agreement with the client and on the basis of a sketch design have his brief clearly established. And then he should be left in peace and given time to get on with the job. If advice on contractual methods is essential for his design he should have authority to obtain such advice, or he might even advise his client to nominate an efficient and reliable contractor.

Each designer would probably gradually assemble a team of collaborators with whom he is used to work – heating engineers and so on – and there would be no objection to some or all of them being united in one firm. But it might be difficult in practice to provide the best possible service in all branches and at the same time provide balanced employment for all departments, unless they were also acting independently in conjunction with other chief designers – and then the problem is more or less back where it started. But there is a value in having a few allied technologists in an office who can deal with smaller jobs or jobs of a particular kind, because it provides a lesson in collaboration for the staff.

The practice of having the contractor prepare his own designs can work very well in such cases where the integration of the design with the method of construction is a major consideration, because that is undoubtedly the best way to achieve it. The Author is here thinking mainly of engineering structures such as marine structures and special industrial structures like chimneys, silos, etc. It can work extremely well, provided the contractors are good designers. To emphasize this it might be better to talk of the designer doing his own contracting. It might even work in housing when a firm has successfully developed its own system of building. But in such cases it would not do to let the firm be responsible for the architecture as well, unless there should happen to be a [Pier Luigi] Nervi or [Felix] Candela in charge.[†] The principle that the client should have his own professional adviser to look after his interest should remain, and for all really important jobs it should apply to all engineering services as well.

To obtain the right design is the important thing, because that is the same as serving the client's true interest. That is exactly the duty of the two professions, a duty which, on the whole, engineers and architects strive to perform to the best of their ability, in spite of the fact that the financial reward happens to be almost inversely proportional to the effort put into the job – an oddity which it may be difficult to do anything about.

Now that practically every occupation is elevated to the status of a profession, designers may have to shed some of their conceit on that score, but the essence of their professional code is to create an atmosphere of professional integrity which is the client's best safeguard, and which should be preserved, whatever happens.

---

[*] R.L. Davies, 'Deeper Knowledge, Better Design', *Architectural Record*, vol.121 (1957), p.185.
[†] Pier Luigi Nervi (1871–1979) was an Italian engineer; Félix Candela Outeriño (1910–1997) was a Spanish architect.

An Account of Progress in Reinforced Concrete Design

This article appeared in the Financial Times Survey, *November 1961.*

Thirty or forty years ago Reinforced Concrete was a fairly well-defined structural material, which had definitely come into its own as a serious competitor to structural steel in many fields. It had been developed from small beginnings mainly in France half a century or so earlier, when [Joseph] Monier, [François] Coignet* and others had the idea of overcoming the structural weakness of concrete in tension by reinforcing it with steel bars; it had been tested in laboratories and a fairly good idea of how the two materials worked together had been obtained. Theoretical analysis had provided a basis for calculation, codes of practice had been drawn up and a body of specialist contractor and craftsmen had gained experience in constructional techniques.

The Design of Reinforced Concrete structures was still suffering from the prevalent conception of this new material as a substitute for structural steel and timber, but imaginative designers like [Robert], Maillart and many others after him had realised that Reinforced Concrete was a material in its own right and should be treated as such. Certain forms (as for instance the so-called mushroom floors) peculiar to this material were gaining currency, and the first shell structures were being erected in Germany and France. Of course Reinforced Concrete was still an 'old-fashioned' material compared with the more precise pre-fabricated steel structures, it had to be laboriously mixed, often by hand, and poured into timber forms mostly made by a carpenter according to rule of thumb, the steel likewise being fixed by hand with varying degrees of accuracy. This meant that one could not always depend on obtaining the desired quality, and this again was reflected in the factors of safety laid down by regulations, which tended to discriminate against conscientious execution or imaginative design. Yet the material had so many good points and was an answer to so many prayers that its use over a constantly widening field was a foregone conclusion, once its potentialities had been realised.

The development which has taken place since then, especially after the war, can perhaps best be understood if we dwell shortly on the great advantages and the considerable shortcomings of the ordinary Reinforced Concrete placed 'in situ', i.e. poured into forms in its final position, as it has been known for more than fifty years.

Reinforced Concrete is the result of an extraordinary happy union between two well-known materials, concrete and steel. Its happiness rests on the lucky fact that concrete adheres strongly to steel, making the two materials collaborate under conditions of stress, and that they react in a very similar way to temperature variations, so that inside the ordinary range of such variations their union will not suffer.

The new material combines many of the advantages of the two components. It has the plasticity of concrete – it can assume any desired shape and can be made into a monolithic structure of any size, because joining different parts of the structure together presents no serious problems, in contrast to what is – or used to be – the case with steel or timber. And it can be given the tensional strength of steel at any desired point, thereby eliminating the one serious shortcoming of concrete. Moreover the concrete protects the steel against its two worst enemies, rust and fire.

We get then a material which can be used architecturally, to enclose space, form the body of floors, walls, silos, dams etc., and which at the same time can resist the forces acting on it. Its plasticity makes it into a willing medium for the designer's wishes – for better and worse.

The drawbacks are, as already mentioned, its dependence on good workmanship, the absence of which causes cracks and blemishes and possibly settlement, its lack of thermal insulation when used in building, its unsightly surface with bad weathering qualities, and its 'heaviness' which is a hindrance to modern factory production.

To these disadvantages should perhaps be added the fact that Reinforced Concrete is apt to present the designer with problems which he may not be equipped to deal with, resulting in much second-rate work. It is a complex, somewhat irrational and fickle material, maturing slowly and subject to changes as time goes on, and if used to its best advantage it naturally assumes forms which defy rigorous analysis or at least are statically indeterminate to a high degree.

These assets and these defects have acted as a challenge to scientists, engineers, architects, contractors and manufacturers to exploit its flexibility and adaptability to any functional structural situation and to eliminate its defects; and this is exactly what has happened in the intervening years.

The points of attack have been many, stretching from improvements in theoretical analysis, and design to those in manufacturing and construction techniques. This has resulted in more and more specialisation and an ever widening field of application. Now it is not enough to talk about Reinforced Concrete – there are so many varieties that one has to be more specific. What has happened is of course in line with what is happening everywhere in industry – a greater use of science, replacement of labour by machinery, of quantity by quality and the introduction of standardisation and mass-production.

The means at our disposal for analysing complicated structures have been much strengthened by new theoretical work (plastic theory, shell analysis, etc.), by the invention of digital computers, by information gained from laboratory tests and by developing the technique of testing models as an alternative to theoretical analysis.

At the same time work has been going on in many countries aiming at the improvement of the concrete quality, and the production of concretes with certain desired and predictable qualities.

This can be done by controlling what goes into the concrete and the treatment it receives in the first weeks of its life.

Ordinary concrete consists of stones of varying sizes, bound together by a mortar of cement, sand and water and allowed to harden. By varying the size, relative quantity and quality of these ingredients in a predetermined and controlled manner and by adding further special ingredients if required, we can now produce a whole range of different concretes for different purposes. [Eugène] Freyssinet[†] produced concrete of a crushing strength approaching that of steel by careful selection of aggregate, cement and water, meticulous grading and steam-curing the mixture under great pressure – an interesting experiment with only limited application in practice, but then his great invention of pre-stressed concrete made it necessary for him to pay special attention to the strength of concrete.

But we can also exchange crushing strength for thermal insulation, by using light-weight aggregates

---

[*] Joseph Monier (1823–1906), a French gardener, was one of the principal inventors of reinforced concrete, receiving a patent in 1867. François Coignet (1814–1888) was a nineteenth-century French industrialist and pioneer in the development of structural prefabricated and reinforced concrete.
[†] Eugène Freyssinet (1879–1962) was a French civil engineer who successfully developed pre-stressed concrete.

or distributing air throughout the mix by mechanical or chemical means; we can use a number of special cements to make the concrete more resistant to chemical action, to water penetration, make it quick or slow setting, make it expand when setting, give it a special colour, etc.

Manipulating the mix also gives us the clue to a satisfactory surface treatment, and now concrete need not look dowdy, on the contrary it presents endless possibilities for artistic expression. But the surface still presents a problem to be solved, it doesn't come naturally, as with stone or brick. Perhaps this stage will also be reached one day when manufacture of concrete has reached reliable perfection.

In steel reinforcement there have also been minor improvements, but the one really outstanding achievement is the amazingly rapid development of a host of 'pre-stressed' and 'post-tension' techniques, making use of high tension steel, wires or strands, to produce controlled artificial compression in the concrete, to counteract any tension which may be produced by external forces.

In ordinary Reinforced Concrete it was not possible economically to take advantage of the greater strength of steel and concrete which could be produced by manufacturers. Pre-stressed concrete however can exploit every extra ounce of strength to the full, making the structures lighter and more slender. And a further great advantage of pre-stressed concrete is that it goes a long way towards solving the problem posed by the growing practice of pre-casting concrete members or units in special factories or in 'ad hoc' factories on the site. Obviously this is very tempting, because it is much easier to control quality that way, working conditions are much better, machinery can be used, and given the necessary standardisation, the forms can be re-used over and over again and can therefore be made very exact and, if required, complicated, without affecting the cost much. But it means that these bits of concrete must somehow be joined together in the structure, which thereby loses its monolithic character. This can however be restored by using tensioned cables to press the bits together.

The practice of pre-casting is in fact changing the whole character of concrete construction everywhere. We have the small highly standardised units of patent floors, roof trusses etc. more or less sold 'off the peg', the more specialised units made for one job to order – in many ways the most significant development – and the very large units consisting of whole walls or rooms or bridge girders often manufactured near the site. Improved means of transport have of course helped this development, which incidentally has a far-reaching effect on Reinforced Concrete design. It implies standardisation, to a larger or smaller extent, but it need not be universal standardisation, which would destroy the flexibility of concrete design: it only requires enough repetition of units on each particular job to make this procedure economically viable. It favours the construction of large jobs as against small – the ideal is a job like a whole town which can make use of the same units and the same processes year after year.

However, the ordinary practice of pouring the concrete in situ is far from superseded yet, and it is unlikely to be so for a long time, if at all. There will always be cases which are best dealt with by this method, and in fact there have been so many improvements in techniques of bulk handling and site mechanisation that they may well ensure it a lasting and considerable share of the work.

Progress in concrete design – the subject of this article – can of course not be considered apart from all these developments, which have unfortunately been very inadequately dealt with here. The designer must know his material, what can be done with it, how it can be produced and put in its final position, and what all these operations cost.

It may be difficult to define the word 'design' exactly and to decide where design stops and execution begins, but in essence 'designing' means instructing the builders *what* to build – in the form of drawings, specifications and so on. But they should be sensible instructions, it should be possible – nay, practical and economical – to build according to them, and if they entail deviations from ordinary practice the designer must instruct the builders *how* to build as well. Because design and method of construction are inextricably mixed up, they must fit each other; and original design may sometimes consist largely in finding a new and practical method of construction, which must inevitably be reflected in the design.

But all this is dealing with the means at the disposal of the designer. The purpose of the design is of course to create a building or structure which will do a certain job; in this respect reinforced concrete design, a branch of Engineering, is itself Architecture, or has its final purpose in helping to create Architecture, with all that this implies in the way of functional and aesthetic considerations. The Reinforced Concrete designer must never forget that this should be his main concern. His knowledge of the means should enable him to do this job economically and practically. But it would be idle to pretend that there is only one right solution, or if there is, that it can be found by a scientific analysis of the available means.

There are far too many possibilities and far too many conflicting considerations. The design represents a synthesis, a compromise between conflicting interests, which requires of the designer an intuitive feeling for the possibilities of the material, an understanding of the underlying purpose of the design, and an act of inventive creation.

This kind of creation can only thrive where there is still room for manoeuvre, where the problem is new, or the site unique (which every site is, to some extent), or where there are special difficulties to overcome. Actually every situation is different, and could well be served by a special solution, but against this there is strong economic pressure in favour of large scale standardisation. This is bound to increase, and has its legitimate place, but it must be remembered that standardisation also is wasteful owing to functional shortcomings. There is no point in building what can easily be built, if it is not what you want. The purpose built structure or building will therefore always be needed and will provide the field in which new inspiration can be found. In fact in many cases it will be possible to have the best of the two worlds: controlled standardisation of specially designed units assembled to create unique Architecture.

Coventry Cathedral: How the Plan Took Shape

This article appeared in The Times *supplement on Coventry Cathedral, 25 May 1962.*

Architectural and structural design are really two aspects of the same thing, but because our knowledge of ways and means of building has been so vastly increased, one designer can rarely cope with both, hence the design of an important building must result from a collaboration between architect and engineer.

The latter looks after the structure – which could be defined as that part of the building which ensures its stability and permanence – but as this forms an integral part of the building fabric and may embrace the major part of it, it inevitably impinges on the province of the architect. In fact the merit of the structure is not judged by its fulfilment of its main purpose – which is taken for granted – but by its economy and by its contribution to the solution of the architect's own functional and aesthetic problems.

Special problems

In Coventry Cathedral the emphasis is very much on aesthetic quality, and this has posed rather special problems for the engineer. There have been, of course, many quite ordinary matters to attend to: the foundations – which in the end were designed to consist of 671 bored piles, 17 in. in diameter and of varying length, to carry the loads down to the sandstone – the loadbearing walls, the floors, the crypt, the ducts, the thermal insulation and waterproofing and other such mundane matters. But when we come to the parts where the structure is visible, the roofs, the canopy, the screen or the fleche, then the structure cannot be considered separately from the architecture; it must be subservient to it. This must not be misunderstood: were the architect to make complete nonsense of the structure, the architecture itself would suffer. A certain structural clarity and crispness is desirable, and therefore a very intimate collaboration between architect and engineer is necessary.

Abstract sculpture

But the problem is not just to design an efficient and economical roof spanning 80 ft. It is to create a visual impact, to create abstract sculpture, if you like. If it were not for the demands imposed by aesthetic or symbolic requirements, there would hardly be any structural problems at all. To span a roof 80 ft. can be done in a hundred different ways. If an acoustic false ceiling is needed under the roof, it can be slung from it. The columns, which in the old cathedrals used to support the roof, are not at all necessary in this case. But that is not a fault in the design. It would be absurd to contend, as some architectural critics are apt to do, that the design of a cathedral should grow out of structural necessity. The structure of the canopy, for instance, should be crisp and elegant and articulated, the details should be controlled, but whether the canopy with its columns should be there at all, or some other way found to create the atmosphere the architect is striving for, is not a matter to be settled by criteria of structural economy.

The design of the canopy has gone through many stages as the architect – aided and abetted by the engineers – worked untiringly for some years to find the form that would satisfy him. To begin with, there were four rows of columns supporting a kind of concrete vault. Then the two rows near the walls were left out and the positions of the two rows of centre columns which converge towards the altar were determined by a system of diagonal gridlines based on a mathematical relationship which also determined the whole plan of the cathedral and fixed the position of a series of ribs in the canopy. For aesthetic effect and for acoustic reasons the spaces between the ribs were filled with concrete panels forming shallow pyramids, which effectively concealed the ribs from underneath, making the whole appear as a kind of concrete shell. Later, the pyramids were pierced then the ribs were partly shown underneath the canopy in the interest of structural honesty and finally the concrete panels were replaced by timber slats, spaced apart to admit light. The canopy now appears as what it was all the time: a free-standing spatial framework of ribs and columns, complicated by the fact that the ribs pursue a somewhat angular course up and down, which never goes from column to column, but, proceeding diagonally from a column, always ends up on the other side between two columns. However, statically the structural system is clear enough in spite of its complication.

The columns were precast, in three pieces, glued together on the floor and prestressed, then lifted into position. Later, when the ribs were cast, the prestressing in the columns was reduced on the inside and increased on the outside to improve the moment distribution between columns and ribs, thus making it possible to increase the slenderness of both.

Design of roof

The most interesting structure from an engineering point of view is probably the roof above the canopy, and especially the roof over the baptistry. The latter covers an area of 100 by 90 ft. and consists of a 4 in. reinforced concrete slab slightly folded, but with a very low pitch, strengthened by ribs and held together by strong prestressed concrete ties concealed in the walls. This roof supports the 78 ft. fleche – a manganese bronze space frame – and also part of the large bronze and glass screen. The latter is hung from the roof in ten ¾ in. inclined rods, prestressed to give the required stability against wind. By this arrangement the screen could be made much lighter, which improved its appearance and saved a lot of money at the same time, which is exactly the sort of thing the engineer is always trying – and sometimes managing – to achieve, especially if the architect and engineer pull together as they have done in this case.

The Design of Bridges

This article appeared in the Arup London Newsletter, *nos. 21 and 22, February and April 1964, and was reprinted in the* Arup Journal, *2009.*

This article is about the design of bridges, and tries to show why in a number of cases certain designs were chosen, and how they were developed. That most of these bridges will probably never be built is regrettable but does not defeat my main purpose, which is to probe into the nature of architecture by showing how in the case of bridge design the architectural form results mainly from the choice of structure and the method of construction. I say mainly, because there will always remain a number of more or less arbitrary decisions about proportions or detail design which do not greatly affect economy or functional efficiency, and which have to be made on purely aesthetic or sculptural grounds. I suggest, however, that the best result is obtained if there are very few of such arbitrary decisions to be made, in other words, if decisions affecting proportion and form at the same time make structural and constructional sense.

When everything thus 'comes naturally', there will be the greatest possible unity between architecture and structure – they will in fact be one and the same thing, which is as it should be. I know that this kind of unity is not always possible, and that it can be perfectly justified to do violence to the structure or to add to the difficulties of construction in the interest of architectural values, but most people agree that such unity is worthwhile striving for. As is well known, what in the end 'comes naturally' is the most difficult thing to attain. It has the best chance of emerging if one mind controls the design process. That is why the great bridges are created by engineers with a feeling for form, but thinking mainly in engineering terms.

Unity between architecture and structure, or perhaps rather 'Unity' in general, has since Aristotle been valued as a mark of great architecture. However, in the case of buildings filled with technical equipment and housing a multitude of human activities – as for instance a teaching hospital – such unity is difficult to obtain or even define. The needs to be harmonised are multifarious and perhaps even conflicting, and structure anyhow comes rather low on the list of priorities. That is why bridges and large engineering structures seem to me a more rewarding field for the study of architectural unity. That a bridge is a form of architecture will probably be conceded; in fact it can have a very powerful architectural impact. But it is architecture with a clear and simply formulated function: to carry traffic of a certain kind from one place to another. All one has to worry about, then, is the stability, durability, cost, and appearance. Or to put it in another way, structure, method of construction, and architecture.

It is, of course, the architectural past which for the engineers may be the most difficult to come to grips with, and this explains my interest in exploring the issue. Architectural theories, I am afraid, do not help much. Unity, harmony, balance, proportion, scale, pattern, truth, structural honesty, fitness for purpose, economy of materials; all these guiding principles are much too general, and can all be violated with impunity in particular cases. They give practically no guidance to the designer who has to resolve an alternative on the drawing board. Fortunately bridge design is fairly immune from infection by warring and ephemeral architectural issues. It is generally accepted that to impose a preconceived 'style' would be out of place. This leaves us basically with a structure with certain sculptural qualities. But this is not the same as a piece of sculpture with certain structural and spatial qualities enabling it to carry traffic from A to B. If an architectural critic looks at the finished result he may be tempted to judge it from the latter point of view. He has a right to do so, of course, but it would be like judging a car by its appearance only. To judge the quality of a bridge – the whole bridge and nothing but the bridge – one should not only appraise its form, but should understand why it has that form.

This brings me to the crux of my argument, which is that to study architecture – I am talking about bridges, but suspect that it applies to all architecture – one should study it *in statu nascendi*.* One should be privy to the working of the minds of the creators. Creating architecture – good or bad – consists of making a great number of choices. One should get to know what these choices were, what was rejected as well as what was adopted, and why. If one selected as example designs of acknowledged merit – and there is much more agreement about what is good, once it has been created, than about architectural theory – then one would come nearer to an understanding of how good architecture was produced and one might perhaps even get an inkling of what good architecture was.

One would derive a benefit akin to that accruing to the pupil who watches his master at work. It would serve the dual purpose of exploring the nature of good architecture and of teaching the making of it. It would be nice to think that that this was generally conceded and that henceforth we would be spared the tedious descriptions of what the work looked like, how many tons of cement and acres of glass were used, how the contract was administered and so on, and that we instead would witness through information 'straight from the horse's mouth', the exciting battle going on in the designer's mind to find the right answer amongst the scores of possible solutions. But I am afraid these are pipe dreams, and that for several very good reasons.

The main reason is this, that it is extremely difficult to get hold of what exactly happens during the largely intuitive process of designing. The material would at any rate have to be edited and drastically reduced. It is also difficult to remember unless immediately recorded. Designers are not authors; they are bent on designing, not on recording. When much later, a reconstruction of the process is attempted, the result is probably a rationalisation more *Dichtung* than *Wahrheit*.† And then in order even to attempt to describe the design process to the reader, it is necessary that he should understand the problem as it presents itself to the designer. The latter will have spent some time and effort getting acquainted with the problem as it relates to the site and other conditions, and only when it has been thoroughly absorbed into his system will be able to survey the field of three-dimensional possibilities in his head.

What he can then see in a flash will need a lot of explanations and 3-D sketches or models to put across to a reader.

I am afraid, therefore, that this *statu nascendi* business will have to be dropped, at least if taken too literally. But I still think that the main idea has validity, and that designers could make a contribution to informed criticism if they could bring themselves to give an account of the path followed – including some of the blind alleys – to reach a particular solution.

This then, is what I am going to attempt, but I am immediately up against two difficulties. One is lack of time and space which will make my effort very sketchy in any case. The other, more serious, is, that in the nature of things I can only talk about my own experiences. What we really want is an eye-witness account of how great architecture is produced,

---

* 'In its original form'.
† From Goethe's autobiography, *Aus meinem Leben: Dichtung und Wahrheit* (1808–31).

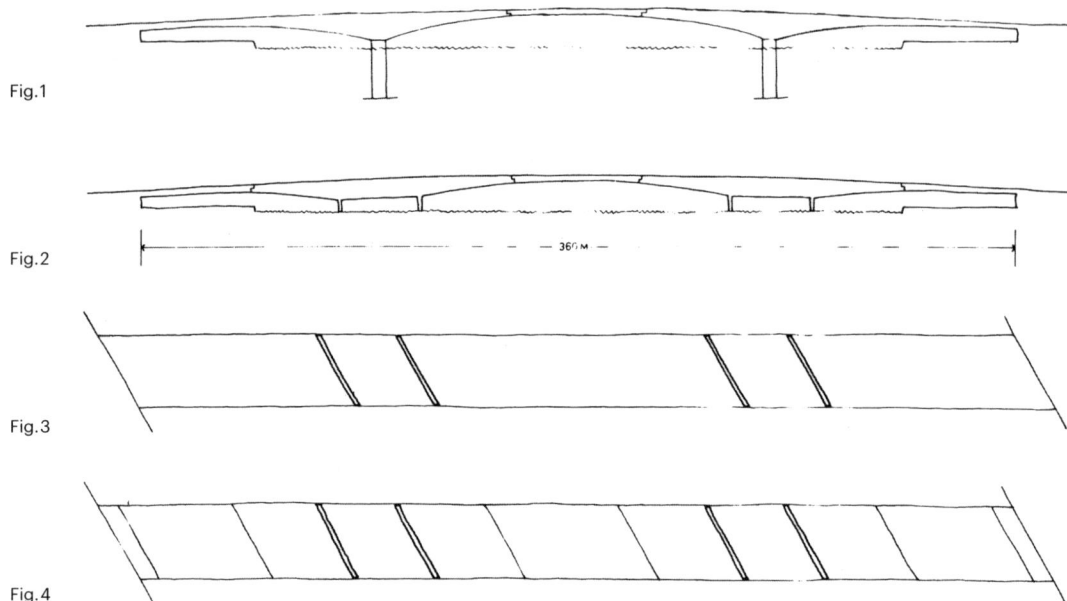

Fig.1
Fig.2
Fig.3
Fig.4

and unfortunately I am far from being a great architect. My only hope is that my example will inspire someone better qualified to make a more valuable contribution on these lines.

Perth Narrows Bridge

The first design, for a bridge over the Narrows at Perth, Australia, never got further than an early sketch stage, but the fundamental decisions about how to build the bridge had been taken and, as will be seen, these decisions, logically applied, resulted in a bridge of a somewhat unusual form.

The task, as presented to us by the clients at the time, was to build a low road bridge 92ft wide and 1300ft long – of which 900ft were over water – between the mainland and a large island. The special feature of this bridge was its skewness – the line of the bridge formed an angle of 60° with the channel it had to span, and consequently with the current. The clients at one time expressed the hope of spanning the bridge in one span, but that could only be done by having the main structure above road level – suspension bridge – and that was not considered desirable for other reasons – landscape. The best that could be hoped for with the construction height available was three spans: a long middle span with two cantilevers and a floating span, and two shore spans.

Considering the method of construction, however, it was very soon found that to provide a temporary staging for the whole bridge would be far too expensive. The best method seemed to be to drive piles from a floating plant for the construction of the piers and then cantilever both ways from these piers, delivering all the materials or precast units to these piers by barge (Fig.1). This would not be easy, considering the depth of water and the skewness of the pier; at the least it would require very heavy and expensive piers. It would obviously facilitate matters enormously if each of the two piers was replaced by two narrow piers relatively close together (Fig.2). These two twin piers would then form natural harbours for supplies by barge and would, when connected, form a stable base from which to cantilever in both directions. Further, it would then be possible to arrange floating spans connecting the bridge with the shore, thus diminishing the height of construction over land, and solving the problem of temperature changes.

However, there was still the skewness to consider. The narrow piers would have to follow the direction of the current, forming an angle of 60° with the centreline of the bridge (Fig.3). If we, in order to preserve the symmetry and the logic of the system, were to cut the floating spans on the skew as well (Fig.4), all sorts of problems would arise. The system would work if the bridge consisted of parallel strips, but that would be wildly uneconomic because each strip would then have to support the maximum point load on its own. Tying the strips together to form a monolithic structure would, however, cause havoc with the orderly distribution

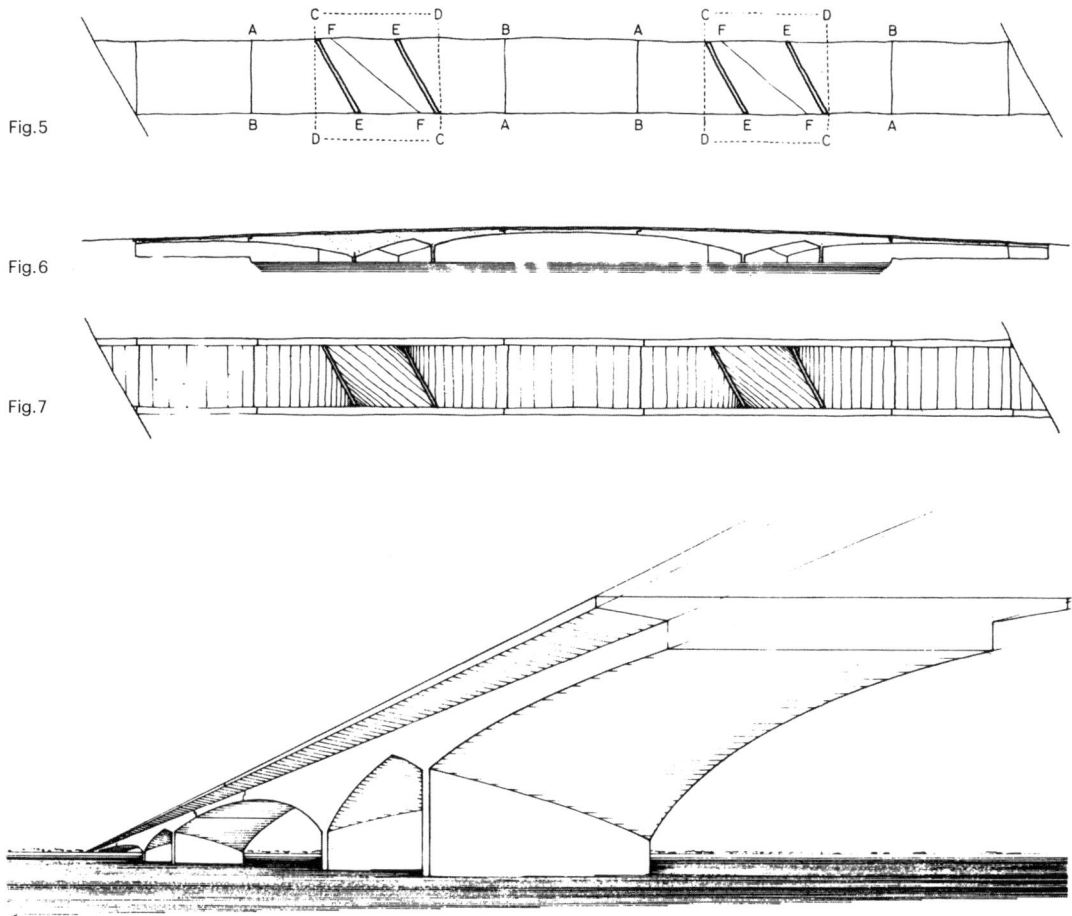

Fig. 5

Fig. 6

Fig. 7

Fig. 8

of moments, certain points would be overstressed in relation to others, in other words, shape would not any more correspond to the forces acting on the bridge. To overcome this, it was proposed to cut the floating spans at right angles to the bridge along the lines A–B (Fig. 5). Now everything is normal outside the areas CDCD around the two twin piers, or at least almost normal, because there is still a small extra deflection of the points D compared with points C which rest on the pier, and this would cause a small torsion in the 'normal' areas. This can be rendered insignificant, however, by making the deflection of D sufficiently small, and this is achieved in a simple way if the curve of the cantilever from B to D is continued downwards to a lower point on the pier at E.

The elevation of the bridge will then look like Fig. 6, with short cantilevers AC and long cantilevers BE, the latter following an identical curve to AC on the stretch BD and then dipping down further to E. From E to C, that is between the twin piers, the soffit is formed by two curves, each being symmetrical to the corresponding cantilever curve and meeting in F. The resulting contour lines of the soffit are shown in Fig. 7. The soffit in the area between the piers will then consist of a vault with horizontal lines running parallel to F–F, a direction still more skew than the piers. It will be seen that the elevation is not symmetrical about the centre of the bridge but follows a rhythmic but syncopated movement from left to right of deep dip, low dip, deep dip, low dip. Seen from the other side, the movement is again the same from left to right, not from right to left, as one would expect. A perspective is shown in Fig. 8. This is as far as we got.

There were of course hundreds of questions left to consider – whether to construct the bridge in situ as a hollow box section or a ribbed construction, of precast and prestressed units – probable – and the size and shape of units, the treatment

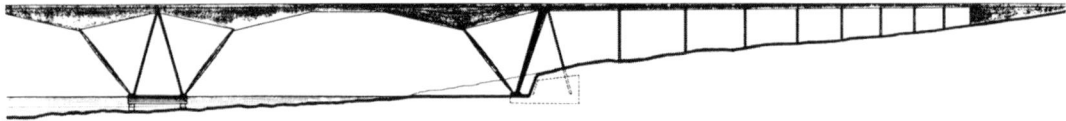

Fig. 9

of the joint between bridge and pier, cantilevered footpaths, if any, railings, lighting, etc. all of which would have influenced the architecture in varying degrees, but none as much as the basic design decisions described above, taken on purely structural and constructional grounds, which really determined the architectural character of the bridge for better or worse. I must confess I felt a bit doubtful myself, when I had drawn an outline of the elevation resulting from my structural thinking, and an architect friend, who came in and saw the thing, thought it looked awful. But after a few days of looking at it I came to like it more and more, and I was very grateful for the skewness of the bridge that made it possible and even sensible to produce something with a distinct character, different from the ordinary run of bridges. But that feeling may of course be peculiar to me.

Bridge in Scotland – over the Tay

The next sketch design is for a bridge in Scotland (Figs. 9–11). The bridge is about 8070 ft long, of which 5510 ft is over not very deep water. The roadway is about 110 ft above high water level, because the roads on both sides of the firth are at that level, and because shipping requires a free height of 82 ft. There are 11 piers in the water, spaced 475 ft apart.

The main consideration in this case was to keep the cost down. It was thought that the height of the bridge above water level would make this very difficult, but in the proposed design this difficulty has been largely overcome by extracting the greatest possible advantage from this extra height. Greater height means of course that there is more room available for the supporting structure, which makes it possible to employ arches, deep cantilevers, or raking struts thus reducing moments, increasing spans, and reducing the number of supports. But the fact remains that more structural material has to be used to raise the road level to this height, and more important still, work at this height and far out over the sea is very expensive. The aim of the designer must therefore be to reduce this extra material to a minimum, and to avoid work in situ.

In this case conditions for prefabrication were favourable, insofar as the length and uniformity of the bridge involved a lot of repetition. This would make it economically possible to invest a fair amount of capital in specially designed floating cranes and other plant that could be used for sinking cylinders and landing prefabricated units. There was also available, near the site, a rather underemployed shipyard, which could be used for constructing and launching floating units, if structural steel were used for the bridge.

These considerations led to a form of cantilever-construction almost on the lines of the old Forth Bridge, with floating spans between balancing cantilevers supported on central piers. Arches were considered, but rejected because of the one-sided thrust they would exert on the piers during construction, but mainly because the chosen system seemed to offer greater opportunities for almost complete shore-fabrication.

The first problem was to establish stable bases from which to work without going to the expense of constructing heavy solid piers. This led to open piers, consisting of four cylinders placed at the corners of an 18.5 m square, and connected by precast concrete bracing, as roughly indicated on Fig. 10a. The lower 'ring' would be cast or assembled at the top and lowered down, the diagonal bracing lowered into pockets at the connection of the piers with the lower ring, and fixed by pouring concrete in the pockets under water, etc. – enough to say here that it would be possible, at a reasonable cost in view of the repetition, to provide 18.5 m wide bases able to resist forces and moments in all directions, and therefore each able to support a portion of the bridge independently of the other piers. The next problem was then to use the available height to spread out the support as much as possible in the most economical way, and the method chosen, with four A-frames that together with the deck provide maximum stability with a minimum of material and minimum wind resistance, could hardly be improved upon.

Having established a desirable static system, there still remained the question of how to build it and what materials to use. I am not suggesting that this happened exactly in that order. When you are designing, the mind is let loose amongst a lot of

The Design of Bridges   75

b

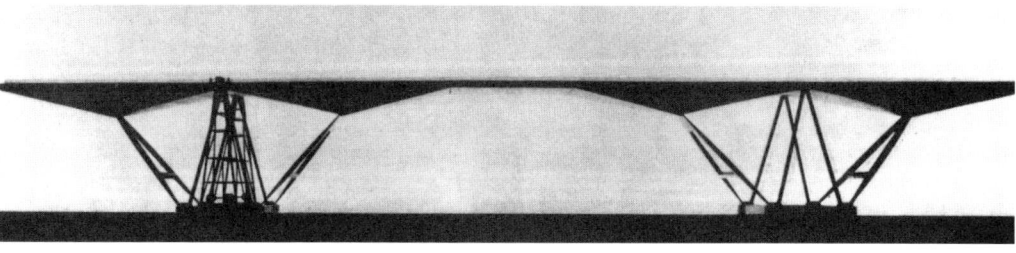

c

Fig.10

possible combinations of statical systems, methods of construction, until an idea emerges for closer examination. Anyhow the idea emerged, based on the preferred statical system, to form the bridge of floating units – which I will call 'barges' – which could be completely finished with paving, lighting, railings, etc., on shore, and which could be lifted up to their final position by making use of the supporting structure of A-frames. If the main A-frames supporting the 'barges' are hinged top and bottom by simple open hinges and the 'barges' are pulled towards each other, they will automatically rise from the water at high tide to the required level, and can be secured to the other A-frames which provide the longitudinal stability (Fig. 9).

It would take too long to describe in detail the various problems involved in this operation, but the forces were all calculated and the necessary plant designed in principle. The winches and hoisting gears were to be fixed to a temporary steel frame formed as a pyramid, which from a couple of 'barges' could be transferred to each pier in turn. A floating crane would transfer the A-frames to the piers and the bridge 'barges' would be guided towards each side of the pier by temporary guides fixed to the piers.

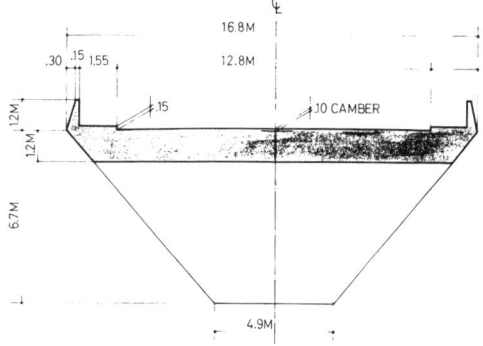

Fig.11

It is obvious that the use of structural steel for the bridge would favour these operations, as the weight of 'barges', etc., would be much less. There was actually no time to investigate a prestressed concrete scheme as well, but had it been decided to proceed with the construction of the bridge, this should have been done. It would have reduced maintenance problems – but actually these were not too bad in the case of the steel structure, because it was to be constructed of hollow units presenting a smooth surface to the outside.

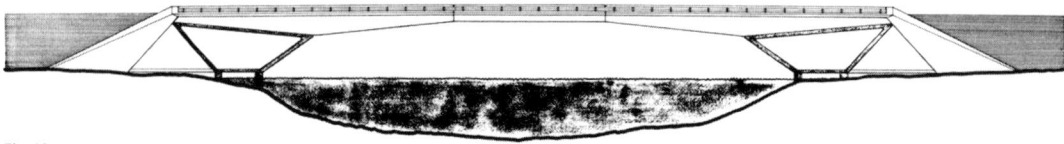

Fig. 12

Actually, later a probably somewhat better way to erect the bridge was thought of. According to this the lifting up of the 'barges' from the sea would take place at the dockyard, and the whole section of bridge resting on one pier, including A-frames but excluding the floating spans, would be brought to the bridge pier on two large barges or ships, total weight about 900 tons. This would mean that the steel pyramid including hoisting gear could remain in one position all the time and would not have to be transferred from pier to pier. The bridge section would be brought to the pier at high tide and guided so that when the tide went out it would come to rest on the pier.

The 'floating span' would of course also be floated out and lifted up in position.

How to design the railing is always a most perplexing problem for the engineer – and I suppose the architect too – because of the danger of its becoming a mere additional ornament not logically or organically part of the bridge. In this case this problem was solved very neatly and naturally by making the railing part of the hull of the barge (Fig. 11), thus assisting the floating and acting as a useful windbreak protecting cars and pedestrians.

Also in this case, the 'architecture' is essentially dominated by the structural and constructional idea. What remains is to look after the main proportions, the detailing of the structural members and their joints, and the design of the two land approaches at each end.

As far as the main proportions go, these are actually largely dictated by the need to strike a reasonable balance between the forces in the members and the distance between piers, but this balance is in my experience arrived at more by eye than by calculation. In other words what looks right, both structurally and aesthetically, is likely to make structural sense. But of course such judgments must be checked by calculation.

The two land approaches were difficult to deal with, because these portions of the bridge, which would best be built in concrete, would be entirely different in character, and the junction between the steel structure and the concrete abutments was obviously of the greatest importance from an aesthetic point of view – in fact it is on points such as these that so many bridges go wrong. To obtain a satisfactory transition it seemed best to complete the 'arch' in steel (Fig. 9). This meant, however, that the last 'barge' and A-frame would not balance against another 'barge', as in the case of the 11 centre piers, and it would be necessary to provide a counter-thrust to take the reaction from the cantilevered 'barge'.

This was done in the simplest possible way (Fig. 9). The concrete approach was designed as a completely plain hollow slab, on plain walls which were spaced closer together as the height became less. This is logical enough – although it may not lend itself so easily to prefabrication – but at any rate I think it is justified aesthetically. This slab was bent down at an angle to form the front leg of an A-frame at the junction with the bridge proper, which automatically enabled the bridge to resist a pull from the 'barge' at this point.

This account is of necessity very brief, dealing only with the basic idea. In fact, all the many detail problems were only solved to the extent required to make sure that the scheme was workable and economic.

Ankobra Bridge, Western Ghana

The next bridge on the list is the Ankobra bridge in Western Ghana, over the river Ankobra, close to the sea. This bridge has been designed down to the last detail, including the temporary staging and apparatus for sliding the main units into position, and tenders have been received, but owing to lack of funds the bridge has not yet been built and it now looks as if it never will be.

The conditions we have to deal with here are: a road, 24 ft wide, with two footpaths of 6 ft each, to be carried over about 302 ft of river, giving a clearance at the centre of about 24 ft over high water. Subsoil is poor, until rock is reached 90 ft down on one side, and about 33 ft down on the other. To provide temporary staging in the river would be expensive and should if possible be avoided.

There is often a salt spray from the sea nearby, and this salt, humid, and warm atmosphere would corrode steel, aluminium, and even concrete,

The Design of Bridges

Fig. 13

Fig. 14

unless the latter were in fairly smooth, solid sections of high-grade concrete, preferably compressed to avoid cracks. So prestressed concrete was the obvious material to use, especially as it would not be justified to rely on proper maintenance in this fairly remote spot.

The desire to produce a bridge which would withstand the ravages of time without maintenance was therefore a major factor in the design. Another was the desirability of avoiding staging in the river. And not least, there was the expressed wish of the government that this should be a beautiful and impressive bridge worthy of the new era in Ghana. A design on the lines of many of the Public Works Department bridges with frequent pile trestles supporting steel or concrete girders was definitely not wanted.

The need to avoid staging suggested cantilevering out from the two shores. The normal method of cantilevering by adding small sections and tying them back did seem to be rather complicated, making high demands on constant good workmanship to ensure that the many joints would not be sources of weakness. I did not feel certain that this procedure would in the given circumstances yield the high quality that I was after. So I was groping for an idea on the lines of the previous bridge with the 'barges' constructed in prestressed concrete instead of steel, but in this case there was not the same height to play with, and there were no two balancing 'barges'. The structural system could easily enough be envisaged, with inclined struts supporting the 'barges' in the centre, so as to

reach as far out into the river as possible and an A-frame with a counterweight at each shore end (Fig. 12) but how to get the 'barge' into position?

Sliding them out seemed a possible solution, and that is in fact the solution which was finally adopted, but it proved to be much more difficult than at first realised, and the design went through many stages before reaching its final form. It would be very instructive to retrace the many alterations made and the reasons for making them, because it would show very clearly that aesthetic conceptions must not be imposed at a too early stage; the final form cannot be determined before the structural and constructional requirements have been met in a direct, clear, and simple manner. But it would require a book rather than a short article to bring that out.

The first scheme (Figs. 12–14) was completed in outline before the structural problems had been properly resolved, because the model was needed for presentation to the clients. Visually, this scheme is satisfactory enough, and brings out very clearly the main components of the scheme: the cradle along which the 'barges' are slid out, the counterweight, and the suspended span in the centre. And this appearance of the bridge could have been kept, the details were actually solved, but the solution was too complicated to be really satisfactory. In this scheme, the inclined forward strut was permanently anchored back to the A-frame and counterweight, and afterwards the three 'barges' on each side were slid out, using the ties as tracks. Naturally the ties would have to be supported during the sliding, and that proved difficult because this cannot be compared with an ordinary launching of a ship or a caisson, as the weight of about 600 tons or so of the 'barge' was concentrated on a very small area. Then the spatial requirements of the sliding made it difficult to transfer the shear satisfactorily from the 'barge' to the inclined strut. And then there was a certain ambiguity in the structural system. To begin with, all the tension produced by the action of the inclined strut on the 'barge' was concentrated in the ties, but later, when the 'barges' were connected with the ties and each other, most of the tension would be transferred to the upper part of the 'barges'. This meant that the steel used for the ties would not be fully exploited. For these and other reasons the scheme was changed and went through a number of stages until it emerged as Scheme No. 2 (Fig. 15).

Here the connection between the inclined strut and the 'barge' is direct and simple, and the 'barge' itself acts as the tie – and is anchored back to the counterweight at the back by prestressing cables. This means that there is no redundancy of steel,

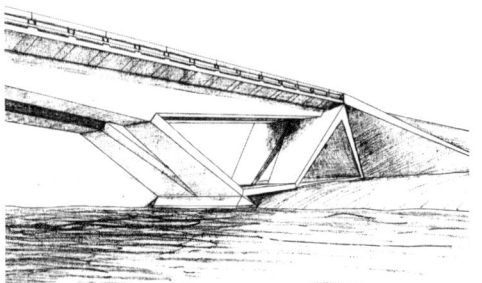

Fig.15

and the statical system is clear. On three rows of piles on each side of the river, a reinforced concrete slab and an A-frame are erected, with a retaining structure at the end which is filled up with boulders and concrete to form a counterweight sufficiently heavy to ensure a reasonable distribution of weight over the pile groups under all conditions of loading. The retaining walls also form a finish to the embankments on both sides but are independent of any settlements of these embankments. How this is achieved will be apparent from Fig.16.

These two structures can absorb the forces transferred to them by the inclined strut and the anchorage of the 'barge'. But this means that the temporary loads induced by the sliding of the 'barges', which incidentally have been reduced to two on each side, will have to be taken up by a temporary structure, made of structural steel. When this temporary structure was gone into, it was found that the slots required to accommodate it in the A-frame weakened the latter to such a degree that it could not act as the anchorage for the 'barges' without considerable complications of reinforcement and anchorages for cables, and the design was changed to Scheme 3 (Fig.17) where the apex of the A-frame has been widened and thickened, and a new aesthetic organisation imposed. Fig.18 shows a model of the final scheme.

The temporary steel structure used for sliding is shown in Fig.19. In order to save steel, the 3 ft high joists used for the sliding are later used in the permanent structure for the suspended centre span. The 'barges' are built on formwork supported on this temporary structure, and when completed, and after the formwork and supports have been removed, rest on a 10 ft cradle that slides on the joists on ball-bearing tracks. Calculations showed that the friction could by this arrangement easily be reduced to a figure that would allow the 'barges' to slide down the ramp by their own weight. All that would be required in the way of plant was a hand winch with a brake arrangement to control the movement. The inclined strut is also suspended from the temporary steel structure in a slightly lower position (Fig.20), and after the sliding of the 'barge' has been completed, this strut is pivoted into position and Freyssinet flatjacks are then placed between the strut and the 'barges'. When the 'barges' have been anchored and the flatjacks blown up, the weight of the 'barge' is taken by the strut and the temporary steel structure is released (Fig.21).

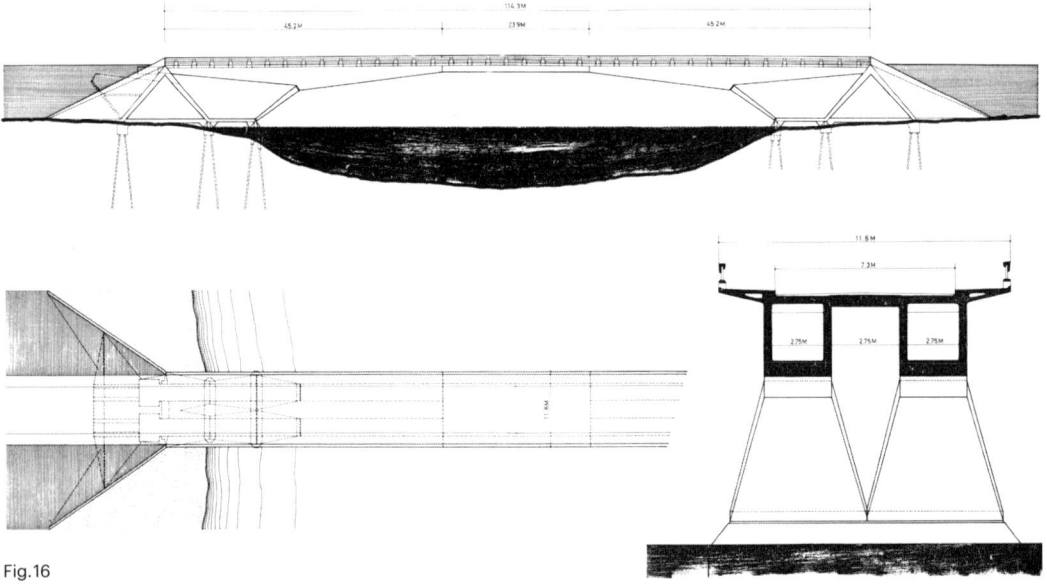

Fig.16

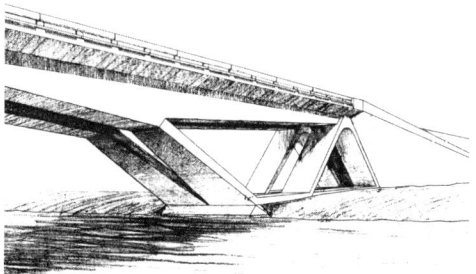

Fig. 17

Fig. 20

Fig. 18

Fig. 21

Fig. 19

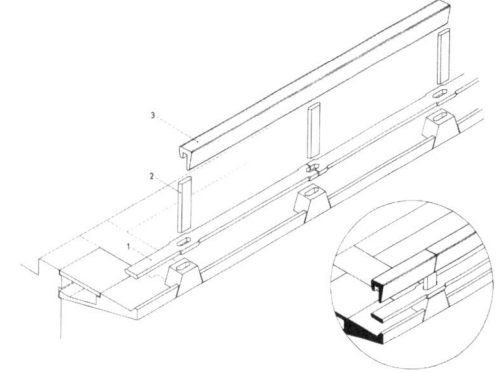

Fig. 22

This explanation is, of course, far from complete but will have to suffice here.

The two footpaths at each side of the bridge provide accommodation for services, and are cantilevered out from the main structure. In conformity with the wish to avoid in situ work carried out under difficult conditions, they are composed of precast units of very dense concrete. The detail design allows for adjustment of the cantilevers to obtain a perfect alignment, and provides easy access to the pipes. The precast units are placed by a mobile 2-ton crane from the bridge.

The design of the railings proved to be a very difficult job. Dozens of designs were drawn up, and several of them might have served, but none of them produced in me the feeling of rightness. This was a purely architectural matter, and my architectural training or ability was obviously no match for my critical sense. On one occasion I showed about 20 of these designs to an audience of architects during a lecture, and asked them for their criticisms and advice. The result was disappointing. Although some were able to argue fairly convincingly in favour of one design or another, the favours were more or less evenly distributed over the various designs.

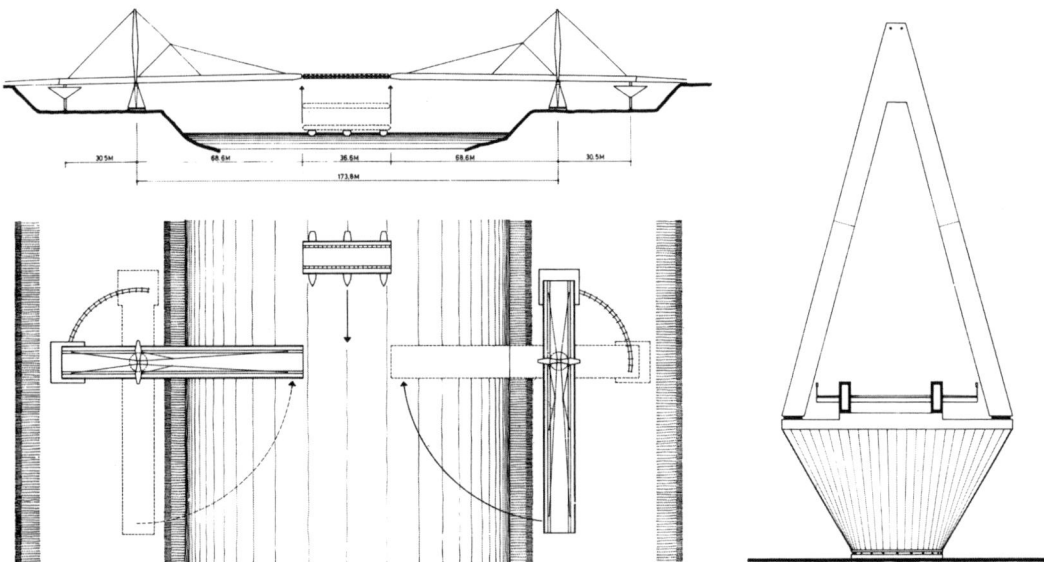

Fig. 23

So in the end I went back to basic requirements. I had been considering various combinations of concrete and hardwood – the only two materials which might do the job – but now on the advice of my West African collaborators I ruled out timber and decided to stick to prestressed precast concrete. This meant the units had to be long, preferably able to be produced by the long bench method. Further, I decided against bolts or joints in situ, which would be liable to deteriorate. The units would have to be placed in prepared holes and fitted together so that they stayed put by their own weight – each unit being completely self-contained, and with rounded corners. This led to the design shown on Fig. 22 which can be produced from three forms. The design now at least has a raison d'être.

The Black Volta Bridge, Ghana

The next scheme, so far only a sketch design, is also for a bridge in Ghana, but in the northern part of the country where the atmosphere is dry, and where steel and aluminium are possible materials to use. The bridge is to span the Black Volta, which is approximately 505 ft wide at this point, but runs in a valley 984 ft wide, which is flooded for three months of the year. The profile is as indicated in Fig. 23, with a 36 ft drop from the outer embankments to the flat valley and further 25 ft embankments down to the river, when it is not in flood.

Again, it is desirable to have as few obstructions as possible between the outer embankments, because the river can rise right to the top of these embankments and the current may be very swift. For the same reason it would obviously be cheaper to avoid staging in the river.

The design should be clear from Fig. 23. In cross-section the bridge consists of two 12 ft high hollow prestressed concrete girders, with steel joists stuck through holes in the girders at 2 ft centres to support the roadway and the cantilevered footways. These are timber decking with a covering of asphalt.

There are only four main piers, two on each side, the span between the centre piers, where practically all the loads are concentrated, being 581 ft. On these piers A-frames of hollow steel construction support two main cables which run from the outer piers or counterweights at the back over the A-frame and then to the outer end of each concrete girder. These cables in turn support a second set of cables as indicated. Between these two cantilever systems a centre span of aluminium construction is suspended.

The girders are, to begin with, interrupted at the main pier and at the point where the secondary cables support the girders. This makes the system statically determined for the dead load and when the cables have been stressed – by jacks under the main counterweights – and the length of cable adjusted to ensure that the different portions of concrete girders form a straight line. Then the

Fig. 24

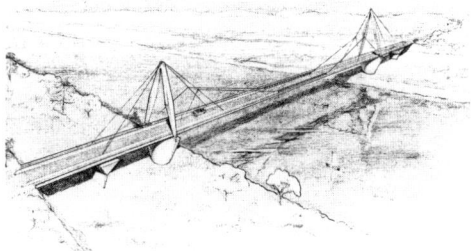

Fig. 25

Fig. 26

the main piers – which are founded on circular caissons 24 ft in diameter – the outer piers which act as counterweights can be pushed along a light circular track, thus turning the whole bridge round the centre piers.

Whilst the details have not been worked out yet, it is not anticipated that any major difficulties will be met with in the detail design. Actually the process of turning the bridge on a kind of turntable is a much easier proposition than the sliding of the 'barges' in the Ankobra design, because the resultant of all the forces stays in the same position. Figs. 24 and 25 show two perspective drawings of the bridge. This design employs four different structural materials: reinforced concrete, structural steel, aluminium, and timber. This is generally a bad thing, but in this case each material is used for a separate and well-defined part of the bridge, for which its properties are most suited. The guiding principle has been economy of construction, and this has certainly been achieved in this case, if one adheres to the decision that it is undesirable to have supports in the river.

The principle of constructing the two halves of the bridge on the banks of the river and then turning them out would in this case cut the cost of the bridge considerably as it would make construction independent of the yearly floods. If the four piers were built in one season, and the steel A-frames, formwork and cables were brought to the site, then in the next nine months' season the prestressed concrete girders and the supporting cables could be constructed, and probably the decks finished as well, because this is only a matter of sticking the joists through the holes in the concrete girders and laying the hardwood roadway.

Conditions here are therefore almost ideal for this method, but there must be many cases where it could be used with advantage, and I am surprised that I have never heard of it being used before. It is at present being used for a footbridge over the river at Durham Cathedral, one of the most beautiful settings in England. Fig. 26 shows one half of the bridge nearing completion along the river bank. Although appearance was of major importance in this case, the form was largely influenced by structural and constructional considerations.

joists are 'frozen' by prestressing and concreting and the girders now take a greater shear in the absorption of the live loads. The system is now statically indeterminate and the calculations somewhat complicated, but the principle is simple enough.

The special feature of this design is, however, that the two cantilevers are constructed on the banks of the river during the dry season in a position parallel with the river, and are then turned round the main piers through a quarter of a circle so that they reach out into the river. As all the load is practically concentrated on

An Artist in Small Matters

Transcript of an interview with Ove Arup by an unknown interviewer for a programme entitled People Today, 1964. It is noted as 'Not Broadcast'.

Interviewer*: Mr. Arup, you're known as one of the leading British Civil Engineers, but though you speak English remarkably fluently, you still have a distinct Danish accent, I think you will agree with that. How did you become English originally?*

Ove Arup: Well, I would not claim to have become English, exactly, but I've become a British subject, by being born in Newcastle, and that was simply because my father at that time worked in Newcastle. He started professional life as a veterinary surgeon, and after practising for about twenty years in Northern Jutland, was asked by the Danish Government to look after their interests in Newcastle. However, soon after my birth the trade in live cattle, with which he was mainly concerned, switched to Hamburg, and he was sent to that city, and that is where I spent the first twelve years of my life, until I was sent to a Danish boarding school in 1907.

You were at school in Hamburg?

Yes. My mother was Norwegian, and at home we spoke Danish or Norwegian, they are about the same thing, or at least they were at that time, except for a difference in accent, but of course the language I came to know best was German. My father did not want me to become German, however; he had been much happier in England, and did not care very much for the German mentality, and that is why I was sent to Denmark to one of the only two public schools – Sorø – run more or less on English lines – we even played cricket. There I stayed till I was 18, taking my entrance exam to the university in Copenhagen in 1913.

How did you react to life in a public school, and being moved to another country?

Not too badly, on the whole. In Germany I had been in opposition, so to speak, resenting the rather blatant German patriotic propaganda – on one occasion my younger brother and I had to fight a whole bunch of boys because we were being abused for being Danish, and had to retreat with as much dignity as we could muster. As a result I came to Denmark as a rather blue-eyed Danish patriot, but that was soon knocked out of me. Or rather, it was just not on the agenda, nobody was interested. Of course, in a public school one learns to keep one's ideals and secret longings safely underground, only to be revealed to a few trusted friends. Also here I drifted into a kind of opposition – my form was rather good at sports, school matches, etc. I was simply not interested. And I am afraid I was not particularly interested in school traditions, I resented any kind of bullying, however hallowed by custom. But I loved the countryside, the beautiful woods, the lake and park and all that, I was glad to escape from a big city. I wanted to study nature, animals, insects, fish, to become an explorer or scientist. But I also read a lot, mostly the usual boys' stories, Cooper, Marryat, Carrit Etlar, Defoe, Jules Verne and that sort of stuff. However, there was no doubt in my mind, when I had to decide at 15, that I wanted to study science rather than classical languages, much to the disgust of my Headmaster, who was a classical scholar of some distinction. At that time I came across Darwin, I read *The Origin of Species* and *The Descent of Man* and that set me thinking of a lot of things. I liked his sober, methodical, scientific approach, and it seemed to me that he had established without doubt, that all species, including man, evolved from lower forms, by whatever mechanism this was achieved. I read other books, the German Haeckel, whose brazen materialism I found very shallow, Spencer and various others, but also Kierkegaard, whose savage attacks on the hypocrisy of official Christianity I could but approve of. And I admired his wit and irony, and the intellectual honesty of his 'credo quia absurdum'. I also got a vague idea of Indian philosophy, and read Hoffding's psychology – and for that matter Thomas Hardy and Bernard Shaw's *Plays Pleasant and Unpleasant* and Danish and German literature, and Ibsen, of course. Not that I was a bookworm exactly, I did many other things, and enjoyed the last years of my schooldays. I was actually very sorry when I had to leave. But all this had left me rather bewildered, there were so many problems to solve: How did life evolve from matter? How to square free will with determinism, Western science with Eastern mysticism? The nature of truth, the foundation of ethical beliefs and behaviour – all that and more. Obviously I had to find out before I could think of a profession. It seemed rather absurd to me that the object of life should be to earn a living. So I decided to study philosophy.

Although you studied philosophy you took up civil engineering. Now there seems some distance between these two. What moved you from philosophy to civil engineering?

Well, I am afraid that I got rather into a muddle, I lived through what the Germans would call a 'Sturm und Drang' period, which really means a lack of control over one's personal problems, feelings and behaviour – altogether taking oneself far too seriously. My friends were a rather mixed lot, seen from a sober bourgeois standpoint, mostly artists. It was very easy to tempt me to attend a party or go sailing instead of reading Kant or Schopenhauer, and I rather neglected my studies or read all sorts of things which had very little to do with them. I re-discovered the old truth, that there is a great difference between knowing what one ought to do, and doing it. But as for Truth with a capital T, that eluded me. And that was really the main reason why I abandoned philosophy. Closer acquaintance had made me realise that it consisted of a series of specialised disciplines, Theory of Knowledge, Ethics, Psychology and so on, all involving a lifetime immersed in books, and none of them answering the questions I had set out to solve. In fact in philosophy there seemed to be no answers, only more and more subtle questions. Science, or any logical reasoning, cannot solve the human predicament: What is the whole thing about? What are we? Where are we? What are we supposed to do? What is good or evil? Can we, or should we teach the tiger not to eat meat? The greatest happiness for the greatest number? And what is happiness, and Truth, and Beauty? I revolted against ideologies, philosophical systems, moral codes, on Kant's insistence on rectitude in preference to kindness. I realised that human relations are important, that art is important; listening to a fantasia and fugue by Bach I felt that here was something that was good in itself no matter whether the mysteries of this world were solved or not. If I could have become a great artist, I would gladly have left philosophising to others, but I obviously wasn't cut out for that. But you could also be an artist in small matters. *To create anything which was good of its kind would give satisfaction.* For a joiner to make any old table would perhaps not be very exciting, but to make a really good one would be fun.

It was some such reasoning which made me switch over to engineering. I was good at mathematics, and this was something I at least thought I could do. I was not so sure that I had enough artistic ability to become a really good architect. I liked the idea of designing some nice bridges, but I cannot say that I felt wildly enthusiastic about it, I disliked the idea of specialising, and felt that I was perhaps giving up too easily.

Then after finishing your studies, how did you get your first job in your chosen profession?

I applied for a job with Christiani and Nielsen, a well-known firm of engineers and contractors, who had been the first to introduce reinforced concrete to Denmark, and who had branches in many countries. I was offered a job in Hamburg, not the place I would have chosen to go to, because I wanted to see something different, but I took the job. It was just after the first world war, and during the two years I was there the mark completely collapsed – it ended up by being one thousand billion marks to a shilling. That led to some pretty absurd situations, with all the big firms printing their own money. There was also a lot of political upheaval, with fighting and barricades in the streets. Also in the literary and artistic world there was turmoil, disillusion turning into extreme pacifism, eastern mysticism, lots of new movements, defiance and grim humour, with new plays by Ernst Toller, Fritz von Unruh and others having their first performance at the Hamburger Kammerspiele – all very exciting and entertaining if not very convincing. My favourite authors were Hermann Hesse and Thomas Mann, both well established before the war.

But in Hamburg I certainly learnt how to design quay walls and all sorts of marine structures. Christiani and Nielsen were pioneers in this field, and I am very grateful for what I learnt during my twelve years stay with this firm, first in Hamburg and then – for ten years – in London. I am mainly indebted to Mr Forchhammer, who was in charge in London at the beginning of my stay, and who was an inspired engineer. He had organised the whole technical know-how of the firm and supplied most of the ideas to start with. They had an excellent system, which we have also adopted in my present firm, of circulating technical reports on interesting jobs, special difficulties encountered and overcome, new methods of calculation, and so on to all branches, so that you really benefited from the firm's experience everywhere. And their emphasis was on good design, as their main means of securing contracts. Of course there are other stratagems involved, but having the best possible design to start with is more than half the battle – or at least it ought to be. Design and method of construction ought to be completely integrated, you see, design is really nothing else than inventing and indicating a sensible method of construction, that is, one that leads to the desired result with the least effort, taking into account all the local and other circumstances. This is fairly obvious if you have to build something in the middle of the sea; how you set about the job, whether you drive piles from a staging, sink cylinders, float caissons or build inside a coffer dam must of course affect the design. But it really applies to all construction, building, and for that matter manufacturing. It has however been my – I almost said bitter – but at any rate often frustrating experience, that the paramount importance of getting the right design is hardly understood by laymen, including clients, is rarely grasped by building authorities and the legal profession concerned with building, often not even by architects who leave the costing of jobs to quantity surveyors and therefore lose touch with the method of building, or by consulting engineers, who concern themselves exclusively with structural stability, but leave matters of construction to the contractor. In the organisation of the building industry, great care is taken through the system of competitive tendering to obtain the lowest price for a given design, but hardly any attention is paid to getting the best design. And it must be admitted, that this is a very difficult thing to do.

I'm afraid you are jumping ahead a bit. Could you tell us what brought you to England?

Well, I never intended to stay in Germany. I was travelling with a British passport, and intended to come to England sometime, but I thought it would be a good idea to learn French first, so I applied for a job in the Paris branch. They had no vacancy for me there, however, and I was transferred to London.

Did you find it difficult to adapt yourself to the English approach?

It was certainly a big change. There were so many exciting things, big coal fires in the waiting room at Harwich station, arriving in London in a real old-fashioned pea-souper, with policemen carrying torches walking in front of a string of buses, coal fires even in the drawing offices, and lots of nice tea and crumpets and roast beef and two veg. But of course London is big. I had an Uncle and Aunt living in Kew, who had been in London for forty years, they were very kind to me, and I stayed there the first couple of weeks until I found a bed-sitting room in Pimlico, within walking distance of Victoria Street. The proprietor was a real butler, complete with side-whiskers; he and his wife had served in a number of big houses, their thoughts seemed to be entirely focused on the doings of the great, and he could hardly talk about anything else. Altogether England at that time, 1923–24, seemed to me rather old-fashioned, young people seemed healthy-minded, innocent, or naive but not a bit interested in intellectual gamesmanship, having never heard about Nietzsche, Oswald Spengler, or even their own Bertrand Russell. But then I did not know London or England, I did not speak the language well, I mixed a lot with foreigners and had no access to any set which might have shared my interests.

So I felt rather lost, although there was much to see and discover. But then I had the remarkably good luck to find a Danish girl, who had been sent over to London by the Rockefeller Foundation to teach domestic science to some Women's Institutes, and that changed my life. We got married in 1925, I found a furnished studio in Battersea, just across Chelsea Bridge – my salary of five pounds a week was just enough to live on, but no more – and I settled down just to be happy. I did not bother much about philosophy, and I was still reluctant to get completely swallowed up by engineering or to take my career too seriously.

So you did not make any plans for the future?

No, I just did my job fairly conscientiously, but no more. I cycled to and from the office, and when the weather was nice, met my wife in Battersea Park on the way home. But then gradually I got more absorbed in my job, and was given more responsibility. Christiani and Nielsen preferred to design their own jobs, but this was not the accepted practice in England, where there was a sharp distinction between the consulting engineers on the one side, and the contractors on the other. The first were professional people, bound by a code of honour to serve the client, the second worked for profit, and had to be carefully watched and supervised so as not to cheat the client. This was forty years ago, of course. Design was therefore the province of the consulting engineer, borough engineers, chief engineers of railway companies and so on, and the idea of designing contractors was frowned upon. So the firm had to a large extent to follow this pattern and carry out work to other people's design. And in the beginning I several times got into serious trouble by suggesting to people that they could save a lot of money by altering the design. On a few occasions our firm was even put on the black list and never asked to tender again.

Did you find that English people refused to adopt new ideas unless you could show the evidence?

I think it is fair to say that that was often the case before the war. It has changed now. And then we were really reinforced concrete specialists, and this was a material which was not much understood then, and which was under heavy suspicion. Not entirely without reason, for the workmanship was often bad. But the code of practice was so conservative that any kind of concrete was strong enough for what was asked of it.

There is no doubt about it, the design which we came across was often shockingly bad. And it is kind of frustrating, when you know that you could save the country thousands of pounds, not to be allowed to do anything about it. And as a contractor, at that time at any rate, you only got about ten per cent of the work you tendered for, and I think that many of my best ideas lie buried in the files of Christiani and Nielsen. Of course as a consulting engineer, your frustrations are of a different kind. If you are appointed for a job, your client will accept your ideas, and if you are able to give him a good job and save him some money at the same time, you are happy, even if he may never discover it, because he has nothing to compare it with. But the frustration comes in when you are never consulted about the kind of job which you feel you could do very well. Bridges and marine structures for instance. But I can't complain, really, I have always had plenty to do, even if not always what I would have liked to do. And a good deal of frustration is the common lot of mankind – nobody has yet devised a system which will exploit the capacity of each individual to the full.

Had this frustration anything to do with your leaving Christiani and Nielsen?

To some extent, perhaps, but it was not as simple as that. I had for some time been dissatisfied with the limitations imposed on a designer in a contractor's office. The main object is, and to some extent must be, to make money. A competitive design must be cut to the bone. To do that, it must be a good design, and design and method of construction must be perfectly matched because this reduces costs. So far so good – excellent, in fact. But when this has been done, something should be added back to improve the design at its weakest points, so as to get a more balanced and sound design. And something should be done to make it more pleasing, more satisfactory aesthetically, to make it better architecture – because after all, all manmade features are also architecture, and must be judged as such. But this the contractor cannot afford, if he wants to remain competitive. And even if he could – and this is quite possible, for good architecture need not necessarily be more expensive, it only needs taking great trouble, and having the right kind of judgement – the contractor very rarely has that sort of judgement, unless he is a [Pier Luigi] Nervi or [Félix] Candela, and if he seeks architectural advice, which costs money and is therefore nearly always ruled out for engineering structures, he probably gets hold of the wrong architect, because he does not know any better. In any case you cannot tack architectural advice on to an engineering scheme, the architecture must be completely integrated with and arise from the structural and constructional concept. So to get all round quality – architectural quality, structural quality, functional efficiency and to keep within the budget – this is very very difficult. It requires that power to control, or at least to influence or persuade, should be in the hands of someone who is able to judge these different qualities, and who has the will to achieve perfection. A quality surveyor with a passion for perfection. This of course is a counsel of perfection, and outside practical politics in all but the most exceptional cases. As it is, building and construction is dominated by quantity surveyors, lawyers, businessmen, bankers, Treasury officials and that sort of person in whose mind the question of good design and architectural quality hardly ever crops up.

But all this hardly justifies moving from one contractor to another?

No, you are right. But you see I had for some time been interested in modern architecture, I joined the Architectural Association, I got to know Lubetkin and through him joined the MARS – or Modern Architectural Research Group* – just after it was founded by Wells Coates, Maxwell Fry, Lubetkin and others. MARS was affiliated to CIAM – Congrès Internationaux d'Architecture Moderne – led by Corbusier, [Walter] Gropius, [Cornelis] van Eesteren and others, and they undertook a complete reappraisal of the function and aims of architecture. The modern architectural movement was very fond of reinforced concrete, in spite of the fact that used wrongly, as it often was, it could be a very unsuitable material for housing. It was more a fashion, a matter of style, but of course that was not officially admitted, as 'functionalism' – fitness for purpose – was the battle-cry. However, I realised that there was a future for reinforced concrete for multistorey buildings, to replace the steel frame, a type of construction much too wasteful of steel, and therefore fundamentally expensive. (There was, but it has taken thirty years for it to sink in.)

I therefore proposed to my firm that we should go in for this kind of construction, but they were not interested. I can well understand their reluctance, because there was not much money in it at the time, but I was interested in the architectural possibilities, so that when I was offered a job with J.L. Kier and Company as director responsible for designs and tenders, I accepted on the condition that the firm would interest itself in what we may call architectural structure. And this started my long collaboration with the architectural firm of Tecton.† We built Highpoint I and II, the Penguin Pond and other Zoo buildings, Finsbury Health Centre and the flats at Rosebery Avenue and Busaco Street, the first examples of what I first called boxframe construction.

But by that time I had already left J.L. Kier and Co. and founded my own firm, Arup and Arup Ltd. together with a cousin of mine. This was in 1938 and war was approaching.

That was when you got interested in the design of shelters?

Yes. Through my connection with Lubetkin I became consultant to the Finsbury Borough Council and was asked to make proposals for their shelter programme. The brief was to provide protection against a direct hit from a half ton bomb for the whole population of Finsbury at a cost which they could afford. Moreover, we were only allowed to build on the many open squares they had in Finsbury, the police at that time objected to street shelters, and private premises were not available. And we could only build down, and not upwards.

There was only one possible solution to this brief, namely to build large multi-storey underground shelters in each of the squares, protected by a thick heavily reinforced concrete slab on top and around the sides. Obviously, if you have to provide this expensive concrete slab to protect everybody underneath from a direct hit, you simply cannot afford to have only one layer of shelter, you must use the slab to protect as many layers as would be practical from the point of view of access, evacuation, ventilation, etc. So we evolved an economical way of building these shelters in the form of large spiral ramps which were so dimensioned, that they could later on be used as carparks. They were fully air-conditioned, subdivided and provided with bunks and lavatories so that they could be used to provide a night's rest under safe conditions. These were the so-called deep shelters.

I believe they caused a certain amount of controversy?

Well, that is certainly an understatement. A hell of a row, I would say, which lasted for years. Tecton's and my proposals were shown at a large exhibition at Finsbury Town Hall, and included an illustrated report where the whole question of shelter construction was considered scientifically, from the point of view of getting the maximum value for money. I could obviously not decide how much money the country could afford to spend on shelters, or how much protection was politically indispensable, but as an engineer I could perhaps suggest how to spend the money wisely, so as to get maximum protection for a given sum, or pay the least for a given amount of protection. And in my report which was subsequently issued as a book, I clearly showed that to give everybody protection against a direct hit from a large bomb would be a very expensive affair indeed. The best value for money would be obtained by constructing multi-cellular 'wall-shelters', as I called them. These would give very good protection against anything falling outside the shelter – and that meant of course the large majority of dangerous bombs. This meant, that I did not really approve of the brief we had been given by Finsbury, but I strongly maintained that the deep shelter was the only possible solution to this brief.

Anyhow, the Government did not approve of the deep shelters, because they objected to large shelters in principle – they were afraid of possible political repercussions or of panic if a lot of people got together, and they refused to support the Finsbury scheme. Finsbury however persisted, and placed the contract for the first large shelter with Peter Lind and Co. with the aid of borrowed money. Strangely enough the war put an end to the construction, because all contracts at that time had a war clause which enabled the contractor to ask for revised terms if war broke out, and the loan which Finsbury had obtained to pay for the shelter did not allow for this contingency. It was a pity in a way, because the method of construction would have made engineering history, and the shelter would not have cost more per person accommodated than the rather inefficient brick street shelters later built by the Government. Also it would have made a very useful car park after the war.

In so far as there was any Government policy about shelters at that time, it consisted in reliance on dispersion. I had pointed out in my report that dispersion only made any sense if people were moved from an area where bombs were likely to fall, to one where they were less likely to fall – for instance from towns to the country or away from likely targets such as bridges, factories, etc. But this was heresy in the eyes of the powers that be – or were – in fact it was even worse than the Finsbury deep shelter proposals, because it undermined all the official propaganda put out at the time. Sir John Anderson, as he then was, came to the exhibition and assured me that his experts could prove to me that I was wrong. I was naturally very anxious to meet these experts, but it was not until long afterwards, after the war had started and Ellen Wilkinson had been put in charge of shelters, that I succeeded in obtaining an introduction to one of these experts, a Civil Servant at the Home Office, I think. I liked Ellen Wilkinson very much, she was honest and sincere and very eager to do the right thing, but she was not exactly a mathematician. I had many long sessions with her about my shelter theories, which were based on the law of probability and certain facts from official documents about the destructive power of different types of bombs, and I had prepared a picture book for her which made the whole thing absolutely clear. She was visibly shaken, and arranged for me to visit this expert. He *was* a mathematician, and a cultured and delightful person besides, and he surprised me by admitting straight away that I was completely right, a fact which the experts were perfectly aware of, but which I could not expect a mere Minister to understand. But there was more to it than that. What matters was to keep people quiet, to give them confidence in the measures taken and prevent panic; this psychological or political aspect was really more important than the safety of the shelters. He went so far as to say that if a board which spelt SHELTER could make people feel safe in any old basement, he would be satisfied. I found this view a bit cynical and was worried about what the consequences might be, but there was not much I could do about it.

---

* The Modern Architectural Research Group (MARS) was an architectural think-tank and the British arm of the Congrès International d'Architecture Moderne (CIAM) founded in 1933.
† The Tecton group was co-founded by Berthold Lubetkin, Francis Skinner, Denys Lasdun, Godfrey Samuel and Lindsay Drake in 1932. The group played a leading role in bringing continental modernism to Britain.

Ove on Kingsgate Bridge, Durham

After the war I think you left Arup and Arup and devoted all your time to consulting work. By this time you had become very well known as a Civil Engineer and a designer in reinforced concrete, who was interested in modern architecture and therefore able to help architects with their structural problems. You had strong views about the relationship which should exist – or does exist – between the architect and the engineer, and you had written articles and made speeches about it.

Yes, I gave up contracting largely because it became more and more impossible to combine contracting with design – and it was design which interested me. Contractors were not supposed to have any ideas, if they had they were not listened to, and if they were they were not paid for them. Their motives were suspect, anyhow. I was sorry in a way, because I still strongly believed in the need to integrate design with method of construction, but as I was getting more concerned with buildings, there was another kind of integration which became important: that of structure and architecture. During the next twenty years this problem was to become of major interest to me, not forgetting, of course, to adapt the structural system to a sensible method of construction. As the firm grew, and we collaborated with more and more architects, I received through this collaboration a practical training in Architecture or at any rate in the ideas and aims of different architects which enabled us in many cases to help them realize their ambitions. I realized that there are many conflicting architectural theories. There are also many definitions of the word architecture – but the simplest might be to use it for any building or structure which is artistically controlled. If we use this definition, then everything built by man ought to be architecture, and by implication, good architecture. But this is not the only thing, and mostly not the most important thing required of a building or structure, it must first of all serve its purpose well, it must not be too expensive, it must wear well, etc., and the difficulty is to strike the right balance between these requirements – a balance which must vary with the nature of the job and the personalities concerned. The aim should of course be to satisfy all of these aims equally well, but this is rarely possible, in most cases some of them are incompatible, and compromises have to be accepted. The difficulty is, that there are so many different people involved in the design of the same building. There ought to be only one, who knew all the answers, as was the case in the old days when building was simpler. Now we depend on teamwork, and this depends on mutual understanding and identity of aims, and very much on strong leadership and a passion for perfection which will not be satisfied with second rate solutions. It also raises endless discussions about the whole organisation of the building industry.

Now I'd like to come to yourself and the buildings you have been responsible for. I know that not one of the biggest but one that gave you the greatest satisfaction, was the footbridge at Durham University, and I know you were involved with Coventry Cathedral and with the Crystal Palace sports centre. I know the next job, which I think is terribly exciting, is the new Sydney Opera House. Which of your jobs would you say have given you most satisfaction?

Well, it would be very difficult to pick from the many exciting jobs we have done over the years, and remember my part in them has only been marginal. The various architects involved have of course had the main responsibility and made the main contribution and then I owe much to my many excellent collaborators – the firm is so big now, that I only know a fraction of what goes on. But if I had to choose, I should like to pick two jobs at the opposite ends of the scale with which I was very much involved personally, the block of flats known as 'Highpoint', built in 1934 with Lubetkin as architect, and the little bridge at Durham which you mentioned. Both are rather perfect examples of the complete integration of architecture, structure and method of construction. In the first case I was both engineer and contractor – or employed by the contractors – and I broke away from the traditional concrete framework which was an imitation of the steel frame and also evolved a system of jacking up the working platform and formwork which was a forerunner of later events. Unfortunately I did not get the opportunity to make more use of these methods which had proved to be very successful. In the case of the Durham Bridge completed last year I was myself the architect and responsible for the method of construction as well – ably assisted by my own collaborators and the very excellent contractors who did the job, and we succeeded between us to produce what I think is a very satisfactory job at a remarkably low cost. Apart from these, we are of course involved in very many jobs, the Sydney Opera House being by far the most difficult and almost too exciting. I still hope that the result will repay the enormous effort which has gone into it.

It seems to me, that great changes are taking place in building technique and organisation. What impact, if any, have they on your work, and how are you dealing with them?

You are certainly right, these changes are our main concern. How to absorb them, use them, and yet produce good architecture. There seems to be a schism developing between the contractor or system-dominated industrialized utility buildings, and the architect-dominated prestige or unique buildings. In Sydney the design has been gradually adapted to allow a large amount of mass-production of units – in other words industrialisation of a unique building. We are very much concerned with developing methods of construction – mostly involving large pre-cast units, pre-stressing and all sorts of new methods and materials – which will allow us to take advantage of modern cost-saving inventions without sacrificing architectural quality. It is still this matter of integration of all the different requirements and all the different skills which is the main problem. The building industry is not sufficiently geared to achieve this integration, and to achieve it and avoid being parochial or narrow-minded we have to concern ourselves with all the aspects of building, including sometimes roads and traffic control, town-planning and the general aims of building. After all, we are building for people, so we must try to understand people, their needs and aims and values.

Mr. Arup, you have told me about your work and you have told me about your life. You are certainly certain about your work. But I still get the impression that you are not really certain about life itself. Is this a fair comment?

Yes, I suppose it is, I am certainly not certain about anything as grand as life itself, whatever that may mean. There are, and have been, a great number of people who claim to have found the meaning of life – they belong to a great many different religions, sects, movements or schools of thought. There are even scientists who think that science will gradually enable us to solve all our problems – or at least there were. There are also people who claim to know all, or a good deal about what everybody ought to do – they know what is good and bad. Then there are people who perhaps are less prepared to generalize, but who have found personal happiness and fulfilment in life, one can perhaps say that they have found their own truth – although some seem satisfied with very little. And then there are people who perhaps have been very unhappy and have made a mess of their lives and yet have managed to give a great deal to mankind – or to be less pompous – to give joy or happiness to many other people. Now it would be nice and simple if one could first find the truth about life, the whole explanation of how it works, how it happened, what it is in aid of, and so on, from which would follow what one ought to do with one's life. Then one would proceed to do it and thus get personal fulfilment and make everybody else happy as well. But it isn't quite like that. Life is complicated and mysterious, so varied, rich and marvellous, cruel and sordid, heroic or mean, it is everything under the sun. But I don't think there is any Truth about life with a capital T. No absolute truth, not one which is available to human beings with their limited understanding. It would certainly not be a logical, scientific kind of truth, this is beyond the scope of science. And if it is a personal, directly experienced truth, it is only a truth for the one who experiences it. But this is a different kind of truth, if it exists, it seems to me that truth should be universal. Every individual is different, is unique – a fact which is sometimes forgotten by scientists and organisers who would like to treat human characteristics as material to feed into a computer. Therefore there is not one truth, not one kind of goodness. It seems to me that one should savour and try to understand, in an artistic way, if you like, the richness and variety of life. That there are infinitely many different kinds of people, different nations, races, languages, customs and artforms, that nature is so rich and wonderful beyond belief, and also frighteningly cruel. That there are so many entirely different kinds of excellence – so many kind of good architecture, for instance, and I am afraid still more of bad – which more or less exclude each other, and which are also inextricably mixed up with all sorts of bad qualities.

Viewing this rich canvas artistically is all very well, but you have to get involved personally, and it seems to me that you have got involved, and that you have created something worthwhile, in spite of your uncertainty. How do you account for that?

Well, I am not so sure about that – or at any rate, I am not so sure it is good enough. It is not really a matter of what people think, it is a matter of what I think, and whether I have used my talents wisely, and that is quite a different matter. But you are of course absolutely right in saying, that one must be involved in life, that is the great challenge which faces everybody. I have perhaps too great a tendency to be merely contemplative, I hate in a way to commit myself until I have investigated every possible course of action or line of thought. It makes me see the other man's point of view, which can be a good thing if it does not stifle action altogether, but it is mostly infuriating and a source of weakness.

The possibilities are so endless, what sort of excellence should one pursue? Should one study art, science, religion, politics, history and social behaviour, should one train one's body, or one's mind, should one be a connoisseur of French wines or an Indian yogi, or lead a life of action, for the good of mankind or just enjoy life? Should one have great humility, be meek – to inherit the earth – mild, charitable, tolerant, kind, self-effacing, or should one be intolerant of stupidity and prejudice and be ruthless in the pursuit of some idea or ideology? It is very difficult to choose. It is very difficult to be dogmatic about what one should do – it depends of course on what sort of person one is – and if one thinks too much about what sort of person one is one is quite likely to make a mess of things. I can appreciate almost any kind of excellence, even if it contains a certain amount of wickedness. For me it is almost easier to say what I don't like. Cruelty to children, greed – in others – pompousness, cocksureness, injustice, as I see it, lack of consideration for others in others, well I don't like to see people or animals suffer – all the usual things, for that matter. And, come to think of it, the reason you have to become involved in life, is really the existence of other people. We are in this together, a fact which one, or I, sometimes loses sight of. You cannot shut yourself off completely from other people – there would hardly be much life left. And therefore human relations are really the most important thing in life. Hunger, illness and all kind of human suffering can be terrible, but the cruelty of one human being towards another is surely worse. And in human relations are also found the greatest possible happiness which can be felt. But – the most important? Creative thought or activity is of course also important, and for some the most important so here we go again – sorry.

The Problem of Producing Quality in Building

This lecture was given to Westminster Chamber of Commerce, 27 April 1965.

Ladies and Gentlemen,

I thank you for the honour you show me in inviting me to speak to you today. I can only hope that your confidence will not prove to be entirely misplaced. The title of my talk: 'The problem of producing quality in building' sounds pretty formidable, obviously you do not expect me to solve this problem in twenty minutes. All I can do is to talk round the subject and to make one or two observations based on personal experience, observations which I am sure you are perfectly aware of already, old stuff which I have been bringing to market for the last twenty years or more, but which still has got some wear left in it.

I need not tell you that building is a very important activity in our society, because it provides the shell which houses most of our activities and makes our kind of life possible.

We are in dire need of buildings – throughout the world. We cannot get enough of it fast enough, our resources are overstrained. This imposes an obligation on us to use our limited resources wisely, to get the most out of them, but in discussing this problem we must not forget that all this building activity is constantly changing our environment, for better or worse, but much too often for worse, in spite of the fact that we have it in our power to make our environment better, if we only would use that power. *I think that our environment has an enormous influence on us, it is a constant source of happiness or misery, and to get the environment we would like to have instead of one which is forced on us by expediency, or by economic forces which we fail to control, is surely a very worthy object to which we all subscribe, even if we do not always agree on what we would like to have.* But that is just part of the challenge, we do not want uniformity but variety, variety to express different personalities, different modes of life.

This complicates the matter. It would be so much easier if we could just get on with organising our building activity efficiently for maximum output and minimum cost, without bothering about artistic effects, the psychological impact of space, colours, textures, light and shade – all these matters which long-haired artists spend all their energies talking about without ever agreeing about what they really want, and which would drive sober and practical men of affairs up the pole if they were ever to take any notice of it. It *is* a complication, but it is a complication we must face, and which I think we ought to give very high priority. There is no need to stress functional and technological efficiency, needs are needs, and will assert themselves, and money we know, talks; but beauty, character, poetry of environment – what shall I call it – is something which has to be fought for. It is highly prized where it exists, especially when people have got used to it – then they will pay fantastic sums for a house in a favoured locality – but they are not so eager to make any sacrifice or to exert themselves unduly to create it, if it should happen to conflict with maximum letting space, for instance, or with the convenience of the almighty car.

There is a fourth and confusing issue which raises its ugly head in a discussion of building activity. All those people who move stuff about with their hands or with the help of machines, those who tell them what to move, those who think out what the second lot should tell the first lot, and those who tell the last lot what to think out, and so on, in an intricate maze of activity – all these people are not really collaborating in a spontaneous desire to create new and better buildings, what they are doing is to make their living according to some complicated rules which have been evolved and fought over for centuries. What they are thinking of, what drives them on, is probably how to improve their status and their share of the common cake. Anybody who would try to eliminate waste by organising the necessary collaboration of many people on a more rational basis is at once up against old customs, established trades and professions and vested interests, and the whole thing moves into a sphere of social organisation and politics. I cannot even attempt to deal with all that here. I must confine my remarks to the *design* of buildings, to the problem of getting the best possible design – which happens to be the way *I* make my living. This leaves out the important questions of Politics, how to initiate or instigate action, Town and County Planning and how to organise the execution of the design, once it is established. It leaves all this out, I say, – but it can't quite leave it out, because everything is intertwined. Design must take account of purpose – and purpose is politics if you like. And design must most certainly take account of execution – in fact it is nothing else than indicating a sensible way of building. So both Client and Contractor are involved in the design. As I use this word here, it is a vital link in the chain that leads to the realisation of a project, in fact it is the key to the building. It includes all drawings, specifications, descriptions and detailed instructions about what should be built *and how it should be built*. Some of these instructions may emanate from Client or Contractor – but they must be absorbed by the designer and made part of the design. If we get the right design therefore we will get the right building – provided the design is executed as intended.

What we want, then, is designs of quality – to produce buildings of quality. Perhaps quality is not the right word – I have used it because the word quality implies something of value, something we prize, it is also related to a purpose, it is the result of a discipline imposed by man, the result of something well done or well organised, as opposed to shoddy work and lack of organisation.

In architecture – and Architecture in this connection covers every kind of man-made structure which forms part of our environment – in Architecture it is useful to distinguish between three kinds of quality, according to the three things we require of a building or structure, namely:

1) That it should fulfil its function in the best possible way.
2) That it should not tax our resources more than necessary.
3) That it should enhance our environment rather than spoil it.

This means that the designer must organise the design from three different points of view – that of the Client, the Builder, and the Artist, and, reversing the order, we can call them the A, B, and C discipline of design. Each is important, but in varying degree, according to the kind of job we are dealing with. The ideal is to combine all three kinds of quality, but unfortunately they nearly always clash – how often do we not see function sacrificed for some aesthetic preference, or cost soaring for the same reason, or because the ideal functional arrangement poses difficult structural problems. Every design is therefore a compromise between the three kinds of excellence, and the problem is to strike the right balance, the balance appropriate to the task in hand.

How we get it is another matter.

I am afraid there is no general solution to this problem, but I should like to illustrate it by reference to the design of engineering structures, where I feel most at home.

The problem here is the same, the same threefold design discipline is needed, but the artistic organisation does not play such a big role here – in fact it is generally neglected altogether – and the function, although it determines the form of the structure, is generally pretty clear and uncontroversial. One knows exactly what is required of a grain silo, retaining wall, jetty or bridge. The designer therefore starts with a clear idea of what the purpose of the whole undertaking is – which is the first requisite for producing a design. The second is that the designer has certain facts at his command. I am thinking of the engineering knowledge and experience which make him a qualified engineer, augmented for the occasion by reference to books or papers or by asking other people's advice. And this knowledge must of course include awareness of all the available constructional techniques and their cost. And then there are all the data peculiar to the particular job, the site, and subsoil, local resources, in short everything which may have a bearing on the design and the method of construction.

The design then emerges as a result of a mental process, a kind of synthesis of (1) and (2). The engineer, knowing his stuff, knowing what has to be achieved and having gathered the local information, sets to work on the problem. His *imagination* juggles with the data, hauls out for inspection various combinations and possibilities, discards them, tries again, – intuition, invention, ingenuity, such as there are, spring to action, tentative solutions emerge, are developed, analysed, adopted as working hypotheses, new relevant data collected, partial decisions made, etc. It is difficult to describe this process in detail, and I think it is quite impossible to replace it with some computerized technique, as has been suggested. And as long as this is the case, the result will depend on three things:

1) The completeness of the data on which the design is based.
2) The quality of the brain in which the design process takes place.
3) The effort applied to the problem.

This is not exactly surprising. It means that the *best designs* are produced by good engineers with plenty of engineering knowledge and experience; and plenty of imagination, ingenuity and inventive capacity who take the trouble to gather all the relevant information and keep on worrying about the design until they are completely satisfied with the result. And perhaps we should throw in a bit of luck and an interesting problem to solve.

I am of course talking about creative design, not about ordinary routine design where not much effort is applied. Excellence follows from intelligent application, you don't get it for nothing. And progress in engineering has always depended on ingenuity and invention, it is a creative thing which cannot be arrived at by statistical methods or any of the latest rational design techniques. This is a fact which is often forgotten by some people, Clients, public servants, financiers, lawyers and others who have no knowledge of design. And there is another thing I would like to stress. Nearly all this invention is concerned with how to do things, finding new, simpler and better ways of carrying out the work. And therefore, as I have said so often, design cannot flourish without knowledge about methods of construction. Designing is indicating a sensible way of building. Any contractor who has suffered from impractical consulting engineer's designs knows this.

I have not said anything about the artistic organisation of the design – except that it is generally neglected, and I am afraid that is only too true. In industrial design – coal bunkers, gantries, purifiers and that kind of thing, any attempt at artistic control would be laughed out of court. And where it *is* considered desirable to add some artistic touch at the end this probably makes matters worse. This is simply because engineers as a rule lack that artistic sensibility which is necessary to produce a work of art. You can't blame them, but the result is that the work suffers from a deficiency of A-vitamins.

Now this is bad. And, in fairness I must say that it is being recognised more and more that this is a bad thing, and engineers are increasingly concerned about adding some kind of artistic education to their curriculum. This is not easy. Artistic discipline is a very personal thing. Art can only be judged by acquiring understanding of artistic culture in general and of the personality of the artist in particular. Art can be criticised, perhaps, but it cannot really be taught. There are no rules – the artist makes his own rules. In this respect it differs from technological or functional quality. The first can be measured in L.s.d. The second can perhaps only be proved in the same way as a pudding – in the eating – which may apply to artistic quality too, but it does yield to research and scientific analysis which artistic quality, or 'delight', does not.

'Delight' can be compared to a coy maiden who will shrink from direct pursuit; but pretend to ignore her and get on with your work and she may come running after you. My advice to engineers is to be good engineers first of all. A brilliant engineering solution is quite likely to be praised for artistic qualities where an attempt to force the design into a preconceived artistic form would fail miserably.

If we now turn to architectural design – with an architect in charge of the design team, we will find that it correspondingly suffers from a lack of B discipline or put it another way, it does not realise the technological potential. This is naturally because the Architect-designer, who has to effect the synthesis between the relevant facts is himself less of a technician, he must therefore rely on technical advisers. Many of the technical and constructional considerations which rightly ought to influence the design are never given the attention they deserve because they never 'surface' in the brain of the designer. He thinks it is better to concentrate on A and C – C, because that is his main duty, the purpose of the whole undertaking, *which he is the only one to take care of*, and A, because he is or fancies himself as an artist and his whole ambition is bound up with the wish to make an architectural – which in this connection means an artistic – 'statement'.

There is a good excuse for this, and there is also a great danger.

The excuse is, that architectural design – and I can only talk about the average in both cases, because there are all kinds of architecture – architectural design is generally much more complicated than structural design – or at least there are many more facts to consider. This is mainly because engineering structures cater for the force of gravity and other natural phenomena, whereas buildings cater for people. And people *are* complicated. The engineer need not bother about the purpose of the design – he is told what is required. The Architect bothers very much, he must study human needs, human reactions to environment, human ways of life, humans at work and play, their need for privacy and social contacts. This is both a complicated and controversial subject. And because he caters for human beings, the artistic organisation also becomes so much more important. And the technical data which have to be considered tend to be more numerous and varied. So naturally the synthesis of aims and moans is more complicated. One mind simply cannot absorb all the relevant data. The synthesis then becomes a synthesis of only those facts which arc uppermost in the Architect's mind – it is incomplete. Or if all relevant facts should be brought to the designer's notice, he is unable to effect a true synthesis – the result is patchwork, which is worse. The situation is sometimes aggravated by an attitude of mind which is frequently found amongst Architects. He is a superior being, his main concern is to keep alive the flame of true Art, and the objects of his attention receive a kind of reflected glory and are raised to a higher category, that of works of Art. He is in charge of function or commodity, as well, of course – but as arbiter of taste he really thinks that he should dictate to the Client what he is allowed to have. And as for technology – well, there are people who can work that out, and thank God for the Quantity Surveyor who can keep him at a suitable distance from such mundane matters. His attitude to technology is that of a husband when it comes to sewing on buttons.

Such arrogance may well produce works of Art which be praised in the technical papers and excite architectural students all over the world. One may even contend that a certain amount of arrogance is necessary for an artist, although some seem to make do with humility instead. But it will not do for the great bulk of building which is so urgently required. If the architect does not knuckle down to trying to understand and guide technical development, the system-boys will take over. There is nothing wrong with industrial building and systems of building for mass production, it is our kind of technique, and the renewal of architecture must come from a study of man's needs and from invention and organisation of building technique. But building technique has its own economic logic. It imposes its own discipline which, left to itself, will take no account of Art or true Amenity. That is the danger. This discipline must be guided, it must be fused with artistic and functional discipline. This can only be done if the designer or the leader of the design team understands all three forms of discipline, and if he is supported by the powers that be in insisting on certain standards of excellence. It is too much to hope, however, that such support will extend to providing much extra finance. You can only put across delight if it doesn't cost anything. Therefore you have to study building methods and see whether you cannot work *with* your material rather than against it. Those who are on the side of the angels must join the battle where it is fought: on the economic front. The architects must stop shielding behind Quantity Surveyors to avoid contact with the mundane world of building, building costs and building invention. Their spatial imagination must be put to use in the service of practical building.

That is all very well, you may say, but how can the Architect possibly manage more than he is doing already. His curriculum is full. It cannot be increased – perhaps it can be changed?

Yes, perhaps. I think it is absolutely necessary that Architects, if they aspire to be the leaders of a design team, should think more about how things are put together. Delight is produced by imposing some kind of organisation on the building structure, and you cannot organise something you don't know anything about. A sculptor must know his material. Bricks and mortar is the stuff that dreams are made on. You cannot produce delight in a vacuum.

But generally speaking the answer is teamwork. The data, the knowledge required, can be found not in one person, but in a number of persons. But how do we then contrive to produce the synthesis, the artistic or human unity which alone will ensure quality. That is the question, and it is much more difficult than most people realise.

I have spoken to you about the threefold discipline which has to be imposed on a design to get what we ought to have. Let us imagine that we accordingly choose a team consisting of a sociologist to define the human requirements, a builder cum engineer to design the body of the building, and an artist, a sculptor for instance, to impose artistic control. It would be hopeless. They would not speak each other's language, and the builder would prevail in the end because it is he who puts up the building.

No. Successful teamwork requires that each member of the team understands what the others are doing and respects them, and that they are united in a common purpose: to produce good architecture. Two heads are better than one, but too many cooks spoil the broth. And, as it would be next to impossible that they should all agree on relative priorities, they must have a leader who gathers all the threads together and makes the decisions. In fact, I don't mind his being a 'prima donna' architect in the best sense, being a true leader, shaping the design and giving orders, but on the basis of acquaintance with and understanding of the fundamental principles of the various disciplines, so that they can understand the advice given, and can assess its relevance to the design.

How difficult it is to realise these conditions. I could spend hours in telling you about the various frustrations occasioned by the present organisation of the building industry, about the impossibility – almost – of ensuring proper integration of the various technical disciplines – let alone the artistic and functional. And that is perhaps where my talk ought to have started.

I have not begun to suggest a solution to the problem – but I am afraid that would take another twenty minutes.

The ABC of Building Design

This lecture was given at the Architectural Association, 28 May 1965.

Esteemed Audience,
 I may as well put you out of your misery and come clean about this title: 'The ABC of Building Design'.
 As you will have guessed, it's a gimmick. A, B and C simply stand for the threefold organisation or discipline which must be imposed on a building or a design for a building in order to produce a building of quality, of all-round excellence, a building which is both delightful, useful and relatively cheap, in short a good building. The architect, or leader of the building team, if you like, must be three persons in one. He must be a *Caretaker* in the literal sense, who takes care of the people who are going to use the building, who studies their needs, what the building is going to be used for, and who gradually establishes the brief, the preferences and priorities and organises the space in the best possible way to meet these needs.
 Then he must be a *Builder* who knows all about the means available to give these spaces and climatic controls physical reality. The term builder here includes Engineers and various technical experts.
 And thirdly he must be an *Artist*, who looks at the thing as a piece of environment which must be subjected to the necessary aesthetic discipline.
 Artist, Builder, Caretaker (or Client, if you object to the last term) --- A, B, C. *Voilà tout!*
 The trouble with titles for lectures is that they are always asked for long before one has decided what to say. At any rate that applies to me. I know that I am very unreasonable; if I am given a title I don't like it, and if I am not given one, I have no idea what I should talk about, and can therefore not produce a title when it is wanted. So the title having been extracted under duress, so to speak, I will not promise to stick to this subject.
 What *is* the subject then?

Well, the other day I happened to read an article by Donald Smith in the *Architectural Review* called 'Towards a Theory'.* He quotes an anonymous author as saying: 'There is still almost a total lack of generally accepted basis for saying that X is a more suitable solution to the stated problem than Y. Until this exists, there is little point in design problems anyway.' This, he thinks, is a very bad situation, and he suggests that it is high time that Architects did something about it. And he, and that goes for many other writers and critics – is trying to help us and is showing us the way to go about it.

After an historical introduction, Mr Smith examines some modern architectural theories, seven of them to be precise, and finds them all wanting because of their great poverty of philosophical invention and because they are, as it were, introspective, because they 'seek to derive an aesthetic programme from the conditions of one set of problems set by the task itself, without any further reference to the external world'. (A pretty good idea, I should have thought.)

We get an inkling of what this means when he later on states that 'architects will persist in doing what they have always done, that is making a species of comment on the world about them.' And he thinks that 'the ambition of architects to make a general comment is a proper one.' To do this, architects must have a theory. And this theory must take into account the world we live in. And the two outstanding qualities characterising our world are Mystery and Danger. It is a smooth, ominous and dreamlike age, there are three thousand millions of us, one thousand million are starving, one thousand million are poor, and the last thousand million spend their surplus resources in accumulating explosives expressly designed to blot out reality for ever.

The role of the architect, therefore, is to wake us *from the dream, that makes this state of affairs tolerable*. It must *give us an awareness of the reality of ourselves*. And so on.

I am sure that this very short summary does not do justice to Donald Smith's argument. If so, I apologise, but in this connection it hardly matters, because I do not intend to discuss the merit of Donald Smith's thesis, for the simple reason that I don't understand a word of it. It is rather sad, for obviously what Donald Smith is after is exactly the same as that which I would like to know. Towards the end of his article he says that a real theory of architecture must be concerned with *how* and *to what purpose* the building obtains its 'delight'. Exactly. I would like to know that too, and that is what I should like to discuss with you. And the reason why I have dragged Donald Smith into it is because he for me is representative or typical of a whole lot of worthy architects and critics who make pronouncements on architectural theory from time to time, and who have this in common, that they are unintelligible to me. I don't understand how a building can 'make a statement on our times', or express the fact that one thousand million people are starving. Does that mean that curtain walling is in or out, for instance?

In a case like this one ought to be very careful to suppress one's natural tendency to declare *that* which one does not understand to be a lot of rubbish. And it would be a most unlikely explanation, really, when one considers the seriousness with which these pronouncements are discussed. Probably the fault lies with me. But I might venture to suggest that these critics perhaps concern themselves exclusively with the artistic organisation of the piece of architecture they are discussing; in the terms of my title, they evaluate A, neglecting B and C. This I think is very wrong, because in architecture these three kinds of organisation are really one, it is the same design which is organised in these three ways. A is expressed through C and B, and these in turn can only be evaluated if one has sufficient knowledge of the technicalities of C and B, and this knowledge is often lacking in art critics. And if you move into pure art criticism, anything goes, meaning takes on a different meaning, we are concerned with making people see and feel, *with propaganda* if you like. I do not intend to get caught in this morass, but I am still interested in the question of how to judge architecture, and how to improve our environment, and I know you all have that at heart.

I think that our environment has an enormous influence on us, it is a constant source of happiness or misery, and to get the environment we would like to have instead of one which is forced on us by expediency, or by economic forces which we fail to control, is surely a very worthy object to which we all subscribe, even if we do not always agree on what we would like to have. But that is just part of the challenge, we do not want uniformity but variety, variety to express different personalities, different modes of life.

At this stage, thinking about what we want of a building, what the word quality means, in this connection, I thought of this ABC gimmick, which is of course very akin to Commodity, Firmness and Delight, except that I am thinking more of the discipline which has to be imposed on the design

---

* Donald Smith, *Architectural Review* (February 1965), pp.101-4.

in the interest of commodity, for instance, not the actual commodity specified, but the elegance with which the spatial jig-saw puzzle has been solved – what I elsewhere have described as 'Excess commodity'. And as for B – it is not so much firmness, which one takes for granted, as again the elegance, if you like, of the arrangement of the building fabric so as to obtain *economy* – the main yardstick – without *shoddiness* – which would be a loss of excess commodity – and without sacrificing A and C quality more than necessary.

It *is* quite a useful gimmick, in a way. You can talk about A, B or C orientated designs, corresponding to different kind of architectural problems, you can talk about a deficiency in A, B or C vitamins, and so on. Developing this theme, I seemed on the verge of propounding another architectural theory, and frankly, I got fed up with the whole thing. A contributing factor, or probably the main reason, was that I read Leonard Manasseh's excellent Presidential address* – my efforts seem futile beside that, why should I waste your time? Or Goldfinger's Vote of Thanks – let me quote Goldfinger†:

> The purpose of building is not to create a spatial sensation but to fulfil a social function with the best means of an up-to-date technology: by doing so, space is delimited and the sensation of space automatically created. If it is an artist who shapes this space, who develops it from the crude by-product of enclosure into a spatial order, not by adding frills or ornaments, but by making the very enclosed space self-evident and clear, that is architecture.

I think that is excellent. Or Leonard Manasseh: I quote:

> No one talks about design any more, in so many words, so I shall, for now that I have rushed in I might as well make a night of it. Truth, proportion, mass, solidity, line, light and shade, texture, contrast, colour, and I mean colour, all the direct definitive words – the very stuff and art of architecture – are hardly discussed.
>
> They are considered jejune – almost corny – understandably perhaps in the Technology Camp where they are busy with *their* half of the problem, skipping along their Critical Paths to new pastures of productivity and prefabrication, spurred on by Management and efficiently insulated against almost everything including architecture. Oddly enough this inhibition prevails in the Art Camp too. Lost in a labyrinth of unsignificant form, swallowing the latest images as if they were purple hearts, they spurn the ties of history instead of using them as guide lines to the future.

and again, I quote:

> System building is fine too, it's the systems that are so awful.

How true, and well put. I like Leonard's snipe at the Technology Camp – we are about to be drowned in a sea of computerised technical data processing and what not, throwing up a whole new 'quantity' of experts who will presumably have their Royal Institutes and professional rules, and who will be able to juggle with incredible efficiency with a lot of code numbers but will know very little about what it is to design or to build.

I am not opposing this, we must use all these techniques, but let *us* use *them*, not let *them* use *us*.

This is by the way, but at this stage I solved the question of the title for my talk, and started all over again – and that was yesterday. And today I have been very busy on rescue operations. The title is:

An engineer's approach to architecture. Not *the engineer's* – and not theory – approach. That solves everything. It's factual, you can't dispute it. I am an engineer, I have spent more than twenty years with contractors and afterwards more than twenty years as a humble servant of architecture, or architects, as the case may be. So I have had to 'approach' architecture.

Let me first tell you about an engineer's approach to design. [Draft ends abruptly at this point with no record of a continuation]

---

* Leonard Manasseh's AA Presidential Address was published as 'The Moment of Truth', *AA Journal*, vol. 80, no. 886 (November 1964), pp. 95–102.
† The Hungarian-born architect Ernö Goldfinger (1902–1987) was an influential figure in the British modern movement. His papers are currently held by the RIBA at the V&A reading-rooms.

Art and Architecture

An address given by Ove on receiving the RIBA Royal Gold Medal 'for services to Architecture' on 21 June 1966. It appeared in the RIBA Journal, *August 1966, with the subtitle 'The Architect-Engineer Relationship'.*

It must have come as a surprise to a great many besides myself that I have been awarded the RIBA Gold Medal.

Since the award was announced, I have, it is true, been told by many friends by word or letter that this decision was unanimous, most popular, well deserved and long overdue.

I am most grateful for these expressions of kindness and sympathy. I do not, in the great majority of cases, doubt their sincerity, and this has warmed my heart. But it would be wrong – for a seeker of truth – to take them too seriously. After all, one knows that ordinary politeness almost demands that such congratulations be couched in somewhat exaggerated language. This is a field where the famous British understatement does not apply, and in any case the majority of people naturally and fortunately did not write. I had quite enough coping with those who did. So my opening statement may still be true. At any rate, it is for me.

This is not due to modesty. I am probably fairly conceited, intermittently at least. I am quite prepared to believe that I *may* have deserved this medal. But it does surprise me that *you* should think so.

On the face of it, I have no doubt rendered some service to architecture of a rather ordinary kind – a little common-sense here and there – but nothing spectacular like [Pier Luigi] Nervi, [Riccardo] Morandi or [Robert] Maillart, and nothing to compare with the giants of architecture. So I can only stammer, like a bashful lover: *I didn't know you cared!*

The knowledge that you do, that my endeavours to further architecture are being appreciated in the quarter which should be in the best position to judge; this fills me with gratefulness and happiness And I can think of no honour that could please me more.

It would probably be a good idea to stop here. Just to add my thanks to all those who have helped me, taught me, supported me, inspired me and without whose help this would not have happened to my parents, my wife, family, the architects I have worked with, my staff and partners and then leave it at that. But this might disappoint you.

You probably expect me to survey the architectural scene; to map out the future of architecture, threatened as it is by industrialization and large-scale planning, and to end up with a clarion call to young architects and engineers to join forces and bring about an architectural revival.

Or do you just want me to show slides of my work and show how the masterly solutions have fully justified the honour you have bestowed on me?

Or perhaps, as has been suggested to me, I should just be myself, which, according to reports, means: patently honest, charming, but slightly muddled and never finishing a sentence.

This last suggestion must I think be ruled out. On an occasion like this I owe it to you to prepare my talk, and that disposes of unfinished sentences.

The second is difficult – I am glad it is not my job to justify the award. After all, for the last 30 years most of my work has consisted in designing structures for buildings designed by architects, and the result is mainly their work, not mine. To try to point out my – or rather my firm's – contribution would be both difficult and tactless.

I am left with the first suggestion: assuming the mantle of an elder statesman guiding the younger generation – a wise counsellor, drawing on his more than 30 years' experience in the service of architecture – but, frankly, I don't feel up to it. I am not all that wise. I hardly know what architecture is. I am still a student, in spite of the excellent, but not exactly consistent, tuition I have received from my many architect friends. And the architectural scene is very complex.

The wind of change is blowing hard, we are in the grip of forces which may be difficult to control. In these circumstances, for me to prophecy or guide would be presumptuous.

But a phrase has been haunting me since the award was announced: *Service to architecture*.

In my long apprenticeship as an architectural student (and, I should add, the slow erosion of my engineering instincts?), have I really served architecture? Can one 'serve architecture' if one does not know exactly what architecture is? What is the fundamental difference between the architect and engineer, if any? When does an engineer become an architect, and *vice versa*? How should architects and engineers collaborate?

Should the engineer's loyalty be to the client, to the architect, to Architecture – with a capital A – or to his own engineering principles, if any? (I don't, here or later, question his duty to look after stability or firmness; that is taken for granted.) But when does 'Service to architecture' degenerate into 'Servitude to architects'?

This is not meant to be flippant, but one can certainly not render any service to architecture just by being polite to architects, or by glossing over any personal or professional rivalries. It is surely good to clarify where one stands.

I know, of course, that in the normal architect-engineer relationship, the architect is the client's representative and must make policy decisions on his behalf if they are not referred to the client himself. The engineer's role is that of a technical adviser to the architect; he should look after stability and advise the architect about the cost of alternative structural solutions. And decisions about the priority or the cash value to be accorded to aesthetic desiderata are policy decisions. This works beautifully in the great majority of cases. But does there come a time, ever, when the engineer ought to say: 'No – this is too silly for words.' How does he know it is silly? It may be Art!

The question may be put this way: *What role should art play in architecture*?; and in that form, the question would certainly split the architectural profession and the architectural critics into several factions. It is a good question for a discourse.

If you will bear with me – and you have really no alternative – I will try to throw some light on this question and the related question of architect-engineer relationships. There are many variants, of course. I have done this often before, but I will try to dig a little deeper this time. This means I must draw on my own experience and hope that it has a message for you as well. I cannot claim to be objective, but I seem to be slowly evolving my own private Theory of Architecture and, partly under pressure of recent events, it tends to revert more to the engineering principles I imbibed in my youth. A clear case of second childhood, perhaps.

The normal image of an engineer is a matter-of-fact, down-to-earth sort of person, who knows what he is doing, who applies scientific principles and logical reasoning to known data, and who leaves nothing to chance; a person who likes his drawings to be dimensioned, who is interested in the weight of things, the strength of things, and the cost of things rather than the effect of moonlight on a textured surface. He is supposed to be the antithesis of an artist, who deals in imponderabilia which nevertheless may have the power to stir the heart of man. And the architect is somewhere in between. He certainly likes to claim that architecture is an art – even the mother of the arts – and to bask in the glory due to him on this account.

This is of course a very crude picture, but there is some truth in it. If we have to generalize, we must recognize that there is a basic difference in temperament which results in the well-known and oft-deplored schism between engineers and architects.

However, when I started my collaboration with architects, the time was in some ways propitious for an approach between the two professions. For the modern movement, the engineer was almost a kind of hero – in theory at least. Functionalism demanded that materials should be used according to their nature and not forced into alien formal patterns. Steel and particularly reinforced concrete were the preferred structural materials and, willy-nilly, engineers had to be brought into the picture to handle these.

I, for my part, had a good working knowledge of reinforced concrete, which was rare in England in those days. I had had the good fortune to spend the first twelve years of my career with a firm of civil engineering contractors specializing in the design and construction of reinforced concrete structures, mainly marine structures; first a couple of years in Hamburg, and then in London. I soon became chief designer with responsibility for design, estimating and tendering, and I can think of no better training for a designer. You've got to make better designs than your competitors if you want the contract. And your own foremen will soon tell you if you've done anything silly. In any case, by cost-control on the job, you get a very valuable check on your design and estimate.

This training taught me one thing forcibly, that: *Good design should embody a sensible way of building.*

It all depends on what you mean by *sensible*, of course, and in this context it mainly meant *economical*, because the emphasis was on price competition (assuming that the object of the exercise was well defined, which it mostly is in engineering structures).

To begin with, coming fresh from college, I could analyse and calculate almost anything in structural engineering which could be calculated in those days, but I knew very little about structures and less about construction. I was surprised to see what reinforced concrete looked like in practice – the placing of the steel bars made a mockery of my carefully worked out drawings, and the concrete was often replaced by air, bits of timber or paper – and yet the thing was much stronger than required. (Things are much better nowadays, of course.) I threw away some decimals in my calculations. I learnt what it costs to make concrete or formwork or erect steelwork under different conditions, and realized that it was not so much the quantity that mattered as the ease of construction. I learnt the economic value of *simplicity* and *repetition,* keys to labour saving. I realized the importance of improving the site organization and control by organizing the *design* so that the sequence of operations gave continuous employment to the different types of labour. Waste of timber was eliminated by design of the formwork, which was at that time generally left to the foreman.

I gained a sense of reality and a sense of proportion, and I came to prefer the direct simple solution not only for its economy in the long run but for its own sake.

These principles are, of course, only plain common-sense and, I suggest, applicable to architecture as well as to engineering structures.

And so is the fact that it is the *design* which is the key to successful execution. Things should not be left to chance, to the hoped-for skill of foremen or craftsmen. The design should embody, foresee and specify all the phases of execution, the layout of the site and the plant used, except when we are dealing with routine jobs. The designer should always think of how his design can be executed.

Our firm also tendered for contracts where the design was done by the engineers of various authorities, or outside consulting engineers, and I am afraid that they did not always observe the above maxim. I was appalled at the waste which this entailed, and, to begin with, rushed in with alternative solutions only to be asked, politely or otherwise, to mind my own business. I have always found that very difficult. But I learnt to be more tactful. Ever since, I have understood and shared the feelings which many contractors harbour towards the designs of impractical consulting engineers.

The system of contractors' competitive design did not, however, allow money to be spent on the aesthetic perfection of the design. Our clients were simply not interested. I know that Nervi holds that economic stringency is a necessary spur to good design – and I agree with that up to a point, but to scrape off the last couple of per cent to bring the cost below that of your competitors can be very bad policy from the client's point of view, if he only knew. It is bad aesthetically, of course, but it may even prevent money being spent on weak points which would make it a more balanced or sounder structure. It is spoiling the ship for a ha'porth of tar. This is one of the objections to the method of contractors' competitive designs, and I felt that strongly at the time.

Already, when I made the decision to become an engineer, I hesitated between architecture and engineering, and I chose the latter because I knew that I had what it takes to be an engineer, but I did not feel sure that I could become a first-rate architect. There is this about Art, or anything connected with art – that it is rather sad to be a second-rate artist. Perhaps it was just youthful arrogance, or my romantic ideas about Art, which were, I suppose, in vogue in those days, and which I'm afraid I have not quite shed. Anyhow, I had at the back of my mind that I could perhaps take up architecture later, and I had kept up an interest in it.

Frank Lloyd Wright once told me that an engineer was only a kind of frustrated architect. Maybe; but I am sure that if I had become an architect I would have been a frustrated engineer. Anyhow, I think that remark says more about Frank Lloyd Wright than about engineers. My experience is that one is always frustrated, but when I tell that to people I get very little sympathy. You might say, therefore, that I was a kind of mixed-up kid with a leg in both camps and my head in the clouds perhaps.

My first real teacher of architecture was [Berthold] Lubetkin. He taught me how good architecture was produced, and what a serious business it was. I was surprised at the trouble he took over every detail. In Highpoint he designed the lift and liftshaft and the plumbing, he lined up all the tiles in the bathroom, he made dozens of drawings to get the proportions of the elevation right, and he did not hesitate to pull down what he did not like. For him, architecture was a battle to be won with every means at his disposal.

To begin with, our collaboration was well-nigh perfect from my point of view, because I was allowed to make a real contribution to the architecture and, through my firm, was able to construct what was designed: an ideal collaboration of architect, engineer and contractor. There was real enthusiasm on both sides – and enthusiasm is a necessary lubricant for any collaboration.

He also taught me that 'sensible building' must be modified to satisfy the claims of aesthetics. This I readily accepted and, as my education proceeded, it became perfectly natural for me to think of any structural form from these two points of view: the structural or practical, and the aesthetic. But there were cases when I got worried about whether my guide really knew the way.

Highpoint caused a stir in the architectural world, especially amongst the modern movement, mainly because of Lubetkin's architectural genius. But, as they say in Denmark, 'When it rains on the priest it drips on the deacon', and a certain amount of publicity descended on me. I joined the newly formed MARS Group; I got to know a lot of architects, and it is not too much to say that my association with Lubetkin and Tecton had a decisive influence on my career. For better or worse, I got caught up in the pursuit of architecture in a subordinate capacity, naturally.

I have now for more than 20 years worked with many architects as their consulting engineer. I have tried to understand what they were driving at, what architecture was. They have taught me much, and I am grateful to them. They have taught me that there are almost as many approaches to architecture as there are architects, and of course there are also an almost infinite number of architectural jobs or situations, from a cottage to a city, a factory to a cathedral.

Whilst I was a member of the executive committee of MARS, we spent a whole year discussing what modern architecture really meant, and what MARS really stood for. It was supposed to mean 'Modern Architectural Research Group', but what kind of research? Apparently, it was supposed to be into heat and sound insulation of walls, acoustics, light angles and so on.

I pointed out that this was engineering or building research and that we, as a group predominantly of architects, were neither competent or equipped to undertake it. We should do architectural research: planning research. Lubetkin maintained that no two architects would be able to agree on architectural questions – that was Art, a personal matter – and that architectural research was nonsense. Hazen Sise produced what was in effect a description of the modern style: walls and glass in one plane, like a taut skin, cantilevers, windows at the corners, etc.; an interesting document, but it was shot down without further ado.

Maxwell Fry was more optimistic, but no result was reached. Actually, MARS later produced a very useful bit of planning research during the war, the MARS plan for London, which was the work mainly of Arthur Korn, helped by [Felix] Samuely.*

Gradually, it dawned on people that functionalism (planning for function and using materials according to the way they are produced, etc.) did not lead *automatically* to good architecture, and it did not take long (through systems of proportion, etc.) to reach a stage which looked like a partial return to the much despised *beaux arts* principle of organizing the facade according to the preconceived 'artistic' ideas.

What Modern Architecture is now I do not know. It can apparently be anything under the sun and there is nothing wrong in that, but it has certainly strayed a long way from functionalism and [Walter]

Gropius' Bauhaus ideas, which I still think, were right, if rightly understood. It seems to me that to read certain architectural critics today is to enter into a fairyland where words have sound but no discoverable meaning, but that may be my fault.

Whatever architecture is, we can call it the organization of building activities to achieve as much commodity and delight as is possible on a generally limited budget. It must therefore be organized from three different points of view. I have called it the A, B and C discipline: A for art; B for building technology, or sensible building; C for commodity, the programme or function. Sensible building would reduce cost. Commodity costs money, and art may or may not cost anything, but generally does, and can even be very expensive, if badly handled.

The importance of the three disciplines varies enormously with the type of job, from the building of a national shrine, where art is everything, to some industrial job to be built on a shoestring. But it seems to me that the aim must be to achieve a balanced design, where all three disciplines are given the consideration which the type of job warrants.

This Total Design[†] is the result of a synthesis, and is the key to the kind of job we are going to get. But architectural design is much more complicated than engineering design. This is mainly because engineering structures cater for the force of gravity and other natural phenomena, whereas buildings cater for people. And people are complicated. The engineer need not bother about the purpose of the design – he is told what is required. The architect bothers very much, he must study human needs, human reactions to environment, human ways of life, humans at work and play, their need for privacy and social contacts. This is both a complicated and controversial subject. And because he caters for human beings, the artistic organization also becomes so much more important. And even the technical data which have to be considered tend to be more numerous and varied. So, naturally, the synthesis of aims and means is more complicated.

The quality of this synthesis depends on two things:

1) The completeness of the data on which the design is based;
2) The intensity and quality of the mental effort expended on it.

Naturally enough most designs, or in fact every design, if you really want to be critical, suffer from defects on both counts. What happens in the ordinary way is that this synthesis is produced in bits. The architect, whose main concern is art and commodity – often in that order produces the sketch-design which is based on the data available to him, and the engineer and other specialists add their solutions of the technical problems. This works and, if the collaboration is good, it can give excellent results. I have been happy in my collaboration with architects on this basis, and in the process have acquired many good friends, and have, I think, been of some use in helping them to achieve their aims. But as a method it is open to criticism.

I am not complaining about the fact that the structure sometimes has to be strained to comply with the architect's aesthetic requirements. So it should be, if it serves the ends of architecture. In [Denys] Lasdun's College of Physicians, for instance, the structure is not exactly straightforward, although quite reasonable – but the total result is in my opinion a masterpiece, and I am happy that my firm has been associated with it. For such special one-off jobs of civic or social importance, which are meant to become focal points in the landscape, there can be no rules; anything is right which leads to the right result. But there are cases where the enforced awkwardness of the structural solution is *not* so obviously justified.

There, one cannot help asking oneself: would it not have been possible to create equally good architecture with a sensible structure? Perhaps it wasn't possible, and if this could be shown, the doubts would be dispelled. But it was never put to the test, because the sketch-design which determined the type of structure to be used, was based on limited information. Had the architect known as much about structural principles as the engineer, when he made it, he might have done the whole thing differently.

Of course the architects vary enormously in their appreciation of sensible building. Most of them are very keen on it, and many are very good at producing it. And I think that is right. *Architects should think of themselves as master-builders*. But what worries me is that great architecture is often produced by people who apparently don't care a damn about sensible building. Architectural reputations are built on art, not

---

* Arthur Korn (1870–1945) was a German-born physicist, mathematician and inventor. Felix Samuely (1902–1959) was a teacher, innovator, engineer and pioneer of welded tubular steel construction.
† This is the first instance of Ove using the phrase 'Total Design'. In the 'Key Speech', which dates from 1970, he refers to 'Total Architecture'.

technology. The architectural press, architectural critics and architectural students all get very excited about new sculptural forms, about Corb's latest visions, Miesian aesthetics or Louis Kahn's towers, but few seem interested in whether they work, in the people living in these masterpieces. We have all heard of unhappy people forced to occupy significant architectural statements. The same audience can easily be taken in by slightly bogus structural ideas or visions – provided there is something to excite the eye. Shells, space-frames and the rest are admired and used for the same reasons – not because they are necessarily the honest solution to the problem in hand.

This sort of thing is, of course, slightly bogus, and it is easy enough to attack it, pointing out that the purpose of the exercise should be to provide commodity at the right price, and no leaking roofs, please. And the majority of architects are fully aware of this. Somebody has spoken about the division of architects into the Art-boys and the System-boys – or was it the One-off boys? No matter, it is about the same thing. What I am worried about is that at the two extreme ends, the system-boys have no art and the art-boys have no system. I don't so much mind art without system, if the money for it is available, but I *do* mind system without art. And I realize only too clearly that, in a competition between the two, that's what we are going to get. Why do I mind about Art? Well, art is a big word, but it's short and can be made to cover many things, so it's convenient. But I will try to explain.

I was lucky enough the other day to be present in Orford Church in Suffolk listening to the first performance of Benjamin Britten's *The Burning Fiery Furnace*. It made a deep impression on me. I wish I could describe it to you or convey to you somehow the feeling of being in the presence of something great, a power for good which can sustain you and remain with you for a long time. You feel grateful to the composer; you feel there is a divine spark in him which is very precious, and if you were in a position to help him to exercise his great gift, it would be a pleasure to do so.

I am trying in a rather helpless sort of way to emphasize the importance and the power of great art – but you are much better able to do so yourselves. As you well know, great architecture can have a similar effect. The masterpieces of architecture have inspired generations – we would all be much poorer without them. No price can be put on them: they are beyond price. But there are many kinds of art, and many kinds of architecture. *It is not all great, it is not all solemn and monumental*; it can be gay and carefree, cosy, sinister, elegant, earthy, stark, primitive anything you like. And I must not forget that it can be repulsive, false, bogus or vulgar as well. It is, however, always human; in some way it bears the stamp of its creator. And it is very important. Architecture does not often rise to great heights as in the Parthenon. But it penetrates everywhere, or should do.

My family get annoyed with me when I take a long time to decide on a place to picnic, trees or shrubs at the back, a view, sun or shade, wind in the right direction, and the topography so that you have a feeling of where you are, that you are somehow in the right place. I am sure that's part of architecture. Siting, spaces, harmony of surroundings, grouping of buildings, and, of course, the organization of the elements of buildings and structures, light and shade, all that is architecture, and nowadays it is the large-scale modelling which is the more important. It creates the environment in which we all live, it has an enormous influence on our lives – it is a constant source of happiness or misery. We have the power to get the environment we would like to have, instead of one which is forced on us by expediency, or by economic forces which we fail to control – if we could only find out how to use that power. This is the *challenge*. This is what we all should work for. It is no good relying on chance – although that has worked sometimes. It needs the imposition of artistic discipline. And that has to be done by an artist. That is the case for having architects in control of building operations affecting our environment – in the hope that they may be artists.

But the enemy is lurking round the corner. You all know the revolution in building techniques which is going on all round us, the gradual dominance of pre-cast concrete techniques, industrialization of building, etc. This again brings to the fore my old plea for the integration of design and construction. In fact, system building and the rest cannot help influencing design. There is nothing wrong with industrial building and systems of building for mass production. It is our kind of technique, and the renewal of architecture must come from a study of man's needs and from invention and organization of building technique. But building technique has its own economic logic. It imposes its own discipline which, left to itself, will take no account of art or true amenity. That is the danger. This discipline must be guided, it must be fused with artistic and functional discipline.

I should like to quote from a speech I made to the British Association in January 1942 – during the war, at the instigation of Julian Huxley:

The problem is the same here as in other spheres of human activity: a wealth of new knowledge, new materials, new processes has so widened the field of possibilities, that it cannot be adequately surveyed by a single mind. Corresponding to this increase of means, there are increased or entirely new requirements to be satisfied. Our needs increase with the means. Standards are raised, new services introduced.

This produces the specialist or expert, and the usual problem arises: how to create the organization, the 'composite mind' so to speak, which can achieve a well-balanced synthesis from the wealth of available detail. This is, I suppose, one of the central problems of our time. How then can we overcome the difficulty?

Well, the situation is still the same. This is generally accepted. And all sorts of attempts are being made to overcome this difficulty. Some pin their faith upon better management, cost control, cost planning, PERT,* critical path, computerized techniques in one form or another, joint design offices, contractors' package deals, modular planning and dimensional co-ordination; the whole situation is very confused.

I think that more emphasis should be placed on the central position of the design. As I pointed out when I talked about my experience as a designer for a contracting firm, the design – and by that I mean the total design, which embodies the manner of execution – this total design is the key to the whole thing. Once you have that, everything else follows: the appearance of the job, the siting, its character, usefulness, cost, durability, everything – even the time it takes to build, provided the execution is properly organized and the designer's intentions respected. I stress this again because it is a fact which seems to be forgotten in many of the discussions about building methods and the rest. All this cost planning, etc., is only important if it results in better designs.

But the design which does justice to all factors relevant to the three-fold discipline of art, building and commodity can only be done by a team. And the question we must then ask is: How can a team produce art?

The architect would say: by putting me in charge. This insistence on leadership by the architect is more than a lust for power, or job-greediness. *It is the natural point of view of an artist.* Artistic discipline is a very personal thing. A sculptor or painter would not dream of letting a partner share his work. And the more 'artistic' an architect is, the more the same applies to him. He feels he must control every inch of the job if he is to be responsible for its artistic quality. Perhaps he tries to communicate a vision which he cannot share with others before it is perfected, so he shuts himself in and on the basis of the data available to him produces his sketch-design for a work of art.

You know what artists are – or perhaps I should say you never know, because they are all different. Personally, I like them, even architects, but this art business is troublesome. Perfectionists are a menace to their surroundings. Perhaps he is highly imaginative, highly emotional, has his ups and downs, needs to believe in himself, needs to be understood, wants to be praised. He is dedicated to his art – it is something higher, better, more important to him than the petty doings of philistines. He is vain, perhaps, not necessarily in proportion to his greatness. He may be generous, lovable, with an insight into the predicament of man, without necessarily being a realist. Living in a world of fantasy he does not like to be brought down to earth by mere facts. He produces sketches which fascinate him as abstract works of art, and pins them on his walls or publishes them, they become almost as important to him as the reality which they are supposed to represent, and which may be unattainable.

You may say that this is a caricature of an artist, and you may be right. I have of course tried to describe an extreme case of what I may call an A-architect – or artitect. My daughter, when she was very small, used to call them royal artichokes, which somehow struck me as funny, and she even drew a picture of one.

But you may perhaps recognize some of the traits. And all I am saying is, that some of them do not make him a good member of a team. It is still worse if he is of the now fairly rare arrogant type who thinks that as the arbiter of taste with a mission to fulfil he has the right to dictate to the client what he is allowed to have. Such arrogance may well produce works of art which are praised in the technical papers and excite architectural students all over the world. One may even contend that a certain amount of arrogance is necessary for an artist, although some make do with humility instead. But again, it does not make him a good member of a team, and sometimes it is the best artists who are the most difficult.

* Program (or Project) Evaluation and Review Technique, a statistical technique for measuring and forecasting progress in research and development. Developed in the United States in the 1950s.

But *architecture is not just a visual art*. Commodity, the programme, is the main object. And unless the cost is right it will simply not be built. So a balance must be struck between the claims of A, B and C; where that balance lies, depends on the kind of job we are dealing with. We need the A-architect but we cannot afford to let him have it all his own way. When he is making his synthesis, giving body to his visions, he is likely to concentrate on the purely visual aspects if he is not pulled up by the demands of the rest of the team. He must accept the facts of the situation. After all, every architect must accept the need for providing stability. The engineer has a veto when that is threatened. So why can the architect not just as well accept the discipline of sensible building. For the great bulk of building this is necessary, and *it need not be detrimental to his art*. It may very well enhance the artistic quality but it requires an extra effort. Those who are on the side of the angels must join the battle where it is fought: on the economic front.

The architect, therefore, must shed some of his habits to make him team-worthy. But he should not be asked to compromise his art. If he works with a team which has been conditioned to think of architecture as the goal, this should not be necessary. An engineer, or somebody else, could even be the team-leader without in the least jeopardizing the result, provided he is just as determined to produce good architecture as the architect himself. He will then lean over backwards to heed the architect's wishes, and the architect will gradually adjust his thinking to respect the claims of sensible building. This way we may even get better art, and we will get economic and therefore viable building – it just needs that extra effort.

The engineer must of course also be made team-worthy. The typical engineer – of yesterday, let us hope – is much too limited in his outlook. Because he knows more about the technology than the architect and, on the other hand, lacks the sensibility to appreciate the value of the architect's work, he considers him slightly bogus – 'viel Geschrei und wenig Wolle', as the Germans might say. His horizon must be widened. He must understand what his team-members stand for. Whatever his opinion of this or that architect, he must be devoted to *architecture*. He must have *enthusiasm*. He must not just be a calculator or analyser, he must be a creative designer, he must be able to contribute ideas. Then he will be able to play an important part in the team. He has something to contribute to the team – a basic integrity or discipline which stems from the fact that he is dealing with facts, with forces of nature which are not impressed by glib talk or beautiful sketches. Art can sometimes border on make-believe, be slightly bogus. 'Why spoil a good story to make it true?' This is an artistic point of view. Insistence on accuracy is the engineer's and philistine's point of view. Both are right, in their proper place, but in building, the integrity of the engineer must reinforce the sensitivity, imagination and humanity of the architect.

About the other members of the team, I have only time to say this, that they must equally be brain-washed or made team-worthy. They must also think of the whole, not just their bit. The heating engineer must study how the space requirements of his services can be integrated with the building fabric in a way which facilitates installation, interchange and upkeep, and which contributes to total architecture. And this applies to everybody contributing to the design. The importance of installations and services is steadily growing and their proper integration in the design has been sadly neglected. Here there is a lot of work to do.

What about the contractor, or the integration of design and execution? This is a problem on a different level. Engineers and contractors speak the same language. The difficulty here is not psychological, but almost physical. How can the design team get hold of and get familiar with the kind of information which determines the real cost of the job, the cost of handling different size units, assembling, fixing, casting under different conditions, the knowledge about how best to organize the job – knowledge which may become relevant to the design? To attach a contractor to the design team is generally no solution, unless he is the contractor who is going to do the job anyway (in which case his views would certainly be useful, perhaps even essential), or if he is a very unusual contractor-engineer-inventor who really knows all about job organization, and is not limited to the experience of his own firm. But should he then be the contractor? How should he be remunerated? It would be best if he was professional, on the same level as the other members, or that the engineers had in their team engineers with the required experience.

We in Arup Associates are going in the latter direction. But where we base our design on a particular method of construction, a kind of *ad hoc* building system especially devised to fit the architectural problem, as for instance in the Birmingham University Mining and Metallurgy building, or Loughborough University, we still have to convince the contractors that we are right. But *provided we are*, it does not seem too difficult. If they are not convinced to start with, they will alter their opinion later. If we are not right, we try again and we gain experience.

The other possibility is the contractor's package deal, or the financial developer who controls everything. I think this is a dangerous path – but this brings in all the problems posed by the awkward fact that the people engaged in the building industry are not really united in a spontaneous desire to create new and better buildings, but are making their living according to some complicated rules which have been evolved and fought over for centuries. What they are thinking of, what drives them on, is probably a wish to improve their status and their share of the common cake. Anybody who would try to eliminate waste by organizing the necessary collaboration of many people on a more rational basis is at once up against old customs, established trades, professions and vested interests, and the whole thing moves into a sphere of social organization and politics. Even the question of architect-engineer collaboration is often discussed as if it were a demarcation dispute.

I have no time to deal with these problems here, and I don't know the answers either. I suppose that many different ways of collaboration will survive side by side, and that the experience gained, and the type of job will decide which is most suitable for each occasion. In Arup Associates we are trying to eliminate the psychological barriers to teamwork, to create a kind of composite brain for each job. We are still at the beginning, but I think the outlook is promising. It has confirmed my contention that art and sensible building can be combined without detriment to the former. In a team working for a common purpose in a friendly atmosphere, it can happen that something emerges which is more than the sum of individual contributions. I do not know what organizational patterns will emerge in future; I do not suggest for one moment that what we are doing in Arup Associates should become general practice, or that the specialist engineering or architectural offices should cease to exist – on the contrary – but I do suggest that, if all the members of all the different offices and firms contributing to our environment could be made aware of, and respect what the others were doing, and could join in wanting to create total architecture in the best sense – could in fact be made team-worthy – then our joint efforts, in whatever combination, might be able to create a better environment for man.

My trouble is really that I am one of those greedy persons who, when asked whether they want mint sauce or jelly with their saddle of lamb, answer, 'both please!' I give the same answer when asked whether I would rather have competent building or good architecture. I want the warm humanity of art to permeate the cold economics of efficient building. It can only be done by artists embracing and mastering efficiency, or being helped to do so.

So I end up with a plea for closer understanding, interchange of ideas and collaboration between our two professions, starting at the university, and not ending – ever – until death us do part!

Builder Extraordinary

This is a transcript of a BBC documentary film first broadcast in 1966. It was directed and produced by John Read, with commentary written and spoken by John Donat.*

Ove Arup: I mean, sometimes I think I'm an absolute idiot, and other times I think, well, I could have done that much better than all those other people have done it. I thought that one could first find out what one ought to do in philosophy – what was right and wrong and what was true and all that sort of thing and then one can organise one's life in accordance with that. You know as a matter of fact I'm not solemn at all, I mean that's my trouble. In a way you see – because I don't take the things seriously enough. And you can get this sort of solemn – everybody being very culture-minded and, and so then getting all what's good for you – and so you can get absolutely fed up with it and – and do something quite desperately vulgar and thing, and that can be perfectly justified as an expression of … of a bit of guts, you see.

John Donat: *Who is Ove Arup? Poet? Mathematician? Artist? Philosopher? Organisation man? Arup is a remarkable engineer who has shared in the creation of much of the best modern architecture in the country – a spry 70-year-old who is father to an organisation that contributes to 50-million pounds worth of building a year. With his partners, associates and staff, Arup has helped in the design of nearly two-and-a-half thousand contracts: but he's no prima donna, not at all the kind of man who seeks to imprint his own personality on everything he does. He's something much more subtle, and much more important: a man determined to bring together architecture, technology and humanity. In a tough world of big business, everything he touches remains essentially human. He has a passion for perfection, carries a pair of chopsticks in his breast pocket, talks about philosophy, people, food, architecture and engineering, plays chess, collects children's paintings, seems utterly unimpressed by his own achievement, and has devoted his life to what he modestly describes as 'helping to make architecture'. So much of what* we build only confirms our worst fears. As our cities are torn down, rebuilt and transformed, we wonder what our place will be in this new world we are making. Yet it's still too easy to pretend that it's nothing to do with us. Telebent [i.e., wedded to 'TV'?] in our comfy suburbs it's too easy to imagine that architecture – like cancer – only happens to other people. But our whole human environment is at the cross-roads. During the next 50 years we will probably build more than in the whole previous history of mankind.

What are we capable of doing? Can we make really marvellous new buildings? Men like Ove Arup, and the many people he has worked with, show that we could build a country for fifty million emperors – if we really wanted to.

Ever since the Thirties he has worked with the best architects in the country, devising brilliant new methods of construction, always deeply involved in how a building is made.

Highpoint was designed in 1934 by Tecton – a group of adventurous young avant-garde architects. In those days it was a glimpse of a new world. The interiors are classics of the period, still evoking that unmistakable Thirties atmosphere: Fred Astaire, Ginger Rogers, Top Hat, White Tie and Tails. At the same time, Arup worked with Tecton on the elegant little penguin pool in Regent's Park Zoo, with its miraculously thin curved ramps intersecting and spiralling down into the water: a witty background to the pompous shuffle of its immaculately dressed inhabitants.

You don't interview Arup – you listen! His ideas follow one another in a merry-go-round of thoughts and associations and he's incapable of finishing a sentence.

Well, you see, you are asking me these questions which are sort of – require me to make pronouncement and what do I think. You see, I had not thought very much about what is the biggest obstacle. I know this that this business of getting various people to pull together and integrating – you know the designs, or integrating or getting people to act harmonious[ly] together for that is a very difficult one and it is psychological and political and all sorts of things.

I believe after that your ambitions as a young man transferred themselves from science to philosophy and finally to engineering. How do you account for this unlikely trio?

Oh – I don't know that it's so unlikely. I mean – I was naturally interested in science like everybody – you know in those days science – Darwin and – and all the discoveries – one thought that one would gradually be able to find out everything and know everything and – and there was a sort of optimistic mood wasn't there about science progressing and gradually wresting all the secrets of nature – and – and I wanted to be an explorer in science. It would interest any boy I should think. Then there was this business about religion and about the ultimate purpose of the whole thing. And naturally one found out, I mean that the science wasn't everything. The main thing was to find out what you – what you really had to do here on this planet. I mean – why are you here – what's the whole thing about and so on. So that you could make a sensible plan for your life. In a way that was quite logical – I was rather logically minded you see and – so that I drifted into philosophy.

How about the transition then from philosophy to engineering as a career?

I would say that the transition from – from science to philosophy is very natural because the science of philosophy – through the theory of knowledge, finding out the basis of science, you gradually drift into philosophy. I mean that is a quite natural process. The – the transition from starting philosophy and then taking up engineering, that's quite a different matter – that's an irrational thing. That's because to put it bluntly, I got fed up with philosophy. I mean – I found, I realised that philosophy could not give the answer to all these questions which one would – mankind has asked since the world – you know since the beginning of days. I mean that you can't really find out all these things by thinking about it. In fact the more you think the more confused you get. You can answer – you can put a lot of questions and philosophy is – is in a way the science of – of putting the right questions and putting more and more penetrating questions. But you never get to the end of it.

Arup's main office is in London, at the foot of the new telephone tower, where there are over five hundred engineers, architects and technical staff;

* John Read (1923–2011) was a British arts film director who worked at the BBC from the early 1950s until his retirement in 1983, producing definitive film profiles of many key figures in British Modernism. John Donat (1933–2004) was a writer, lecturer, broadcaster and architectural photographer. Trained as an architect, he contributed to more than 100 programmes on radio and TV, and was part of a new wave of photographers who applied a photojournalistic ethos to architectural photography. Donat's archive is now held by the RIBA Library.

he also has offices all over the world in so many places that they sound like a trans-world airline schedule – over 10-million pounds' worth of work is done abroad each year. A meeting of senior staff is so crowded now that there's hardly room for everyone, but they come to discuss and criticise current work to keep in touch with the remoter corners of a far flung empire. But the emperor is more like a father, the empire more like a family. You might expect such a formidable outfit to be spartanly efficient, a vast cold place with serried ranks of human calculating machines busily grinding out miles of technical calculations. In fact, a genial, paternal atmosphere pervades the place, that is casual and friendly. The partners maintain little personal traditions like sending presents to staff who are off sick, flowers to proud new mothers, wedding presents to brides and grooms, and premium bonds to all the staff's children at Christmas. One of them said 'Even though we are probably the largest consulting engineers in the country now, this is still a very nice place to work in.' Arup can't organise – he can't even organise his own car, but he has a genius for attracting people who can. I asked him why his firm had grown to such a size.

I've got some very good people. You see they – I realised from the beginning that it is very important to get the right people to collaborate – to work with. It's most important and I – for a long time, – not any more I'm afraid, but for a long time I took on everybody myself. I mean I interviewed them, I spoke to them and you get an impression from whether you like the man or not. It was not only a question of whether he was a good engineer or like that, it was just as much a question whether he was the sort of person you could work with or would fit in with other people [and] so keep the right atmosphere in the place. Because the office is the place where these people spend most part of their life and unless the atmosphere is right and friendly, I mean it's very silly the whole thing isn't it? I mean it would be idiotic to go to a place for most part of your life where you hated the other people – you hated the – you know – the whole place and what you did and so on. It's one of the sort of quite obvious essential ingredients of having a, reasonably happy life, isn't it? What I like most is to get into a sort of problem and thrash it out with some people I also like and try to get something out of it, you see, and then you sort of forget time and you are not – you're not – well but if you have all the time to think about all the things that happen and you are responsible for – for the administration of the whole thing, then of course that is very distracting and it's difficult to find time. It's only rarely that I actually sit down and do the whole thing myself – that I still haven't got enough time for, I feel. And then the trouble is that all these other people in my office, they're so much cleverer than I now. You see I mean I have forgotten how to calculate things and I you see I know what can be built and how – what is sensible. I can make sensible proposals and I have got a certain amount of imagination and things like that, but as regards the actual – as regards the calculating, you see it would be a waste of time because there are other people who can do it much better and they do it with computers and things like that which I don't really know anything about.

Why do we distinguish between engineer, architect, contractor? The men who created great architecture in the past were master builders – the Greeks drew no distinction between designing and making something – the architect was artist, craftsman, mathematician, philosopher, engineer. His architecture was an indissoluble marriage of art and technology – that mirrored a triple image of the art, science and culture of his day. For the Romans too, architecture was the art and science of building – they stretched their materials to greater and greater limits in the service of power and empire. The great Gothic cathedrals of the Middle Ages were constructed by master-masons, scientists of building and engineers of the emotions who conquered space with stone. Their magnificent structures were subtly fused with the art of a great Religious culture; art and science were one, and indivisible. But by the nineteenth century the architect had sacrificed his birthright as master-builder and transformed the gothic dream into something more like a gothic nightmare. It was not the first time the architect appeared on the scene as an intellectual artist-designer, but the culmination of a long process of fragmentation in the building arts. While the architects were pursuing these romantic gothic dreams, the engineers were creating a new world with a new material, cast iron, literally behind their backs. The engineers were the new men, a new breed born of the industrial revolution who ruthlessly jerked architecture back on to the rails of history.

The engineers; they were trying to do things which you couldn't do before. I mean to span longer than before. I mean, spanning bridges or make tunnels or whatever it was of that kind of thing, they jolly well had to consider how to do it, and find out how to do it. They were battling with nature – I mean they were considering means and methods and their engineering, their designs were at one with the – conceiving ways of doing things – of how to build or how to raise bridges. These pioneer engineers, [Isambard Kingdom] Brunel and these people, they invented everything. [Joseph] Paxton in building the Crystal Palace, he designed every detail. He decided what carriage should be used, what lifting gear – he designed all that sort of thing. The same with Brunel. He designed the machines to do the work which he wanted done and so on. And therefore they did the thing in the most natural, the best way they could conceive and so on and there was this close integration. There was therefore a unity about the whole thing. That is something which of course the engineers have always realised and especially of course if they have been contractors at the same time and have been designing – designers and contractors – then of course this combination comes completely natural and is necessary for good design and it's becoming necessary for good design in building because building is being more and more industrialised and you're using engineering principles and you're using – there is such an enormous wealth of new materials, new methods and so on so you hardly know how to build a building any more.

Today a new technocracy is devising hundreds of technically brilliant industrialised systems which no-one will want to live in, while the architects produce superb one-off, tailor-made designs that are an invisible drop in the great ocean of building. The dilemma is that without systems, increased productivity and mechanisation, we haven't a hope in hell of constructing all the buildings we need, and without creative imagination we have even less hope of making a world worth living in. Arguing about two cultures in architecture isn't just an intellectual game, the divorce of art and science will have to be reconciled if we're going to make places for people.

It's this question of man v. machine and whether the machine is the servant of man and man remaining the master, or whether the machine gradually takes over. You could create that kind of thing because really when you are coming to computers and that kind of thing, you really want all people to be the same, or – in America all their brainwashing, all their questioning of personnel – they want people who fit into their organisation, who will take the business of that Corporation and that would be their sort of main aim in life, and they should all be – they must – they don't want any exceptional people, they want all people who fit together and can do that sort of thing. Now against that, all the artists and the, people, they revolt and they remind one of the essentials of life and – looking at flowers and stars or painting or things on canvas, and expressing their personalities in different ways and getting more and more crazy. There's a reaction against that pressure for uniformity.

Paxton looks down an avenue of trees on the old Crystal Palace site towards a new National Sports Centre built for two million pounds by the London County Council. Arup, his partners and staff, have worked with many of the best architects in the country – created together – shared knowledge and experience. This design began as a dialogue between Arup and Leslie Martin, then architect to the L.C.C., and was developed by their partners and staff – a close collaboration between architect and engineer in which design and construction combine to produce an architecture of pleasure. The stadium, an amphitheatre carved out of the landscape, wraps around a football pitch and athletics track. Even the structure is athletic, like a taut gymnast, poised in space on the parallel bars. The steel canopy sails out over the stands without obstructing the movement or the view of twelve thousand spectators. The stadium is linked to a huge indoor sports hall by broad promenades above the ground. A structure had to be devised to enclose three swimming pools, indoor tennis and badminton courts, squash courts, cricket nets and several gymnasia, all in a vast space, two hundred and seventy feet square. The structure stands in the centre like an athlete with his legs apart and his arms stretched out to carry the roof over a hundred feet of clear space fifty feet above the water. This Crystal Palace of Sport was designed as a national training centre for our top athletes but is also available to everybody from the humblest amateur to the most serious professional. Olympic champions, hundreds of school-children and all kinds of sports clubs can enjoy the superb facilities that are fully equipped for international competition.

The structure and form of a building can appear very simple and direct, but its simplicity conceals the nightmare of technical and functional organisation that goes into the planning of a complex building. Mechanical services, air conditioning, dozens of different functions, the spectators and the players, have all to be served by the total design. A setting for people and activities that is more than merely functional must itself celebrate the idea of sport and enjoyment.

Architecture doesn't always involve spectacular engineering gymnastics. A building like the Law Library in Oxford also designed by Leslie Martin can be routine for the engineers. It was the architect who ingeniously combined three large libraries on an awkward site into a single building that asserts its own tough individuality. When you get there you really feel you've arrived somewhere. The interiors are discreet and cool: a quiet setting for quiet work. Just down the road from the Law Library is St. Catherine's College, designed by the Danish architect Arne Jacobsen. Not just a single isolated building but a complete place for a community of scholars. Jacobsen's powerful intellect matches Arup's passion for perfection with an almost pathological demand for precision, quality and excellence. Everything he touches is refined, distilled and purified to the limit – dare one describe it as the architecture of immaculate conception? It's full of the sheer pleasure of something that has been beautifully made. St. Catherine's has a curious atmosphere: like the meeting of two worlds. The luxury and comfort of a superb modern hotel combined with the spartan finishes and monastic gloom of a mediaeval Oxford College. The dining hall is imbued with an atmosphere of age and tradition rare in a modern building. Even though the architect has handled everything with such determination, it doesn't mean to say that the engineers had nothing to do. It's often much more difficult to design even a simple structure that must be seen as a visible and natural part of the whole design, particularly when a 72-foot beam, 5-feet high, must be accurate to an eighth of an inch. Jacobsen designs all the furniture, knives, forks and spoons in his buildings so that his pursuit of excellence is evident in every detail.

Even homely old bricks look as though they had been laid by computer. Architect, engineer, contractor and manufacturer have to work very hard together to achieve this quality, so that the basic structure goes hand in glove with the finished building.

Of course the crunch comes when we realise that architecture of this quality is so rare that for most of us it might just as well not be there at all. A few isolated masterpieces can show us what can be done, but they don't begin to answer the question of how we can influence our whole built world.

The question is really how to influence it for the good, isn't it? And again we come back to what is the good and so on. But there is an enormous amount that people can do about their environment, obviously. And an architect must see that his part is part of the town planning of the whole environment and town planning is a way of planning one's life at the same time, and that could – leads into the – you know, the aims and what – what should we aim at – how should we live and all that kind of thing, you see. So that building is in a way in a sort of central position. On the one side it connects up to – it's applied science – to all the science, all the techniques, all the mastering nature and all that sort of thing. To the other side it comes to re-integration with all the other people who're concerned with building to create an environment – the town, the country, the kind of life you want to live – philosophy, religion, the lot.

Architecture touches everything in our lives. As much as anything else Britain needs good modern buildings for its industry. It's typical of Arup's philosophy that the places we work in are every bit as important as the places we live in. When his firm was asked to design this factory at Duxford his first move was to bring architects into his office.* It led to a new parallel partnership called Arup Associates in which architects and engineers collaborate as a team on the total design of buildings. Designing for industry means finding technical answers to technical problems, but that's not the whole story: the buildings must also be organised together not only to work well but to make a reasonable place for people to work in. These buildings put Arup Associates on the map as factory designers and they have built many buildings for industry that are a far cry from the shambles of old corrugated sheds that are only too familiar in our industrial landscape.

They aren't only involved with factory buildings. They have designed some marvellous new rooms for the dons of Corpus Christi in Cambridge, set in a beautiful old English garden. Enormous windows roll back to bring the pleasure of the landscape right into your room. Each room is poised above the garden behind a slender concrete structure that takes unmistakable delight in the way buildings are made. The structures are linked together in elegant pavilions that play hide and seek with the trees.

But architecture isn't only third programme stuff.† Arup's architects designed this tower of council flats at Bracknell New Town that makes Room at the Top for everyone. Bracknell Tower is really a remarkable achievement, providing for all the needs of modern life at incredibly low cost. You can park your car underneath, stroll to the lifts under cover, and rise up 18 storeys to your castle in the air. From the privacy of your own living room you command a view across the town and over miles and miles of country landscape.

Without Ove Arup, none of these buildings we have seen would have been quite the same; but perhaps the irony of his life is that while his organisation has grown and prospered he has found himself at the top of the tree, more and more remote from the actual process of design. Though he is one of the world's great engineers and has profoundly influenced building in this country, there are hardly any examples of his work of which you can say: 'Yes. This shows the hand of the Master.'

Of all the things you've done, what do you feel has pleased you the most – given you the most satisfaction?

Yes I have been asked that before. It's really very difficult to say. I think I must try to think that out one of these days. You see – in a way I can say that this little bridge which I did recently at Durham has given me very great satisfaction because I had time and was given peace to work on it, you know, for a long time. There was no hurry about it at all. I have of course always wanted to do bridges. I've done them in the old days but we have never had any bridges to do and this was given to us on the distinct understanding that I myself should design the bridge – of course it was very nice for me because then there was no argument about it and we had plenty of time.

Across the River Wear, at the foot of Durham's great mediaeval cathedral, Arup designed his little masterpiece, a footbridge linking the university to the town, supported on slender concrete fingers high above the water … an object lesson in how to build, a true work of art by an artist engineer. The footbridge at Durham only cost 55-thousand pounds – but in Australia in sight of the magnificent Sydney Harbour Bridge, Arup is staking his career and his reputation on the twenty-million-pound Sydney Opera House, designed by the Danish architect Jørn Utzon to stand on the site of an old tram station on a promontory in the harbour. As the old building was demolished, the politicians were so impatient to get the building started that construction had to begin without a single correct drawing. No-one watching the Premier of New South Wales laying the foundation stone could guess the fantastic history that lay ahead. Utzon's seductive competition sketches showed two amphitheatres side by side covered by gigantic floating sails. When Arup analysed these intuitive free forms, he found that they just couldn't be built. But Utzon's optimism, fired by Arup's enthusiasm, set in train an incredible process of structural analysis in which a whole series of ideas were explored, analysed and rejected. It took Arup's firm seven years, three-hundred-and-fifty-thousand man-hours, and at different times two hundred engineers to do all the work before the final structure emerged. Arup was convinced it could be done without destroying the spirit of the architect's idea. But the free shapes of the roof had to be brought into a geometric discipline if they were going to be built. The break-through came with a telephone call from Utzon in Copenhagen: he had discovered that all the main shells could be cut from the surface of a single sphere. This was a real turning point, because it meant that the ribs would all have the same curve and could be made with hundreds of similar units cast in moulds on the site. It made possible the industrialisation of a unique building. During this long process, three computers were used for a total of eighteen hundred computer hours. One man could have done the work with a calculating machine – but it would have taken him ten-thousand years. Arup and his staff made flying visits to Sydney where they set up an office on the site to supervise construction. The costs were rising at a fantastic rate. But the whole venture had captured the imagination of the Australians who set up an Opera House Lottery to help pay for their ninth wonder of the world. It was an immediate success and brings in nearly a hundred thousand pounds a week. Arup's wife Li won fifty pounds herself.

What were you saying before about the unusual aspect – all the different unusual aspects of the building?

Well – you see, it is really, I suppose, Utzon who is unusual, first of all when this – well everything is unusual – the site is unusual. The method of paying for this opera house by lottery is unusual. And, as I said the architect, the clients are unusual because I've never met cli … – I mean they're very understanding. They all want to help to create this masterpiece. As I say, the architect because he is a – I think he's a very unusual architect; I mean, and he's very gifted. He's a very good sense of space – very quick in the uptake and he sort of goes to the – to the bottom of things, I mean or – he has got a very good sense of all the

---

* The CIBA Aero Research Ltd complex at Duxford, designed by Barbara Priestley with Ove Arup and Partners, and completed in 1958, was a prime example of a building where structure and services were the primary drivers to the building form, in order to accommodate industrial processes.

† The BBC Third Programme first went on air in 1946 and acquired a reputation for being 'highbrow'. In 1970 it became Radio 3.

architectural – what shall I say – the bricks with which you make architecture – I mean colour and – and – and form and so on and things. He really knows how it affects people. He has got very strong views on that without having any particular style or anything like that. You know there are no – he's completely open to any kind of suggestion but he's very – determined to have it right – to have what he thinks is right, you see. I mean he will not compromise very easily and he will go to – he will – if I say well, of course, if you do that this will take six months longer or will cost more then he says all right it must take six months longer then, they can wait for this house – this opera – there won't be another opera house built like that for the next hundred years so I mean, what's six months, you know. That's sort of more or less his attitude. He's rather go on working six months more than – than have it not so good. Now that enormous sense of form and space, and the colour and texture of these things and that great simplicity, you see – that mustn't be spoilt. In fact you have an extremely complicated thing. Now to make a very complicated thing look very simple, that is much more difficult to – than to make a simple thing look complicated which lots of people can do. But that has really been the main task of the opera house. Apart from these rather striking structural things which are fantastically difficult and something which has never been attempted before and we are not out of the wood yet.

'Not out of the wood yet' may be putting it mildly. The sheer scale of the operation has had everybody fooled. Arup's partner-in-charge said: 'When I look at it now, I shudder. If I'd known three years ago what we were in for I wonder if I'd have had the guts to go on. This building has changed all our lives – we're wrecking our business, our family life and our reputations because we all want to make it marvellous.' The practical business of constructing this concrete giant is right on the boundary of what is technically possible. In order to lift the two-and-a-half-thousand segments of the roof – each weighing ten tons – a world survey had to be made just to find the right crane. As just one example of Utzon's demand for quality: a Danish firm has spent two years developing a special tile to cover the roof: there are over a million of them. They are cast into five thousand panels and hoisted up on the roof by crane. Needless to say, this fantastic adventure has stirred up a hornets' nest of critics, it has been described as an engineer's folly, a tour de farce, an unmitigated bitch to build. Songs have been written about it sailing down the harbour in a fair wind; but the loudest cries condemn building for pleasure with twenty million pounds when half the world hasn't even got enough to eat. Arup is its most passionate defender – his replies are quiet and restrained.

I don't hold with the view that you can't – as long as there is anybody in the world starving or not having a house you are not allowed to build a theatre or a monument or a thing like that. I mean it's – it's going too far, you see, because you can't do that – people need that kind of thing. They need a bit of uplift and they need an Inspiration and they need – need something and if you can build something which is good and which is marvellous and which is a monument for all of them, you are doing more than just building this thing. It's a spiritual thing. It's a spiritual thing to have this sort of example of perfection or of – of something grand, and big which will be classified as one of the great buildings of the world. After all our whole outlook our whole – you know, the whole mental atmosphere or milieu would be different if we hadn't got the Parthenon and this – all these big buildings all the big events or the big epics in – if they'd all just been hundreds of millions of families who all had a nice house and were all happy and – and – but there would be nothing – you know really to talk about.

Arup regards this as one of the most creative collaborations he has ever had with an architect. It is both unique and industrialised, so it was not surprising, when Arup was speaking to me, that he returned to the theme of Art and Science, man and machine.

Some people like to have the thing in order and streamlined and everybody knows what he should do and everything is sort of organised well and functions and – and it's, you know, legally correct and it's all that kind of thing and there are other people who are sort of rebels. I mean they delight in – in things not – not – not being orthodox and having different – and – and – and being inefficient. I mean it's a question of – almost you see the value of efficiency, as such, you see. I mean of – efficiency is of course a means to something. But efficiency as a sort of moral virtue or a thing like that – that's doubtful, isn't it? Because, after all, the enjoyment of life consists in waste, perhaps. I mean, you – you – you – consume things – you throw things away – you waste things – you do all kinds of unnecessary things when you play or when you have your – do your whatever hobby you have – climb mountains – complete waste of energy. I mean you could reckon it out in ton-feet and so on but in the – you'd have to come down again and then – and the thing is senseless, isn't it. You can obviously maintain that the man who doesn't want to be efficient doesn't want to work – who wants to laze in the sun and think about, you know, flowers and one thing and another – then he's a very sensible sort of person. I mean you can't argue against him can you?

What I'm thinking is, coming out of this argument in a way is what you might call a doctrine of inefficiency – sort of in praise of inefficiency. I mean you talk about mountain climbing as being something inefficient, you talked about the people becoming more and more uniform for the sake of the system and that it's the few creative sparks which still give life to a situation.

Yes.

It's almost as though – any direction away from uniformity is in fact the – the last sort of creative gesture one can make.

Well, I don't know if – suppose it's because I have really always been a rebel by nature you see. It – it's a you know – if I get into any solemn situation or somebody – talking and making speeches or official dinners or anything of that – I mean – it's simply – it – it sort of turns inside me. I like to make a scandal or do something completely unheard of. I don't do it because I'm very timid and shy and – and – I behave very well as a rule, except – you know in ordinary manners I am not very good but then, you know – I sort of – toe the line and do as I am told generally but – I have this feeling of – that – I want to debunk all this solemnity – all this sort of and – I want to – any kind of – what is it – any kind of hypocrisy and intellectual dishonesty or – dis … – I like – I don't mind people doing whatever they like to do for the hell of it, you see. That's all right but if they then pretend that they're doing it because of something quite different you see, because it's for the good of mankind, or something like that, then I say no, it isn't. It's because you like to do it. You see, I say that in fact to architects when they come with all sorts of spurious reasons. They want me to give them a structural reason for doing what they want to do. They say – no I say – economical – the other would be much cheaper – cheaper, but I agree that what you want to do is rather nice and I think you should do it, but you should do it because you like to do it, not because you think you can justify it by some bogus reason.

It means that in fact the architect is carrying an extraordinary sort of social responsibility, which he's never had before.

Yes. The architect must sort of bridge this gap because there can be a difficulty about society getting the environment it ought to have because it doesn't know how to get it and it can't create it and the architect must tell them. But they cannot hardly create an environment for the society which is against what the society wants. Now but how do you do it? That is the problem of architecture isn't it, how do you do that and I think therefore an architect has to have a very great understanding for people and how they live and work and he must have great sympathy – he must have love for the people he builds for and think like that – he must understand them.

Everything Arup has done reflects his own love of life and of people. He has shown us how we could make a marvellous tomorrow. It might help if we had a thousand more like him.

Aesthetics and the Engineer

This address was given to members and guests of the Institution of Municipal Engineers at the Town Hall, Oxford, on 24 November 1966.

In asking me to speak on 'Aesthetics and the Engineer' you have really set me a pretty stiff task. Aesthetics or art, is a vague and slippery kind of subject, nobody can define it, there is nothing to get to grips with, it means different things to different people, and yet it seems impossible to get away from it. Even hardboiled engineers are beginning to realise that this is something which they have perhaps not paid enough attention to in the past – or rather in the recent past – because the great engineers of the last century certainly were very much concerned with making their structures look beautiful. And it is presumably this renewed interest in the subject which has led to your request.

Actually I reluctantly turned down a similar request from the Secretary of the Civils* five years ago. What he said was something like this:

> We have come to the conclusion that something must be done to improve the appearance of engineering structures. Engineers lack training in the aesthetic aspects of design. If architects are not to muscle in on the engineer's domain, this deficiency must be remedied. We want you therefore to write a paper or a series of papers which can be issued to structural engineers and perhaps form part of their curriculum, and which will teach them to design beautiful as well as efficient structures.

I naturally felt flattered that the Secretary and to some extent the Council should think that I might be a suitable person to perform this task, the more so as in my view the task goes far beyond what any person could possibly achieve.

I pointed out that I myself, in common with other engineers, lacked training and knowledge in this field. The only thing which I may claim to have in preference to some other engineers, is an appreciation of the importance of the problem, but that is obviously not enough to solve it. In fact, as I have said, I don't think it can be solved this way. But as my objections were not heeded – Mr. McDonald is a Scot and very persistent – my resistance was gradually worn down to the extent that I promised to think about the problems.

It may save me a lot of trouble if I give my reasons for turning it down as I explained them at the time to Mr. McDonald:

> I will begin by trying to survey the task before me – to see what can be done and what cannot be done.

The first thing which should be attempted is to establish to everybody's satisfaction that there is – and always will be – a *need* for improvement. That the task is important. I will not try at this stage to define the task precisely – that will probably prove to be impossible in any case – I only submit that when all the functional, structural and economic requirements of a structure or building have been satisfied there is still something left to do – call it to create beauty, to give aesthetic satisfaction, to impart character, unity or integrity to our physical environment, to express our civilisation or our cultural values, to satisfy certain psychological needs for symbolism, monumentality, humanity, inspiration, calm – call it what you like, there is still a spiritual need to attend to, and the task, the truly formidable task, is to improve the ordinary engineer's ability to attend to this need.

The majority of engineers will no doubt agree that this need exists. But they don't feel passionately enough about it. They don't – I submit – attach sufficient importance to it.

Naturally if you are to succeed in anything, you must first *want* to succeed. The first part of my task is to make engineers *want* to create what I for short will call more beautiful structures – although beauty is almost a dirty word amongst art critics!

This will have to be sheer propaganda. We are here in the realm of value judgments. Nobody can *prove* that one value should be given priority, one can only try to persuade by contrasting good solutions with bad and by inducing people to relate their particular engineering problems to a wider framework to think about the long-term effect of what they are doing on the more permanent human values.

This part of my task may be difficult enough – it involves choosing the right illustrations and the right words – but it is at least possible, although I am painfully aware that I am not likely to be very good at it.

The second part of my task is, I am afraid, quite impossible. Logically, if your professed aim is to make engineers design more 'beautiful' structures – again I use this word for simplicity, to denote the elusive quality we are after, and not to indicate my preference for any particular theory of art – then you should be able to tell them what beauty consists of.

The question has exercised mankind for centuries but has never been solved, and never will be. Ethical and aesthetic pronouncements are not capable of logical proof – if anything is – they can only have a relative validity inside a certain cultural circle. This circle can embrace a large portion of *homo sapiens* in space and time or it may consist of an esoteric coterie – but only with reference to such a framework do they carry weight.

So our task is to find out what in our time and with our background we consider 'beautiful'. We would naturally turn to our architectural critics or philosophers for guidance.

'My abysmal ignorance'

Again, my abysmal ignorance about the relevant literature is a severe handicap, which I hope to reduce a little before I finish this paper. But I don't think one needs to be an expert on the history and philosophy of art to realise that art critics don't always agree. So the guidance they are able to give is not available in any final and authoritative form. There are a great many movements and theories and principles supported and held with strong convictions, strong feelings and even stronger words – but they are not the same, they differ widely.

This is the sort of thing which leads many a layman and many an engineer to incline to the view that 'beauty' is a matter of taste, and that one man's taste is as good as another's. 'I don't know anything about art, but I know what I like.'

Now this is a most dangerous view and it is most definitely wrong. One man's taste is *not* as good as another's. I may not be able to prove this, but if the gaudily coloured linos, carpets and plastic ware exhibited and bought with avidity in the average provincial soft furnishing shop are supposed to be 'beautiful' because they apparently must be liked by some people – then I revolt with all my being.

The danger of this view that taste is a purely personal matter is that it absolves one from trying to improve one's taste. And it certainly needs to

---

* Alexander ('Sandy') McDonald (1903–1968) became Secretary of the Institution of Civil Engineers in 1954.

be improved. As with other skills, the latent ability of people to acquire good taste, to become good judges of aesthetic quality, varies widely, but latent ability is not enough. It has to be brought out by application to the subject. Ability plus hard work is the formula. It is no good thinking that you can apply a formula or go to a book of rules to solve your aesthetic problems, as you can to some extent when you want to find the necessary size of a structural member. You have got somehow to get a feeling for what is right. But how? What work has one got to do?

'Surely' – I can almost hear the Secretary of the Institution of Civil Engineers saying this – 'surely there must be some aesthetic principles which can be put down on paper and taught to people, surely it must be possible to give some guidance to the students!'

Well, I admit it is most difficult. I can't really think of any such principles or at least I don't know which to choose. And yet I am convinced that there are good designers and bad designers – from an aesthetic point of view – and that some of the good designers have at some time in their career been bad designers, which seems to indicate that the ability to design well can be acquired … somehow.

I must admit, therefore, that it is very natural to look for some guiding aesthetic principles, and I am far from postulating that they do not exist or cannot be found.

Disagreement among critics

A little while ago I pointed out that architectural critics do not always agree. That is of course unfortunate and it certainly complicates my task but I do not thereby mean to imply that all architectural criticism is rubbish, and I am painfully aware that part of my task here ought to be to provide a review of what has been said by architects and architectural critics or eminent engineers on this subject, and to try to extract what is common ground between them. A kind of critique of architectural philosophy, obviously that could be done and ought to be done, but it is a big job and – need I repeat it – it is a bit hard to ask an ordinary engineer to do it.

Leaving aside this question for the moment, there is still one difficulty which troubles me. Most aesthetic principles are of a somewhat general nature, naturally enough, and I find it most difficult to translate these general principles into practical decisions on the drawing board. Mostly I have no hesitation in deciding that one solution is better than another, but I would in most cases be hard put to it to explain what aesthetic principle is involved. Moreover, I have had a very extensive experience of advising diverse architects on structural matters, and I am grateful to them for what I have learnt from our collaboration on architectural matters. But I have learnt to be very sceptical about the various architectural or aesthetic maxims put forward to justify particular decisions. There is very often no compelling connection between the two, it may be quite easy to twist the argument round the other way, and great fun can be had by all – or by me, at any rate. I have seen the most excellent principles turn into good, bad or indifferent architecture, and I have seen good architecture – or bad – produced without recourse to any principles at all.

The crux of the matter

Again, I am not saying that there aren't any valid principles, but unless we can find a way to translate them into good designs, they are really not much use.

And now I am coming to the crux of the matter. I have a feeling that good design, to be taught, should be studied '*in statu nascendi*' – when it is emerging on the drawing board or even in the imagination of the designer. If we could see what is actually happening when a good designer is at work, if we could follow the emergence of the idea, its development and purification, study the rejects and compare them with the chosen solutions, and if possible hear the designer's own explanation of his preferences – then we might learn something. It would perhaps enable us to test the various architectural theories, to expose the hollow ones and embrace those which had a more than ephemeral validity. I have often felt it would be interesting to have representatives of the various architectural viewpoints present at the birth of a design and hear their comments on the various steps taken. Perhaps this could be attempted?

This is what I consider to be the most promising approach – but again, a most difficult one.

It is difficult for three reasons:

Firstly, design decisions are often arrived at intuitively, without any conscious argument for or against – it will often be very difficult for the designer to explain why he prefers a certain general solution or certain details. Or, if he has an idea of why he does it it may not be easy for him to put it in words.

Secondly, a writer who wishes to analyse a process of creation has only direct access to his own experience. I can perhaps with some difficulty explain how I have arrived at certain structural solutions – but it would obviously be much better to draw on the experience of those who really have created undisputed masterpieces. It may be possible to find in print a few such explanations – but I have not come across any which really go into details so that one can understand what happened at the time of creation.

Best way to design

There is a very good reason for that – and that is my third difficulty. The reason is simply that it is a very complicated thing to do. You have first to make the reader understand the whole of the design problem – all the different considerations and conditions affecting the design, and to make him see the whole thing in space. It may have taken the designer some time to get really familiar with the spatial possibilities so that he could start designing in his head without the help of the drawing board – and in my experience, at any rate, that is the best way to design.

To make the reader follow this process requires a very clear exposition, with numerous three-dimensional sketches and photographs of models of all the various stages and the various rejected possibilities. And that means that it could take a whole book to explain thoroughly even one design. Naturally one must try to reduce the thing to essentials – but it will be no mean job.

Undoubtedly we will come to the conclusion in the end that the way to produce a good design is to put a lot of thought and work into it, and let the solution be determined strictly by the nature of the problem, without pre-conceived ideas or reference to common practice. If the solution is right – functionally, technically and economically – then the battle is at any rate almost won. But this is an example of a general maxim which does not give guidance to the practising engineers unless it is explained by reference to practical examples.

To sum up the task is:

1) To explain that it is important to pay attention to 'Beauty'.
2) To survey the many different architectural theories in order to find out whether one can extract some guiding principles.
3) To explain by examples how an engineering structure is really conceived and perfected, describing all the many considerations which influence the choice between different possibilities, and possibly to test the architectural precepts in relation to the actual process of creation.
4) To draw whatever lessons can be obtained from the foregoing exercises.

I wrote this five years ago. I intended to write the paper – or book – but I really was too busy with various jobs – the Sydney Opera House especially – where I could perhaps help to realise in the flesh what I was supposed to talk about, and this seemed to be to be more important. Examples are more convincing than talk.

The situation is therefore more or less the same as it was five years ago – I still have not developed my philosophy of architecture or what you may call it, and I ought perhaps to have turned down your request as well, to avoid wasting your time. But at last I have not undertaken to teach you anything.

And perhaps I even know a little more about the subject now, at any rate I know what I would advise a young engineer to do about it now, and that is to become a damned good engineer first of all and not worry too much about aesthetics.

Perhaps I should explain this a little.

Well, in the foregoing, when I have talked about engineers, I had of course particularly in mind structural or civil engineers who together with architects are responsible for the design of the many structures which clutter up the landscape and determine the character of our environment. Many engineers are of course engaged on research, analytical calculation, administration, organisation and so on, but the people who above all influence our environment are the designers or those who take decisions having a bearing on the design – whether large-scale planning, framing of by-laws governing the height of buildings, fire regulations, zoning or the design of individual structures. For the design is the key to what we are going to get.

Results of good design

Design is a creative activity. It can of course be mere imitation or routine – and this may be justified if it imitates something good and if it fits into the particular context – but this is hardly design in the proper sense.

We demand of a good design that it results in a 'thing' which:

>   functions well
>   lasts well
>   looks well

and
costs as little as possible.

I think most people would agree to this proposition, and that 'looks well' is an essential part of what we are aiming at. There are of course people and amongst them engineers who think it does not matter two hoots what a strictly utilitarian structure such as a grain silo or a gasholder looks like – or perhaps what happens to the back of buildings. But that is surely a very short-sighted view. Such people may be engineers, but they are not creative engineers, they are not original designers. A creative engineer is one who cares about his design, who aims at quality, at excellence. He cannot help being interested in what his brain-child looks like. As I mentioned before, good engineers have always been concerned about this kind of quality and it should really be quite superfluous to stress the point.

Consider for a moment the design of cricket-bats, tennis racquets, saddles, golf clubs and other sporting articles, a field where British designs have been outstanding – what is the reason for their success? Not the application of an aesthetic theory. The success is due to the fact the British love their sports, they lavish their care on perfecting the implements, choosing the right woods, achieving the right 'feel' or balance, taking it all very seriously and striving for *perfection*. Perfection, that is, of function. The aesthetic perfection follows from this personal involvement.

I should like to read to you an extract from a report made by Charles Eames to the Government of India 'recommending a programme of training in the area of design which would serve as an aid to the small industries'.*

Designing a Lota†

Of all the objects we have seen and admired during our visit to India, the Lota, that simple vessel of everyday use, stands out as perhaps the greatest, the most beautiful – the village women have a process which, with the use of tamarind and ash, each day turns this brass into gold.

But how would one go about designing a Lota? First one would have to shut out all preconceived ideas on the subject and then begin to consider factor after factor:

The optimum amount of liquid to be fetched, carried, poured, and stored in a prescribed set of circumstances.

The size and strength and gender of the hands (if hands) that would manipulate it.

The way it is to be transported – head, hip, hand, basket, or cart.

The balance, the centre of gravity, when empty. When full, its balance when rotated for pouring.

The fluid dynamics of the problem not only when pouring, but when filling and cleaning, and under the complicated motions of head carrying – slow and fast.

Its sculpture as it fits the palm of the hand, the curve of the hip.

Its sculpture as complement to the rhythmic motion of walking or a static pose at the well.

The relation of opening to volume in terms of storage uses – and objects other than liquid.

The size of the opening and inner contour in terms of cleaning.

The texture inside and out in terms of cleaning and feeling.

Heat transfer – can it be grasped if the liquid is hot?

How pleasant does it feel, eyes closed, eyes open?

How pleasant does it sound when it strikes another vessel, is set down on ground or stone, empty or full – or being poured into?

What is the possible material?

What is its cost in terms of working?

What is its cost in terms of ultimate service?

What kind of investment does the material provide, as product, as salvage?

How will the material affect the contents, etc., etc.?

How will it look as the sun reflects off its surface?

How does it feel to possess it, to sell it, to give it?

Of course, no one man could have possibly designed the Lota. The number of combinations of factors to be considered gets to be astronomical – no one man designed the Lota, but many men over many generations. Many individuals represented in their own way through something they may have added or may have removed, or through some quality of which they were particularly aware.

The simplest problem of environment has a list of aspects that makes the list we have given for the Lota small by comparison. The roster of disciplines we have suggested can bring about measurable answers to some measurable aspects of the problem, but in addition they must provide the trainee with a questioning approach and a smell for appropriateness; a concern for quality which will help him through the immeasurable relationships.

But to say this does not unfortunately get us anywhere. We must face the fact that any engineer who aspires to become fit to take charge of a design for a structure or 'feature' which will form part of our environment has a duty to develop his feeling for form, colour, texture and sensitivity to landscape and local atmosphere, etc. And one could go further and say that any citizen has this duty – because in the end it is the general level of aesthetic awareness which determines the quality of an architectural epoch.

Aesthetics: not so simple

This may appear to you somewhat exaggerated – and perhaps it is. But it illustrates that this question of aesthetics is not so simple – that there is much more to it than we engineers generally realise.

We have abandoned the craft method of working – machines do the job for us. But we control what we want made through the design. The design must make use of the most efficient production methods – but we must decide what we want, we must care for the design, we must want to make it perfect, we must lavish on it all the care which the good craftsman used to lavish on his work. If we do that, as good engineers, then the result will be as good as we can make it – and that is all we can do.

Art in design

It is unfortunately not always enough. A structure which is right from a functional and economic point of view can still be marred if the designer is not sensitive to certain sculptural or aesthetic values – but there is nothing he can do about that except perhaps accept advice from outside – and that is a very doubtful proposition. 'Art' is not something you can add to a design. It emerges during the design, by accepting the logic of the particular situation, the site, the people and the function you design for, the local conditions, the technological potential – and by striving for a synthesis which in as simple and direct a manner as possible achieves the desired result.

* Charles Ormond Eames (1907–1978) and Bernice Alexandra 'Ray' Eames (1912–1988) were American designers who made major contributions to modern architecture, furniture and design.
† A Lota is a small, usually spherical, vessel of brass, copper or plastic, used in parts of South Asia for cleaning and ritual purification and to store or transfer small amounts of milk or water.

Architecture Is Sick: Should It Be Revived?

The lecture is dated 2 January 1967, but there is no indication of where it was given.

This is the statement and the question we are supposed to discuss this evening. Unfortunately the statement is so vague as to be almost meaningless, and yet so categorical that it can't be true in any case, whatever it means.

The answer to the question, on the other hand, is easy, and is in the affirmative – obviously we can't have sick things lying about.

I suspect that what the, to me unknown, author of the motion had in mind was to invent a title which would be so sensational as to attract a large audience, and so provocative as to lead to a lively discussion. But he made a slip. He chose the wrong speaker.

I can associate myself fully with his aim, but not with the motion. Not only because I don't really know what it is supposed to mean, but also because I am constitutionally unable to support anything which sounds so definite. I am one of these unfortunate people who must see a thing from all sides. The advocate's role doesn't really suit me. Rather do I aspire towards the detachment of a judge summing up. Not very successfully, I am afraid.

The result is that when I have finished, it is all so fair and reasonable and qualified that you all have to agree with me – which of course is *not* what was intended.

If after this you feel that you have been lured to the meeting under false pretences, I feel sorry for you – but I am afraid I can't do anything about it. Each bird must sing with its own beak – as they say in Denmark.

But seriously, it *is* difficult to speak to this motion. It could mean *so many things*, and it covers such a wide area. It could mean simply that the author doesn't like what is being built today. Many people don't – and for the most varied reasons. Some of these boil down to the fact that they don't like living in a modern welfare society where we have to cater for thousands in place of the hundreds we catered for before, which leads to overcrowding, noise, lack of privacy, and destruction of the human scale by bulky building blocks, brutally disposed.

And for this they blame the architects. Understandably enough, because architects have so successfully advertised themselves as the only people fit by training and disposition to guide our building operations that the public can be excused for thinking that they actually do so.

But, coming back to the motion – I suspect that the author meant more than that.

The question: 'Should it be revived?' seems to contemplate with some equanimity the possibility of letting it die.

But in that case architecture cannot simply mean 'what is being built today', because obviously we cannot stop building. Architecture must here mean: architecture as a Discipline, as Art, or Building in accordance with Architectural Theory. And what he is driving at may be simply that there are no generally accepted architectural standards any more, architecture is confused, sick – and further, all this talk about making an architectural statement, etc. is so much tommy-rot, we can very well build without it.

If this is what the motion means, I cannot wholeheartedly support it. We may be able to build without any conscious architectural theory, but technology alone, even when it does satisfy man's functional requirements, is not enough. Architecture is concerned with the creation of our urban environment, and this environment somehow becomes imbued with the personality of its creator, it has character or it lacks character, it speaks to us, affects us, we are elated, stimulated or oppressed – we may hardly be aware of how it comes about, we only know that we like this place, this building, this room, – or we dislike it.

To create the right atmosphere, a psychological climate inducing contentment in some form or other, this, I take it, is the business of architecture *as an Art*.

We have also the physical or physiological climate to look after – control of temperature, air pollution, light, sound, statical electricity and so on – and we must above all ensure the fitness for purpose of the whole undertaking, and we must achieve this at a cost we can afford. These latter requirements undoubtedly come first, in the sense that bread comes before 'the circus'. But we need to satisfy both our physical and spiritual needs. The growing power of technology gives us the means to satisfy the former, but how do we create the elusive quality which is the soul of Architecture?

It has sometimes developed almost without conscious effort, as the accidental by-product of a set way of life and a set way of building; but now that mechanisation has taken command, and scores of new materials have been invented, we can certainly not rely on chance; It must be deliberately created as a result of an artistic discipline imposed by the designer.

Unfortunately we have no recipe, no set of rules or methodical approach which will ensure the desired result.

In common with the other arts, architecture at present enjoys or suffers from a complete emancipation from accepted norms. There is not even a general mood – romantic exuberance and puritan self-discipline exist side by side. You can call that being sick, if you like. But I cannot square the idea of sickness with the vigorous or sensitive architecture which *is* being created today where conditions are favourable. The best, I think, is better today than it has been for a long time.

The fact that there is no generally accepted style is in itself not a bad thing – or is it? This may be a point for discussion. But after all, we need different kinds of architecture, to express different moods. Modern living imposes severe restraints, and it is certainly not fashionable to add to them by moral or aesthetic codes which curb the free unfolding of our personalities – we have a complex about creating complexes that way – and that again may be unfortunate or may not. I really can't tell – the thing becomes far too involved, because if this is a sign of sickness, it is our whole civilisation which is sick and not just architecture. I only know that if I were to build anything, I would resent any fashion or imposed stylistic restraint which did not arise naturally from the nature and purpose of the job, the site and local conditions, the atmosphere of the surroundings and the means at my disposal for carrying out the work – anyhow, as I said, different kinds of jobs, different circumstances, call for different kinds of Architecture.

What can be bad is to mix them indiscriminately. Just as in human intercourse some jokes or some attitudes are out of place in some situations. We need sensitivity to atmosphere, to what is appropriate, we need what I have called artistic discipline. So that we are *not* entirely free after all. If we were, there would indeed be no architecture. But artistic discipline is not the same as imposing a style. Consistency, harmony, proportion, balance, unity, a clear expression of function or structure, a feeling for form, texture, economy of means – all these vague general principles are not the prerogative of any one style, they *are in fact very difficult* to translate into definite decisions. But they are not therefore completely meaningless, they are attempts to express in words what various artists have been striving for.

Architects as a whole cannot be accused of being indifferent to these values. And some have shown that architecture is very much alive still. To suggest that architecture is sick would, I therefore think, be barking up the wrong tree.

But I do agree that what is being built is unsatisfactory. We are *not on the whole* making the best use of our resources, and we are *not* creating the environment we would like to have, and could have.

But the remedy is *not* a better theory of architecture, a new and better style, or the abandonment of architecture altogether. If I may anticipate, it lies in creating the opportunity for architecture to flourish – which again presupposes that this becomes the serious concern of a much larger section of the general public than at present.

But if we are going to discuss the shortcomings of the building and allied industries, *with its causes* we will certainly have enough material to carry on the discussion all night – with very little prospect of getting anywhere. For it will involve a critique of our kind of society, our whole civilisation.

I can only throw out a few ideas on the subject for your consideration.

The construction of a building, an engineering structure, a group of buildings, or a whole town with its communications etc. is the work of a great many people, some working on the site, some in factories and offices, some labouring, some organising, directing, making drawings and so on. If all these people are going to work together *efficiently* for a common purpose they must

1) have an incentive to do so, and
2) they must ideally be directed according to a pre-conceived plan.

Every action, every disposition in this intricate pattern of events must fit together like pieces in a jigsaw puzzle, its place in space and time foreseen by the master-plan.

A master-plan presupposes a master-mind to conceive it. A *master-mind* who would combine in himself all the knowledge and experience of the architects, engineers, builders, technicians, manufacturers, scientists, economists, town-planners, sociologists, public authorities – in fact of everyone who could contribute to the problem.

A master-mind who would know:

1) What was best for society to have.
2) What would be the most efficient way of getting it.
3) How many people could be induced to collaborate to create it.
4) How much of it we could afford to have inside a given time.

– all looked at from the point of view of society as a whole in a way which was just and fair to everybody.

The master-mind would then proceed to embody the whole master plan in what I would call the *Total Design*.

This design would take the form of drawings, specifications, descriptions, lists of things to be ordered or specially manufactured and precise instructions as to what should be bought or done.

This Total Design would be *the key* to everything which had to be built, to every change which had to be made in our environment, to achieve the desired result.

Having created this Total Design, he could then proceed to organise the work of all the people who would bring the plan to *fruition*.

The master-mind would of course also have to be an artist. He could then see to it that his solutions of the many technical problems did not offend against his artistic sensibility – the design as a whole would be seen as an organic whole, and every part would take its place in the whole pattern and would also be an artistic object in its own right. In other words, his total control of everything would make it possible for him to exercise artistic discipline.

In order to avoid any misunderstanding I should perhaps add here that I fully realise that such control by a master-mind is neither possible nor desirable. I do not share Plato's belief in the possibility of government by philosopher-kings.

I am also aware that this whole idea of an ordered, artistically controlled environment would be anathema to many people. They may want freedom to do what they like, diversity, vigour, expression of the life-force, perhaps anti-art – whatever that may mean. The trouble is that people differ, and want different things. But at least they want *something better*.

Well, we are concerned with how to get whatever we want in the most efficient way, and the idea of the Total Design, produced by a master-mind, is only introduced to show up the imperfections of our present practice.

Instead of one master-mind we have a host of government bodies, institutions, agencies, corporations, firms and individuals divided in their aims, each seeing only their side of the picture, each beset with their own difficulties and problems which are ignored by the others, each perhaps pursuing their own sectarian interests, or if their motives are impeccable, each having their own idea of what is good for society or how it should be achieved.

And instead of master-minds we have just the average imperfect individuals. And the idealistic urge to create better conditions for mankind has to compete with common or garden greed, vanity, laziness and stupidity. In this context idealism doesn't always win.

The result is that the Total Design for a particular entity – for of course in the end there is in effect a Total Design if the entity is completed – that this Total Design is not the work of one master-mind or of one close-knit team which considers all the relevant factors and reaches decisions in a wise and logical manner according to the weight to be attached to each – on the contrary we find that *important decisions are taken independently by different sets of people, and are therefore based on a limited number of facts falling within their particular sphere of interest, and are not related to other equally relevant facts.*

Most of the theoretically avoidable botchery of our environment can be attributed to this lack of integration and artistic control of the Total Design – or, what amounts more or less to the same thing – the fragmentation of what *ought* to be a Total Design into too small units.

Of course, many of these bad decisions are not caused by ignorance, but by the sad fact that incentives are not obviously married to quality of performance at *any* level. The Trade Unions are not primarily interested in quality or output but in maximum pay for any kind of performance. The architect *need* not be a *good* architect to be financially successful – it is more important that he knows how to get and handle clients and how to cut down his office expenses. The consulting engineer gets paid more if he turns out a safe but expensive job which he can do with a minimum of effort. The 'get out quick' developer makes more money by overcrowding the site.

This is unfortunate but still more harm is done by legitimate interests and laudable loyalties concentrated on too narrow a front.

We all know how the servants of different official departments can be much more interested in interdepartmental fights than in interdepartmental collaboration for the benefit of the people they are supposed to serve. Similarly with professional bodies, pressure groups, or individuals – their interests are sectional, not concentrated on the customer but on perfecting whatever they are interested in.

It is a sad tale, and the worst of it is that there is very little we can do about it, short of changing human nature! There is no simple, or single cause of all this, no single culprit, no single remedy. Even the whole Building Industry is not primarily responsible – it is only the servant of others who decide what should be built. Our whole society is involved. It is a case of Society getting the architecture it deserves.

The touchstone will be the way it deals with the motorcar, which threatens to strangle every attempt to create or preserve a human scale in our environment.

But what about the architect. Surely he is the designer of our buildings, he creates our environment?

I have already mentioned that there are many other cooks involved, owing to the growing complexity of modern life, and that some of the most important design decisions are taken out of the hands of architects. But it may be useful to look shortly at the historical development.

There was a time, not so long ago, when the term architecture applied only to the more monumental or prominent buildings, mostly commissioned by wealthy private clients. Then the Architect really had control of the design – subject to the possible rows with his Client who controlled the purse, and who might not only want to have a say in what should be built in terms of commodity, but might fancy himself a bit of an architect, and perhaps rightly so. But the Architect then knew at least how buildings were made, and so did everybody else in the game. So that he was able *himself* without any other interference to arrange his materials so as to satisfy the brief and produce his architecture – guided by the conventions of his time. All then depended on whether he was a good architect or not.

This is of course how any artist likes to work. He must have undisputed control of what he is doing. You cannot imagine two painters making the same picture, or two sculptors working on the same statue except in a relationship of master and pupil or servant. The same is true of any work of Architecture which aspires to become a work of Art – the artistic control should preferably be left to one master.

And this is how Architects still like to work. But many things have happened lately to make this difficult. We live in a rapidly changing world – mostly due to the enormous progress in science and technology, especially after the war. It is nothing less than a technological revolution, and it is changing not only the way we build, but the way we live, and therefore what we need to build.

The rigid class structure is breaking down – it is the age of the common man, the Welfare State. The rich private client of taste is disappearing, the client now tends to be anonymous – it is Society, the State, or the people!

The domain of Architecture is extended to cover everything we build or construct. The centre of gravity, the bulk of the work is now the provision of mass accommodation for the masses – housing, schools, hospitals, factories, the communications network, harbours, power stations and so on, to which increasingly industrial or mass-production techniques will be applied – necessitating larger building units.

The Architects were among the first to see this coming and that is what the modern movement, what functionalism, was about. It accepted with enthusiasm the new materials: steel, concrete, glass, and hailed the pioneering work done by engineers. And it stood for a new social conscience for Architects, it made it the concern of the Architect not only to interpret and execute the brief, but to be a party, at least, to creating the brief. The Architects became the defenders of the interests of the anonymous client, the people, and they reacted violently against the idea that it was the main business of Architecture to create stylistic masterpieces. If only this line had been pursued consistently, and if the gradually emerging new techniques had been studied and absorbed by Architects – admittedly a formidable task – much might have been different. But something went wrong, on several levels. Inside the architectural profession Gropius's Bauhaus ideas could not compete with the enormous impact of Corbusier's artistic genius. He was the hero and also the seducer of the modern movement. He was mainly interested in technique as a fountain of artistic inspiration, and the same can be said of many of the other idols of articulate architectural opinion. They are praised as artists, for their visual or sculptural impact, not for improving the soundness and cheapness of buildings. This is natural, for sound building is not nearly as exciting as artistic innovation, but if it is neglected, Architects are not doing their job.

It can perhaps be said, therefore, that the architectural profession as a whole has tended to neglect the practical business of sound building in favour of the more glamorous pursuit of artistic, expression. But this again would be taking a much too narrow view – it is like picking out one thread in a weave of intricate design. There are all kinds of architects, and only a small minority could be accused of not caring for sound or economic building. The majority care very much, some to the extent that they are prepared to abandon any attempt at artistic control where it conflicts with the logic of technology. But what is happening, and what gives rise to this accusation of incompetence, is that the architect is losing touch – unavoidably one can almost say – with the way things can be built nowadays. He used to know all about brickwork, damp-courses, slate or copper roofs, lead flashings – and there were experienced craftsmen to support him. It is different now. He is faced with a multitude of technical innovations, new materials, new ways of constructing even the carcase of buildings. They are developed outside his ken, in laboratories, factories, the backyards of inventors' homes. He has not the same intimate knowledge of his material, he has to rely on technical advisors, on experts in different branches of engineering. And even they may not be of much use to him when it comes to assessing the *cost* of different 'untraditional' ways of building. The contractor might know – but he is generally not available at this stage. There is a growing gap between design and execution. Designing means inventing, choosing, fixing priorities effecting a compromise, a synthesis of conflicting aims. It is difficult to effect a synthesis of facts which are largely in other people's heads, and can only be imperfectly communicated. A designer must know the cost of what he is doing. To a growing extent, that knowledge is not within his grasp.

Of course the situation changes from job to job. The tide of technical progress is advancing very unevenly. There are large areas of building almost untouched as yet, small jobs, jobs in out of the way places, individual prestige jobs for which special techniques can be developed. These can remain for a long time under the architect's control.

And the situation changes from year to year. In fact, the promise or the threat of technological advance is as yet potential rather than actual. It will first engulf the mass-repetition jobs. So many new techniques are as yet untried, or unproved in practice. There is a great gap between what we could do, and what we actually do. The computer is only beginning to make its impact felt. We have one in the office, but so far it only helps us to make intricate calculations – it hasn't yet started to tell us what to do. But the signs are in some respects ominous. Pre-planned large scale industrialised jobs will tend to follow their own technological or economic logic. Can artistic – or any kind of control in defence of humanity be exercised in these circumstances? Certainly the old organisation of the building industry will not be adequate, the position of the architect and of everybody else will change. *Teamwork* will be the answer. But successful teamwork is rare and difficult. The minimum that is required is that everybody contributing to the design should at least get together and make their special problems and possible solutions known to the others, but even that does not always happen.

The enthusiasm which must drive the whole effort in the right direction must in the end be a disinterested enthusiasm for the work itself, the oldfashioned pride of the craftsman, the creative urge of the artist, the social conscience and moral drive of the reformer. There is a lot of it about, but will it be enough?

Advances in Engineering

This article appeared in a special Financial Times *supplement on cement and concrete on 11 July 1967.*

Assuming that we are talking about advances inside the last 10 years or so, or at any rate since the war, there is nothing radically new to report. Concrete is still the same old material produced by mixing cement with sand, stone or other aggregates, adding water and stirring the mixture into a porridge and pouring it into forms. It will then harden into a stone-like material of a shape determined by the formwork. This has been known since Roman times. And the two main inventions which have laid the foundations for the use of concrete as a modern structural material by overcoming its weakness in tension, reinforced concrete and prestressed concrete, were both made before the war.

But this does not mean that there has been no progress since then. On the contrary – one may even call the progress spectacular if one compares it with the slow progress before the war, and if one accepts the fact that progress is always much slower than it theoretically need be.

This especially applies to a material like concrete, which depends on so many factors for its success, and which for that reason can be a very primitive or a highly sophisticated material. It is like the girl with the curl – when it's good it's very very good, and when it's bad it's horrid. Improving concrete construction is in a way like improving agriculture – it is not enough to improve the quality of grain or the milk yield of cattle – you have to pay attention to soil, weather, pests, weeds and especially to the whole complicated economic proposition of increasing yields with limited and expensive man-power necessitating mechanization, rationalization, larger units, etc., and you have to square this need with human factors, with ingrained habits and existing social organizations.

Fickle material

It is the same with concrete. It is not enough to show theoretically how various combinations of steel and concrete can result in a building material of excellent properties, it is necessary to create the technology which can transform a primitive and fickle material like the original handmade mass-concrete into a precise, controlled product with predictable qualities, dimensional stability and acceptable appearance, worthy to enter into union with steel, the structural material par excellence, on which the whole of our industrial revolution is based.

It has long been clear that if this could be achieved, if the valuable properties of steel and concrete could be combined and the shortcomings eliminated, we would be on to a very good thing, because the two materials complement each other. The main weakness of concrete is its unreliability in tension, the second, its dependence on good workmanship. The first can be completely cured by adding steel in one form or another, the second by strict control and mechanization. Steel on the other hand is liable to rust and to weaken under fire, and these faults can be eliminated by encasing in concrete.

The composite material has great strength which can be varied and concentrated exactly where needed. It has the necessary body to form walls, floors, ducts, containers and any other desired shape, and its raw materials are readily available in bulk. This makes it an exceedingly versatile material.

Before the war all this was known; it was also known how to make high quality concrete where required, and with experience stretching back over 40 years there had been an impressive development in the design and construction of reinforced concrete structures by engineers, specialist firms and engineering contractors, whereas the ordinary builders were hardly involved. But unsightly cracks, rusting reinforcement due to insufficient cover, an unpleasant surface, etc., were so common that it brought the material into disrepute. It didn't pay to make really good concrete, because in ordinary reinforced concrete it was not possible to make use of the greater crushing strength which could be obtained by improved cements and more scientific mix-design, or of the greater tensile strength of the latest high tension steels. The ordinary run-of-the-mill concrete was quite adequate for its purpose even if it didn't look so good.

New development

The invention of prestressed concrete changed all that. Now every additional ounce of strength in the constituent materials could be exploited, and when after the war the traditional building methods could no longer meet our needs, engineers and contractors rushed over to Paris or Brussels to learn about this new development. It was quite amazing to see how strongly contractors were represented at the various congresses. Many of them equipped themselves to meet this new challenge even before the economic implications were known, a welcome change from the cautious attitude to new ideas shown by contractors before the war.

This interest in prestressed concrete set off a chain reaction which far exceeded the importance of the new material itself – at least in its first stages. Because now it became necessary and profitable to study and to practise the making of high quality concrete, and to develop still stronger high tension steels, cables and strands and improved anchorages.

Monolithic character

The new invention also stimulated the practice of precasting concrete elements away from the site under more favourable conditions. This had often been advocated, especially by architects, as a means of improving the quality or appearance of concrete, but it had generally foundered on the hard fact that the method could not compete with in situ concrete, and because it destroyed the monolithic character or continuity which was one of the valuable features of r.c. [reinforced concrete] structures cast in situ. However, prestressing can overcome this latter deficiency, in fact, with a continuous structure formed by stressing together a number of precast units, the designer has a much greater control over the stresses induced in the structure. The two processes, precasting and prestressing, complement each other, and they also fit in with the general trend towards replacing quantity by quality, labour by machinery, craftsmanship by automatic control – in short: rationalization, or the rational use of our resources.

In fact, advances in concrete construction form only a part of a general technological advance and they are dependent on and greatly helped by advances on other fronts. That is why it is so difficult to discuss concrete in isolation. The advances could not have happened without, for instance, the digital computer which allows more accurate analysis of structures, statistical analysis of concrete strength leading to economies in cement, and makes the use of limit state design a practical proposition. Improvements in cements, the development of special cements for special purposes (phosphor resistant, water-repelling, expanding, etc.), new and more reliable lightweight aggregates and the methodical study of the nature of concrete and its behaviour during curing and maturing are, of course, directly relevant to this development, but so is the development of special steels, of epoxy resins and other jointing and waterproofing materials, of phosphor bronze for sliding joints and especially of all the different kinds of machinery for use on the building site and in the factory, from the largest tower crane and complete industrial plants to the hundreds of small gadgets which contribute to the economy of the various processes.

Economic methods

It would be hopeless to enumerate all these advances here. It is of course not primarily a question of producing better quality concrete – that can be done if we pay for it – it is really a search for economic methods of building, which incidentally, through mechanization and control, lead to better quality, at least on the technical level. The most spectacular advances are therefore the new construction methods or production techniques – I am thinking of the diaphragm wall cast in a bentonite-filled trench which has supplanted steel sheet piling for basement excavations down to 75 ft. and more in city centres where noise and vibration are problems: or the improved sliding formwork for tower block cores with door openings, etc., or the many other forms of moving formwork – the free cantilever construction for bridges and the development, already mentioned, of precasting larger and larger units and of the factory production of complete housing sections such as bathrooms and kitchens with all fittings and finishings done in the factory.

Most of these methods have been used even before the war on a smaller scale and in a more primitive form. What brings them to the fore now is not only advances in technology, but the different economic circumstances – the higher cost of labour, the greater demands for housing and all kinds of engineering structures, the greater emphasis on large-scale planning, leading to bigger jobs and to bigger design offices and contracting firms to deal with them, and the fact that these bigger units make it possible to introduce a greater amount of repetitive processes or units, which again is the basis for any rationalization of building.

What has hindered this development and what is still one of the principal obstacles in the way of rational building, is the fragmentation of the building and construction industry, which has its roots in history, but which ill accords with modern technology. In no other industry is design completely divorced from production, or are design decisions taken by so many different authorities, professions or firms, who are each a law unto themselves. In times of traditional building – when building methods remain stationary over a period and are known to everybody – this is a possible way of dealing with things, but it is totally unsuited to a state of flux, where new materials, new inventions, new methods of building tumble over each other.

Best use

The design must then be firmly anchored to the method of construction, and the implications of a given choice must be understood by the legal, financial and political authorities if the best use is to be made of our technological potential. There is no easy way to achieve this, but the progress which has been achieved lately is, I believe, largely due to the fact that the interdependence of the different professions and institutions dealing with building is better understood.

Teams for Total Design

This article appeared in The Times, *15 July 1968.*

The involvement of civil engineers or structural engineers in building is of comparatively recent date. The art of building flourished thousands of years before the idea of structural engineering as a discipline arose. Building developed by trial and error, by experiment and experience handed down the generations as established practice.

When the Institution of Civil Engineers was founded 150 years ago, the members had already considerable achievements to their credit but their domain was the design and construction of bridges, railways, harbours and tunnels. This was only gradually extended to include such utility buildings as cotton mills and other factories, waterworks, railway stations and exhibition or market halls, where the new building materials, cast iron, wrought iron and then steel, used in engineering, could be usefully employed to increase spans and reduce costs.

These were constructed on strictly statical and economical principles to do a necessary job efficiently and economically, and did not rank as Architecture with a capital A. It is significant that many of these utility structures designed by engineers were later acclaimed for their architectural merit.

Ordinary houses were at that time – and are still to some extent – the province of builders. Architecture was confined to mansions or important public buildings and these were designed by architects on quite different principles. The architect then had a client who knew – or thought he knew – what he wanted, and a well-established tradition of building based on a few materials and supported by craftsmen who knew their job and were proud of it. He could therefore concentrate on creating architectural masterpieces according to the prevailing rules of the game.

The industrial revolution and the whole technological advance after that, the social revolution, and the change in architectural philosophy which gave rise to functionalism and the modern movement have changed all that. And the change has been so drastic and is accelerating so fast that it would be difficult to paint a picture of the present situation, because so many stages of development co-exist.

The client is increasingly the community as a whole, expecting to be decently housed and catered for in all sorts of ways undreamed of before. The scale of buildings and of building operations is growing, except for a few tailor-made individual houses. The demand for central heating, air conditioning and services of all kinds is growing at an even faster rate, making building a matter of increasing complexity. Add to this the wealth of new, partly untried, materials and technical aids available to us and we can hardly wonder that a somewhat chaotic situation has arisen.

It is obvious that we can only cope with this situation – we can only get all the things we would like to have – by making effective use of the new knowledge and resources at our disposal. We must do more with less and this is exactly what engineering, what technology means.

Among the various branches of engineering knowledge relevant to buildings, structural engineering is possibly the most important because it is concerned with the whole carcass of the building, its stability under all foreseeable conditions, its durability, its adaptability to the functions of the building and above all, its cost, for cost is the essence of engineering, doing more with less.

Using advanced techniques involves pre-planning. One must know what has to be done before doing it, so that one can organize the work properly. The key to a building operation ought to be what one might call the total design – which foresees and plans every stage in the operation. This total design must nowadays be the work of many people, each contributing his particular knowledge, and this team should be controlled by a strong leader or an executive team with power to decide priorities and reconcile conflicting claims.

Without this the technological potential will not be realized and without this, artistic unity cannot be created. This is important, for we ought to build to create a happy environment for human beings to live in; this means more than the prescribed number of square feet of gadgets, and will not be achieved without a strenuous effort to reconcile it with the discipline imposed by technology.

We cannot avoid the splitting up of the business of building among dozens or hundreds of collaborators. Specialization is the way civilization moves forward – and perhaps it is the way it will destroy itself. Faced with a complex entity we split it up, catalogue the parts, study and develop them separately and then fail to put them together again. That is what happens to buildings. We are still encumbered with the old set-up suited to a more leisurely time, of architects, builders and various consultants, all independent firms, barely speaking to each other.

The client, if he can be identified, often issues a brief without understanding its implications for the design, and expects the building to conform to his innermost wishes. He does not realize that he has an active role to play in the development of the brief, a professional role which he is rarely organized to play. For, taking building as a whole, building the right things is much more important than building things rightly – and that is where we chiefly go wrong. But this is a political and controversial matter.

Then there is the total cleavage between design and execution which is hardly paralleled in any other industry. This makes it difficult to know the cost of different operations, a knowledge any designer must have. The building industry is more like a battleground for sectional interests than a meeting place for a combined effort to find the best solution.

This leads to frustration all round. The structural engineer is in a difficult position – his loyalty is divided between the architect under whose direction he works, and the client who does not realize that the engineer's chief headaches are created by the architect for possibly perfectly good reasons and that he has no power to decide what should be built as long as it stands up.

What the architect and the others have to put up with would fill a book. The authorities and most laymen suffer from the curious delusion that building can be improved by more accountancy, cost planning, etc. These obviously have their use but chopping something off a design by lowering standards does not create anything. For that you must go back to the drawing board and make a better design. To get the right materials in the right place is what gets building costs down. Designing is creative accountancy.

Of course, the whole thing works after a fashion. One could even be quite complacent about it and revel at how much progress we have made and how much excellent work is being done by hundreds of dedicated architects and engineers. Many new experiments in team-work are being made. The need for integration, for breaking down barriers, is generally recognized and talked about. Something is bound to crystallize out of this turmoil, and this is perhaps how things must develop in a democracy, but it is a slow process.

It is difficult to feel happy about the way we are developing our heritage. The opportunities which seemed to exist after the war for a radical change have on the whole been missed, but if one knows how much more could be done with our present know-how one cannot help indulging in Utopian dreams of all the creative forces in the industry combining in an unselfish effort to build a better environment. But they must be given more power, and we must make up our minds what we want. This technology cannot do.

The World of the Structural Engineer

The 'Maitland Lecture', given to the Institution of Structural Engineers at the Purcell Room, South Bank, London, on 14 November 1968 and subsequently published in The Structural Engineer, *January 1969. Partly autobiographical, Ove Arup selected this lecture to lead off an abridged selection of writings, produced to celebrate his ninetieth birthday in 1985. The Arup Papers archive in Cambridge contains four distinct drafts of this lecture, indicating some of the rigour and process that he dedicated to preparing his lectures.*

I am sure you all agree that the structural engineer needs no introduction to this audience. But actually it is a bit hard to define the term 'structural engineer'. It could be one who has passed certain examinations, who is a member of this Institution – in which case he would even be a Chartered Structural Engineer – or one who holds a certain position or does a certain job. For the purpose of this talk, I would prefer to define the structural engineer simply as one who is competent to design stable and economical structures of different kinds to meet the requirements for which these structures are needed. This means of course that one can be more or less of a structural engineer, and that civil engineers, mechanical engineers and some who are not called engineers at all might be so called.

But the world of the structural engineer cannot be thus defined – it would vary with each individual, and they vary widely, as a glance at this audience will show. The structural engineer can only be an abstraction, a figment of the imagination.

Since, therefore, we must imagine this structural engineer of ours, let us at least imagine a man who will serve our purpose this evening – who will provide us with a critique of his professional milieu. We'll make him a civil engineer specializing in structures, and we will make it his job to design structures in different circumstances, as employee or employer, as contractor or consulting engineer, as principal or consultant to an architect. He should also be a difficult, critical sort of chap, always thinking that things could be better than they are. Being a mere invention, he can of course afford to be outspoken. Perhaps we should make him a foreigner – that would after all explain a great deal. But all the same there must be some sense in what he says, for if not the whole exercise becomes pointless. We'll make him, also, a bit of a dreamer, a man to whom dreams are at least important, and not too much a man of action; for action distracts from thought. As it says in Ecclesiasticus: 'The wisdom of a learned man cometh by opportunity of leisure: and he that has little business shall become wise.'

And while we're at it, we really must give him a name, otherwise we'll never get to know him. I think Ernest would be a good name for him; it is not impossible that he may turn out to be a bit of a prig.

I imagine that even as a child Ernest had an inquisitive sort of mind, a curiosity about what's inside things, how they work, how they're made. And this being so, he was naturally attracted to science. You must remember that this was a long time ago, when Science stood for Truth, and Art for Beauty, and when Goodness was the purpose of life. They were absolutes – to begin with. And for him they never quite lost that aura. Especially truth: he thought he would one day be able to discover the secret of Kant's *Ding an sich*, the secret of being.*

Of course he was disillusioned. He soon ceased to expect any absolute solution. But truth remained important to him, and so did beauty – or rather, art. Still, he was no artist, and he decided to become an engineer. But of course: a good engineer; because he chose this way also in search of an opportunity for artistic fulfilment, the satisfaction of a job well done. This was not surprising. Young people are often idealists, they believe they can do better than their elders. Ernest realized that he wouldn't solve the world's problems, no matter how much science he studied; and he saw engineering in terms of solving problems that *could* be solved. Engineering is not a science. Science studies particular events to find general laws. Engineering design makes use of these laws to solve particular practical problems. In this it is more closely related to art or craft, as in art its problems are underdefined, there are many solutions, good, bad and indifferent. The art is, by a synthesis of ends and means, to arrive at a good solution. This is a creative activity, involving imagination, intuition and deliberate choice, for the possible solutions often vary in ways that cannot be directly compared by quantitative methods.

But I had better let Ernest get on with his career. He studied mathematics, physics, chemistry, mechanics, and the rest, learned about materials and their properties, about forces, stresses, and all the other things, mostly theoretical; and he took his degree in engineering, specializing in structures.

Designer and contractor

He was particularly interested in the potentialities of a comparatively new material called reinforced concrete, and therefore joined an international firm which specialized in the design and construction of reinforced concrete structures. This firm had come in on the ground floor, so to speak, building quay walls, jetties, bridges, silos, water towers, coal bunkers and so on, in competition with firms using established structural materials – mostly steel, timber and stone. It seemed a wonderful opportunity for anyone wanting to use his imagination and creative power.

He got a bit of a shock when he first visited a building site and realized how far reality is at variance with theoretical assumptions about the placing of bars, the density of concrete, and dimensional tolerances. (These were early days, remember – concrete looks different now.) And he soon realized the futility of pressing calculations to an exactitude which exceeds that of the basic assumptions.

It also very soon dawned on him that what he had learnt at school didn't get him very far when it came to designing, for instance, marine structures. If you are faced with building a breakwater in deep sea, with huge waves rolling in, what on earth do you do? You know there are various possibilities, blocks, caissons, piling; and you can at a pinch decide which will stand up when it is built – although it proves difficult to get anyone to commit himself about the force of waves. But how do you get it there? Won't it be smashed to bits before it is built? And above all, how much does it cost? Because, so far as his firm was concerned, the whole point was to find a solution that they could offer at a lower cost than that of competitive schemes, so securing a job and making a profit.

Fortunately older members of his firm were well versed in the practical business of building in difficult circumstances, and he accepted their guidance with gratitude. After a couple of years he grew quite good at designing plus estimating. He found out about the cost of materials from the buyer, and about the labour expenses involved in each type of operation from the firm's weekly cost sheets. So far he had nothing to do with deciding about overheads and profits, dealing with customers or visiting sites. But he did learn one useful lesson that he was never to forget: namely that *a designer must have a clear idea of what he wants to achieve; and must know the means of execution available to him and how to evaluate their effectiveness, both theoretically and practically.*

There was no difficulty so far about the first part: he simply had to fulfil the client's requirements for less money than his competitors could, while providing a stable structure with no obvious defects and satisfying the building authorities. With whatever imagination and ingenuity he could summon he had to battle with the facts and possibilities, and try out alternative solutions, costing every step to make sure he was not taking a wrong or expensive turn. It required an effort on his part if the result was to be good. A sudden inspiration could help, of course; but it very seldom came without prior intense absorption of the relevant facts.

Let us now imagine that one day Ernest, this structural engineer of ours, was posted to London. He arrived in mid-winter in the early 'twenties in a real old-fashioned pea-souper, policemen in white nightgowns armed with flares or white sheets walking carefully in front of whole rows of red double-decker buses. There were coal fires in stations, even in drawing offices, cosy and dirty, roasting one side, freezing the other. Surveying in gumboots on the mudbanks of the Solent, staying at a little pub, darts, warm beer, kippers, joint and two veg; a hot humid December, tea with crumpets, lovely old Christmas carols – he was enchanted with it all. I don't suppose he was actually asked whether he thought our London policemen were wonderful – but of course that's what he did think.

After a while he grew more used to the ways of the natives. His firm had lost heavily on two major contracts, because their estimates were based on continental rates for output per man-hour; and reinforced concrete was looked on with the greatest suspicion by the majority of potential clients. But Ernest learned, and eventually he became chief designer in the London branch of his firm, responsible for designs and tenders. He soon realized that his chief headache was not to design the structures, but to get the *chance* to design them. In order to get enough work the firm tendered for jobs designed by consulting engineers, city engineers, railway engineers, etc.; and much that Ernest saw appalled him. He frequently saw marvellous opportunities for suggesting much more economical solutions. But he discovered the naiveté of assuming that engineers would be interested in his ideas, even if they led to better solutions to their problems: they very rarely were. A contractor who dared to offer an opinion on the design of a consulting engineer might find his firm excluded from tendering at all.

To begin with he put his foot in it good and proper, and was several times shown the door. It would be too much to say that Ernest learnt tact from such experiences; but he learnt some caution, and scored some successes. There was a design for a wharf put out to tender by a railway company, which proved to be a mechanism that would collapse as soon as the backfill was placed. Ernest managed to get an interview with the chief engineer, and indicated delicately that his firm was worried about taking responsibility for the design because of so-and-so: would the chief engineer perhaps be good enough to explain, or would it be in order to put forward an alternative solution? The chief engineer saw the light, and whilst not admitting that anything was wrong, refrained from kicking Ernest downstairs, and agreed that he could put in an alternative solution provided that everyone else was allowed to tender on it as well. Of course there would be no question of paying for the design commandeered in this fashion. Ernest was none too happy about it; and when the QS was called in and estimated that it would take him six weeks to prepare the bill of quantities for the alternative design – which would not therefore be ready until long after the date of tendering – things looked black indeed, and Ernest wondered whether the chief engineer had really understood the situation. But a bargain was finally struck. Ernest would quote on the unworkable original scheme in competition with the other firms, and only if his firm submitted the lowest tender would his alternative scheme be considered, and probably accepted if the price were lower still. Other firms would after all not have to quote on it.

The rest was easy, because the alternative was indeed cheaper, even with a good profit; and Ernest could safely put in too low a price for the official scheme, knowing that it would not be built. And so it came to pass.

I am sure Ernest could tell you many such interesting stories, if there were time for them, and if we could rely on the accuracy of his memory. But we must return to his career. He began to feel that as a contractor he was rather frustrated. He remained a novice in the subtle art of cultivating clients, and at that time people were just not interested in ideas. He had many such; but he couldn't get manufacturers, crane-makers, or brickworks to collaborate in evolving new handling plant or new facing materials for concrete unless he had bulk orders to place. He couldn't try out new methods, for nobody would take any risk; he couldn't even get the firm's own foremen to make really good concrete with a decent surface,

---

* In his *Critique of Pure Reason* (1781) Immanuel Kant argues that we are never able fully to know the 'thing-in-itself' but are only able to perceive things as phenomena, through the senses.

since it cost more, and profit margins were narrow. And when he did succeed in getting out a design that ought to beat all competition, it still didn't mean that his firm would get the job or that it would be built if it did. Sometimes the client sent the design to all his competitors, so that they could quote on this idea as well. Sometimes an appreciative but just a little too greedy head office abroad, to which all important tenders had to be submitted, clapped on an extra 10 or 20 per cent, thinking to cash in on an opportunity which was thereby lost.

I am afraid that Ernest is given, in some moods, to complaining that all his best ideas came to nothing. No one takes him too seriously; he has had his frustrations – who hasn't? – but he achieved a good deal, and most people would consider him lucky. But I must say I can sympathize, for I sometimes feel the same way myself. I have rather surprisingly reached a position where I am – for instance – honoured with this invitation to give the Maitland Lecture; and if only certain designs I produced as a younger man had been carried out, I might not feel quite such a fraud.

A minor annoyance was caused by the growing practice of extending quantity surveying as known from the building trade to steel and reinforced concrete structures. When his firm received a bill of quantities – a thick volume, beautifully printed, which had taken months to prepare – they had laboriously to pick out all the small bits of concrete, steel etc. from hundreds of different entries describing different members of different sizes; collect them all together; and prepare an estimate on their own model, perhaps two or three pages long, giving the amount of concrete of different mixes in cubic yards, the different kinds of formwork in square yards, the reinforcing bars in tons, plus whatever excavation and extra items like pipes, bolts, and whatnot had to be provided. Then, after it had been decided how to lay out and organize the job, the cost of plant, staging, sheds, foremen's time, and so on was added. And then came the tedious business of distributing the tender price over the thousands of items in the bill – including things like 'extra over for rounded edges', though no one has ever put in a rounded edge without placing the concrete at the same time. The trouble was that there could be no correspondence whatever between the items in the bill and the information the contractor received from his weekly cost sheets – and that, after all, was where he got his costs.

Of course the idea was to make the bill a legal document defining the job, so that the consulting engineer or architect could obtain a price without having to finish the drawings. A thoroughly bad excuse for a bad practice, thought Ernest. The whole method breaks down if you are faced with an original design introducing new methods – which was what Ernest was always *trying* to achieve. And he couldn't share the QS's faith in these rates as cost indicators, since he well knew that the way the total price was distributed over the different items was guided by political motives rather than by devotion to accurate accountancy. Ernest used to claim that in the time it took his staff to deal with all this clerical work they could have designed the job, taken out *their* kind of quantities, and priced it. But then he wasn't very fond of clerical work. And besides, the business of multiplying a quantity of steel expressed in tons, hundred-weights, quarters and pounds, by a rate expressed in pounds, shillings and pence, using a ready reckoner, seemed to him faintly ludicrous.

The modern movement

At this time, still before the war, Ernest happened to meet some of the pioneers of the modern movement in architecture, because some of them approached his firm asking them to tender for some buildings in reinforced concrete.

Here he met a number of young people who really *were* interested in new ideas, who in fact had plenty themselves, and were very fond of discussing them. It was stimulating, amusing, and also puzzling. The puzzling part was that these architects professed enthusiasm for engineering, for the functional use of structural materials, for the ideals of the Bauhaus, and all that; but that this didn't mean quite what you might suppose. They were in love with an architectural style, with the aesthetic feel of the kind of building they admired; and so they were prepared and indeed determined to design their buildings in reinforced concrete – a material they knew next to nothing about – even if it meant using the concrete to do things that could be done better and more cheaply in another material.

But here was a group that both welcomed and needed Ernest's ideas. He joined the MARS group and the Architectural Association, and started to help architects with their reinforced concrete schemes – mostly on paper only. He also helped some architects to win some competitions, and they celebrated together with a trip to Paris to look at modern architecture. Corbusier's Swiss Pavilion* made a deep impression on him. This *was* something. But what was it? Why did it have that effect? He shared the enthusiasm of the architects, but not perhaps their reasoning. He suspected that what mattered was not that the building was 'modern', but that it was great architecture, architecture produced by an artist.

He joined a new firm in order to have the opportunity of working with architects; and he was busy designing, tendering for, and obtaining contracts for all kinds of structures, including reinforced concrete frames for buildings in imitation of the more usual steel frames. Ernest deplored this method of using concrete, and in the building carcasses which the firm designed for modern architects he adopted what he at that time called 'slab construction'. This attracted the attention of at least the architectural profession, for and against. But his position as designer of the reinforced concrete structure, when he was at the same time employed by a contractor who tendered for the building, was really quite untenable. The architects wanted Ernest's firm to get the job, because they wanted him as designer; and he had to persuade his firm to quote a low price, so that the architects could in turn persuade the client that the job would be cheaper than traditional building. Whereas it really should have been more expensive, if it were to be done properly, in view of all the innovations it contained. Ernest was far from happy about the whole position, and realized that if he were to help architects to design buildings, it would have to be as a consulting engineer. And in any case, he had had enough of this political game, of the pressure to temper truth with expediency, and the assumption that he had done so whatever he did.

Contracting and consulting

Nevertheless, when he was offered help to set up as a contractor himself, he did so, planning at the same time to act as a consulting engineer independent of the contracting firm, and hoping to use some surplus profit to initiate new methods of construction by design-research combined with practical tests. For he was still convinced that the designer should be able to choose and control the method of construction, to achieve the proper integration of the two. He had seen enough of impractical designs produced by consultants. This was before the war, of course.

He was in fact trying to ride three horses at the same time:

1) as plain contractor – to make a living;
2) as designer-contractor, carrying out structural work to his own design;
3) as consulting engineer for the design only of structures, in the first instance to help modern architects who mostly wanted to use concrete as a structural material.

To the outsider (and Ernest remained something of an outsider) the proposed combination looked fairly sensible; but it was in a way an act of defiance. He was perfectly aware that it would meet with resistance and suspicion; but he hoped to overcome it by sticking strictly to the rule of *not* involving his contracting firm if he was chosen as consultant. He wanted of course to give up carrying out other people's designs as soon as he could afford it, because it was design he was interested in, and he only wanted a link with construction in order to improve design. It worked for a time, but war intervened. This put an end to architecture, other problems loomed ahead.

I think we must skim over Ernest's experiences during the war. There were satisfying moments, and there were frustrations; and in a situation where the nation needed more than ever before to husband its resources, the frustrations could be hard to bear. Suffice it to say that at the end of the war Ernest took the plunge and set up as a consultant.

Two reasons impelled him. The first was that this seemed the only way in which he could really concentrate on design. Construction was useful both as a stimulus to and as a test of design; but in itself the exacting task of organizing all this complicated activity with its trivial setbacks and conflicts did not appeal to him – which in no way diminished his admiration for professional and dedicated building contractors. And the second reason was that for him all the excitement had gone out of contracting during the war. The sporting element, the adventure of getting an idea, the thrill of beating your competitor on merit, the risk of offering a lump-sum price for the job, all that buccaneering spirit had gone. You were paid for so many quantities at controlled prices, with controlled labour, extra for canteen, bus transport, and what not, all registered and counted up, and whether or not you made a profit depended entirely on whether you were able to persuade the client's quantity surveyor to allow extras for difficulties encountered: bad weather; increased haulage; too little or too much rock-excavation; supply of too little or the wrong kind of labour by the Ministry of Labour; acts of God – it was quite unbelievable what could be done. He found contracting at that time a thoroughly uninspiring, even distasteful business.

* The Pavillon Suisse was a student accommodation building in Paris, designed by Le Corbusier and Pierre Jeanneret in 1932.

The period after the war started with great expectations and also a good deal of apprehension. The brave new world might be round the corner, but large parts of Europe were in ruins, and austerity reigned unabated. Yet there was a new spirit abroad. In the contracting world, and among architects and engineers, the atmosphere was certainly different. New ideas were actually welcomed, or at least considered. Prestressed concrete swept the country with unprecedented rapidity. Contractors and engineers undertook in scores and hundreds the pilgrimage to [Eugène] Freyssinet in Paris and [Gustave] Magnel in Ghent.

Structural consultant

At first he worked almost exclusively as structural consultant to architects. He was sorry to leave marine work, which (compared to building) offers so much more scope for dramatic cost-saving through inventive design; and he was sorry to lose the life-giving connection with actual construction; but a consulting engineer cannot choose his work. And he was determined to join in the adventure of helping to create a new and better architecture. He first had to try to learn what architecture was about.

He soon realized that architecture is a very personal thing. Architects are certainly influenced by theories – some, indeed, have to find theoretical justifications for almost every decision; but theories can't produce good architecture. Only good architects can do that. Ernest's job would be to help the architects in their task. Of course it would have to be left to the architect to decide what constituted good architecture; for *he* was the principal who had to interpret the client's wishes. The architect might certainly experience a conflict of loyalties: loyalty to his art; to the client who commissioned him; to the people who would use his building. Since visual or sculptural art – delight, for short – is what an architect's reputation depends on, and what he is most praised for producing, it was not surprising that architects were generally most excited about their loyalty to art, sometimes at the expense of function or economy. This might make it difficult for Ernest, too, to see where his duty lay; but in general he saw it as his task to side with the architect in his battle for good architecture against the prejudices of clients and authorities.

He brought to this task his experience in handling reinforced concrete, and in using its plastic qualities; and he was often able to surprise the architect himself, showing him possibilities he had not dreamt of. He therefore fulfilled a need, his help was appreciated, and his practice grew. He found plenty of enthusiasm for new ideas – his battles were not with the architects, but with the authorities. But very often his task was one of debunking, of putting a brake on ideas that were too advanced or fantastic, of fighting for sound construction.

He accepted, of course, that the aim of designing a structure that would convey the forces to the ground in the simplest, most direct and economical manner would have to be modified by the additional demand that it should form an acceptable – perhaps a vital – part of the architect's composition. This might mean that the structure should as far as possible remain hidden; or that its arrangement, the size and form of its members, might be determined by other than structural and economic considerations, so long as stability was not endangered. But sometimes he could not help thinking that equally good architecture might have been achieved without loss of structural efficiency by a little extra effort. Sometimes even some of the best architects made demands leading to structural contortions which could have given Ernest the satisfaction of difficulties surmounted, had he not suspected these difficulties of having been artificially created. But the architect would be pleased and appreciative, and his faith in the omnipotence of reinforced concrete was confirmed; not necessarily a good thing. The firm even got a reputation for making complicated structures – which was hardly what they aimed to do.

Basic anomalies in the building industry

Nevertheless his collaboration with architects was on the whole very happy and satisfying. The jobs involved were of course limited in scope: single buildings or groups of buildings, designed to a brief, inside a given budget, and making use of the existing resources and organization of the building industry. Within this framework it was possible for a good architect to make buildings of architectural merit. But from a technical point of view, the framework was too narrow for more than variations and minor improvements of routine solutions. It was difficult to make effective use of the new techniques and materials which were being developed by the building industry at a rate impressive by pre-war standards. Such things as the increased use of factory production and site mechanization, new and improved materials, new methods of jointing, scientific thinking applied to organization and communication – they could all enable us to build better and more with less; but *only if the framework was widened*. And the need was pressing. We could not meet our targets – desirable projects were being cut down and postponed. But as structural adviser to the architect there was not much Ernest could do about it.

On the one hand design decisions belonged to the architect. Any alteration in the technique of building would affect the way in which the architect built up his artistic concept from familiar structural elements, he might have to change his intuitive thinking, follow the lead of the new technology and familiarize himself with its details instead of dictating to it – which was both distasteful and troublesome. Architects were not master-builders any more, cut off, as they were, from the grass roots of practical building and building costs by the interposition of quantity surveyors and technical advisors. In this Ernest saw a danger to the renewal of architecture.

On the other hand, there could be no proper integration of design and construction, owing to the complete segregation between the two, which is such an odd characteristic of the building industry. As long as Ernest stuck to routine designs, all was well; and that was what he had to do in the majority of cases. But where he saw an opportunity for introducing new or improved methods, he needed the collaboration of the contractor, and he needed cost-information *before* his designs were finalized. With the growing variety of available methods, this information was increasingly essential for choosing the right design, and increasingly difficult to get hold of. Contractors were reluctant to plunge into the unknown, departures from normal would be discouraged by high rates, and in any case costs were guarded as a secret. Understandable, perhaps, in a competitive world. But Ernest felt that there was something wrong with a system that allowed costs to be withheld from the designer. *Engineering design is creative accountancy*. And architects, too, design buildings that have to be built. If the hard facts of building do not form part of the artistic vision, architecture is brought into disrepute.

But Ernest realized early on that the real fault lay neither with the architect nor with the contractor, but with the whole way in which the building industry was organized, and geared to an out-dated technology. The new technology required assured markets to allow mass production, larger contract units, discarding of old habits and professional and other barriers, multidisciplinary teams given steady employment, standardization, time and capital for research, testing of prototypes, and other things which taken together would amount to a drastic change in the whole social order. This would take time, it could not be forced through by government action without unacceptable dictatorial measures, and it lay in any case outside the sphere of structural engineering. Only concerted action by the building industry might have speeded things up, and this was effectively prevented by its fragmentation.

On this somewhat pessimistic note we will abandon our account of Ernest's career. He has served his purpose, his grumbling has highlighted some problems which, more than 20 years later, are still with us. Much has happened in these years, technology has advanced in leaps and bounds. The building industry for a long time lagged behind, but we are now all aware that great changes are upon us.

The situation today

I should now like to review the situation as it exists today, not statistically, for I have not got the figures, but intrinsically, as I perceive it to be from my undoubtedly somewhat restricted viewpoint.

For most of the work designed by architects with the help of consultants, the situation has not changed much since Ernest's days. More precasting, more factory production, more mechanization has been squeezed into the existing organization of the building industry. It is still difficult to surmount the barriers between authorities, professions and private interests with fingers in the same design-pie and this causes frustration to designers who want to break with routine. The best architecture has improved partly at least because architects have now become more familiar with the new materials and techniques, but quantitatively the urban scene is dominated by bulky building blocks, disposed as dictated by financial and political pressures, and to this must be added the devastations caused by the motor car, indiscriminate proliferation of street furniture, and the vulgarity of much private display. Uniform mediocrity tends to destroy the identity of our cities.

Good architecture has always been produced by good artists, and it is the same today. The impact of an architectural composition is produced somehow by the creation of spaces, sculptural relationships, light and shade, colours and textures and not least by the clarity or ingenuity with which its functional and structural problems are solved. Exactly how, we do not know – and we cannot know – beforehand. There is no infallible recipe. Were it otherwise, we could do it by computer. It is the artist's sensitivity, his humanity or personality which speaks to us, if we are receptive to it.

But artists differ even more than structural engineers, and there are many ways of producing good architecture. And that is how we wish it to be – we would soon get tired of uniformity.

Value for money

But we don't build to produce art. We produce useful hardware to fulfil various functions. And we want to get it with the least effort, the least expense. We want value for money, and we can therefore measure efficiency by the simple formula

$$E = \frac{Commodity}{Cost}$$

where 'commodity' stands for what we want to achieve.

In 1945, in the first number of the *Architects' Yearbook*, I proposed a modification of this formula to:

$$E = \frac{BC + EC + D}{Cost}$$

where BC stands for 'basic commodity', EC stands for 'excess commodity', and D stands for 'delight', recognizing the fact that what we are getting as a result of a particular design is not only the basic commodity defined by the brief, but many other qualities or features peculiar to this design, and that these have a commodity value positive or negative, which we must take into consideration when comparing different designs. Likewise, the 'delight' produced, which stands for all the intangible values associated with good architecture, should certainly also be considered, even if it is impossible to put a money value on it. This may apply to the more material 'excess commodity' as well, for if you haven't asked for something you may not be prepared to pay for it, even if it is useful – for instance, extra thermal insulation, longer life, more adaptability, etc.

It is a normal thing that 'excess commodity' becomes 'basic commodity' as standards are raised.

Of course commodity, delight and costs are interrelated in all sorts of ways. I mentioned that an ingenious and simple solution of the structural and functional problems can itself produce delight without incurring extra cost, and that therein lies the art of designing. It may even be produced at less cost. *But unless drastic measures are taken to pull the whole design together and provide a balanced and total design, embodying all the available knowledge, wherever it resides, and knitting it together in an artistically controlled pattern, it cannot be achieved*. Without it, art tends to be expensive.

The trouble is not lack of talent, enthusiasm and idealism. They are to be found in plenty in the architectural profession, mostly amongst younger architects, who will work day and night to produce quality. Naturally, the best human endeavour: that which produces outstanding quality, delight, the great works of art, the really human and satisfying environment; that which lifts humanity above the soulless efficiency of an ant-heap – with due apology for a possible injustice to ants, this is rare and cannot be bought. The driving force behind it is a passion for perfection, a dream of a better world, an artistic urge or something equally absurd to the proverbial hard-boiled business man – apologies again – but naturally mixed in various proportions with ambition, dreams of fame, recognition, applause.

But in a world increasingly dominated by technology yet bedevilled by fragmentation and sectarian interests, the odds against such endeavours succeeding are formidable. The bulk of what we build is subject to severe financial restrictions. Rightly or wrongly, private and public finance is not prepared to put a high value on excess commodity and delight. In most cases those who control the money have no strong feeling for architecture, certainly their ideas of delight are likely to differ from those of the architects who naturally have given the subject much more attention. It is difficult to break through this crust of indifference. The fact is that if art is expensive, it can survive only as a kind of luxury for the few. Technology will then take over, and it is happening now.

Technological demands

What can we do about it? To get what we want and not just have to want what we get, we must control technology, and therefore we must first understand its needs.

What are its needs?

Technology achieves economy in three ways: by invention; by repetition or mass production; and by specialization.

Invention requires freedom from convention, an ability to look at a problem with fresh eyes. Accepted ideas are not easy to escape from. In the very first motor cars, the driver's seat remained high up, so that he could see what his non-existent horses were up to; and he had a little tube fixed to the board in front of him, in which he could deposit the whip. Similarly, when reinforced concrete replaced structural steel as the structural material in buildings, the familiar three-dimensional orthogonal frame was retained, with its secondary and tertiary beams of different sizes. The first Building codes were based on this conception; concrete panels had to be supported by this frame, in spite of the fact that they formed the stiffest members of the whole assembly. And walls in coal-bunkers, reservoirs, etc. were treated as panels and set back from the frame, sometimes in several steps – an architectural anachronism adding unnecessarily to the cost of formwork. Or again: when extruded aluminium sections were introduced as a replacement for steel under certain conditions, the industry issued catalogues showing angles, channels, and I-sections similar to those made in structural steel. They had failed to grasp the basic fact that this was a different material, which could be extruded, and which could therefore be manufactured in quite different shapes. It was only by exploiting this potential, to save material and produce sections to serve several functions, that extruded aluminium sections could be made competitive.

There is a German tag I have often found useful: 'Umgekehrt ist auch was wert' – or, in English: 'The other way round may be equally sound'. Invention comes from forgetting how a thing was done before, so that apparently insoluble problems cease to be problems at all when they are seen from a new view-point. And each new invention creates a whole row of redundancies, posing problems of change and resistance to change. Every solution to a problem is made possible because other solutions to other problems have been made previously; and it in turn affects solutions to quite different problems, without regard to boundaries.

This *Integrality of Technology* is matched by, and partly identical with, the network of means and ends. A structure may be made to stabilize a building, a building to shelter human activities – the education of children or the manufacture of tools – to make other things to serve other ends. And you can't solve a problem in a really new way without first knowing why you want the problem solved; you must be able to see the problem from a distance of at least one step along the network. In this way technology is a radical force, demanding fluidity of outlook and freedom from preconceptions.

The second important ingredient in economic production, *Repetition* or *Mass Production*, is of course bound up with invention. If you can repeat the same process, use the same component or the same detailed solution over and over again, you can facilitate production and carry out complex processes cheaply; and, in particular, you can save skilled creative labour, which is suspect because it is fickle, unreliable, slow and expensive. In its demand for standardization, technology has a built-in tendency to megalomania.

A friend of mine with a very large farm wished to rationalize the milking of his herd of several hundred cows. Cows are creatures of habit; and he trained his cows to come every evening, in a long file, always in the same order, to the milking shed. Here they climbed, one at a time, on to a huge circular revolving platform. One man or girl put on the milking machine as each cow arrived; and another took it off again when the platform had completed a round. The speed was adjusted so that one round corresponded to the milking time for an average cow.

The only snag was that the cows varied. Cows with exceptionally high yields were an expensive nuisance. They could not stay on the milking platform for a whole second round; they had to be disconnected, and milked dry by hand. So very good cows – like very bad ones – had to be replaced; the whole herd had to be normalized.

It would obviously be a great advantage if human beings could be standardized in the same way, so that they were all of the same size, weight, and shape, had the same preferences and tastes, and never asked for variety. They wouldn't be human any more; but think of the money we'd save. And already we sacrifice functional and aesthetic amenity in thousands of ways for the sake of standardization and economy. The only question is: where should we draw the line? Technological megalomania is evident in the expanding size of building operations. Whole towns, town centres, residential or industrial areas, new universities, are designed by one team. Or in industrialized building, one system is used to build identical high-rise flats, for example, in many different districts. Under such conditions we may ultimately save money and labour; but we won't do even that unless we get the design right and unless we solve the total design before operations begin. Standardization is, I think, an evil *per se*, though it is so powerful a tool that we cannot afford to neglect it. But at least let us refrain from making standardization an end in itself. On the other hand we cannot expect the benefits of standardization unless we are willing to create the conditions which are needed to bring them about. *Specialization*, the third ingredient of successful technology, is not peculiar to technology, of course, it is a characteristic of all progressive human activity. Concentration on a narrow field makes it possible to achieve the mastery, the penetration in depth, upon which progress depends. The need for specialization is obvious enough. But whereas invention and repetition must disregard boundaries and demolish barriers in order to be effective, specialization *creates* barriers.

We are all familiar with the proliferation of learned societies and institutions clamouring for their Royal Charters, of congresses discussing their esoteric mysteries in terms unintelligible to outsiders, of administrative bodies on Ministerial and local levels cherishing their particular author-ity and jealous of outside interference, of specialist occupations, industrial lobbies, trade associations, and private firms. Each has its special axe to grind.

There are good reasons for all this. Like so much else, it is understandable, justifiable, beneficial – and harmful. It breeds narrow-mindedness, it hinders the effective use of our resources.

Design deficiencies

The result is that most designs fall into one of the following categories:

Starved designs
Deprived of the benefit of technical knowledge which could have improved them. As when engineers are called in too late to an already 'frozen' design, or when the designers simply do not know their job or do not take the trouble to consult those who do.

Forced or lopsided designs
When put into a strait-jacket of architectural formalism or structural acrobatics or client's prejudice, disturbing the balance of priorities.

Loose designs
When no proper synthesis is achieved for lack of effort or collaboration, hardening into:

Split designs
When the design is being handled by different authorities or firms who barely communicate with each other.

Pinched designs
Due to economic stringency, when the ship is spoilt for a ha'p'orth of tar.

Patched up designs
When the brief is altered or added to by clients, or the architect has a better idea or additional information comes to hand which is somehow tacked on to the design without taking the only course that can assure a proper digestion of the new data: that of starting all over again with the new information in mind and reconsidering the decisions made. Naturally this is in many cases not possible, but this does not alter the fact that the result is patchwork.

This judgment may be considered too harsh. I admit that I am measuring against an ideal that is unattainable, that much excellent work is in fact being done today, and that you could criticize any design, however good, from some or all of these points of view. Architectural design is by its very nature a compromise. I am only trying to pinpoint some of the defects which could be remedied by better organization, a freer exchange of knowledge, less divided responsibility. These defects are not so noticeable in 'closed' designs or limited design objects. It is when we move towards comprehensive design, large-scale planning, that these barriers have a crippling effect. But more of that later. I will first deal shortly with some of the attempts which are being made on a smaller scale to overcome them.

The multi-disciplinary team

That multi-disciplinary team work is necessary is now generally accepted, and everybody is eagerly climbing on to the bandwagon. A number of multi-disciplinary group practices have been formed, most of them led by architects or at any rate endeavouring to promote good and efficient architecture, total architecture.

Some large contractors, on the other hand, point out that large jobs nowadays demand above all efficient organization and co-ordination, using the latest scientific techniques, which necessity has taught them to perfect; that construction and design belong together, and that the most natural solution would be to let them handle the whole matter from A to Z, and let them deal directly with the client – the so-called package deal.

Lately the quantity surveyor, who has been busy acquiring a new look, has also put in a tentative claim for the leadership. It has been pointed out that his position as disinterested go-between, acting in a quasi-judicial capacity in disputes between client and contractor, fits him excellently for this role, provided he acquires a little extra understanding of the points of view of architects and engineers. His familiarity with money matters would endear him to the client, who would feel that his affairs would be in the hands of a practical man who would not be led astray by artistic aspirations and would know how to deal with dubious claims for extras.

As far as I know no engineers have so far claimed the leadership of mixed design teams – except where the job falls into the category of civil engineering. But that engineers must play a prominent part in the creation of total design follows from the fact that all modern and progressive design must make use of technology based on scientific knowledge and method, and this is the province of the engineer.

The situation reminds me a little of a group of children clustered round a box which one of them is trying to open. All want to have a go – 'let me try', 'let me', 'let me'! Grown-ups, if they are active and creative, never lose this urge, it is something elementary in human nature. It can, however, be an impediment to successful collaboration, especially between colleagues – two architects, or two engineers, for instance. It would tempt a consulting engineer to insist on solving a problem his way, rather than asking advice from a more experienced colleague. And it could make collaboration between two architects quite impossible, because art is personal and different points of view can rarely be resolved by hard facts or logic.

But apart from that, any of the suggested arrangements could work successfully, depending on who was involved. But if we want to find the best arrangement we should not make the accidental division into professions, etc., our starting point, we should look at what we want to achieve, and then decide what training the participants should have to fulfil their roles.

Requirements for integrated design

Don't forget we are talking about a design team, and we want them to produce a total, balanced, efficient design which can help to produce a better environment than the one that seems to emerge from our efforts at the moment.

The first condition is that all members of the team subscribe to this aim, that they all want to help to produce good architecture, architecture in depth so to speak – not just artificially imposed formalism or applied make-up – as well as efficient function and economy. Each of these demands imposes its own and quite distinct discipline, this must be understood by all, and this takes time.

The concern of the leader would then be to create the overall balance, to assess priorities, he must be a creative designer or at least a connoisseur of creative design who can fuse the different parts together. The architect would be the natural choice provided he respects the need for technical efficiency, without which his art cannot survive.

But in a closely knit group subscribing to this philosophy – to use, or misuse a now popular word – the leadership tends to be shared by the group, or changes according to the subject being debated.

But it takes time to reach this stage. This is because all the members have to forget part of their training and acquire new understanding and skills. Barriers – which are astoundingly solid and high – must be broken down. The engineers must understand that there are other things between heaven and earth than their rigorous calculations. There are values which cannot be measured. And they must learn to understand the practical craft and technology of building, to organize the production of the job as they are designing it – or the team must include engineers experienced in the methods of contractors, who are able to assess their real cost, helped by the quantity surveyors, whose function is drastically changed and should change much more. What is needed are costs to help in the making of design decisions. Costs are of three kinds:

1) the rates quoted by contractors which are both unnecessarily detailed and a mixture of labour, plant, overheads, profit, etc., and do not apply to new ways of doing things;
2) the contractor's actual costs, which are difficult to obtain;
3) the intrinsic cost of the operation if tackled in a rational manner as intended by the designer, and at reasonable rates for labour and profit – which can to some extent be estimated by planning the operation in detail, with the appropriate plant, labour gangs, etc.

All three are of some interest, but for the designer who is breaking new ground it is the last that measures the fundamental soundness of the proposition. However as long as the usual bill of quantity is retained the quantity surveyor must master its complications. But I must admit that I think a better way would be to let the designers organize the job through the *design*, which would make taking out quantities a simple matter.

For it is a fact that today the artistic, functional and technical unity must be created by the design.

The design records the constructive forethought which must precede any action in a complex situation. Nothing can be left to chance. We cannot rely on creative craftsmanship guided by a universally accepted architectural idiom and a settled way of life; it is the responsibility of the designer or the designers to create harmony out of a chaotic material. *Their control must therefore extend over the whole area of design, from the smallest detail to the position of the whole in relation to adjoining areas.*

Another essential requirement is that the designers should be dedicated to the interest of the clients and society as a whole. They should not have a financial interest in using certain materials, plant or methods, they should be unfettered in their choice. They may use proprietary methods but only if it is the best choice in the given situation.

This was the position when Brunel [1806–1859], Telford [1757–1834], Paxton [1803–1865] and others created their masterpieces. They controlled even the labour to a large extent, they certainly invented the plant and tools to be used in the operations. Forty years ago designers had largely lost this close connection with execution, but they still exercised firm control over what was built. Today the large contractors have a much greater influence on the design, simply because they may be the only people who really know how to build practically and economically. But that leads to a fatal split in the control over design decisions, which will lead to loose, patched-up and uneconomical designs. So either the contractor must take over the whole multi-disciplinary team, which for many reasons is undesirable, or the designers must in their organization embrace the knowledge needed to make practical designs. The latter is by far the easier to achieve, for it is not so difficult for engineers to understand the principles and the practice of economical design.

It follows that the designers should organize the job, in fact should take over this role from the general contractor, and contractors should become specialists in different types of construction or assembly techniques, working more on a professional basis. Building would, according to the nature of the job, be divided into:

1) site works, i.e. excavation, roads, drains, foundations, etc., which would be mechanised and organized to provide continuity of employment of labour and equipment;
2) the main structural carcass, executed by specialists in concrete or structural steel construction;
3) all the 'infilling' – walls, partitions, main ducts or spaces for services, stairs, lift-shafts, etc. – if not included in the main structure. These should be mainly factory-produced, brought finished to the job and inserted in the spaces allotted to them, independent of each other;
4) services and equipment divided into their respective kinds – air-conditioning, electricity, etc.

The important thing is that all these items should not interfere with each other, and this condition can be met if the designers have visualized and drawn up the way the job should be built before the design is frozen. Structural grids, partition grids and service grids should by-pass each other. The critical path studies must be woven into the design, and should follow logically from it. It is too late if they show up deficiencies in the design after the contract is let.

The designers should have adequate information at their disposal about the relevant structural methods and manufacturers' products, and should deal directly with these firms so that they can together develop new methods or new products to suit a particular large-scale job, and place orders early enough for inclusion in the construction programme.

The construction should not begin before the design is sufficiently advanced, and the decision should be the responsibility of the designers. Clients should understand that good design takes time – but will speed up and cheapen construction. If speed is of the essence of the whole undertaking, this must be understood from the beginning. It will affect design decisions and it must be accepted that it will increase costs or reduce quality – although the opposite can happen in certain circumstances. Naturally this puts a great responsibility and extra work on to the design team, which will have to be supported by experts in soil mechanics and foundation methods, costing and communication techniques, computers, analytical research, formulation of contracts and so on, servicing several design teams. The latter must be kept fairly small to retain their intimate character.

These are dreams and idle speculations, and highly controversial as well. If anybody should get upset about them, they can draw comfort from the fact that they will most likely have no effect whatsoever. And in any case, even I do not think that there is only one answer. Think of how many different ways of organizing these things co-exist today. Whether they work well depends more on the people involved than in the methods used.

I am suggesting this line of attack because I am concerned about retaining an artistic control over what we build, and about the need to combine quality and economy in building. My suggestion would enable a closely-knit design team to obtain the experience, the 'feel' for the practical problems of building, and the control, which would enable them to integrate all the relevant facts. If led or advised by good architects – and sociologists as well – there would be a good chance of producing viable masterpieces, and not just white elephants.

What to build

However, so far we are still dealing only with closed designs, where the brief is given. Today the design of single buildings, or even groups of buildings, is less important than the artistic organization of much larger units – which must then deal with transport, location of industry and dozens of other problems as well. Town and country planning, in fact. Our efforts in this direction have not been outstandingly successful. There are plenty of plans, but little action. We put all our best brains in a committee or Royal Commission, or we ask an eminent architect to produce a plan for London or Oxford or replan the area round St. Paul's or Parliament Square, or the British Museum or Piccadilly Circus – and then forget about it. Mainly, I suppose, because we don't know how to pay for it. We rightly do not want to dictate to people, and we cannot get the various bodies concerned to look much beyond their own narrower interests. And also because we don't really know what we want. This is by far the most difficult problem of all.

Engineers have not had to worry much about that, they nearly always work to a well-defined brief. Architects are not so lucky. Their briefs have always been less well-defined and their criteria for excellence the subject of controversy. And the modern movement brought a change in outlook, which made the architects concern themselves with the needs of society, with providing a worthy setting in which people could live, work and play. The right setting would, it was hoped, improve the quality of their life. But the setting must in turn be a reflection of the way people live. This has always been so, and it has happened mostly without the intervention of a conscious design. Can we now reverse the process and shape it by deliberate planning? This seems doubtful. What is happening now can hardly be so called. The economic and technological forces which now shape our environment – are they controlled by man, or man by them?

Technology has a habit of creating its own ends. We do things simply because we are able to do them. We glory in our power. And having created the machinery we must keep it going, and think of more things we can do with it. And, like the sorcerer's apprentice, we can't stop the process.

But if we want to curb the excesses of technology we must play the game according to its rules, for we can't do without it. We must do it with better technology. And in any large-scale planning the barriers must go, human boundaries – even eventually those between countries – must be surmounted.

System engineering

In the USA, this is beginning to be accepted. The whole March 1968 issue of the *Consulting Engineer*, a weighty volume, is devoted to something called 'System Engineering'. Senator Robert F. Kennedy contributed an inspiring article to it. The method is applied to five major problems of our time:

saving our cities;
urban revival;
untangling urban transportation;
water supply;
air pollution.

Its basis is: 'A recognition by society that its major social problems cannot be solved by looking at each problem separately, they are in fact "systems" of interacting problems.'

System engineering has developed from operational research analysis as practised for years by Federal Defence Establishments. It operates with multi-disciplinary teams, it aims at 'providing a scientific basis for management decisions' and of course: 'The systems approach stands squarely upon a quantitative description of the proposed system [...] this quantitative description is reduced to a set of relationships, which frequently are represented by mathematical equations.' These can then be solved by computers.

Of course it operates through the existing private enterprise system. The idea is that 'do goodism' is made to pay by introducing legislation that provides the necessary incentives in the form of tax rebates, equity investment, etc.

So in a way it does solve the whole problem of how to get it done. No sticks, just carrots. Profit for everybody.

A somewhat similar development in England is called 'value engineering'. A journal of that name was launched last April, and also stresses the need for teamwork, and a rational scientific approach to design.

System engineering is an interesting and significant development. To me it is also slightly alarming. There are two things I am worried about: first, the *quantity syndrome* – the idea that everything can be measured multiplied with a unit rate to arrive at a value in dollars. This is the so-called scientific method, and it is invading territories where it simply does not apply. Jacques Barzun* is quite right in claiming that we do not live in a world of [C. P.] Snow's 'two cultures', there is only one – the universal acceptance of science – even in such unlikely places as literary criticism.† I think it was Galileo who first formulated the scientific principles:

1) measure everything which can be measured;
2) make measurable what cannot be measured.

We are taking this too literally. The area of what can be measured is being extended all the time, but it doesn't mean that we can ignore that which can't be measured. It may even prove to be more important.

To me it is surprising that so many people have no difficulty in ignoring the fact that stares us in the face, and which has been stressed by poets, saints and thinkers throughout the ages, that what has most value for man cannot be measured, bought, or obtained by force, but must be given freely. And that whether our man-made environment pleases us or not depends on unmeasurable qualities which can be created only by artistic inspiration and dedication.

The other thing that worries me about system engineering is the complete reliance on the profit-motive. Of course the sponsors and the politicians and others who get the necessary legislation passed are moved by a wish to improve their cities. And I must admit that it is a realistic approach, and I know of no very realistic substitute. But I distrust the dominance of money over man's mind. Think of the lobbying and the bargaining that will precede legislation. What price will society have to pay?

It is interesting that in both cases the role of the engineer is stressed. Engineering has of course always been value engineering for that matter, and system engineering is much the same as what I and others have called 'total architecture'. I think both these developments show the way things are moving, but the difference in wording may be significant. The word 'architecture' somehow suggests a concern about the brief, about what we should build, about function and delight, whereas 'engineering' suggests efficiency in fulfilling the brief. Both are needed, for whatever we build. Civil engineering is of course also architecture in this sense. But the need for efficiency is accepted by everybody – the need for artistic control over what we build is not. Not until there is a public feeling against leaving litter about will we be successful in cleaning up our environment – therefore I prefer the phrase 'total architecture' where it applies.

We all know the fairy tale about somebody who had been granted three wishes and the disastrous consequences of that.

To wish sensibly, to dream the right dreams, is important. We have today the ability to make our wishes come true. But as soon as some of us have reached this point – we step up our wishes. It could be dangerous.

But I am afraid I am getting out of my depth – and I am sure that you are looking forward as much as I am to an end to this ordeal.

But what is the moral of all this? I am afraid that my talk may have confused you more than it has enlightened you. I can offer you no solution to the problems facing mankind, but I think engineers have an important contribution to make, and I think this contribution will be improved if we look beyond the narrow confines of our metier, if we understand that we are part of a team, each contributing his special knowledge to a common aim, which must ultimately be to help to improve the lot of mankind. Only loyalty to this aim can make our contribution meaningful.

---

* Jacques Barzun is a French-born American historian of ideas and culture and a philosopher of education. He was influential in post-World War Two training of schoolteachers in the United States.
† In his 1959 lament on the gulf between scientists and 'literary intellectuals', C. P. Snow argued that the breakdown of communication between the 'two cultures' of modern society – the sciences and the humanities – was a major hindrance to solving the world's problems.

An Engineer Looks at Architecture

This lecture was given at the Leicester University Arts Festival, 11 February 1969.

The title for my talk tonight is: 'An Engineer Looks at Architecture'. The engineer is me, of course, and the only reason for bringing him into the title is to indicate that I am *only* an engineer, and cannot claim to be an expert on architectural theory, so what I say about architecture may not meet with the approval of the pundits. But I have had a great deal of experience in helping architects to design buildings and other structures, and I have tried my hand at the latter myself, and it was always the intention that the result should rank as architecture – preferably good architecture. Unfortunately that doesn't mean that I can give you any satisfactory or generally accepted definition of the term, and I doubt whether anybody else can. I can only give you my own point of view.

A building can be a piece of architecture. But of another building, some might say that it isn't architecture. In other words, buildings are architecture only if they fulfil certain conditions. Which conditions? – General confusion.

Architecture can also mean a discipline, like philosophy, medicine, law, building science, sociology or Art – with a capital A. In fact architecture was once considered the mother of arts, a valid art form like painting, poetry or drama, and many attempts have been made and are still being made to produce a theory of architecture which will enable us to distinguish architecture from mere building, good from bad architecture, and which will be a guide to the *creation* of architecture.

These attempts to distil the volatile essence of architecture from the many tangible proofs of its existence encompass such acknowledged landmarks as Vitruvius's *De Architectura*, and [Christian] Norberg-Schulz's latter day *Intentions in Architecture*, many less systematic but more impassioned pleadings by actual and 'would be' architectural practitioners, and the weekly outpourings of esoteric critics in architectural journals whose claim to fame rests on their being incomprehensible – or so it appears to a mere engineer.

What all these have in common is:

1) That they are all different – if that isn't too Irish.
2) That they deal almost exclusively with aesthetic considerations of order, balance, spaces, forms, light and shade, textures – in short, the visual organisation of the material, and are less concerned with function or economy. and
3) That although they may be a very valuable aid to the understanding of different architectural viewpoints, they are too vague to be a guide to architectural creation. What I mean is, you cannot look up in a book on architecture where to draw the next line on a drawing board – as the engineer can if he has forgotten the formula for analysing the strength of a beam. Books and drawings may enable an architect to produce a building in the Gothic or even Miesian style, – but that is not nowadays considered an acceptable substitute for true and original architecture – whatever that may mean.

No, the architect nowadays is definitely on his own, in an ocean of complete permissiveness and an almost infinite choice of means. It can be a relief, therefore, if his choice is limited by impossible site conditions and a shortage of materials or technical resources.

A corollary, or in any case in keeping with this chaotic state of affairs, is the fact that architecture cannot be said to have progressed from old times till now. Few would argue that modern architecture is a marked improvement on the architecture of earlier epochs, that our great architects are greater than their ancient confrères. Perhaps such a comparison is meaningless. But look at the contrast in engineering. Here there is steady progress in the achievement of engineering aims, and a very much greater agreement about what is good and bad engineering.

What is the reason for this difference?

And how can it be maintained in view of the fact that there is no clear border line between engineering and architectural structures. Whether you call a bridge architecture or engineering is optional – if we attach the normal vague meaning to these words it is both. And that in fact applies to all manmade structures – they are both structures – i.e. engineering structures and pieces of architecture, in different proportions, if you like.

The question arises, can one separate the structural from the architectural part? Can a structure be a bad engineering structure and good architecture or vice versa? That is a very important question, which I will return to later, when I have dealt with my first query.

The reason for the difference between the architectural and engineering 'climate', so to speak, is very complex. It is partly a matter of terminology, partly a matter of historical accident, and the consequent training of architects and engineers, and mostly a matter of what is commonly supposed to be the difference in content – or context – architecture being concerned with producing works of art, engineering with utility structures.

If we continue to use the word structure in its widest sense, in which it can mean a building, a silo, a bridge, dam or road, in fact anything built by man which stays put – for a time at least – so as to avoid 'static hardware' or some such concoction – we have seen that to call some of them architecture and others engineering structures is rather arbitrary.

We demand of all of them that they should

function well
last well
look well
and cost little

but if we survey the whole field of possible structures, the emphasis placed on these four demands differs widely.

They must all fulfil their particular function, for that is the reason for building them. But the functions vary, from those which are easily defined but difficult to fulfil, for instance to build a bridge over a gorge, to others which are easy enough to fulfil if only we could manage to define them – a teaching hospital, involving several authorities and a large number of doctors all with their different and often conflicting demands, and which moreover may very likely become obsolete before it is finished, owing to changing demands, belongs to the latter category.

They must also all last well – that is, they must be stable and able to withstand wear and tear by natural forces or imposed loads. But this may be a simple or a very complicated matter – the latter a characteristic of daring engineering structure.

They should also all look well – they create our manmade environment which is of concern to us all. But again the emphasis varies widely – between, for instance, a retaining wall and a cathedral.

And finally they should all cost as little as possible, but again, the need for economy varies. Economy is a matter of devising a sensible way of building the structure – and even the richest client doesn't want to spend more than necessary.

Roughly speaking engineering structures are those which have an easily defined and undisputed function and which present structural problems of some intricacy, whereas those where aesthetic and functional problems dominate are classed as architecture.

Or we could say that the first are those where a civil engineer is in charge and responsible for the design, whereas the second are designed by architects.

These two ways of classifying structure lead to more or less the same result, and correspond to the difference in training and background of the two professions. At least this was the case before the drastic changes brought about by the modern movement in architecture and the technological advance since then. Engineers built bridges, railways, harbours, dams, tunnels, factories – in fact all the utility structures called into being by the industrial revolution, whereas architects were concerned exclusively with 'fine' buildings, with Building as an art, an art which could trace its origins back to antiquity. Ordinary houses were at that time – and are still to some extent – the province of the builder. Architecture was confined to mansions or important public buildings and these were designed by architects on quite different principles. The architect then had a client who knew – or thought he knew – what we wanted, and a well-established tradition of buildings based on a few materials and supported by craftsmen who knew their job and were proud of it. He could therefore concentrate on creating architectural masterpieces according to the prevailing rules of the game. In fact the highlights of architectural achievement were felt to lie in the past rather than in the future. Engineers looked the other way.

It was in part the great engineering achievements in the last century which triggered off a change in architectural philosophy. The Banhams,* the whole Modern Movement accepted the new structural materials and the technological advance with enthusiasm and dreamt about building a new and better world. It partly misfired, for enthusiasm for the visual manifestations of technology was not enough to effect a radical change in architectural thinking – the Modern Movement in many cases amounted to no more than a new style. But one radical change in outlook took place which changed the way we look at architecture today. Architects acquired a social conscience, they were no longer content to cater for the whims of rich clients, they dreamt of a better world where technology could make everybody share in the good life. The client was therefore society as a whole, and the people actually using the buildings. They felt it as a duty to help in formulating the brief, a task which grew more and more complicated, and which demanded the expertise of architects and engineers. The field of architecture was widened to include housing, schools, hospitals – and gradually all structures which clutter up our environment, for their architectural quality concerns us all.

At the same time engineering technology also invaded the whole field of building and construction. In fact the realisation of architects' dreams depended on engineering knowledge. The whole way of building has changed – it will soon all be engineering.

This demands collaboration of architects and engineers, a topic which has been discussed ad nauseam these last thirty or forty years.

To begin with the civil engineering consultants, the heirs of Telford and Brunel, were reluctant to enter the field of ordinary building – there wasn't much engineering in it, it was fiddly, unremunerative work and they were certainly not prepared to act as mere assistants to architects – they didn't think much of them anyhow.

The architects, on their side, naturally wanted to retain complete control over the design – you have to, when you are producing a masterpiece, you cannot tolerate interference from people who know nothing about the finer points of architectural composition – or for that matter, from those who do. But a new proletariat in the form of structural engineers grew up, somewhat more narrowly based than civil engineers, but with a deeper knowledge of engineering structure, and willing to offer their help under the architect's direction. The normal process of specialisation. And many other kinds of engineers and experts are coming into the picture. Buildings nowadays are full of services and gadgets which account for a greater and greater part of the total cost.

All these changes have brought about a pretty chaotic state of affairs. People, old habits, old ways of thinking, do not change so rapidly. There are powerful personal interests at stake. New ways of building demand larger jobs to be tackled by larger organisations, different financial arrangements, collaboration of different departments not in the habit of speaking to each other, in fact a complete reorganisation of the whole building industry. At the moment every possible combination of new and old methods and attitudes exist side by side.

---

* Reyner Banham (1922–1988) was a prolific architectural critic and writer, best known for his theoretical treatise *Theory and Design in the First Machine Age* (1960).

It would take far too long to sort out this complicated situation tonight – and I am just as lost as anybody else anyhow. But one thing is obvious – what we build is always a whole, an entity – a building, a precinct, a town with roads and all – and all these entities interact and influence each other. If you split the design of these entities amongst a number of specialist designers each acting more or less independently, you won't get an entity, but a hotch-potch. There must be coordination, integration, a proper assessment of priorities based on the true interest of the community.

At the moment we are far from achieving this integration. We are just about drowning in specialisation. It is perhaps the biggest problem we have to face.

It means much more than the much discussed collaboration of the design team. Design decisions are taken by all sorts of authorities, financiers, etc. outside the design team proper. It means for instance that the Ministry of Transport must collaborate with local planning authorities, that city architects must work hand in hand with city engineers and extend other hands to those who frame our bye-laws and building regulations and to government on a local and national level. And it means further that the gap between design and execution which is such an ingrained feature of the building industry must be bridged somehow. For the designer must be familiar with the means of execution and their cost. It is a fallacy to believe that more accountancy and cost planning will in themselves make building more efficient. These obviously have their use but chopping something off a design by lowering standards does not create anything. For that you must go back to the drawing board and make a better design. To get the right materials in the right place is what gets building costs down. Design is creative accountancy.

To use our resources efficiently there are two kinds of question we have to make up our minds about: What to build, and how to build, needs and means, more or less! Of course they are intertwined in various ways, for what we decide to build depends largely on what we can afford to build, and this depends again on the means available or employed. So that those who decide what to build must be advised by those who know how to build. But I think this distinction can help up to throw some light on the role of engineers and architects in building.

How to build will more and more become a matter of engineering, it will at least have to employ engineering methods and will need an attitude of mind mostly found among engineers. That the designers must be thoroughly familiar with the means of construction and their cost has already been mentioned – as I have said so often, designing means indicating a sensible way of building.

The engineer, however, is used to working to a definite brief, what he has to achieve is fairly easily defined – to span a river, to store grain, etc. He is dealing with 'the art of directing the Great Sources of Power in Nature for the use and convenience of man' – but he does not give so much thought to whether it will in fact benefit man. He will see to it that the thing functions well, lasts well and costs little – provided somebody tells him what the function is going to be. And the 'looks well' part is not always his strong suit. He has both feet on the ground, not given to dabbling in airy-fairy aesthetic notions – or so it is generally assumed.

The modern architect, on the other hand, is endeavouring to design an environment for people to live in and work in and enjoy – a very different and very much more complex business – for we humans enjoy so many different things.

'A house is a machine to live in' – Corbusier's dictum, which has loomed large in the public image of modern architects, has perhaps not always been rightly interpreted, as Joe Chamberlin[*] pointed out in his lecture to the RIBA the other day. The machine part is largely the engineer's business – but 'to live in' is not a simple matter. Man lives not by bread alone. Man needs life and company as well as calm and privacy, he needs the sun and air and green plants and birds singing as well as the excitement of the metropolis, he needs work and play and relaxation – he wants to be able to drive his car anywhere – but he doesn't want his peace disturbed by other cars. And his needs tend to grow faster than our means to satisfy them. Man is quite a problem.

Architects have long been grappling with this problem. It cannot be solved by computers or technology – it is a question of sensitivity, of understanding the deeper needs of human nature.

Amongst these experts the architects should play a decisive role, for it is their task to ensure the artistic quality, the character, the visual harmony of our environment.

For me, then, everything we build is architecture – different kinds of architecture, even when the structural problems dominate. An engineering structure is not a good structure if it is not also a pleasant thing to look at. And a piece of architecture is not perfect if the structure is second-rate, if the roof leaks and the heating fails.

---

[*] This is probably a reference to Peter ('Joe') Chamberlin, founding partner of Chamberlin, Powell and Bon, who designed the Barbican Estate in London which was under construction at this time.

Architects, Engineers and Builders

The Alfred Bossom Lecture was delivered to the Royal Society of Arts on Wednesday 11 March 1970. This text has been transcribed from the Journal of the Royal Society of Arts, *vol. 118, June 1970.*

The title of my talk doesn't sound promising. 'What, again!' would be a natural reaction. It was suggested in order to make the title suitable for a Bossom lecture, it being implied that as long as the title was correct, what followed didn't matter. But somehow this way out doesn't appeal to me, so we are stuck with the title, and I had better consider what can usefully be said about this much-laboured theme.

The trouble is that the terms Architect, Engineer and Builder are beset with associations from a bygone age, when building was something very much more primitive than it is now; and they are inadequate to describe or discuss the contemporary scene. The Building and Construction Industry, to which they all belong, is in a state of flux. If I delve into this chaotic conglomeration, I will find myself overwhelmed by its complexity, and can certainly do very little justice to the theme in one lecture.

What then is useful? The word only has a meaning in relation to an aim, and the aim in this case would naturally be to suggest ways in which the building industry, which term I shall use this evening to include the construction industry, could do whatever it has to do more effectively than at present.

To do this one would have to define *what* the building industry should do, *how* this could best be done, and *what* reforms this suggests – indeed a tough proposition.

If you look at the building industry in a global sort of way it embraces all the activities which shape our physical environment. But the environment is the product of our way of life, and it again influences our way of life. In the past the environment, the landscape in all its natural and urban forms just happened, it was never before deliberately created by man, except in small patches. The technological revolution is changing all that. Man's battle with nature has been won. Whether we like it or not, we are now burdened with the administration of the conquered territory. Nature reserves, landscape, townscape: they will all be wantonly destroyed, to the ultimate ruin of man, or they must be deliberately planned to serve his need. Much has been destroyed already and more will be destroyed, but the alarm has sounded. Pollution, population explosion, etc., is news. The battle is on, and it is a crucial battle for mankind. Those who long to return to the good old days must be told firmly that that road is now closed.

Logically, we would now have to define man's needs to enable us to discuss the means to provide them.

This, I am afraid, is beyond the wit of man. How we want to live is a matter of values, and values are under debate. Even if a vague ideal way of life could be agreed on – and it could only be vague – the way to achieve it would be equally debatable. Any hope of defining the task of the building industry on the basis of some such ultimate aim must, I am afraid, be abandoned, at least as far as this lecture is concerned.

The purpose of life is like that of a work of art, it emerges only during the making.

This doesn't mean that we can do nothing. I think we can give a push in the right direction, and if enough join in, it may even have some effect.

We could start from one of the entities or structures produced by the building industry, as for instance a bridge, a water reservoir, a harbour, or a factory, school, town hall or other building, and consider how such an entity is planned, designed and finally built. We know it can be done in many ways, some good, some bad, and some indifferent, measured by the result. If we can find out what is needed to produce a good result, the best possible result, an entity of quality we might say, then what applies to one entity might well apply to most, and might also give us a clue as to how the organization of the building industry could be improved to facilitate the production of such entities of quality. We have to realize, of course, that we don't necessarily get the best total environment, the best town, for instance, by ensuring that each of its constituent parts is a perfect example of its kind. These parts must also be integrated and priorities assessed, to produce the right environment. But it would certainly be an improvement if the parts taken separately were satisfactory. And as the need for proper integration of parts is a feature of all design – whatever sized entity we are dealing with – the experience we gain on a smaller scale may help us to tackle the larger.

To treat such an entity as an independent whole is of course a device to limit the area of attention, it is the only way by which the human mind can deal with the chaotic material presented to it. The danger is, that we forget to switch the mind back to the connections which we have so ruthlessly severed.

Everything in nature hangs together in various ways, and the same applies to the artificial world of human creation. The connection may be a matter of proximity in space, of generations supplanting one another or of different species that feed on one another.

In our building activity we are mainly interested in three such relationships:

1) The relation of part and whole,
2) That of means and ends, and
3) What I might call the spiritual relationship between inanimate objects, usually thought of as aesthetic, though I don't think this word covers it entirely.

This last is a very difficult relationship or quality to define, describe or manipulate – but is of the greatest importance. The words 'art or 'artistic' are vague enough to cover it, perhaps. I will return to it later.

In the total building activity relating to an entity or a job, it is usual and indeed useful to distinguish between two stages, design and execution.

Design can be simply defined as 'constructive forethought'. *Designing* is a mental activity devoted to 'figuring out' and *deciding* how to make or build a thing or an entity, what it should be made of, what it should look like, how it should be made, etc.

A *design* is the sum of all these decisions recorded in the form of drawings, sketches, models, prototypes, instructions, specifications, etc., covering all the facts which must be known and the processes which must be gone through to realize the project.

Defined in this way, the design is obviously the key to what is built. The actual building or execution is equally important, or more important if you like, but it does not add anything to the concept of the thing, if it is carried out as visualized in the design.

What I will call '*the total design*' defines the entity completely.

I use the word 'total design' to distinguish it from what usually goes under the name of design, or is called a sketch, scheme, blue-print or plan – which are generally only partial designs, ranging from a mere recording of a tentative idea to what almost amounts to a total design which only needs to be supplemented by the detailing of certain parts or site arrangements carried out by manufacturers, contractors or specialists. Such definitions are always somewhat arbitrary or blurred at the edges, but the idea of total design implies that sufficient decisions have been made and recorded to enable others skilled in organizing such work to carry it out.

As mentioned, most things are parts of other larger things and consist in turn of many smaller things, and their designs are therefore also organized in a kind of *chain or hierarchy of part and whole*. The designs of part and whole are always interdependent, but in varying degrees. Some entities are fairly self-contained, and are thought of mainly as wholes – for instance a building or water-tower. Others have only meaning as parts – a concrete beam, for instance. But the designer or designers of one thing can't also design all the other wholes or parts in the chain, he must stop somewhere; the stopping is done by giving him a brief. The designer of a bridge need not bother about the larger context, the road-net, etc., if he is given a brief telling him where the bridge is to be built, what traffic it will carry etc. The design is then a *closed* design – upwards. Downwards he must know all *relevant* details – for instance he may have to know the quality of cement – but not necessarily how that quality is obtained in the factory. He must simply know everything which would or could affect his design, including of course the cost of different possible methods of construction.

The *hierarchy of ends and means* sometimes coincides with that of whole and part – for instance the foundation is part of a building and also a means of enabling it to be built on that spot; but generally the path diverges: a crane is a means of building a tower, but not part of it, a building is a part of a village but a means of educating children or manufacturing shoes. Obviously the ends and means relationship affects the design very much, and if this is closed upwards it too, must be defined by the brief, which must specify exactly what the entity is going to be used for.

The chain of means and ends generally, ends up in some spiritual sphere implying value judgements. We build a school for the education of children – for what? Value judgements, whether in the sphere of art, ethics, religion or politics tend to be controversial. Therefore the further we go along the line to search for the ultimate ends, the more difficult it is to reach agreement on what these ends are.

We are faced with the paradox that the pursuit of value of some kind or other is undoubtedly the mainspring of action, and yet if people really went about thinking about the ultimate purpose of all they did nothing would ever get done, there would only be a glorious fight about what ought to be done.

This kind of thing is not unknown in human affairs, but fortunately it is not what people normally do. In most cases they don't think at all – and that is perhaps going a bit far in the other direction. They are quite happy to pursue means without bothering about the end – let alone anything so remote as an ultimate end. In fact means have a habit of becoming ends in themselves. This saves thinking, and encourages action. But, seen in a wider context, it could be the wrong action.

The *artistic relationship* of things may also affect the design – the whole in relation to its surroundings and its parts – but is of course also often controversial.

A *part design* is either a part of a total design or a total design of a part, in relation to a given entity.

In theory the total design includes all its part designs, but in practice the obligation to define all its constituent parts is mostly discharged by making use of already designed and mass produced parts and partly processed materials readily available. We are moving strongly in that direction; it simplifies design, encourages mass-production of standard components, thereby lowering cost, and if coupled with such practices as using standard computer programmes for statistical calculations it can speed up everything – but it also reduces the freedom of the designer and the possibility of matching the parts to the whole – so necessary for artistic excellence. A proper integration may therefore require a needed part like a window or partition to be specially designed by the design team in collaboration with the producers of the article. As manufacturers are often backward in applying rigorous functional or aesthetic criteria to their products, the result can be a great improvement in the design of this part, thus both lowering costs and raising standards. But it can only be done for large repetitive jobs.

Since the start of the Modern Movement architects have toyed with the idea of a standard, prefabricated kit of parts which could be assembled into different types of building: strangely enough, for it would kill what is generally understood by architecture, and anyhow it is, and has always been, nonsense. You can design a system of limited flexibility with a limited number of standard parts, but the parts can then only be used for that system.

We started this inquiry by considering a particular entity, its position in the chain of things, and its design, by which it is defined.

How then is a design of excellence or quality produced?

I described designing as a mental activity. It is set in motion by the challenge of a particular practical problem, that of satisfying a brief with means which are available, or can be made available.

To meet this challenge the designer's mind must be stocked with a great deal of knowledge about available materials, their behaviour under various conditions, their cost, their durability and the manner in which they can be used, about processes and construction techniques and a host of other things which are far too numerous to mention here. He must have the ability to supplement this knowledge and experience with new data relevant to the particular problem – for instance site conditions, local resources, etc. – and if his own resources are insufficient, he must get advice elsewhere. Lack of expert knowledge is not conducive to excellence. He must have a thorough look at the brief, absorb it in his mind, question it and criticize it and have it supplemented if necessary. Having marshalled sufficient data to start with, he sets to work on the problem. His imagination juggles with the data, hauls out for inspection various combinations and possibilities, discards them, tries again – intuition, invention, ingenuity spring into action, tentative solutions emerge, are developed, analysed, adopted as working hypotheses, new relevant data collected, partial decisions made, etc. It is difficult to describe this process in detail, and I think it is quite impossible to replace it with some computerized technique, as has been suggested. The result will depend on three things:

1) The completeness of the data on which the design is based.
2) The quality of the brain in which the design process takes place.
3) The effort, devotion and enthusiasm applied to the problem.

This is not exactly surprising. It means that the *best designs* are produced by good designers with plenty of knowledge and experience and plenty of imagination, ingenuity and inventive capacity, who take the trouble to gather all the relevant information and keep on worrying about the design until they are completely satisfied with the result. And perhaps we should throw in a bit of luck and an interesting problem to solve.

What the designer is trying to do is to produce a structure or building which

1) Functions well,
2) Looks well,
3) Lasts well,
4) Costs little,

but if we survey the whole field of possible structures, the emphasis placed on these four demands differs widely.

All structures must fulfil their particular function, for that is the reason for building them. But the functions vary, from those which are easily defined but difficult to fulfil (such as bridging a gorge), to others which would be easy enough to fulfil if only we could manage to define them (such as those of teaching hospitals, involving several authorities and a large number of doctors all with their different and often conflicting demands which are, moreover, likely to change before the building is finished).

All structures should also look right – they create our man-made environment which is of concern to us all. But the importance of this varies widely – between, for instance, a jetty and a cathedral.

All structures must also last well – that is, they must be stable and able to withstand wear and tear by natural forces or imposed loads. This again may be a simple matter, or in the case of daring engineering structures a very complicated one.

And finally, all structures should cost as little as possible, but again, the need for economy varies. Economics is a matter of devising a sensible way of building the structure. It therefore depends on engineering design and construction – not on costing, which is a means of guessing more or less accurately what the cost will be. Even the richest client doesn't want to spend more than necessary.

Corresponding to this difference in emphasis we are wont to divide structures into two categories, architectural and engineering structures.

Roughly speaking, engineering structures are those which have an easily defined and undisputed function but which present structural problems of some intricacy, whereas architectural structures are those where aesthetic and functional problems dominate.

And of course architectural structures are supposed to be designed by architects and engineering structures by engineers.

This division has done a great deal of harm, because it has diverted attention from the fact that *all structures* must be submitted to the threefold discipline of functions aesthetic and structural or technological organization. But it has its roots deep in history. Architecture, building as a 'fine' art, can trace its origin back to antiquity. It concerned itself with the design of mansions and important public buildings according to varying principles or theories which had more to do with forms, spaces and proportions than with strains and stresses. Engineering structures – bridges, tunnels, harbours, etc. – were classed as utility structures. They were built on quite different principles and did not have anything to do with architecture. Ordinary houses were, and are still to some extent, the province of builders.

The traditional differences persist in the differences in background, training and outlook of the two professions. Fifty years ago they didn't even speak the same language. Each profession lacked understanding of the values the other profession stood for, which naturally led to a neglect of those values in their own designs. The natural tendency of a designer to care for the appearance of what he creates was actually thwarted rather than encouraged in the education of engineers, with predictable results. And the emphasis on the spiritual quality and the preoccupation with architectural theories in architectural schools sometimes made pupils forget about how their beautiful drawings were to be transformed into real buildings.

Even the firms which carried out the work – the split between designers and constructors having occurred centuries before – were divided into builders, working for architects, and engineering contractors, working for engineers.

The Modern Movement changed all that in theory. It was discovered that the work of bygone engineers was in fact architecture. It is now accepted that bridges and factories and all that are architecture. So is housing, in fact everything built is architecture. And the same spirit which is supposed to be moving architects is behind town-planning and landscaping as well as interior design and furnishing. Everything made by man for man's use now has to be designed. And in all these spheres dedicated engineers are trying to conjure forth that mystical spiritual quality which is the essence of art.

The difference between builders and civil engineering contractors is also disappearing. Buildings are just as much constructed as are bridges or radio-masts. If we add to this that technological advance has produced a host of new experts and specialists, and computerized techniques for dealing with all this bewildering detail, it is clear that in large complex jobs we cannot manage with one designer on each job, we need dozens.

This brings us to the very topical subject of teamwork.

I have earlier emphasized the need to integrate all design-decisions relating to a job. The growing specialization makes that very difficult, but it also makes it *more necessary than ever* if we are to produce the perfect job – or let us say a job which is as good as we can make it. I am quite convinced that lack of proper integration of design decisions is largely responsible for the mediocrity of much of what is built to-day. What we build should always be a whole, an entity, and the job of designing it is very much the job of giving it the wholeness of a work of art, and the inevitability of the perfect tool. If you split the design up amongst a number of specialist designers each acting more or less independently, plus various clients and authorities who do not even realize that they are making design decisions which may affect the design adversely, you won't get a whole but a hotch-potch. You don't get quality that way, anyhow.

I come back to what I said before, that the quality of a design depends on three things:

1) The completeness of the relevant data;
2) The quality of the brain of the designer;
3) The effort, devotion and enthusiasm applied, except that now we are not dealing with one brain but with many.

(As I expressed it about thirty years ago: 'The problem arises how to create the organization, the "composite mind", so to speak, which can achieve a well-balanced synthesis from the wealth of available detail. This, I suppose, is one of the central problems of our time.')

'A composite mind which can achieve a well-balanced synthesis from the wealth of available detail' is of course an abstraction, an ideal which cannot be achieved. Even a single mind would rarely achieve a well-balanced synthesis – if such could be defined. The various ideas are emotionally charged. Even the most rational engineering solution is only one out of many possible solutions, and is preferred by its author on the basis of some intuitive feeling which he would find difficult to explain. Designing is not a science, it is an art – but an art confined by the nature of its medium and the aims to be achieved.

The idea of a composite mind is useful, nevertheless. To be effective, the participating minds must collectively span over an area of knowledge and experience which covers all the knowledge needed to produce the best possible design. Each should preferably be an expert in his own field – or at least have easy access to supplement his knowledge if required – and the fields should overlap so as to leave no gaps, and to facilitate communication. But equally, or even more important, they should share a common aim, that of creating 'total architecture'. This is not an aim which can be defined – anything which has to do with art is emotionally charged and therefore *personal*. But there must at least be agreement about one thing: that total architecture is not just a matter of creating a sculptural monument which enhances our visual environment, or a matter of fulfilling certain functional requirements or satisfying the need for 'firmness'. It is all these things together, and moreover they have to be achieved at a cost the client or the community can afford, and must therefore embrace the art of building in a practical sensible way. As I said before, the relative importance of these claims varies, but they cannot be neglected on any job.

I would define architecture as: 'A way of building which delights the heart', because this emphasizes the two essentials, that it is a way of building, and must therefore be judged by the standards of competent building, and that it must touch the heart – it must give us a shock of delight.

But delight is not only aesthetic delight. There is delight in economy of means, in the recognition of inventive simplicity, of directness and clarity of structure, in the appropriateness of the spiritual quality expressed in the combination of forms and spaces. Architecture can transmit to us the human emotions which inspired it – perhaps unconsciously, perhaps even accidentally – it can appear as forceful, bombastic, exuberant or modest, restrained, controlled, it can be serene or exciting, cool or giving warm welcome – or it is just right – why, you cannot say. And this spiritual quality, which can neither be defined nor created according to a formula or recipe, but which can contribute so much to our happiness, this quality is the result of personal involvement, of enthusiasm. And of many other things as well, but enthusiasm must be the impelling force.

It is clear, then, that even agreement on the ideal of Total Architecture leaves plenty of room for disagreement on what kind of architecture and which claims should receive preference, for that they frequently clash is obvious. It is therefore also necessary that the members of the team are on the same wavelength, that they are excited by the same things. If two people come together who recognize that they share the same enthusiasm, then there is great joy, then a bond is created, then they can collaborate and fructify each other's minds.

Perhaps not necessarily, if they are on the same level. I am sorry, but I can hardly begin to make a statement without thinking that the opposite may be equally true. It is not my fault, really, for that's how things are. After all, two sculptors, or two architects, on the same job is really not so hot – or should I say too hot? They have to be very intimately attuned to make a success of it. But there are all sorts of fruitful relationships. If, for instance, one acknowledges the other's pre-eminence, and the relationship is that of master and admiring disciple – and it need not go to that extreme. If there are several members who cover the same field of expertise, it is desirable that there is an acknowledged line of command, but it is equally desirable that it should hardly be noticeable. If each member of the team is encouraged to contribute his share to the total solution and is not just told to shut up and do as he is told, ideas will trigger off other ideas, and there *will* in creative moments come into being a kind of composite mind, superior to the sum of its components.

It is not so difficult for members of different professions to collaborate, because their pride is not affected by having to accept the expertise of another profession. But what is absolutely necessary is that they should respect each other, and each other's point of view. They should recognize that each has a valid contribution to make, that the goal is not yet reached if the solution of one part or one aspect is second rate. Great architecture can be created from a tortuous structure or at inordinate cost, but it would be greater still if structural clarity and ease of construction could be added to its virtues. And who knows that this might not be achieved by further effort? Complete perfection is unattainable, but if we are satisfied too early we are not even attaining what is possible.

To reach this state of understanding between members reared in different establishments where no thought is given to other than their own disciplines, takes time. *Ad hoc* teams, hurriedly thrown together for the duration of one job, are useless for the production of quality, unless the coordination of the work takes place at a higher level between principals who agree on the total aim. They have to get acquainted with each other's territory, to understand at least the principles followed and the aims pursued. They have to approve of these aims, and they must come to like each other, or at least accept with tolerance and humour each other's idiosyncrasies. They must to a large extent be prepared to sink their own personalities in that of the group, forgetting status, position, and personal or professional pride. In a choir a member will enjoy making his or her own contribution, but it is the performance of the ensemble which matters and which all members are proud of – even the one who moves the chairs about. This sharing of enthusiasm and pride in the work of the team is the team is the best seed-bed for nurturing a work of quality.

Of course, enthusiasm is not enough. It must be tempered with realism, with the ability to apply critical analysis. It is an advantage of team work that where enthusiasm is leading one astray, as it easily can do, other members of the team may be able to supply the antidote. For my whole argument rests on the fact that if you want Art in building you cannot afford to neglect mundane, practical matters.

There must of course also be some organization and leadership, so that the whole thing doesn't degenerate into a talking shop.

The fundamental design decisions will nearly always be taken by a small nucleus of people representing the disciplines primarily involved. You have to start with an idea, a tentative proposal and then investigate the implications. The important thing is not to freeze any decision until its consequences for the detailing can be assessed. If new factors emerge – the client changing his mind, for instance – the whole position should be reviewed afresh.

To generalize about the organization of the team is, however, quite impossible and to attempt a survey of the many forms it can take would take too long. It depends on the nature and size of the job, the personalities involved and the whole social setting.

The ideal would be a relatively small closely knit team, working in the same place and having a continuity of work on a few jobs at a time, so that the members could really learn to appreciate each other's qualities, or if necessary shed those members who didn't fit. In such a team the question of leadership need hardly arise, each member taking the lead in his own subject. Even the professional demarcations may fall away – at least in the discussion of the main design decisions. But generally there will be a natural leader, an architect for architectural jobs, an engineer for structural jobs, or a manager type understanding what it is all about and almost representing the client inside the team.

But such a small team has its limitations. Jobs are getting bigger and bigger and more like machines to work in, full of installations of different sorts. Or large engineering jobs may call for scientific research, the invention of construction techniques, extensive computer services etc. Top level men in all these fields cannot give their full time to work on a small team – yet their advice may be crucial to the problem in hand. So unless such a small team, or several such, can be embedded in a very large multi-disciplinary engineering firm with free access to all kinds of advice, it will have some difficulty in obtaining this special help.

Large, technically complicated jobs may therefore require a different organization – the design will have to be organized on different levels and be split up in parts to be designed by well coordinated teams. To paraphrase the well-known tag:

> Large parts have small parts,
> The art is to unite them,
> And small parts have smaller parts,
> And so *ad infinitum*.

But the important thing is the human element in whatever organization adopted, the determination to succeed, the agreement about aims, at least among the leaders of the design team, *and the powers that direct their work*.

This brings me to my last task, for which unfortunately hardly any time is left, to see how these conditions for producing excellence can be realized in the rough and tumble of the real world.

For it is not enough to have the will to produce a work of quality, and the insight and ability to know how to do so, you must also have the power to get it done.

Unfortunately the three are seldom combined.

The power to initiate action rests mainly with a small minority wielding political or financial power. Their main preoccupation is, however, with the maintenance and extension of this power. Improving the quality of our environment is not likely to come high on their list of priorities unless it can be made to serve their primary objective. And with the best will in the world, their power to act depends on their voters or shareholders, and *their* support can only be won by appealing to their pocket. And even where idealists among them are prepared to use their power to the utmost for a good cause, their ability to choose the right advisers and the best cause is questionable.

This is not surprising, for even those who are concerned with building, with planning and design, those who have both the insight and ability, and often the will, do not agree on their objectives. Apart from the fact that they differ in their likes and dislikes, each can only have a limited and varying knowledge of *all* the factors – local, national and worldwide – which have a bearing on, or would be affected by, a planning decision. As regards large-scale planning they must to a large extent be guided by intuition, by a kind of Utopian vision. Where their views carry weight is in relation to a limited objective which they have made a special study of, a design of a neighbourhood, for instance. It is heartbreaking for them and for others who share their values to see their hard-won success in reaching a good solution brushed aside by those in power for reasons which have nothing to do with and completely ignore their own objectives, as happens frequently. The advisers may of course not be wholly disinterested, and the powers may possibly be right, or may have no choice in the matter – but one feels that they so often are wrong because their priorities are wrong, at least seen from the point of view of long-term benefits. But this, I am afraid, does not only apply to those in power – it applies to everybody. The will – or rather the wish – to see our environment improved is fairly widespread in so far as the matter is given any thought at all. But it is not very strong. At least there are a number of other things we want still more. First of all, we must make a living – we have to, otherwise we can't make anything. Just as the Government first of all must try to stay in power – otherwise it can't influence matters for good. Making a living is quite a job in itself, and while you're at it, you had better lay something aside for your old age, and look after your family. And whilst you yourself may be content with only a modest place in the sun, you see no reason why your wife and children should be worse off than your neighbour's. And so on.

And if it isn't money we are after, it is recognition, prestige, status – we want our fellow-beings to love us, if possible, but at least to respect us. And if we are more discerning, we may realize that the applause of the uninformed is worth less than the respect of those who share our values. And that the values themselves are more important even than the respect of others, that what matters is that we can respect ourselves. And we move into the sphere of other motives which generally would be classified as less selfish, but which perhaps are even more selfish, because they satisfy a part of ourselves which we would like to see win. We move into the sphere of ideas, and their motive power, of compassion for suffering humanity, of allegiance to a cause, of identification with a larger unit, town, country – mankind. And we come to the pleasure of exercising our faculties, the satisfaction of the creative urge – which is bound up with the quest for quality. Self-fulfilment, if you like. As Maria Callas said in an interview recently: 'How can you exist if you do not do things, and how can you exist with self-respect if you do not do things as well as lies in you? And how can you achieve that if you do not work at it?'

That, as I have already pointed out, the attitude of those creative people who could make a contribution if allowed to. But occasionally you see this attitude allied to a thirst for fame which can lead astray. That is the trouble with all these motives – they are hardly ever pure, they are mixed with all the other motives, and taken in all, it is the grosser, simpler motives which are strongest. We have to accept this fact and use it. To realize a 'higher' aim, we must attach it to a 'lower' one, and it must at least not go against the business of making money. That is why ambition, a striving for recognition and status, can be so useful for begetting the right kind of action. And that is why if we want quality, at least of a spiritual kind, we must master the economy of construction.

This digression into the tangled complex of motives is not irrelevant to our theme, for it is motives which beget action, and it is action guided by deliberate choice we are seeking. But you will agree that it is hopeless for me to attempt a review of this tangle. I would only say this, that in the discussion of world affairs, attention tends to be focused on measurable things, gross national product and the rest. The importance of 'imponderabilia', of the dreams of mankind, are neglected in the interest of 'realism'. Which is very unrealistic. For it is the power of these dreams which will decide our fate. And it is the unfortunately fragmented fraternity of people with imagination and a perhaps irrational concern for humanity which is our hope for a better world.

The divisions within the building industry do not help matters. All the many economic units, professional firms, builders' manufacturers, etc., of which it consists are in business to make money. Prestige, status, etc., comes next – but also mainly as an aid to profit. Collaboration therefore collides with competition. The same rat-race is repeated inside the firms themselves. The business of designing is split up among a number of autonomous units concerned with safeguarding their interests, and clients and government agencies knowing little about the business of building. The gap between design and execution is almost unbridgeable, preventing the designers from obtaining first-hand knowledge of the cost of various means of construction, an essential requisite for original, inventive design. The prevailing system of quantity surveying only makes matters worse. It erects a barrier between the architect and the builder, thus widening the gap between design and construction. It enables construction to start before the design is completed, a very bad habit leading to confusion, delay and extra expense. It encourages architects in their besetting sin, the delusion that they can create original masterpieces without soiling their hands with such mundane matters as how the pieces are put together. And it lulls the client into the delusion that his affairs are in safe practical hands, wont to deal with money and real estate and such solid realities. Whereas the fact is, that these over-elaborate bills of quantities are a clumsy method of defining the contractor's obligations, which can be better done by drawings and specifications; that costs should not be based on what other contractors have quoted on other occasions for various fictitious items taken out of their context, but on the operations, plant, materials and manpower needed to carry out the job in hand; and that it is too late to find out that the job costs too much after the design is finished, and then proceed to muck around with the design.

As it is the design which, apart from fluctuating factors, determines the cost of the job, costing, which of course is very necessary, must be an integral part of designing, and the quantity surveyor – and that incidentally is a bad name, for the taking out of quantities is in itself a very simple job if it is not unnecessarily complicated to impress the layman – must immerse himself in the prime cost of various site and factory operations, etc., to become a useful member of the design team.

That individual quantity surveyors can be very useful indeed in the present situation is another matter altogether. I have always maintained that character and intelligence are more important than letters after the name.

It is quite impossible for me to deal with all the other factors which inhibit integrated design – private property rights, the fragmentation of public authority, the restrictions too freely imposed in the form of bye-laws and regulations, etc. I will just say a few words about the dichotomies between design and building, and between professional and commercial.

Over a large area of the building industry design is undertaken by professional firms for a fee, and building by commercial firms for that they can get in the market. This difference in remuneration widens the gulf between them and inhibits collaboration, because a free and frank discussion about design and construction methods and costs is bedevilled by the reluctance of the builder to put the cards on the table for fear of the financial implications. In any case both methods of remuneration are highly unsatisfactory – but it is not easy to suggest any better. To award the contract to the lowest tenderer in open competition is a very risky undertaking for the client, as has been shown over and over again. It is the quality and efficiency of the firm that matters to him.

And *vis-à-vis* the professional designer, the architect or consulting engineer, the client is in some respects helpless, he must take him or his firm on trust, as you must your doctor, dentist or solicitor. The choice of consultant is obviously very important for the client, yet is often undertaken very lightly. This method of remuneration does not call for competition in design, which could be stimulating, but is at the same time fraught with danger. In fact, the less the consultant spends on the design, the more money he makes, and the worse the design will be, probably without the client being any the wiser. This is perhaps not quite so serious as may appear, because firms depend for their commissions on their reputation and standing in the profession, which is built up gradually through their performance. But the client, as an outsider, can easily be taken in by experienced client-charmers.

The professional Institutions exist to:

1) protect the public by ensuring that everybody entitled to practise has the necessary qualifications and obeys certain rules of conduct;
2) advance the disciplines and skills on which the profession is based and enhance the reputation and social status of the profession;
3) prevent competition by unscrupulous or undignified means likely to mislead the public, or by unqualified persons, and one could perhaps add:
4) thus fix a scale of fees and conditions of employment from a position of strength.

As you see, this is a mixture of public and private benefits – the only way a thing like that can be made to work at all – and it has on the whole worked well. It encourages professional pride – which is both good and bad. It is good because it embraces pride in your work, the essential quest for quality. But when the pride leads to pomposity and sectarianism it is bad. Specialization is necessary, the practice of 'apartheid' between professions is absurd and harmful.

I should like to see the various Institutions pulling together more to fulfil their role as *guardians of quality*. And it seems to me that the organization of construction or building ought to be a profession, and should gradually be merged with the activity of designing. Then nothing would hinder the free exchange of information. This would in my opinion be a better way than making design a commercial activity and merging it with building, as in the contractor's package deal. The latter gives the public no protection – and the quest for quality, for artistic wholeness, would suffer a serious setback, in competition with soulless efficiency.

After all, the professional man has his standards of excellence, his pride in his work, for which he is usually prepared to make a great effort, even if it does not pay. I expect most professional firms lose on those jobs they are most proud of. A commercial firm's first duty on the other hand is to pay a dividend to its shareholders.

That the public as a whole does not understand that design is a creative activity which determines the quality of the job is shown by the attitude of clients and government departments, of lawyers and administrators. Of course there is a good deal of routine design, which is just a repetition of previous designs, according to given rules. But quality can only be produced by personal effort, and that takes time. That time is seldom available. The difference between a good and a bad design can be tremendous – but the client pays the same for both, and as cash is the only acknowledged yardstick for value, they are assumed to be equally acceptable. A great mistake. The cost of the fee is actually insignificant compared with the cost of the job and the effect of the design on the job. But unfortunately one cannot be sure of getting a better job by paying a higher fee – as might be the case with sculptors or opera-singers. The effort must be given freely from an inner compulsion. But the extra cost involved for the designers may of course be inhibiting. In fact, fee scales are much too low to allow for the effort to produce a masterpiece; it's a luxury one indulges in for one's own pleasure. They are too high for the far too frequently mediocre design: they are too low for small jobs, too high for large. They are too low for service engineers to do their job as they should, which they as a consequence seldom do – they get the contractor to do the detailing. And they are too high for quantity surveyors. But as you can't measure quality or the real value of the service to the client, there is not much you can do about it. All this is of course my personal opinion, and I have said enough already to get my neck wrung.

I have dealt rather perfunctorily with the obstacles to a good design – I have no time to look at the other side of the coin. It would present a picture of great endeavour by many designers to improve the quality of design. The best architectural and engineering design is getting better all the time, and is setting an example which will have a greater effect than mere talk. And powerful corporations and firms who seek to increase their prestige by the way they build are realizing that vulgar display is less convincing than all-round excellence. In the end it will be the general level of understanding of what good building could do for us, which will decide what we get.

The Key Speech

On 9 July 1970 Ove Arup spoke to a meeting at Winchester of his partners from the practices around the world bearing the Arup name. His talk was in response to the collective desire to continue working together, despite the changes that would take place as the founding partners progressively retired and gave up ownership, handing over control to the successors they would choose for these practices. The title of 'Key Speech' for this talk has endured, in recognition of the fact that, in it, Ove both states the aims of the firm and analyses in his very distinctive way the principles through which they may be achieved. The 'Key Speech' is required reading for each person who joins Arup.

In its pre-natal stage, this talk has been honoured with the name of 'key speech'. It is doubtful whether it can live up to this name. What is it supposed to be the key to? The future of the firm? The philosophy? The aims? At the moment, sitting in my garden and waiting for inspiration, I would be more inclined to call it: 'Musings of an old gentleman in a garden' – and leave it at that.

I have written before a piece called 'Aims and Means' for a conference of Senior and Executive Partners in London on 7 July 1969. It did not manage to deal much with means, however, and it is of course difficult to generalize about means, for they must vary with circumstances. The first part of this paper was published in *Newsletter* 37, November '69.* This you may have read – but I will shortly summarize the aims of the firm as I see them.

There are two ways of looking at the work you do to earn a living:

One is the way propounded by the late Henry Ford: Work is a necessary evil, but modern technology will reduce it to a minimum. Your life is your leisure lived in your 'free' time.

The other is:

To make your work interesting and rewarding. You enjoy both your work and your leisure.

We opt uncompromisingly for the second way. There are also two ways of looking at the pursuit of happiness:

One is to go straight for the things you fancy without restraints, that is, without considering anybody else besides yourself.

The other is to recognize that no man is an island, that our lives are inextricably mixed up with those of our fellow human beings, and that there can be no real happiness in isolation. Which leads

---

* *Newsletter* is the name of an internal Arup circulation that is still today sent to all members of Arup staff, summarising recent news from around the firm.

to an attitude which would accord to others the rights claimed for oneself, which would accept certain moral or humanitarian restraints.

We, again, opt for the second way.

These two general principles are not in dispute. I will elaborate them a little further:

The first means that our work should be interesting and rewarding. Only a job done well, as well as we can do it – and as well as it can be done – is that. We must therefore strive for quality in what we do, and never be satisfied with the second-rate. There are many kinds of quality. In our work as structural engineers we had – and have – to satisfy the criteria for a sound, lasting and economical structure. We add to that the claim that it should be pleasing aesthetically, for without that quality it doesn't really give satisfaction to us or to others. And then we come up against the fact that a structure is generally a part of a larger unit, and we are frustrated because to strive for quality in only a part is almost useless if the whole is undistinguished, unless the structure is large enough to make an impact on its own. We are led to seek overall quality, fitness for purpose, as well as satisfying or significant forms and economy of construction. To this must be added harmony with the surroundings and the overall plan. We are then led to the ideal of 'Total Architecture', in collaboration with other likeminded firms or, still better, on our own. This means expanding our field of activity into adjoining fields – architecture, planning, ground engineering, environmental engineering, computer programming, etc. and the planning and organization of the work on site.

It is not the wish to expand, but the quest for quality which has brought us to this position, for we have realized that only intimate integration of the various parts or the various disciplines will produce the desired result.

The term 'Total Architecture' implies that all relevant design decisions have been considered together and have been integrated into a whole by a well-organized team empowered to fix priorities. This is an ideal which can never – or only very rarely – be fully realized in practice, but which is well worth striving for, for artistic wholeness or excellence depends on it, and for our own sake we need the stimulation produced by excellence.

The humanitarian attitude

The other general principle, the humanitarian attitude, leads to the creation of an organization which is human and friendly in spite of being large and efficient. Where every member is treated not only as a link in a chain of command, not only as a wheel in a bureaucratic machine, but as a human being whose happiness is the concern of all, who is treated not only as a means but as an end.

Of course it is always sound business to keep your collaborators happy – just as any farmer must keep his cattle in good health. But there is – or should be – more in it than that. (We know what happens to cattle.) If we want our work to be interesting and rewarding, then we must try to make it so for all our people – and that is obviously much more difficult, not to say impossible. It is again an ideal, unattainable in full, but worth striving for. It leads to the wish to make everybody aware of, and interested in, our aims and to make the environment and working conditions as pleasant as possible within the available means.

This attitude also dictates that we should act honourably in our dealings with our own and other people. We should justify the trust of our clients by giving their interest first priority in the work we do for them. Internally, we should eschew nepotism or discrimination on the basis of nationality, religion, race, colour or sex – basing such discrimination as there must be on ability and character.

Humanitarianism also implies a social conscience, a wish to do socially useful work, and to join hands with others fighting for the same values. Our pursuit of quality should in itself be useful. If we in isolated cases can show how our environment can be improved, this is likely to have a much greater effect than mere propaganda.

There is a third aim besides the search for quality of work and the right human relationships, namely prosperity for all our members. Most people would say that this is our main aim, this is why we are in business. But it would be wrong to look at it as our main aim. We should rather look at it as an essential pre-requisite for even the partial fulfilment of any of our aims. For it is an aim which, if over emphasized, easily gets out of hand and becomes very dangerous for our harmony, unity and very existence.

It costs money to produce quality, especially when we expand into fields where we have no contractual obligations and can expect no pay for our efforts. We may even antagonize people by poaching on their domain or by upsetting and criticizing traditional procedures.

It also costs money to 'coddle' the staff with generosity and welfare, or to lose lucrative commissions by refusing to bribe a minister in a developing country, or to take our duty too seriously if nobody is looking.

Money spent on these 'aims' may be wisely spent in the long term, and may cause the leaders of the firm a certain satisfaction – but if so spent it is not available for immediate distribution among the members, whether partners or staff. So aim No. 3 conflicts to that extent with aims 1 and 2. Moreover, if money is made the main aim – if we are more greedy than is reasonable – it will accentuate the natural conflict about how the profit should be distributed between our members – the partners and staff or the different grades of staff.

The trouble with money is that it is a dividing force, not a uniting force, as is the quest for quality or a humanitarian outlook. If we let it divide us, we are sunk as an organization – at least as a force for good.

So much for our aims. As aims, they are not in dispute. What is debatable, is how vigorously each shall be pursued – which is the most important; how to balance long term against short term aims. Let us first see what these aims imply.

Obviously, to do work of quality, we must have people of quality. We must be experts at what we undertake to do. Again, there are many kinds of quality, and there are many kinds of job to do, so we must have many kinds of people, each of which can do their own job well. And they must be able to work well together. This presupposes that they agree with our aims, and that they are not only technically capable but acceptable to us from a human point of view, so that they fit into our kind of organization; and that they are effectively organized, so that the responsibility of each is clearly defined and accepted. In short, we must be efficient – individually, in all our sub-divisions, and as a world organization.

I have tried to summarize the foregoing in a number of points. Like all classification, it is arbitrary and rough – but may nevertheless be useful as a help to understanding and discussion, if its imperfections and its incompleteness are borne in mind.

The main aims of the firm are:

Group A

1) Quality of work
2) Total architecture
3) Humane organization
4) Straight and honourable dealings
5) Social usefulness
6) Reasonable prosperity of members.

If these aims could be realized to a considerable degree, they should result in:

Group B

7) Satisfied members
8) Satisfied clients
9) Good reputation and influence.

But this will need:

Group C

10) A membership of quality
11) Efficient organization
12) Solvency
13) Unity and enthusiasm.

Of course there is not really any strict demarcation between aims (Group A) and means (Group C) and the results (Group B) flowing from the whole or partial fulfilment of the aims in A. And it is not absolutely certain that these results are obtained. For instance, A3 and 4 (a humane organization and straight dealings) can as well be considered as a means, and in fact all the points are to some extent both aims and means, because they reinforce each other. And there will be members who are dissatisfied no matter how good the firm is, and the same may apply to clients, who may not appreciate quality at all. But on the whole, what I said is true. We should keep the six aims in A in view all the time, and concentrate on the means to bring them about.

But before I do this, I will try to explain why I am going on about aims, ideals and moral principles and all that and don't get down to brass tacks. I do this simply because I think these aims are very important. I can't see the point in having such a large firm with offices all over the world unless there is something which binds us together. If we were just ordinary consulting engineers carrying on business just as business to make a comfortable living, I can't see why each office couldn't carry on, on its own. The idea of somebody in London 'owning' all these businesses and hiring people to bring in the dough doesn't seem very inspiring. Unless we have a 'mission' – although I don't like the word – but something 'higher' to strive for – and I don't particularly like that expression either – but unless we feel that we have a special contribution to make which our very size and diversity and our whole outlook can help to achieve, I for one am not interested. I suppose that you feel the same, and therefore my words to you may seem superfluous; but it is not enough that *you* feel it, everybody in the firm should as far as possible be made to feel it, and to believe that we, the leaders of the firm, really believe in it and mean to work for it and not just use it as a flag to put out on Sundays. And they won't believe that unless we do.

On the other hand, who am I to tell you and the firm what you should think and feel in the future when I am gone – or before that, for that matter. It wouldn't be any good my trying to lay down the law, and I haven't the slightest inclination to do so. That is my difficulty. I dislike hard principles, ideologies and the like. They can do more harm than good, they can lead to wholesale murder, as we have seen. And yet we cannot live life entirely without principles. But they have in some way to be flexible, to be adaptable to changing circumstances. 'Thou shalt not lie', 'Thou shalt not kill', are all very well, generally, but do not apply if for instance you are tortured by fanatical Nazis or Communists to reveal the whereabouts of their innocent victims. Then it is your duty to mislead. What these commandments should define is an attitude. To be truthful always, wherever it does no harm to other ideals more important in the context, to respect the sanctity of human life and not to destroy life wantonly. But where to draw the line in border cases depends on who you are, what life has taught you, how strong you are.

In the following 13 points, which I must have jotted down some time ago – I found them in an old file – I am grappling with this question, perhaps not very successfully. I give them to you now:

Principles

1) Some people have moral principles.
2) The essence of moral principles is that they should be 'lived'.
3) But only saints and fanatics do follow moral principles always.
4) Which is fortunate.
5) Are then moral principles no good?
6) It appears we can't do without them.
7) It also appears we can't live up to them.
8) So what?
9) A practical solution is what I call the *star system*.
10) The star – or ideal – indicates the course. Obstacles in the way are *circumnavigated but one gets back on the course* after the deviation.
11) The system is adopted by the Catholic church. Sins can be forgiven if repented – it doesn't affect the definition of good or evil.
12) That this system can degenerate into permanent deviation is obvious.
13) One needs a sense of proportion.

Incidentally, they should not be taken as an encouragement to join the Catholic church!

I found also another tag:

'The way out is not the way round but the way through.' That's rather more uncompromising, more heroic. It springs from a different temperament. It's equally useful in the right place. But the man that bangs his head against a wall may learn a thing or two from the reed than bends in the wind.

The trouble with the last maxim is that it says something about the way, but not about the goal. The way must be adapted to the circumstances – the goal is much more dependent on what sort of person you are. I admit that the last maxim also says a good deal about the man who propounds it, a man of courage, of action, perhaps not given too much to reflection, perhaps not a very wise man. The wise man will consider whether this way is possible, whether it leads to the desired result. Unless of course his goal is to go through, not to arrive anywhere, like the man in the sports car. But this only shows that it is the goal which is important, whatever it is.

The *star system* is an attempt to soften the rigidity of moral principles. But it doesn't really solve this dilemma. It is a little more flexible than moral precepts as to the way, but surely the 'stars' must be fixed – for if they can be changed *ad lib* the whole thing wobbles. And that in a way is what it does – I can't do anything about that. I should have loved to present you with a strictly logical build-up, deducing the aims for the firm from unassailable first principles. Or perhaps this is an exaggeration – for I know very well that this can't be done. All I can do is to try to make the members of the firm like the aims I have mentioned. I would like to persuade them that they are good and reasonable and not too impossible aims, possessing an inner cohesion, reinforcing each other by being not only aims but means to each other's fulfilment.

'Stars' like goodness, beauty, justice have been powerful forces in the history of mankind – but they so often are obscured by a mental fog – or perhaps I should say the opposite – they are created by a mental fog, and when the fog lifts, they are seen to have been illusions. They are man-made. I do not rate them less for that reason – but they are too remote, too indefinable, to be of much practical use as guide-lines. They sustain or are born of the longings of mankind, and belong to the ideal world of Plato – which is fixed for ever. Rigid ideologies feed on them. Not so practical politics.

Our aims on the other hand are not nearly so remote. We will never succeed in fulfilling them *in toto*, but they can be fulfilled more or less, and the more the better. And they are not grasped arbitrarily out of the sky or wilfully imposed, they are natural and obvious and will, I am sure, be recognized as desirable by all of you: so much so, in fact, that the thing to be explained is not why they are desirable, but why I should waste any words on them.

I do, as I pointed out at the beginning of this argument, because our aims are the only thing which holds us together, and because it is not enough to approve them, we must work for them – and the leaders must be prepared to make sacrifices for them. Temporary diversions there must be, we have to make do with the second best if the best is not within reach, we have to accept expediencies – and from a strict point of view all our activities can be considered as expediencies, for in theory they could all be better still – but the important thing is that we always get back on the course, that we never lose sight of the aims. Hence the name 'star system' derived from comparison with old-fashioned navigation. But I propose to abandon this expression, partly because its meaning in the film industry may confuse, especially as it is very opposed to our point of view, which is in favour of teamwork rather than stardom: and also because it suggests 'star-gazing', which I find uncomfortably near the bone because I might with some justification be accused of it. So I am afraid we have to fall back on 'philosophy'. Having dabbled in this subject in my youth I have been averse to seeing the term degraded by talk about the philosophy of pile-driving or hair-dressing, but it is of course useless to fight against the tide. The word has come to stay – and in 'the philosophy of the firm', it is not used quite so badly. So that's what I have been giving you a dose of.

I will now discuss what we have to do in order to live up to our philosophy. And I will do it under the four headings 10 to 13 in my list of aims and means:

10) Quality staff
11) Efficiency
12) Solvency
13) Unity and enthusiasm

but it will of course be necessary to mix them up to some extent.

Quality of staff

How do we ensure that our staff is of the right quality, or the best possible quality?

We all realize, of course, that there is a key question. The whole success of our venture depends on our staff. But what can we do about it? We have the staff we have – we must make do with them, of course (and I think we have a larger proportion of really good people than any other firm of our kind). And when we take on new people – the choice is limited. Again we have to take the best we can get. We cannot pay them a much higher salary than our average scale, because that would upset our solvency and sink the boat. Naturally our method of selection is important, and what we can do to educate our staff and give them opportunities to develop is important, but I can't go into details here. All I can say is that staff getting and staff 'treating' must not degenerate into a bureaucratic routine matter, but must be on a personal level. When we come across a really good man, [we] grab him, even if we have no immediate use for him, and then see to it that he stays with us.

The last is the really important point, which in the long run will be decisive. Why should a really good man, a man – or woman – who can get a job anywhere or who could possibly start out on his own, why should he or she choose to stay with us? If there is a convincing and positive answer to that, then we are on the right way.

Presumably a good man comes to us in the first instance because he likes the work we do, and shares or is converted to our philosophy. If he doesn't, he is not much good to us anyhow. He is not mainly attracted by the salary we can offer, although that is of course an important point – but by the opportunity to do interesting and rewarding work, where he can use his creative ability, be fully extended, can grow and be given responsibility. If he finds after a while that he is frustrated by red tape or by having someone breathing down his neck, someone for whom he has scant respect, if he has little influence on decisions which affect his work and which he may not agree with, then he will pack up and go. And so he should. It is up to us, therefore, to create an organization which will allow gifted individuals to unfold. This is not easy, because there appears to be a fundamental contradiction between organization and freedom. Strong-willed individuals may not take easily to directions from above. But our work is teamwork and teamwork – except possibly in very small teams – needs to be organized, otherwise we have chaos. And the greater the unit, the more it needs to be organized. Most strong men, if they are also wise, will accept that. Somebody must have authority to take decisions, the responsibility of each member must be clearly defined, understood and accepted by all. The authority should also be spread downwards as far as possible, and the whole pattern should be flexible and open to revision.

We know all this, and we have such an organization: we have both macro, micro and infra-structure. It has been developed, been improved, and it could undoubtedly be improved still further. We are of course trying to do that all the time. The organization will naturally be related to some sort of hierarchy, which should as far as possible be based on function, and there must be some way of fixing remuneration, for to share the available profit equally between all from senior partner to office-boy would not be reasonable, nor would it work. And all this is very tricky, as you know, because, as soon as money and status come into the picture, greed and envy and intrigue are not far behind. One difficulty is particularly knotty, the question of ownership, which is connected with 'partnership'. There is dissatisfaction amongst some of those who in fact carry out the functions of a partner – dealing with clients, taking decisions binding on the firm, etc. – because they cannot legally call themselves partners but are 'executive' partners – or have some other title. I have discussed this problem in my paper 'Aims and Means'. If some viable way could be found to make 100 partners, I wouldn't mind, but I can't think of any.

In the Ove Arup Partnership we have all but eliminated ownership – the senior partners only act as owners during their tenure of office – because someone has to, according to the laws of the country. And I wish that system could be extended to all our partnerships. It no doubt irks some people that the money invested in the firm may one day (with some contriving) fall into the turban of people who have done nothing to earn it – but what can we do? The money is needed for the stability of the firm, it makes it possible for us to earn our living and to work for a good cause, so why worry?

It may be possible to devise a different and better arrangement than the one we have now, more 'democratic', more fair: it may be possible to build in some defences against the leaders misbehaving and developing boss-complexes and pomposity – and forgetting that they are just as much servants in a good cause as everybody else – only more so. This is partly a legal question depending on the laws of the country. But I have neither the ability nor the time to deal with all that here. What I want to stress is the obvious fact that no matter how wonderful an organization we can devise, its success depends on the people working in it – and for it. And *if* all our members really and sincerely believed in the aims which I have enumerated, if they felt some enthusiasm for them, the battle would be nearly won. For they imply a humanitarian attitude, respect and consideration for persons, fair dealings, and the rest, which all tend to smooth human relationships. And anyone having the same attitude who comes into an atmosphere like that, is at least more likely to feel at home in it. And if the right kind of people feel at home with us, they will bring in other people of their kind, and this again will attract a good type of client and this will make our work more interesting and rewarding and we will turn out better work, our reputation and influence will grow, and the enthusiasm of our members will grow – it is this enthusiasm which must start the process in the first place.

And they all lived happily ever after?

Yes, it sounds like a fairy tale, and perhaps it is. But there *is* something in it. It is a kind of vicious circle – except that it isn't vicious, but benevolent, a lucky circle. And I believe that we have made a beginning in getting onto this lucky circle. I believe that our fantastic growth has something to do with our philosophy. And I believe our philosophy is forward-looking, that it is what is needed today, is in tune with the new spirit stirring in our time. But of course there are many other and dangerous spirits about and too much growth may awaken them. Too much growth may also mean too little fruit.

My advice would be:

'Stadig over de klipper', or if you prefer:
Take it easy!
More haste less speed!
Hâtez-vous lentement!
Eile mit Weile!
Hastvaerk er lastvaerk!

It's the fruit that matters. I have a lingering doubt about trying to gain a foothold in various exotic places. Might we not say instead: Thank God that we have not been invited to do a job in Timbuctoo – think of all the trouble we are avoiding. It's different with the work we do in Saudi Arabia, Tehran and Kuwait. There we are invited in at the top, working with good architects, doing exciting work. We are not hammering at the door from outside. But as a rule, grab and run jobs are not so useful for our purpose. I think the Overseas Department agrees with this in principle, if not in practice.

It's also different with civil engineering work, provided we have control – complete control – over the design and are not 'sharing' the job or having a quantity surveyor or 'agent', etc., imposed on it preventing us from doing the job our way. The general rule should be: if we can do a job we will be proud of afterwards, well and good – but we will do it our way. In the long run this attitude pays, as it has already done in the case of Arup Associates. And incidentally, the control of such jobs should be where our expertise resides.

To export Arup Associates' jobs is much more difficult, for whilst we may be able to build a bridge or radio tower in a foreign locality, good architecture presupposes a much more intimate knowledge of the country. Long distance architecture generally fails. But that does not mean that the ideal of Total Architecture is irrelevant to our purely engineering partnerships or divisions. In fact they have been founded on the idea of integrating structure with architecture *and* construction, and in Scotland for instance they are trying to give architects a service which will unite these domains.

Coming back to my main theme, I realize that when I have been talking about quality, about interesting and rewarding work, about Total Architecture, and attracting people of calibre, you may accuse me of leaving reality behind. 'As you said yourself', you may say, 'our work is teamwork. And most of this work is pretty dull. It is designing endless reinforced concrete floors, taking down tedious letters about the missing bolts, changing some details for the nth time, attending site meetings dealing with trivialities, taking messages, making tea – what is exciting about that? You are discriminating in favour of an elite, it's undemocratic. What about the people who have to do the dull work?'

Equality of opportunity

You have certainly a point there. Of course I am discriminating in favour of quality, and I would do anything to enable our bright people to use their talents. You cannot equate excellence with mediocrity, you cannot pretend they are the same. We would be sunk if we did that. We need to produce works of quality, and we need those who can produce them. One perfect job is more important for the morale of the firm, for our reputation for producing enthusiasm, than 10 ordinary jobs, and enthusiasm is like the fire that keeps the steam-engine going. Likewise one outstanding man is worth 10 men who are only half good. This is a fact of life we cannot change. It is no good pretending that all are equal – they aren't. There should be equality before the law, and as far as possible equality of opportunity, of course. But the fact that you are good at something is something you should be grateful for, not something to be conceited about. It doesn't mean that you are better as a human being. And there are probably many other things you are hopeless at.

No man should be despised or feel ashamed because of the work he does, as long as he does it as well as he can. What we should aim at, naturally, is to put each man on to the work he *can* do. And, fortunately, there is nearly always something he can do well. We will have square pegs in round holes, we shall have frustrated people, unfortunately – those who are not frustrated one way or another are in the minority. But fortunately people vary, as jobs vary, and few would want to do the job another calls interesting if they are no good at it.

If we can reach a stage where each man or woman is respected for the job they do, and is doing his or her best because the atmosphere is right, because they are proud of what we are and do, and share in the general enthusiasm, then we are home. And each job is important. Secretaries, for instance. They could have a tremendously civilizing influence on our staff. They could teach them to write English, for instance, a most important and necessary job. But secretaries who can do that are of course at a premium. We must try to find them. It is even more important than that they are good-looking – and nobody could accuse me of being indifferent to that.

Our messengers and cleaners – how important it is that they are reliable and likeable, human, with a sense of humour. A cheerful remark can brighten the day. All our people are part of us, part of our 'image', create the atmosphere we live in.

But it doesn't alter the fact that the services of a messenger are less valuable to the firm than those of a gifted designer or an imaginative mechanical engineer, a fact that even the messenger will understand.

But there are of course people we cannot employ usefully. Masses of them, in fact.

Those we should not take on, obviously, except on a strictly temporary basis. But sometimes they are found inside the firm. They may have been good once, but are on the way down. I am a case in point myself. But their loyal service, their place in the hierarchy, makes it difficult to de-grade them. To deal with them requires much tact, and is embarrassing. But they should not be allowed to pretend to do jobs they are no good at. They must not prevent the good ones from functioning.

It's a problem all firms have, it's one of the cases where humanity and efficiency clash. To resolve it tactfully may be expensive, not to resolve it is fatal.

So far I haven't said much about solvency. Stuart Irons can tell you something about that.* I compare it to stability in engineering structures – without it the whole thing collapses but if you have much more money than you need the usefulness of it declines until it becomes distracting and dangerous. That danger need not worry us for the time being.

At the moment the need for solvency is restricting, and is the most frequent cause of having to compromise. That we may have to do – but let's not do it unnecessarily, and let's get back on course.

And Unity and Enthusiasm, the last item, is in a way what my talk has been about. It is a question of giving the firm an identity. What do we mean, when we speak about the firm, about 'we' or 'us'? Is it the whole collection of people in dozens of offices in different places? Are 'we' all of them or some of them, and which?

I think it is unavoidable that 'we' should mean different things in different contexts. Sometimes what is said is only relevant to the upper layers of management, sometimes it is meant to include everybody. What we must aim at is to make 'we' include as many as possible as often as possible. To increase the number of those who have a contribution to make, however small, who agree wholeheartedly with our aims and want to throw in their lot with us. We might think about them as members of our community; the others, who come and go, might be called staff. Of course there can never be any clear line of demarcation – it is not a question of signing a form or bestowing a title – it is a matter of how each feels and what we feel about them. For it is a two-way business.

But what binds our membership together must be loyalty to our aims. And only as long as the leaders of the firm are loyal to these can they expect and demand loyalty from the members. This speech is too long already, and I have not even touched on what you perhaps expected to be the main subject of my talk, the relationship between the Ove Arup Partnership and the Overseas Partnerships. But from the foregoing my point of view should be clear.

The fact that we have these outposts all over the world is of course an enormous source of strength to us and to you, it helps to establish our reputation and power for good, and opens up opportunities for all our members. This is however only because the leaders in these places are our own people, bound to us by common aims and friendships. But as the old leaders retire and growth takes place mainly locally, the ties that bind us together may weaken. We should prevent this by forging more ties, forming new friendships, and always being true to our principles. Improve communications – the universal injunction nowadays. Absence does not make the heart grow fonder, unfortunately. There will always be a need for a strong coordinating body – which is at the moment formed by the senior partners – which has the power to interfere if our principles are seriously betrayed. For should that happen, it would be better to cut off the offending limb, lest the poison should spread. Our name must not be allowed to cover practices which conflict with our philosophy. But at the moment there is no danger of that, and we can take comfort from what has been achieved. Perhaps that should have been the gist of my talk? But you are seeing it for yourself. I could also have dwelt on how far we have still to go; it would perhaps have accorded more with my star-gazing habits. But my time is up – my speech should have been condensed to one-third – but it is too late now. I hope at any rate that I haven't deserved the warning which the Duke of Albany addressed to Goneril in *King Lear*:

How far your eyes may pierce I cannot tell.
Striving to better, oft we mar what's well.

---

* Stuart Irons was the first Financial Director of Arup.

The Architect's Human Role

This paper was prepared for the conference of the Board of Education on 2 October 1970, which was a follow-up to the Board of Education's Cambridge Conference, 2–4 April 1970. Ove was unable to deliver it in person, but it was made available to conference members in advance and appeared in the RIBA Journal *for November 1970.*

My first simple proposition is that the aim of architectural education is to turn out good architects. This is naïve, I know, but it is not really so simple as it sounds, if we consider our doubts about the meaning and future role of 'the architect'. But what the statement says is that the education we are talking about is not for education's sake but is a training or preparation for playing a part in the business of building (in the widest possible sense). This will be hotly contested.

I do not deny that the study of architectural theory, the history of architecture and all that, may be useful academic subjects, as long as practitioners are not required to take any notice of them. It would probably do no harm if civil servants and secretaries studied architecture instead of history and English literature. I also admit that we need many kinds of architectural and planning research, just as we need engineering research, to use the old labels. But I suggest that it will both simplify and clarify matters if we push these very interesting subjects aside for the time being and concentrate instead on the needs of those students who intend to take an active part in the shaping of our new environment.

Presumably, man will continue to build, and the great majority of the many people who will take part in this activity will have to be trained for their roles. This training is not first and foremost an academic but a vocational training. What you call it does not really matter, of course, and the two kinds, if they could be defined, would no doubt overlap. But the usefulness of the training must be judged by whether it fits the student for the job he will have to do or – since this is only vaguely known – whether it fits him to do a useful job in the sphere of building. This leaves the question of what is useful entirely open. But I submit that academic respectability is of no use. In fact I am appalled at this preoccupation with status, which seems to reveal an inferiority complex produced, perhaps, by uncertainty about the future. Or perhaps it is part of the scientific mumbo jumbo, the mania for research and computers, which threatens our civilisation.

The conflict between professors and practitioners should therefore be resolved by letting architectural schools inside or outside universities be responsible for training practitioners and then deciding on the criteria for university courses which deal with architectural theory and related subjects deemed to be suitable as general education to rank with (say) history or classical languages. The two kinds of requirement may overlap but are not the same. I admit that I am not competent to pronounce on architectural theory, which to me often appears as a collection of unverifiable statements of obscure meaning. But architecture, if it means anything, and indeed all design, is an art rather than a science. It seeks solutions to specific practical problems with the aid of scientific knowledge and research, but is not itself a scientific discipline, and none the worse for that.

If this is agreed, we are left with the question of what role the architect can, should, or is going to play in the near or foreseeable future. Because this question cannot be answered with any certainty in a situation where the architect's role is rapidly changing under pressure of technological advance and social revolution, it opens the floodgates for a discussion about multidisciplinary education, extending the meaning of the word 'architect', new directions and so on. So we are almost back to where we started. But I hope at least we have got rid of academic respectability.

I can no more predict the future than can anybody else, but I can recognise a trend. I can see or feel which way the stream is flowing, and the force and volume of the flow is such that it could hardly change direction very rapidly. This gives me a basis for saying something about the immediate future, at least, for recognising the problems which are facing the 'progressive' part of the building industry now and will affect a greater part of it later. I can do this simply by seeing what is happening inside my own firm.

This year alone we have been entrusted with four jobs, each running into tens of millions of pounds and each embracing a large number of structures of very different kinds which normally would be designed by many different firms. That is, they are 'comprehensive' multidisciplinary jobs which require the collaboration of planners, traffic engineers, road and bridge engineers, harbour and dock engineers, architects, heating and ventilating engineers, electrical engineers, soil and foundation experts, a chemist, financial advisers, manufacturers and others in various combinations. In other cases, we are handling a single aspect of such comprehensive jobs.

Universal trend

Our experience is, of course, shared by others and is not confined to this country. It does indeed represent a universal trend which has been gathering momentum slowly, and it is a logical consequence of technological evolution. In housing, and office and school building, the trend is toward industrial production of repetitive units, leaving the orthodox architect at the mercy of forces he cannot control, because design control has to be extended into the factories. This has caused the interminable and very necessary discussion about multidisciplinary collaboration which has been going on for years. But, actually, all jobs have been 'multidisciplinary' as long as different disciplines have existed. It is the size and complexity of the jobs and the changing nature of the required hardware which poses the problems.

To try to discover the new role of the architect by sending out forms to different architects asking them how they spend their time seems to me utterly futile. It must be the scientific 'bug' about research, collecting data and processing them with a computer, which is at work. We know the trend all right: it is about the only thing we do know. We know that there are a number of new and changing roles to play, but the question is, who should play them, how should the players be educated, and which of them could suitably be called architects? It is not a matter of finding out and passively accepting where we are going, for we are trying to understand the development in order to influence it. That is very difficult, especially as we hardly know where we want to go to, but unless that is what we are trying to do, I don't know what we are talking about.

Now the proof of every pudding is in the eating, and the eating will not be pleasant unless all the ingredients are of the right quality and they are combined in the right way and in the right proportions. I know from experience that this very much applies to building of any kind. This combination or integration is controlled by the design. And because the design is normally split into parts which are farmed out to different professional or commercial firms, each with its own axe to grind, the result is patchwork. This is the most frequent cause of relative failure; the different professions have never learned to look at the design as a whole.

Each tends to exaggerate the importance of his contribution, often without any understanding of, or respect for, what the others are trying to do. This is one thing which we should try to put right by better education. The interdependence of the various part-designs should be thoroughly understood by everybody who contributes to the total design. Each designer should be good at his own subject, for a failure of any part can spoil the whole thing, but the excellence which should be pursued by all is the excellence of the whole. This is nearly always a result of compromise, for you can't have everything, as the various desirable design objects often conflict. The judicious allocation of priorities is the job of the leadership, which is again intimately mixed up with 'clientship', for it is for the client to decide – if he could be defined, that is – what, for example, he is prepared to spend on capital cost in order to reduce maintenance costs.

In other words, no design decisions which affect the total design should be taken in isolation, but there should be an informed leadership whose role it is to co-ordinate these design decisions to produce the best possible total design. To do this successfully, the leadership must be given power to make these decisions. Now where does the architect fit into this?

If you examine all the physical parts of a modern comprehensive job, they are more and more the products of industry – all science and engineering, in fact. Many people conclude from this that there is no need for architects or architecture: just string the various science controlled detail designs together on the basis of a valuation in dollars of design objectives, and use computerised techniques to find the optimum solution. This is called value (or system) engineering. But such a process confuses means with ends, a mistake that is constantly made. These techniques are useful means, but they cannot yet tell us how we want to live, and I hope they never will.

Right material

Architects, worried about their role in the future, seem to clutch at two solutions. They either proclaim their natural right to the leadership of the design team, a position they have held and still hold in all those jobs traditionally classified as architecture, or they strive to transform architecture into a science, to give it the respectability of a scientific discipline by widening the curriculum to include research which uses status augmenting, computerised data processing techniques. Or perhaps they want to do both, and hope that the latter method will reinforce the claim to leadership. It may be asked, are these stratagems really necessary?

You can't educate a whole profession to become leaders. You can't educate for leadership at all unless you start with the right material. Even now, the majority of architects are not leaders but assistants. The same applies to engineers, of course. Besides, I am not referring only to the jobs traditionally classified as architectural, but to all kinds of jobs, and especially the comprehensive ones which embrace a whole environment, some of them predominantly of a civil engineering nature. Who should be leaders of the design team for such jobs, what should be the structure of leadership, the line of command and so on are questions I can't deal with here. But there is no point in any one profession automatically claiming the leadership. It will require very special qualities to fill such a position satisfactorily.

Human needs

The architect, like every other member, will be certain of his position in the design team only if he has something to contribute to the design which he can do better than the others. And it is incredible that there could be any doubt about the value of the contribution he can make. I see his job as essentially the spatial organisation of things to serve human needs and aspirations. That means that he must be an expert on space, on human needs, and on their relationships. To be an expert on space – what does that mean? It would be useful if he knew a great deal about the mathematical disciplines of solid and analytical geometry, of course, but to be a good mathematician is certainly not enough. What is needed is spatial imagination, an ability to think, sketch, and communicate in three dimensions, to juggle mentally with things in space, imposing an order which will satisfy a number of partly conflicting desiderata which range from well defined physical functions to the complicated human reactions to space, form, light, and texture. The possible solutions are many, and to find a really good one may be difficult, but when it is found, it makes all the difference.

It is really silly of me to try to explain to architects what the architect can contribute. But I know this, that if a factory manager tries to be his own architect for the extensions to his factory, perhaps with the aid of a contractor or engineer, the result is generally deplorable from every point of view. A good architect can transform the situation drastically. I mean, of course, the architect as designer, for I am dealing with his contribution to the design team, and this sensitivity toward forms and spaces is needed in practically all jobs affecting our manmade environment. It may be nothing more than solving a jigsaw puzzle. It is that, but more than that. For the order to be imposed is not given, it has to be created, and it is governed by artistic sensitivity as well as by an understanding of the fickleness of human nature.

We are really talking about whether there is such a thing as Architecture. 'Art' and 'architecture' are almost becoming dirty words in some advanced circles. And it is true that they are often a cloak for amateurism, lack of expertise, failure to make use of the scientific means at our disposal. They may even be a cover for personal pride and arrogance. But if we leave all to technology, which we could do, human nature will rebel in the end. We must retain the ability to decide how we want to live. We must meet the challenge of writing the brief ourselves: otherwise it is the writing on the wall.

Technocratic nightmare

Even if 'art' is out, even if we all resort to living in intercommunicating capsules slung from a mile-high structure or in some other technocratic nightmare, there will presumably be some capsules which are better than others, some sort of 'preferred dwellability', to quote Buckminster Fuller. The possible solutions will still be endless. To find the best one will still be the problem. To build wisely, with sensitivity toward human needs and joys, with an ear to the ground and a hopeful eye for the future, is what architecture is all about.

Thus defined, of course, everything is architecture. And so it is, and everything is also structure, and involves planning, and probably services of different kinds. Spatial imagination and sensitivity are not the prerogative of architects. The structural and civil engineer needs them too but is generally not so good at them, for two reasons: because he has never been taught anything about their importance, and because those who are gifted in this direction generally study architecture. Conversely, some architects have more sense of structure or basic structural layout than some engineers and may be more sensible about heating or planning too. As the individual members acquire more experience about the practice of building and learn from their co-designer, the total pattern becomes clearer to them, which is as it should be. But as I have pointed out, everybody engaged in building design should already at college have been given an understanding of the total picture, of the principles which govern the design of allied disciplines and their importance for the whole, which will help him to place his own contribution in the right perspective. The principle of strict trade demarcation would be fatal for building design – we need the opposite – but it is to be hoped and expected that those who have chosen to specialise in a particular subject are better at it than the others. This isn't always true.

That every artefact is architecture is true in the sense that everything is arranged in space and takes on a certain form, and the possible arrangements and forms can be judged from a functional and an aesthetic point of view. But often the word 'architecture' is reserved for the latter aspect. This is unfortunate, for it is a constant source of misunderstanding, strengthened by critics and the architectural press, because the appearance of a structure can be taken in at a glance. This is what makes the architect's reputation, and when the practical philistine discovers that this reputation can be achieved and, as he at once concludes, is generally achieved at great extra cost and a disregard for function, he ends up by having a very low opinion of architects. Such an opinion is not entirely unfounded, because a (fortunately dwindling) number of architects are undoubtedly failing to keep a judicious balance between the conflicting aims.

Everything we build must function properly, and the cost must be kept within the budget. Spatial arrangement and form must be adapted to the function of the structure in the most economical way. I have said that this is the architect's contribution, but this statement must be modified, for the architect cannot nowadays assess the needs of all kinds of function. To contain and utilise the forces of nature is predominantly the engineer's domain, and the architect must accept the spatial consequences of such functions. The architect's domain is the human aspect. He must soften the edges of 'technocratic space' to make it bearable, or preferably enjoyable, for human beings. This means that he should try to influence the spatial pattern from that point of view, but he must try to understand and respect the engineer's point of view – and vice versa – so that a reasonable compromise can be found.

Better world

It is the type of function, then, which determines whether a job is classified as architecture or civil engineering. Housing, schools, offices, churches, town halls – all the structures which mainly shelter the activities of people – belong to the first category. Factories are on the borderline, with large portions technically defined. Bridges, dams, roads, harbours; these are engineering. But people penetrate everywhere, and so does the force of gravity, the need for economy, and the importance of appearance and amenity. The type of job will influence the leadership, of course. The leader should be a designer – or have been one – for it seems to be very difficult to make lawyers, financiers, or even psychologists understand the nature and needs of design. But the claims of the client, that mythical figure, need to be stressed.

Why are we building at all? To use the skills we have laboriously acquired to make a living by getting a job in the building industry from a client with money to pay? Or to make this planet a better place to live in for ourselves, our children, our country, mankind? The two have to be combined, somehow. But fortunately for the country and the world, there are many of our students who want to stress the second aim. They are not happy with our present social structure, they want to change it, to improve it. They want to build, but for a better world. And so they ask, what should we build? To answer this, they need to know more. Therefore they want to study sociology, psychology, political science, and allied subjects, which they hope can help them decide what should be built, and they want the syllabus for architects to include these subjects.

Ruthless logic

I can understand and sympathise with these demands. They link up with the demand for extending the meaning of the word 'architect', which I earlier treated somewhat roughly and perhaps unjustly. The advice of the architect is very much needed in the councils which take political decisions about how to use our resources and what to build, for two reasons. First, because the architect, who represents the human aspect, is in a way the counsel for the people, who should be the client, ultimately. And second because if he doesn't speak up, there is nobody else to put the case for humanity in an informed way. The twin forces of high finance and technology have their own ruthless logic, and the human point of view can so easily get lost. Afterward there would be complaints and revolutions, but they can't improve the situation without someone who possesses the vision and expertise to show what can be done, and the will to do it.

In spite of that, I don't think it is the architect's job to study sociology and the rest. He is a designer, an artist. His research is of a different kind. Let us by all means make the extended architectural course available to all and sundry, including those architectural students who can afford the time, but don't let us call anybody an architect unless he knows something about building. An architect must be trained to deal at least with minor jobs not yet swallowed up by the technocratic machine – of which there will be plenty for a long time and then, as his experience grows, to graduate to the leadership of the major multidisciplinary jobs. He must be trained to deal with a host of minor but very important practical problems – waterproofing, weathering, jointing, byelaws, fire escapes and such – which otherwise are in danger of falling between the stools of highpowered experts.

My advice to architects would be, for heaven's sake don't queer your pitch by being incompetent at your job. Nobody will listen to your advice about how to run the state if you can't run your own business.

I Am Not a Prophet

A transcript of an interview that appeared in Contract Journal, 29 October 1970. The identity of the Interviewer was not recorded.

Interviewer: *The title of your Bossom lecture at the Royal Society of Arts earlier this year was 'Architects, Engineers and Builders'. You said then that these terms referred to a bygone age and that the building and contracting industry was in a state of flux. In what direction do you think the industry is moving now?*

Ove Arup: I am not a prophet. You can discern the trend just as well as I. Everything now is more thought out, more mechanised, more planned and more scientific whereas in the old days you relied on personal experience. Now you have new techniques available and it is a different situation.

The difference between the construction industry and the building industry is also disappearing though small builders will probably go on for ever. There is a need for small jobs, for maintenance of, and addition to, buildings.

Do you believe in the larger area that the distinction between the civil engineering contractor and the building contractor is vanishing?

I think it must be; it's gradually going. You wouldn't now have a firm with its own joinery works which makes all the doors and connections which the architect designs. In a building which may have a thousand doors all alike the doors are made in a factory. The business of plumbing, putting pipes together, making beautiful welds, cannot exist any more in large scale economic building.

You design beforehand and get new materials which can be put together quickly and you try to eliminate sitework altogether.

The so-called general contractor can really degenerate, or advance, to a position where he doesn't do anything himself, where he is a manager of specialist firms.

That seems to be a sound development in many ways because building is too complicated and if you want quality it cannot really be left to either a foreman, an agent, or a business firm which doesn't know anything about building.

In your Bossom lecture you also referred to the need for integration between design and construction.

That of course is the key, and has been ingrained in me from the very moment I started in an office, which was a designing and contracting office, when I realised how much theoretical design differs from practical building. The two must be integrated: they belong together.

You also said at the Bossom lecture that on a modern site you might have scores of designers involved. Who do you think [should lead the project, the] architect, the engineer or perhaps the contractor's professional manager?

I don't think you can answer that question at all, because it's not really a question of a man being an architect or an engineer. It depends on the man himself, on his personal qualities and his experience.

If I take a man on here in the office I look at his qualifications and at what he has done – it's important that he knows certain things – but what really matters is how he turns out, what sort of person he is, whether you can rely on him.

If you are a contractor and out to make money, it is quite natural that you want a man who can get what you are contracted to do done in the cheapest and most efficient way possible so that you can get your profit on top of it.

That is only a limited aspect, but I am talking about how we could get better design, better buildings and a better environment altogether.

There the leader must have a certain understanding of the whole. He must not have a biased view, he must not be an architect who only thinks of making an aesthetic monument for himself, or a contractor who only thinks of making the maximum profit. He must think about the client and about the people who are going to use it.

He must measure the question of cost against what is available in this particular case but also how much value for money he will get.

You mentioned your early experience in a contractor's design office and you also said in the Bossom lecture that there is still a divergence between the training of engineers and architects. How can the industry develop a man with this comprehensive knowledge which you seem to be suggesting will be needed?

I haven't got the answers and I can't lay down the law but I know from my own experience what is needed to make a good job. One man cannot master all the details of a project therefore you must have people who are educated in depth in one line, but no expert is really any good unless he knows the position of his expertise in relation to other experts. The expert must have knowledge of the neighbouring fields so that he can understand how his job relates to the whole. And the man who is going to have the final say must still have a widespread and overall knowledge, but it would be best if he was also expert in something.

This is certainly a theme that is developing amongst consultancies, in general. You, for example, have Ove Arup and Partners and Arup Associates, which involves an architectural function. Today we are seeing other engineering practices moving into, say, traffic management, and one firm doing economic studies and management consultancies are coming into the management of construction projects. Do you see this as a general development over the whole field of consultancy?

There is a very great danger. Because we want to do the right thing in a particular case we are forced into the multi-disciplinary area. We have traffic engineers and foundation experts, we have chemists and sociologists and though this has excellent results it also tends to produce very complicated communication problems. We must not lose the human touch for there is a tendency nowadays for scientific jargon to creep into everything. Take computers, for instance, they should be used to help people to get what they want. The computer can't tell us what we *should* want.

You mentioned the drawbacks of the present system of quantity surveying during your Bossom lecture: how do you think this could be replaced?

I think the designers should know about costs – when you are designing you are choosing a way that will ultimately reduce costs. Engineering is really accountancy if you like. The engineer's whole purpose is to design something which can be made more cheaply than it could be made before.

There's nothing in this business of taking off quantities if the purpose of the exercise is to help contractors to estimate the cost of executing a particular design. It is the attempt to turn the Bill of Quantities into a legal document defining the contractor's duties and measuring his performance which makes the whole matter so complicated.

This unnecessary complication then requires the setting up of a special profession – Quantity Surveyors – but it is the whole system that is wrong. The job should be defined by drawings and specifications, which should be ready before work is started.

The job is a totality, not a series of different items which can be added to or chopped about while the job is being built. And these over-detailed quantities actually make estimating more difficult, because the labour content, the plant, organisation and overheads can't be estimated rationally on this basis. What you call a 'Quantity Surveyor' or costing expert should have a different function and should be part of the design team, for the only real way to save cost is to make a better design.

What sort of impact do you think package deals will have?

I think they will have a big impact, but it is very important that the purpose of the designer should be idealistic and unbiased.

There are enlightened developers who realise that if they can produce something of quality they may actually make some money, they may get artistic satisfaction from the feeling that they are doing something good.

Looking at the question of quality, in your lecture, while you paid tribute to the professional institutions you also said you would like to see them develop their role as guardians of quality. How would you see the institutions functioning?

You are asking very difficult questions. I don't know myself. Unfortunately I am more able to cast a critical eye on these things than to put them right. But it is a fact that the institutions are concerned with status, with the status of the engineer, the public image of the engineer and the social standing of the engineer. It seems such a childish game in a way. What they should understand is that if you can do your job well you needn't be a professor or have a degree or the status of a Royal Charter.

You wrote to The Times *about the need for an inquiry into 'the building regulations'. Do you think the Government should play a greater or lesser role in legislating for better and safer construction?*

That is a very doubtful question. There are nearly always two sides, a whole lot of sides, to a question. This business of legislation is another matter that is very controversial. I know a good designer would be frustrated because the building regulations which deal with things in general cannot take a particular case into account.

Would you want to go back to the days when towns just developed organically?

There is a lot in that. But then we come to the whole question of planning and what we want to have.

We have got to have industrialised building, for example, but I think one has got to find ways of producing industrialised building which leave freedom for the design of something special even if it makes it a little more expensive. It's not at all bad to have the discipline of having to do a job for a certain amount, because it can improve the design.

You don't necessarily get something better because you spend a lot of money. What you should do is spend a lot of talent and thought on it. But you shouldn't be hampered by bringing it down for the last five or ten per cent.

Surely the present system of tendering for contracts should add to that cost-consciousness?

In a way that is wrong because you do not know what you are getting. A low price can mean that you are getting a bad job and it can be not only a bad job but a very expensive one. If there are those who because they are efficient make a big profit that doesn't matter. But if you get a firm that is muddling, trying to get out of their financial difficulties by skimping on the job, then you very probably end up by getting a job that is both bad and expensive.

Would you favour the negotiated form of contract?

Yes, but I would prefer the designer to deal directly with the different specialists in either manufacture or construction, those people who have the plant and know-how to do a thing well. You can then discuss your detail designs with them and adapt it to their method of construction or manufacture, and then try to arrive at the right price for the job. But then you have to deal with people you can trust. It's part of the stock in trade of a good adviser, whether architect or engineer, to be able to advise the client which people to avoid and which people not to avoid.

Future Problems Facing the Designer

This paper was given at the Royal Society discussion meeting on 'Building Technology in the 1980s', 4 November 1971.

I am aware of, and grateful for, the honour you show me by asking me to address you on the subject of 'Future Problems Facing the Designer'.

I am afraid, however, that you may have overestimated my powers. Like the Danish cartoonist Storm Petersen I find it very difficult to prophesy – very difficult indeed – and especially about the future.* But I can tell you straight away what I fear may happen: that designers in the future will even more than now be working under constraints which will make it impossible for them to give of their best. And I could add that even more than now their best may not be good enough because it is too narrowly based. This I think is by far the gravest problem facing designers, and it is a problem for all of us, unless present trends are reversed.

This is a somewhat pessimistic answer, and probably not what you expected. My opinion is of course based on my own experiences as a designer of sorts, and it is therefore a very personal one. Let's hope I am wrong.

Meaning of design

The word 'design', used as a noun or verb, can mean many different things. Here we are concerned with design as a link in the process of building and construction. Incidentally I make no distinction between the two; such distinctions have become obsolete with growing mechanization and factory production.

It would not do, however, to limit the discussion to structural design only, using the word in its narrower sense, for whereas everything we build or make must have structure to keep its intended

---

* Robert Storm Petersen (1882–1949) was a cartoonist, writer, animator, illustrator, painter and humorist, to whom is attributed the remark 'It's tough making predictions, especially about the future'.

shape, the structure itself is only a means to an end; its merit cannot be judged without reference to the thing of which it forms part.

Designing – and we could add planning – which is roughly the same thing, on a larger scale – plays a central and increasingly crucial role in technology; it is the key to everything which is made or built. For in modern construction everything is thought out beforehand, no unauthorized action is allowed. So any feature of the finished job which is not purely accidental must be due to a decision by somebody. As a matter of convenience, I call these decisions design decisions, and the sum of them the *total design*. The total design is seldom recorded *in toto*, it is more an idea than a reality. But the idea of total design implies that sufficient decisions have been made and recorded to enable others skilled in organizing such work to carry it out. The total design must, by definition, be viable, i.e. it must be possible to carry it out as intended. And it completely defines the finished job.

This cannot be said of all so-called designs. These are often only preliminary designs, sketches, plans or architectural perspectives showing certain aspects of the intended total design, but one cannot always be sure that they are viable, or practical, before the details have been worked out and all the implications considered. This leads to the often lamented gap between vision and embodiment. It is a wise precaution to bring the design to a stage when you know for certain that it can be built and what it will cost, before embarking on work on the site or in the factory.

Our designs, as executed, make our environment, and this in turn makes *us*, partly at least. Designing therefore assumes an importance not far short of that which belongs to scientific enquiry. In fact the two are intimately intertwined, one of them would get nowhere without the other. The whole of our technology is based on scientific knowledge, and scientific observation, and research depends in turn on sophisticated hardware. Both are complex mental activities, set in motion by a stated objective, and based on a stock-in-trade of knowledge and experience, augmented by fact-finding, classification, interpretation, analysis and synthesis in various proportions – a process where imagination, intuition and invention are of vital importance. However, the two differ in their objectives.

The *scientist* wants to *explore* nature, to find out how it works. He is looking for general laws. The motive may be pure curiosity – when we call it pure science – or he may hope that the acquired knowledge will help him to run the machinery himself. In this case it is not so pure, and approaches the kind of research which may form part of designs breaking new ground.

The *designer* wants to *change* nature to suit his convenience. He is trying to solve a practical problem here and now. But his problem is underdefined. There is not just one, but many solutions, good, bad and indifferent. He must choose. The bad solutions come easy to hand, the good he must search for, and work for. And *that is the designer's real métier*, that is his real problem, to find the best solution. Or, as you can never be sure that there isn't a better solution, to find at least a good solution, a solution of quality. And this is a problem in more than one sense – for *what is quality*? What is goodness?

The 'goodness' of a total design must be the same as the goodness of the finished structure, for the total design completely defines the latter. And the goodness of a structure, using this term about any product of the building industry, must be related to its purpose, and the consequences flowing from its being constructed in this particular location. The structure must obviously be fit for its purpose to be good. But that is not all that is implied by quality, as I hope to explain. The purpose behind the whole undertaking does not emanate from the designer, and may not even be disclosed to him. As far as he is concerned, it takes the form of a brief given him by his client and telling him in more or less general terms what is wanted. The designer then digests this information and disgorges it again in a form which will enable the builder to construct what the client wants.

This is the highly simplified version of the building process which is generally used when writing or talking about the subject. The reality is infinitely more complicated and we will come to that later.

Formula for excellence

The brief, supplemented by reference to the client if necessary, is obviously a very important document. If it could really explain exactly what was wanted, the question of quality would be solved. The best design would simply be the cheapest of those satisfying the brief. The formula measuring efficiency or excellence would be:

$$E = \frac{C}{P}$$

where C stands for commodity as defined by the brief and P stands for cost in pounds. And this is in fact what the whole of the modern obsession with cost-efficiency is based on.

All possible factors, even such imponderables as a saving in time for busy executives, are evaluated in money terms, and optima are produced by the computer and used as a basis for what are in effect political decisions. This is very crude, and potentially very dangerous, for it entirely ignores the quality of the product, which we do at our peril. Even the best of briefs cannot begin to define quality. The brief can be satisfied both by good and bad designs. You can specify that you want an elegant structure or a friendly house, or a town hall which is the envy of neighbouring cities, but that does not help you much. The client buys the cat in the bag. All he can do is to choose a good designer. That is why it is tempting to hold a competition for the best design, except that the submitted designs necessarily must be in the form of sketch-designs, which may not fulfil what they promise, and the assessors may not recognise nascent quality when they see it.

As the Danish author Piet Hein has said: 'Art is solving problems that cannot be formulated before they have been solved. The shaping of the question is part of the answer.' And designing is essentially an artistic process. Of course collection of data, research, analysis, calculating, quantifying, costing, etc., and especially previous experience, play their important part, and in engineering structures perhaps the most important part – and some of these activities can be eased by computerized information processing, analysis and mathematical simulation. But the essence of designing is to effect a harmonious synthesis of partly conflicting aims and obstinate facts. It is largely to find the right spatial arrangement of parts. Designing can be likened to the solving of a gigantic three-dimensional jigsaw puzzle – except that there is not one but many solutions, and not one but many designers. And they have got to find or shape the parts themselves, keeping always the object in mind.

A designer has his own standards. He is a professional, a craftsman, and if he is good himself, he knows when he has done a good job. It must be all of a piece, have wholeness, clarity, it must not be too strong at one point and too weak at another – but, as I said, it is useless to try to define quality. All we can say is that its emergence results from the involvement of the designer, from his passion for perfection, from the fever which grips him when he sees the chance of producing a really good job, and which makes him sustain the effort involved. I believe, perhaps naively, that such enthusiasm is a pre-condition for creating a structure or an environment which is not as cold and inhuman as much of our modern environment, but in which we can feel at home.

But enthusiasm is not enough. It can even be dangerous if too narrowly based. Designers – besides knowing their métier – must have an understanding of what other people need, and not just of what they want to give them, and sometimes perhaps what they need is a chance to build their own shacks – disregarding aesthetics.

Design in practice

I am aware that all this must sound a bit high-falutin' to you. What has all this to do with the client? He doesn't necessarily want an architectural or other kind of masterpiece. Maybe his object is to sell out quickly. Let's say a rural council wants a water tower. They have not much money – but they are in a hurry – for the matter has been debated for several years. They know what they want: so they go to an engineer who has designed water towers before and say: One of these, please, so high, so many gallons, for so much money, or less. And we would like the tenders to go out in six weeks time. It can be done. A sketch design, approximate quantities which can be modified later, the contractor starts digging. But he hasn't had the working drawings yet. And so on. The water tower stands in this village for a long time. It is its most prominent feature. You cannot avoid seeing it. A pity – but we must have water.

This is, on a small scale, what happens most of the time, more or less. But it is not the way to get the environment we like.

Of course most designs are more or less routine designs. They must be, we can't invent our technique afresh every time we build. But even if the bulk of what is built relies on previous experience slightly adapted to present circumstances, it is the fresh look at the evidence which initiates progress and improves quality. The natural instinct of a true designer is to ask himself: How can I do this thing better than it has been done before? Let's forget how it is normally done. By concentrating on the essence of what is needed and the most direct of all the ways of achieving it, perhaps I can find a simpler, cheaper and a better solution, fitting into surroundings better, pleasing the people I am serving. If these aims clash – as they will – perhaps if I try harder, some insight, some idea, will come to me in the middle of the night.

It may quite likely happen, of course, that the designer, after such an excursion, falls back on a traditional solution because it is in fact the best in the given context. He has wasted time and effort.

But he has gained the satisfaction, valuable to any designer, of knowing that he has chosen rightly.

The brief, and the formula:

$$E = \frac{C}{P}$$

cannot even settle the dispute between alternative solutions, if they happen to cost the same. For instance, if the brief can be satisfied by using either structural steel, reinforced concrete or aluminium as the basic structural material, the three schemes will differ in many respects which cannot be measured with the same yardstick. Durability, thermal conductivity, ease of effecting alterations, cost of upkeep, weathering, suitability for possible mass production, use of local resources and labour and many more, all will vary. Even the shape would be affected, and they would certainly look different. We would have to modify our formula to:

$$E = \frac{C + EC + D}{P}$$

where EC stands for commodity in excess of that required, but still of some value, and D stands for delight, the artistic quality. EC and D cannot be objectively measured in money terms, yet they cannot be ignored either.

Brief, design, execution

The brief cannot define quality. But it can prevent quality being produced by the designer, and often does, either by being so vague that the designer has not really understood the client's needs and therefore comes up with the wrong answer, or more often by being too detailed, thus pre-empting design decisions which ought to be taken by the designer, or which at least ought to be integrated with the other design decisions and modified as a result. It is wrong to treat brief and design as separate documents. The brief and the basic design decisions should result from a collaboration between client and designer. You cannot decide what to build without finding out what can be built for the money available, what the options are. The client's job is to explain his situation and his needs as fully as possible to his professional advisers, but not to propose, or at least not to dictate the solution. Just as a patient should explain his symptoms to the doctor, but should not suggest the cure, far less prescribe it, the very thought is preposterous in this case. The relationship should be one of openness and trust in both cases.

The same intimate relationship should exist between design and execution. The designer must know where he is going, he cannot design unless he can judge whether his design can be built, *how* it can be built and roughly how much it costs, at least enough to enable him to compare the cost of alternative solutions. Otherwise he proceeds blindfold. To complicate the execution through ignorance or neglect of the ways and means of construction is bad design. True economy demands that the design indicates a practical way of building.

I hope I have explained the need for integration of brief, design and execution. But there is much more integration to be done. If we look at the real situation we find that jobs are getting larger and more complex and that the total design is split between dozens of different professions, experts, manufacturers and contractors, each at best pursuing his own particular kind of quality. Communication between them is inadequate, and not much concerned with a rational appraisal of the design. But although the quality of the overall planning, services, the structural design, the architectural conception and detailing and the economic efficiency are all important, it is the synthesis of all these partly conflicting aims which constitutes the quality of the whole job. We need all-round or comprehensive quality, wholeness, which is really nothing else than a closer adaptation to human needs.

Total Architecture

But who is going to do the integration? The job is too big for one man. Team work is the answer, but is difficult when the members of the team so to speak live in different countries and speak different languages. It requires teamwork of a much higher order, whose members collectively embrace the experience needed for the job, understand each other and have the same desire to create what I elsewhere have called Total Architecture. In such a team enthusiasm can survive, and can even spread and flourish.

Total Architecture does not mean that cost is neglected. It only means that quality is not forgotten. The only hope I see of combining low cost with quality is to spend more time over the design. By more constructive forethought the time and money spent on the site can be reduced. Saving money is done by better design, better job organization and less waste, not by more accounting.

Post-design costing can be a useful check on a design before work is put in hand – but it comes too late – it means re-design if the design is too expensive. And in any case the present over-elaborate Bills of Quantities are a clumsy and time-wasting instrument for this purpose, as progressive quantity surveyors will admit.

But the present vogue and esteem for pre-design cost estimation, where definite sums are allocated to various parts of a non-existing design, rests on a curious delusion. Where does the estimator obtain his superior knowledge of what the right design should cost? It is really an insult and an obstacle to designers; their work is dismissed as of no importance.

Of course, designers may not be good enough – if you are strict you can say that of most designers. But before you bring in somebody else to do their job for them, you had better be sure that these others are better designers, for it is better designs we need, not better costs. A feasibility study by designers is the way to get an idea of costs beforehand.

No, costing must be an integral part of designing. We need cost-conscious design. And that is in fact what all engineering design is or ought to be – to find the cheapest solution to a given problem. This can be said to be the definition of engineering, and everything we build is engineering of one kind or another.

Cost-conscious design is the way as I see it – but the situation is not propitious for its adoption. Spending *more* on design goes against the whole trend, against official policy. We are trying to reduce the cost of design by mechanizing it, applying cost efficiency techniques, which cannot distinguish between good and bad design.

Naturally designers should work as efficiently as possible – but to prevent them from designing in the true sense is counterproductive, to put it mildly.

The client

The 'client' has changed as well. He has lost his identity and accessibility, being replaced by a board of directors responsible to their shareholders, or by government departments administering directives from on high, both represented by agents who can only administer official policy, no matter how inappropriate to the situation. But are these the true clients? Do we not design for the people who use the structures and live in the environment? This view has certainly been gaining ground among designers; it was one of the planks in the programme of the Modern Movement in architecture. This means that the critical look at the brief, for which we felt the need in the interest of wholeness, must penetrate deeper. When the client is the public, the brief must defend public interests. That means that we must take into account the wastage of scarce resources, the cost of preventing pollution, the spoliation of our environment, the harm done to fauna and flora – in fact all the things people have warned us about, and which are the pet theme of our more serious publications. We cannot afford to neglect them, even if only partly well founded. The total design must be truly comprehensive. We must add to our formula another factor: SP – the social price we have to pay, if we execute this design, and we had better put it below the line this time:

$$E = \frac{C + EC + D}{P + SP}$$

You may object that the formula gets less useful for every addition, and you are right, for it is very difficult to put a value on EC, D and SP. But we have to do it, or at least we have to make decisions which take account of these items, and the sooner the better, if we can believe the prophets.

This is a matter for politicians rather than designers; it directly affects only the brief, and therefore the client's right to build what he wants. But, as I hope I have made clear, brief and design cannot be separated, and scientists and designers must be brought in as advisers, to decide why we build and *what* to build.

This is a much more difficult and controversial question than how to build. To get strong and concerted action by independent national governments in this matter seems beyond the reach of man, at least not [sic] until disaster stares us in the face. But at least people and governments have begun talking.

But that we must stop glorying in waste seems obvious. Waste can be glorious – but it leads to waste land. We must preserve our heritage, conserve our resources, build for permanence, not for scrap. We must reduce our production of unnecessary gadgets. Simplify our lives where possible so that something is left over for those in need.

Does this invalidate the quest of quality in design? I don't think so. To do one's job well is good for one's self respect and good for one's fellow beings, and it can't do any harm as far as I can see even if it doesn't solve all the problems of mankind.

After all, it only means using our resources wisely.

The Built Environment

This paper was given at the Building Services Engineering Society inaugural meeting, held at the Institution of Civil Engineers on 26 October 1972.

When I was asked to speak at this inaugural meeting of the BSES I little knew what I would be letting myself in for. I was told that the Society was formed by 10 sponsoring bodies and seven affiliated bodies to advance and disseminate knowledge in the field of building services engineering and to foster co-operation between all those involved with the total 'built environment'. But when I found that neither the RIBA, the Institution of Structural Engineers, the Institution of Heating and Ventilating Engineers, the Institute of Builders, nor the Royal Institute of Chartered Surveyors were to be found among the sponsors, I was puzzled. It was explained to me that the RIBA was on the original Organizing Committee of the Society, but was, in the event, unable to become a sponsoring body but that it was hoped that they would come in before long.

This explanation still left me puzzled, and I said I would have to investigate this matter further and discuss the result of my investigation in my speech. I confirmed this in a letter to Garth Watson* which I will read to you:

> Following our telephone conversation today I think I ought to put on paper the conclusions we reached, so that there is no misunderstanding.
>
> I said that I could only speak at the Inaugural Meeting of the BSES if I could voice any conclusions I might reach after thinking about the whole matter of the Building Services, and discussing it with members of the various bodies connected with the building industry as a whole.
>
> Whilst I concede the need for close integration of the work of all those concerned with the production of buildings, I have doubts about the value of a society which does not embrace the key professions represented by the RIBA, the Institution of Structural Engineers and the IHVE. As you say, discussions can do no harm unless they are a substitute for action, but what

seems to be needed is an institution which can map out a better training for those concerned with building services of all kinds. It could most naturally be based on the IHVE, and it might be wrong to deny them a Charter, provided their standards are raised and provided only those taking the new degrees can call themselves Chartered Engineers.

I understand that you would want me to speak at the Inaugural Meeting even if I should reach some such conclusion. But if you are doubtful about this I am very willing to withdraw.

I received a reply to this letter saying that the Chairman and Garth Watson were in no doubt whatever that they wanted me to speak at the meeting as the Society was a forum for discussion and was not in itself taking any particular point of view on what were certainly controversial matters. Which I must say is a laudable attitude.

I also received a statement of 925 words on the origins of the BSES and the actions taken by the CEI in regard to the learned society and the qualifying role, ending up with an announcement that I had accepted an invitation to speak at this meeting on a subject of my own choosing *within the theme – the built environment*.

This last qualification is not exactly what I agreed to, but let that pass.

In the meantime I had had other letters and messages, and I had talked with various people concerned with the matter, and it was obvious that there was a large number of people who thought that the forming of this new society was not only useless but directly harmful. They regard it as a clever device by the big three, the Civil, Mechanical and Electrical Engineering Institutions, to divert attention from what was really needed and what they wanted to prevent: the granting of a charter to the IHVE. Opinions differed about what should be done instead, but whatever it was it would be very difficult to achieve because the other fellows wouldn't play ball.

The whole situation is extremely confused, to put it mildly, with institutions, charters, societies and other bodies proliferating, but never dying. Unity is extolled, apartheid practised.

I am telling you all this to enlist your sympathy for the difficult situation I find myself in.

I could, of course, confine myself to talking about the need for collaboration between all those concerned with the built environment. I seem to have done that all my working life, stretching over half a century or so, and I suppose I could so some more of it. But isn't it a bit unkind to trot out this old war-horse? After all, we all agree on that. In all my years of campaigning I have never found anybody who disagreed with it. But *talking* about it doesn't seem to have much effect. One must somehow create the conditions which will *allow* such collaboration to take place, and one must educate members of the building team to see their own contribution *not* as an end in itself, but as a part of a common endeavour to create comprehensive, total architecture. That is what we have been trying to do inside our own firm. And therefore we know how difficult it is. And yet we are particularly fortunate in being able to foster such experiments – and they have gone far beyond that experimental stage now – inside a large engineering firm able to supply the necessary engineering experience and finance. But we are, of course, all the time up against the reluctance of clients and government departments to change established rules and procedures. Especially our insistence that our quantity surveyors must be part of the design team causes uneasiness. And yet it is so obvious that accountancy cannot create anything unless it guides what is being designed and therefore what is built. The system of over-elaborate bills of quantities produced after the design is made, or worse still, before the design is made, is directly harmful in many ways, among others because it erects a barrier between the designer and the builder.

One thing we ought to be able to agree on is, that the designer must know how his design can be executed, and the approximate cost of it. If, instead, priced bills of quantities are treated as secret documents which must not be shown to the designer, as happens sometimes, the whole thing becomes absurd. Designing is indicating a sensible way of building, among other things.

All this is by the way, but it reinforces my opinion that more talking is not what is needed. There are enough societies and journals where people can and do talk and write. The Joint Building Group and the Junior Liaison Organization have more or less the same aims. And if the institutions most intimately concerned with building oppose this venture, it indicates that the most pressing need is not the forming of this society, but to bring some order into the chaotic state of separate institutions, chartered or otherwise, which have been created in a very accidental way in response to technological development and specialization, or else because groups of engineers have been dissatisfied with the conservatism of old institutions.

* This is thought to refer to Garth Watson, past Secretary of the Institution of Civil Engineers.

Now, it is obviously not very pleasant for me, having been invited to speak at the inauguration of a new society sponsored by so many worthy people, to come and tell you that the whole venture is worthless, to put it much too bluntly. It is, to say the least, an odd way to inaugurate a new society.

It would make it easier, of course, if I could also tell you what you *should* do. But I am not as clever as that. When it comes to the unravelling of the tangled network of institutions I am singularly inept, in fact. I know only a few of them, most of the letters behind names are meaningless to me. I am a bad institution man. I could, perhaps successfully, put forward excuses or rationalizations for this, but it would be a waste of time, it wouldn't alter the fact.

The Royal Charter

When I look at the list of 15 chartered engineering institutions forming the membership of the CEI I feel tempted to scrap the lot and begin afresh. Divide the whole field of engineering into sections according to the nature of the work they have to do or the knowledge they have to have, and then perhaps group neighbouring sections into a number of institutions which together would cover the whole field of engineering, united by the CEI at the top. Inside each institution you would then have different grades, Chartered Engineers, Technician Engineers and Technicians, if you like. The Chartered Engineer would have a more broadly-based knowledge of mathematics, physical sciences and of all the various branch disciplines inside his particular institution, specializing in one of them, but able to represent them all on the conceptive stage of original design. And so on. New techniques or fields of operation would then originate inside one of the institutional territories and might ultimately warrant the creation of separate institutions. And some old workings might be closed down.

That is what I would be tempted to do, I said. But I am totally unequipped to do it and in any case it can't be done, and it is very doubtful if it would be desirable to do it. For when it comes to dealing with human beings logic breaks down. To force them to do what they don't want to do is counter-productive. To destroy their traditional links with the past would be wrong too. But to build on the present haphazardly disposed foundations is a very complicated business. The creation of the CEI was, however, a very significant step in the right direction. Let us hope that it can gradually sort things out. But if it is intended to limit the number of charters to 15 for all eternity, as some people believe, it can only make sense if there is a re-shuffling of existing charters or if it is a step on the way to total elimination of charters.

All this is of little help. But let me try to establish what we, I hope, can agree on, and what we are up against.

The trouble appears to be this: The Institution of Heating and Ventilating Engineers want a Royal Charter and membership of the CEI. On the one hand they feel they deserve it. They are on the way up, their importance in the building team is growing and generally recognized, they are expanding over a wider field and want to embrace all the building services, and they are doing all they can to improve their service. On the other hand, they feel they need it, they find it difficult to attract the right kind of student unless they can dangle a charter in front of him. If the building services engineer – or more ambitious still – the environmental design engineer – has to study another two years to join a member institution of the CEI to get charter status, however irrelevant those studies may be to his chosen career, it will have a most disastrous effect on recruitment, to quote Mr Pullinger.*

But unfortunately it is getting more and more difficult to get a Royal Charter. When the CEI was created in 1965 they were given eight years in which to raise the standard of the Chartered Engineer. By 1973 they will have to satisfy the Privy Council that the corporate members of all the chartered engineering institutions in the CEI have reached the required standard, otherwise *their* charter may be withdrawn. And they have had a look at the qualifications of the present corporate members of the IHVE to find out whether they meet the criteria for constituent membership of the CEI.

Unfortunately an *ad hoc* committee decided that less than the required 75% did so, so they could not recommend the IHVE for membership of the CEI. And as a result they could not get a Royal Charter either. It seems to be the case that no engineering institution will in future be able to obtain a charter without satisfying the CEI criteria.

Whether the BSES was launched by the Civils as a sop to the wounded IHVE I don't know. It has really nothing to do with the charter business, because the BSES is supposed to be only a talking shop, or perhaps I should say a learned society, and not a qualifying body. And it was meant to include the architects, structural engineers, heating and ventilating engineers and builders, of course.

But now these last four have withdrawn from sponsorship and any form of participation. They all feel that the IHVE should have a charter, that it is absurd that such a vital section of the building team should, so to speak, have a lower status than the other members of the team. And they believe that the formation of the BSES is distracting attention from the much more important question of improving the status and performance of the heating and ventilating engineer.

This seems to me to be a fatal blow to the BSES. For it would, I think, make sense to have a society which embraced architects, heating and ventilating engineers, structural engineers and builders, for they are the four *main* members of the building team. But a BSES without them is nonsense.

I am not claiming any great accuracy for this rough outline of the problem, and I should not be surprised if both the contending parties were dissatisfied with my expose. But it wouldn't do any good losing myself in all the pros and cons – the fact is, that *this fraternal dispute is a setback to the much needed mutual understanding and collaboration between the various professions engaged in building*. And the whole thing is rather silly when you consider that everybody agrees that:

First: There is a great need for a professional building services engineer with a wider education, who, as a member of the design team alongside the architect, structural engineer, etc., can make a creative contribution to the design at the conceptual stage, before the options are frozen, and that such an engineer, by studying on a scientific basis those subjects which would be most useful to him in his work, should be able to become a Chartered Engineer, and have his professional home in a chartered institution adapted to his needs.

Secondly: It would be a very good thing to have a forum, in the form of a learned society, where all the professions and trades who work together to shape our environment could come together and exchange views.

The difficulty in the first case is, of course, that the IHVE seems to put the cart before the horse when it demands a charter before the majority of its corporate members have reached the required standard – if that is in fact the case. But they can certainly claim that there is a precedent for such a procedure – in the case of the structural engineers, for instance, and probably in the case of most of the other CEI members too. So why should the IHVE be penalized? And they *need* a charter *now* to boost morale – and on balance it would, I think, be better to let them have it even if some of them were elevated beyond their proper station – after all, it is not the presence of bad but the scarcity of good engineers which is the trouble, the bad will be found out in time, and the supply of good engineers would be stimulated. But the CEI is, on the other hand, right in upholding the calibre of Chartered Engineers, it is their job to do so, and it would be wrong to devaluate the *designation* C. Eng. in the eyes of other nations. And the alternative of elevating only some of the IHVE corporate members to the blessed state is politically unacceptable. So that's where we are stuck. When we turn to the question of the BSES, I must admit that I cannot understand why its launching should actually *delay* the granting of a charter to the IHVE. On the other hand there are, as mentioned, other societies and institutions who are already now engaged in such multi-disciplinary discussions, so why should the Civils, Mechanical and Electrical Engineers suddenly presume to lead in a domain in which until recently they have not shown much interest? Other bodies, especially the RIBA and the IHVE, would consider themselves more entitled to take the lead in this sphere. And, of course, if it really is only a Building Services Engineering Society, then the IHVE would have a strong claim. But that is another thing I don't understand:

Why should it have this name? I thought it was to 'foster co-operation between engineers and others in all the disciplines concerned with the design, operation and equipping of buildings' – or in another version 'with the total built environment'. So why not call it the Society for the Built Environment?

To sum up this part of my talk: The quarrel is not about what is needed, but about who should do what, and what labels to put on people. And that is really a sorry state of affairs.

Motivation

It stems, of course, from the schism in the motivation of a professional man. On the one hand he wants to do a good and useful job.

On the other hand he wants to – and must – make a living. These two aims tend to conflict, and that gives rise to no end of trouble. In any situation where many people possessing different skills have to produce an artefact – and that practically covers the whole of human endeavour in the building field – their work must be integrated if it is to produce a whole which possesses any kind of quality. This requires unselfish collaboration, and this means collaboration aimed at producing a good job and not hampered by considerations of personal glory, status or reward. But the quest for status, profit and

---

* This is thought to refer to Sir Alan Pullinger, chairman of the engineering group Haden Carrier and president of the Heating and Ventilation Contractors' Association and of the Institution of Heating and Ventilation Engineers in 1972.

the rest is a fact we have to live with, and it *does* interfere with the quality of practically every job, and with the quality of the whole of our environment in fact as our pollution problems testify.

Of course the two aims *need* not conflict. Quality of environment is being produced in patches without endangering the livelihood of those taking part in its production, indeed the opposite is just as likely to result. But only if the natural acquisitiveness, greed and personal ambition of man is kept under control and the quest for quality is given first priority.

Our real problems begin, however, when we realise that it is not enough to create quality in a few favoured locations, that our survival depends on our ability to create tolerable conditions for the whole of mankind without upsetting the balance of nature. But this is by the way, although it is of course this danger ahead which ought to bring us to our senses.

Through a long evolutionary process, civilized man has to a large extent learnt to keep his natural aggressiveness under control, at least in his personal relationships. We associate quite amicably with our potential rivals for jobs or promotion in our professional institutions. In fact the common interests form a bond between us, we feel friendly even towards unknown colleagues. We become a kind of brotherhood pursuing common interests, a mutual benefit society. And then the devil crops up again, our aggressiveness is transferred to the institution, internal unity is stimulated by cultivating a feeling of superiority towards lesser breeds in other institutions. Personal ambition is camouflaged as concern for the status and public image of our profession, our officers are unashamedly pursuing a policy of extending the size, the influence and the field of operations of our particular institution. It is their duty, they feel proud to do battle for what they have no doubt is a righteous cause. We move into the sphere of politics, decisions are reached through a tug-of-war between rival lobbies, not by disinterested reason.

Power struggle

This is a well-known phenomenon which applies to all kinds of groups able to exact loyalty from their members, whether tribes, nations, corporations, companies, religions or political factions or what have you, and it applies in a mild and comparatively innocuous form to professional institutions. This is what lies at the root of the present impasse, and this is how the affairs of the world are generally conducted – by a struggle for power of conflicting interests – and it appears to be the only way. But we know also that it can be a dangerous way, it can even lead to the destruction of mankind. Vietnam represents the ultimate in de-personalized aggression.

One could perhaps imagine a Utopia where affairs were managed more wisely. Loyalty to a narrow circle of friends, compatriots or confrères, which is a good thing in itself, would then not be allowed to detract from our loyalty to a wider entity, that of this whole planet of ours and the life it supports. We are not living in Utopia, however. But perhaps it is not too fanciful to suggest that architects, engineers and the producers of our artefacts could forget their interprofessional rivalries and concentrate on how to improve our habitat.

They all profess to do so – why not do it? It entails in some cases a widening of their horizon and a sacrifice of cherished inessentials.

Titles, letters behind your name, are these decorative features so important? Status, what does it mean? Let's get this thing in perspective. Can we not agree that it is the reality behind the façade which matters? Of course we need some labels. It's no good taking your shoes to the butcher to get them repaired – one must know or must be able to find out whom to go to. Modern society depends on advertising, and its usefulness is immensely enhanced if it is truthful. But how much of it is? In most cases a label tells you very little about what you really want to know. That so and so is a doctor, yes. But is he a good doctor? Will he kill you or cure you? Someone else is an architect. But is he a good architect? Of all those with the same qualifications some are good and some bad – or shall we say not so good. It can make an enormous difference to the job you get. And when you employ somebody or consult somebody you want to know not only his technical qualifications but what sort of person he is. Can you rely on him? Does he mean what he says, is he truthful, reliable, honest, bright, friendly, easy to get on with? Titles and labels are not much use as a guide in this respect. The Honourable So-and-so could well be dishonourable, and the engineer who is a Doctor of Science may well be useless as a designer. We all know that, so why take these letters so seriously?

I know the answer, of course. Many employers take them seriously, institutions and Government departments take them seriously, your family take them seriously, so they can really mean something, even in hard cash, at least at the beginning of a career. And patience is in short supply nowadays. I grant all that. But then we should try to make them really mean something. Make them truthful advertising.

And another thing. What is even more important than a C.Eng. is the reputation of an engineer among those who know him personally and know his work. If I wanted some really useful information about a man, I would try to find somebody whose opinion I valued and who knew the man. But that may not be easy. Then the only reliable way is to try him out. The proof of the pudding is in the eating. Of course reputations, status, fame can also be misleading. The only status worth bothering about is your standing among those who know you and whose opinion you value. And not least, your opinion of yourself – although even that could be the opinion of a fool!

These reflections are, of course, intended as a plea to concentrate on the essential thing: *to improve the value of our work to society, and that means without a shadow of doubt, learning to collaborate*. And improving the value of our work is not a bad way to improve our status, either. This may sound smug and banal – but nobody can deny that it is true. To those bright boys who are supposed to hesitate before studying to become building service engineers because there is no Chartered Engineer status in sight at the end of their studies, I would say that they need have no fear that they can't get a good job at the end of it all. There is, and will be for a long time, a crying need for them.

So relax, and concentrate on your studies. For I hope that you haven't interpreted my words as a disparagement of what the title C.Eng. *should* stand for. To learn what the title demands you should learn is very important, in fact I think the standard should be raised, and that we should demand of Chartered Engineers both more basic science and more knowledge of adjoining fields. But long experience has told me that it is possible to pass an examination without deriving much benefit from it. Your ability to learn while you are working is more important. That an examination you passed as a young man or boy should mark you for life and put you in a certain category is a rather absurd over-simplification.

The architect and the engineer

The same can be said about the sharp division between the image of an architect and an engineer. The terms were coined in an earlier age, but they don't fit any more, and this leads to misunderstandings. I am not suggesting that we should abandon them but that we should now realize what they mean or should mean *now*.

We are in the midst of a transformation of the building industry. Arts and crafts are being replaced by science and technology – or should I say science-guided design and mechanized production. The process was in its early stages when I joined the fray, but now the rate of what we like to call progress has increased to such an extent that we must change our old ways of thinking.

Science-guided design and mechanized production – technology for short – is the domain of engineers.

It is advanced through engineering design. As the art and craft of building is being swamped by technology, the engineer muscles in on the building field. This is as it may look from an architect's point of view. He was once a master-builder. After he had ceased to be a builder himself, he was still master, he knew the art and craft of building, and he could design competently and tell the builder how the work should be done. But submerged by technology he had to learn new tricks, he was bewildered, insecure. He had to listen to advice. He was still master, but he did not master the technique of building any more. And a general who doesn't know his army, an artist who doesn't know his medium, and a designer who has to choose among unfamiliar materials and processes is in an insecure position. He cannot design with confidence. And he is in danger of losing the respect of those he commands.

But the architect wanted to remain master at all costs. For he had a sacred duty to perform. He represented the client, the user, the public. It was his responsibility to see that the building served its purpose, fitted into the neighbourhood, was a joy to behold and live or work in, did not cost more than his client could afford. All this, and more, as expectations of comfort rose, all the multiplying claims of the perfect architectural solution, including his own dreams of artistic wholeness and integrity – all this had to be achieved with the ever-increasing technical aids at his disposal.

But the engineer didn't see it this way. He could see where the architect blundered, his technical inadequacies, his squandering money on architectural or aesthetic aims which the engineer did not understand. He suspected that what the architect was doing was simply pandering to his own ego at his client's expense. And he didn't see why he, the engineer, couldn't go it alone, with the aid of the contractor, of course. He could get the foundations, the walls and the roof constructed, all sound and solid and waterproof, he could put in the required services, enclose the required number of rooms with access and exit – the lot. Why should he need a longhaired architect to tart it up and add to the expense – he knew what he liked, and if necessary he could always hire a tame architectural assistant to make a nice perspective for the client.

Artistic values

The client and the quantity surveyor, being concerned with value for money, were often inclined to share this view. Artistic values change, what one generation cherishes the next despises. To decide in the surge of new -isms what is *'timeless'* art is difficult. Although this adjective is not infrequently bestowed by critics, it is often doubtful whether it will stick. The average client cannot be expected to share contemporary artistic sensitivity, he likes what he is used to, so quite apart from technical and economic considerations, he dislikes modern architecture. He expects the architect to provide cosy old-world cottages with all modern conveniences, access by car, etc., and available for millions of new customers. Or so one would think if one read some of his complaints.

One could not expect the architect to accept this valuation. He still believed in his mission and struggled to keep aloft the banner of Architecture with a capital A.

This, I know, is a travesty of the present complex state of the engineer-architect confrontation. Like the image of Uncle Sam and John Bull, such caricatures have, however, a long life, and I wonder whether in the depths of the engineering jungle there are not tribes who still see reality in this way. And would this, I wonder again, be at the root of the idea that a successful integration of all the building services, or even a meaningful discussion of such integration, could be achieved without the participation of the architects, or the heating and ventilating and structural engineers, for that matter? Of course one must grant that there is a great deal of truth in this caricature, otherwise there would be no problem. But I believe in the architect's mission. All the same, some, or many architects, if you like, may not be good enough, cling to outworn ideas. *But architecture is important. It is about time engineers realized that engineering is useful, necessary indeed, but not enough.*

Specialization and the environment

I suppose I will have to try to explain and support this statement. But it should not be necessary for me to go into the whole question of pollution, squandering of scarce resources, overpopulation and the rest. That mankind is in a precarious situation we all realize by now. And, as Barry Commoner* so convincingly argued at the recent RIBA annual conference on 'Designing for survival', the root cause of the trouble is the massive introduction of new technologies, impelled by greed and fear.

The environment created by natural forces acting in compliance with their own laws, by fauna and flora in equilibrium or by the dwelling or tilling patterns of a pre-industrial era, all speak to us in some way – it can be awe-inspiring or sinister, squalid or pathetic, it can lift up our heart or welcome us. But the environment created by uncontrolled industrial processes, the ravishing of our countryside, the pollution, the insensitive building for profit, simply disgust us. To feel at home we must feel the impact of the human mind on our environment, not the mind of the rapist but the lover.

What could save us is also technology, but wisely guided to serve humanity. But how do we, and can we, guide technology wisely? That is the question. Technology is guided by design, and designing is decision making. These decisions are made by people. And if only these people would make the right decisions we would be home and dry.

What are the right decisions? A designer, to make the right decisions, must know:

1) What he should try to achieve, and
2) How to go about achieving it.

Aims and means, for short. The engineer is not used to worrying his head very much about the first of these problems. His task is set for him – to span a river, invent a machine to make buttons, produce an insecticide to kill certain pests. He throws himself enthusiastically into the problem and comes up with an answer. The best answer he can think of. Until recently, at least, it didn't occur to him to doubt the value of his work. In fact he saw himself as a benefactor, liberating man from drudgery and fear of want. Did he not harness the forces of nature for his benefit? Did he not increase man's power, force the earth to yield its riches?

These achievements were based on specialization. And the more the engineer specialized, the narrower was his aim, the more he shut himself off from any global view of things.

Recently I attended the Fourth Fluid Science Lecture at the Royal Institution. The speaker was Mr Braikevitch, one of the world's foremost water turbine engineers, one of those who need no introduction, but whose name I had never heard of, typically enough. He talked about the development of the water turbine.† He had apparently devoted his life to the improvement of this very important tool, continuing the work of previous generations. And a very full life it was, too. According to the speaker, there is more to this machine than meets the eye. Water is a fickle mistress, it has to be coaxed, but like a human being it works better when given a little freedom. As every part of a turbine is inter-connected hydraulically with its neighbour, fluid engineering has to be applied right the way through so that a harmonious whole is obtained, and the efficiency is at the maximum. The research field is therefore much wider than the lecturer was able to indicate.

Obviously, trial and error, science, and feeling for the totality, the soul of the machine, all this and more went into it. Obviously he was an artist in his domain.

The aim of all that effort was to increase the output of electricity which could be obtained from a given variation in water levels.

Who could possibly object to this aim?

I remember as a child staying with my maternal grandparents in Norway and hearing people discuss a proposal to harness the largest and most spectacular Norwegian waterfall, the Rjukan, to provide electric power. I remember the sorrow and dismay they felt at the possible loss of this awe-inspiring national monument. I was sad, too, for I would for ever by deprived of the possibility of seeing this sight. It was, I suppose, the first time I had an inkling of the ecological consequences of technology, although I didn't exactly put it that way.

A trivial matter? Perhaps. But have you ever been spell-bound by the majesty of such a display in a setting of great natural beauty? It does something to you. It teaches you humility. Have we a right to deprive mankind of such an experience forever, everywhere?

One could mention hundreds of such specialized disciplines or technologies exacting complete devotion from their acolytes, with their institutions, congresses, trade journals and their heroes who need no introduction but are unknown outside the charmed circle. And all have impeccable aims. Aims which obviously benefit mankind.

And yet, when you add it all up, there seems to be something wrong. The undoubted progress seems to be somewhat patchy. It is good in parts, like the curate's egg – but taken as a whole, the curate's was a bad egg. What went wrong? Obviously, in pursuing their aims, engineers also achieved a great number of other things. Some of them perhaps relatively harmless on a small scale, but catastrophic if large-scale interference upset the balance of nature. Like the medicine that cured the fever and killed the patient. We must understand that everything we do affects everything else, and that we must consider the consequences of our actions. Efficiency in achieving our narrow aim at the lowest cost to us or our client cannot remain our only yardstick. Systems engineering and value engineering attempt to take into account the effects of a given technological decision when assessing its merit. But merit is still equated with cost-efficiency. This is something entirely different from human welfare. Engineers have been very successful in solving the problems they are faced with. Almost too successful, for we cannot resist the temptation to show off, to do things just because we are able to do them, without considering whether we really need them. During the war we were told to ask ourselves whether our journey was really necessary in view of the need to save resources for the war effort. We have a war on now, and we would do well to ask the same question. In other words, we must pay more attention to the first problem.

What should our designs try to achieve?

We must take a critical look at the brief, make it more comprehensive. We must look beyond the narrow object and ask ourselves: What will be the ecological consequences? What about the working conditions for those who carry out the work, including their spiritual well-being; will the work provide useful employment or cause unemployment – perhaps in other countries? What effect has it on other industries? What is the cost in scarce resources? We must ask ourselves what would happen if everybody else did what we do. Would that serve humanity? The Kantian criteria for ethical conduct.

Taking this global view is a daunting task. Engineers have a big role to play in this discussion about aims, for just as it is no good doing things which serve no useful purpose or are harmful to humanity, so it is no good aiming at things which can't be done. You cannot alter the law of gravity, for instance.

I am afraid I have spent too much time in proving the obvious: that the failure of our civilization is not a failure to increase our power, but a failure to use it wisely. We must bring technology under the control of man for the benefit of man. This has been said a thousand times, of course. Both architects and engineers see themselves as fulfilling this role. Both are right, to a certain degree, but to understand

---

* This possibly refers to Barry Commoner, the American biologist, who wrote about the negative ecological effects of above-ground nuclear testing.
† M. Braikevitch, 'Straight Flow Turbine', in T. J. Gray and O. K. Gashus (eds.), *Tidal Power* (New York, 1972).

their respective roles better, we must study them in the milieu in which they cannot avoid the necessity of collaborating, the urban environment.

Design

Architects and engineers both see themselves as designers. And although the majority of engineers and a great number of architects can hardly be called that, it's the designers I am concerned with here. For the design, as I use the word, is the key to what is built; it is the record of all the decisions which have a bearing on the shape and all other aspects of the object constructed. These decisions are unfortunately not all taken by the designer but they must be known to him and integrated into a total design.

We must distinguish between routine design, which does not require any creative thinking, and what may be labelled original, innovative, conceptual or creative design. Creative design must, of course, build on previous experience and contains and employs predesigned parts, and it may even consist almost entirely in assembling such parts to create an entity. But building is always tied to locality and to the people one builds for, and they vary from case to case. The synthesis required to create an entity, a whole which economizes in means yet fulfils the aims, is an artistic process.

Art, as the Danish author Piet Hein has stressed, is solving problems which cannot be formulated before they have been solved. The search goes on, until a solution is found, which is deemed to be satisfactory. There are always many possible solutions, *the search is for the best* – but there is no best – just more or less good. *Quality is produced by the search, it doesn't stop at a second-rate solution but continues until no better solution can be found.*

The artist who knows his stuff – literally – knows when it clicks. Then he knows: this is the best I can do. He has his own artistic yardstick – and if he is satisfied there is a good chance that his work will make other people happy – for he should be his own most severe critic. But this statement carries no guarantee with it, for sometimes he isn't.

This extra exertion is not dependent on monetary reward, and frequently goes without, but it is indispensable if the result is to possess any quality.

All this applies to engineering design as well as architectural design – in areas where both act as prime agents. In both cases the designer is responsible for a structural entity, and in both cases he is trying to make it function well, last well, look well and cost little, or to put it differently: make it fulfil all the requirements of the brief including the aforementioned social and ecological aims, at the least cost to the community.

An engineer who doesn't care a damn what his design looks like as long as it works and is cheap, who doesn't care for elegance, neatness, order and simplicity for its own sake, is not a good engineer. This needs to be stressed.

The distinctive features of engineering are mainly matters of content – the nature of the parts and the aims.

Engineering structures are mainly concerned with the forces of nature, overcoming difficult soil conditions, retaining earth and water, containing grain and liquids, spanning rivers, creating terra firma in deep water, moving mountains and taming rivers. All very difficult but with easily defined aims.

Architects, on the other hand, have to deal with people. Cater for them, cosset them. Would you like a little more heat, or light? Do you like your living room facing west? Or would you prefer the view on the golf course? And as the people can't reply, they have to choose for them, and get the brick-bats later.

People are fickle. They differ. They quarrel. They flock together. They want privacy. They want to drive their cars everywhere. They hate other people's cars. It is quite a difficult problem. Compared to that, the actual physical obstacles to overcome are generally trivial.

But enough of that. Besides this kind of difference there is the difference in background and education and the resulting values of criteria. What the engineer sees as a structure, the architect sees as a sculpture. Actually, of course, it is both.

In building, the entity we want to perfect is not the structure or the air-conditioning as such – although that as well – it is the sum of all these parts. The engineer only designs a part of the total. His ideal structure may occupy space which is required for other purposes, it is also part of the architectural composition and therefore subject to other criteria. The ideal air-conditioning system cannot be installed because there is not enough money or because it is deemed more desirable to enable the windows to be opened, etc. The search in this case is for a comprehensive quality which is a sum of particular qualities, each measured with its own particular yardstick, but modified to fit into a general pattern.

The success of the whole undertaking depends on the right allocation of priorities and whether the resulting entity has this quality of wholeness and obvious rightness which is the mark of a work of art.

And as this sounds a bit high-falutin I will try to show you some slides which may throw some light on what I mean, or at least will relieve the tedium.

The Built Environment

Examples

I recently found some prewar photographs and press-cuttings in an old folder, and I will show you a few of these.

Fig. 1) The first example is, I think, the first building I had anything to do with. It is a small café and shelter built just behind the river wall in Canvey Island in 1932 or '33, by Christiani and Nielsen, specialists in the design and construction of reinforced concrete structures.

I was employed by them as their chief engineer in the London office. I functioned both as architect, engineer and contractor – but was severely restricted by lack of funds and lack of architectural training. But as you can see, I had an architectural 'image' derived from the Modern Movement – a kind of mock Mendelsohn, or perhaps Tecton.* The steel columns supporting the canopy of the shelter roof, introduced here to restrict the view as little as possible, definitely remind me of the Penguin Pool at the Zoo – and other Zoo jobs. Although I think these came later – so perhaps I went to the fountain head, Le Corbusier. Anyhow, the circular cafe with windows all round, everything supported on a concrete cylinder on piles, and its extension upwards through the cafe in the form of six columns supporting the roof, all this couldn't be simpler, and was certainly cheap – and, I am afraid, also rather nasty. Anyway the one time I was allowed to visit the job – my place was in the office – I was depressed by the shoddiness of the cheap standard metal windows, the concrete which had received only the normal contractor's rubbing down with cement grout and cement wash or perhaps a coat of *Stic B*, the bare columns supporting the concrete drum at the back, the cheap lino and desk, the bad detailing. But I couldn't do anything about that.

The moral of it all? That architecture on the cheap by an amateur architect employed by a contractor, and a client with no money to spend, is not a good way in which to achieve perfection.

Fig. 2) The next slide shows a model of an ambitious scheme to build a spiral tower at the end of Clacton Pier. Visitors would enter through a central lift and then gently meander down a spiral concrete ramp, passing the shops, stalls, etc.

Fig. 1 Café and shelter, Canvey Island

---

* It is possible that Ove is referring to the De La Warr Pavilion in Bexhill-on-Sea, constructed in 1935 and designed by Eric Mendelsohn, although the competition for this project was not announced until two years after the completion of Canvey Island Pavilion, and Arup's collaboration with Tecton on the Penguin Pool, Highpoint and the Finsbury Health Centre also date after the pavilion.

Fig. 2 Model of spiral tower for Clacton Pier

Fig. 3 Water tower

(including peeps at what the butler saw) which were arranged on the inside. Much the same idea was later adopted by Frank Lloyd Wright for his Guggenheim Museum in New York but I am not suggesting he got the idea from me! The construction was very simple, a cone of inclined columns supported on pile groups or cylinders, and supporting the double cantilevered concrete ramp, which in turn contributed to the stability. It was much cheaper than making a long pier deck to house the stalls. I took the model to Mr Kingsman, the owner, who resided on the Riviera in the winter. He and his family were enthusiastic, but later saner counsel prevailed. The scheme was never built.

Moral? That bright ideas too much removed from the ordinary run of the mill hardly ever get adopted. Certainly not in prewar Britain.

Fig. 3) The next is a sad story, for this monster was actually built. The client wanted a water tower with the tank divided into five compartments, four of equal size and one larger. As his architect was unfamiliar with water tanks or reinforced concrete, he asked my firm – J. L. Kier and Company – to give him a price for design and construction.

I came up with a scheme with four circular tanks on slender circular columns, flaring at the top to support the tank walls. The fifth tank was formed by the space between the interconnected tanks. It was a monument beautiful to behold. But then the architect got the bright idea of using the space in between the columns for an office, adding some decorative features, rims at the top and bottom of the tanks, etc., which considerably complicated the formwork.

Moral? The intervention of an architect, even if he succeeds in pleasing the client, is not always helpful.

Fig. 4) Highpoint by Tecton, is quite a different story. Here was an architect, who knew what he wanted, and how to get it. An architect, I say – there were seven young architects, all equal, trading under this name, but one was more equal than the others. His name was Lubetkin, and from him I learnt among other things that architecture involves taking infinite care over every detail, including services, fittings, and other installations. Every tile was placed in an orderly pattern of unbroken squares, floor tiles lined up with wall tiles.

Lubetkin detailed the liftcage and shaft in tubular steel and netting, light and elegant, and between us we dealt with waterproofing, insulation, surface treatment of concrete, etc., in a very dilettantish way, I am afraid. It had to be cheap, and shoddiness gradually resulted, as with all these modern Corb-inspired buildings.

I dealt with the structural design, suggesting doing away with columns and beams inside the

Fig. 5a Brynmawr Rubber Factory, aerial view

Fig. 4a Construction of Highpoint 1

Fig. 5b Brynmawr Rubber Factory, interior

Fig. 4b Highpoint 1, interior

concrete box – which pleased Lubetkin – and organizing the construction, devising a special moving platform raised by jacks from which the formwork was suspended.

And I had to fight the authorities about the bye-laws and concrete regulations. So between us it was complete integration of design and construction. The heating was done by Hadens, hot water tubes being embedded in the concrete floors, a new development at the time.

Moral? Taking pains gets results.

Fig. 5) The fifth is Brynmawr Rubber Factory, designed by four young architects, the nucleus of the later ACP, or Architects Copartnership. It bubbles over with shells, as Jane Drew described it at that time.[*] What I would like to point out is the way the heating and ventilation were integrated with the roof structure of the main hall. The two main ducts blowing hot air into this area were housed inside two edge beams of adjoining square domes and the

---

[*] Dame Jane Drew (1911–1996), English modernist architect and town planner, was a leading exponent of the Modern Movement in London. She also worked in West Africa, designing schools and universities.

Fig. 6 Sydney Opera House

point is that the whole form of construction was especially chosen to make this possible, so avoiding the usual ugly ducting. That among other things, is what integrated design means, and I can't see how that can be achieved without the architect and the structural engineer coming into the picture beside the heating consultant.

And that is the moral.

Fig. 6) Lastly I show a few slides of Sydney Opera House. Utzon believed in the architect having control of every visible detail, like Lubetkin, and he undoubtedly was an architectural genius. But the organization he built up was not capable of dealing that way with a job of this complexity and magnitude. All went well as long as he was only dealing with the structure – the architecture in this case is the structure, he used to say – but integrating the unbelievably complex installations and furnishings with the structure in his exacting way could only have been done by a much more expert integrating team. The thing had to be completed without him, but it could not be done by anybody – or by Utzon himself, for that matter – to Utzon's standards. But Utzon's brilliant spatial conception has secured him a place in the architectural firmament.

The design team

Lubetkin and Utzon are what are generally referred to as *prima donna* architects, and this is meant as an insult, the image being associated with egocentric soloists throwing tantrums. Their contribution, however, is more that of a conductor – to choose another metaphor from music, so I will use the term architect-conductors. A conductor must know the score, obviously, and he must achieve a balance of sound which is faithful to the score but adds his own artistic touch to the whole. This must be hammered out in rehearsals. The conductor who only strikes attitudes and lets the orchestra get on as best it can does not deserve the name.

What does happen when the architect-conductor is mainly a visual artist, which is generally the case, is that he will allot too high a priority to sculptural or aesthetic quality. On the other hand his critics in most cases have also the wrong priorities, for they underrate visual or spatial quality for lack of visual training or sensitivity. You can't make a deaf man appreciate music. Yet spatial music *is* important. For we must build in space and in light, we appreciate the relationships of things in space and move in space and we create our own space. So a visual artist is not a bad conductor in this case, provided he has humanity and builds for people.

Leaving it to the architect-conductor to solve all his problems with the aid of his own team of architectural assistants and the specialists he consults, and the manufacturers he guides, can therefore give excellent results, depending on the master mind. But it breaks down in the case of large, technically sophisticated jobs. He must then at least have advisers and collaborators who are constantly at hand, also at the conceptual stage, for the whole way of tackling the job may depend on their advice – he cannot any more impose a visual pattern, it is the parameters, to use Lionel Brett's phrase, which govern the conception.*

But as long as the various disciplines and trades involved are represented by different firms, it is difficult to involve them all at the conceptual stage. And in any case you can only involve a few key men at that stage, otherwise the whole affair develops into a design by committee. And most important, those key men must share the conductor's view of what the aim is, and must try to achieve 'the complete integration of structure and services which will best serve that aim'.

This can as a rule be best achieved if they are independent consultants and not representatives of commercial firms. But they must not be specialists in a narrow field only – otherwise there will be too many of them. They must represent a broader section of the total technological knowledge required, able to produce – from inside their own firms, or by calling in from outside – *ad hoc* specialists as needed. They will in fact be assistant architects. Not on paper but in action. For not only should they understand the conductor's architectural ideas and approve of them, but like the architect they each represent a team covering a multiplicity of detailed knowledge and experience in a particular area of related subjects. They are also synthesizers, like the architect. It would not be a bad idea to recognize this and call them structural architects, building services architects, etc., etc., if they really are capable of fitting that role.

In the past, there have always been large lacunae in the combined knowledge of architects and consultants, which were covered by hunches and rules of thumb. That's why the fabric deteriorates, and the services don't work. This must stop; responsibility must be squarely placed in one camp or another.

The integration will then be effected from the top, so to speak, by the architect-conductor in conclave with his chief assistants and specialist co-architects, who then each will see to it that his particular team, including the *ad hoc* advisers needed, carries out the leader's agreed intentions.

Such a system can work very well, it is the parallel working which in a more or less incomplete form is generally practised.

The question has often been raised whether another profession could not fill the role of the leader. Of course, but it is not a profession but a person (with his team) which is the leader – and it depends on that person. He must then have the necessary qualifications for such leadership. He must be able to assess the priorities and effect the synthesis, be in effect an architect-conductor – in my sense.

I have not time now to discuss which technical co-architects will be required and what their role should be. There will obviously be a structural architect, for the structure and fabric of the whole building is the physical expression of the architecture. And there will equally certainly be a building services architect. As the name implies, he should cover all services, but should also understand the architectural and structural implications of their spatial requirements and the psychological and physiological effect on human beings of light and glare, of humidity, heat and radiation, noise vibration, acoustics – as well as the economic and ecological aspects of different sources of power. It is a very wide field and is largely dealt with by architectural hunches – which are very important, but can hardly deal with modern technological sophistication. One man cannot deal with all these aspects – but he should be able to call on the needed expertise as required. He would be of immense help to the building team, in fact without him expensive blunders are inevitable. And, of course, he should be able to achieve chartered status, but his status would be assured, anyway, If he could fill the role.

And may I say again that encouraging high calibre people to fill this role is much more important than any inter-institutional rivalries. If giving them chartered status furthers this aim, ways should be found to give it to them. If no more charters are available, they should combine with the Structurals, who also provide a building service, or with the Mechanicals, or some of the other institutions should combine – Structural with Civil for instance, which would be sensible – or what about Mining with Mining and Metallurgy, Marine Engineers with Naval Architects – leaving a space open, so to speak. This may be utterly naive, but those who know the ins and outs should find a way.

I wonder, are institutions created to prevent us from doing what we want to, or to give us an excuse for *not* doing what we ought? Surely not, so let bygones be bygones, kiss and be friends and let Fred have his lollipop. And if you think I am not serious you are wrong.

There is a third chief adviser who I think is needed, especially when the design stretches into untrodden territory. It is a production engineer, or operational costing expert. But this is a chapter in itself, and highly controversial to boot. I have probably offended enough people for one evening, and I have no time, either.

---

* Lionel Brett (1913–2004), architect and town planner, was president of the RIBA from 1965 to 1967.

There are, of course, many ways of working other than the way I have just described, in fact the possible permutations are legion. There is, for instance, the contractor's package deal, and there is the multi-disciplinary team working as we practise it in Arup Associates.

The latter is probably the best way to eliminate professional rivalries and create the right enthusiasm straight down the line, but it takes time. The quality of people plus enthusiasm is what matters, much more so than the type of organization. But the latter should be of a kind to encourage and not thwart enthusiasm.

The comprehensive view

Just one thing more – to set up an organization which is able to effect the integration of diverse elements of the environmental fabric is one thing. But its usefulness is severely restricted by existing bureaucratic boundaries.

Every time a major surgical operation disturbs established environmental patterns it sparks off side effects which may even make the proposed operation obsolete before it can fulfil its function. Where people live and work determines the transport network that establishes routes for underground services that feed the buildings with light, heat, water and telecommunications. These in turn generate new and inter-related problems and so on almost *ad infinitum*. A comprehensive view is essential. But departments keep on dealing with one aspect at a time.

The establishment of the Department of the Environment is the Central Government's answer to this problem. But will this enormous conglomeration of civil servants and professional gentlemen be able to cope with it? It seems almost too much to expect.

We must hope that they will learn by experience, it is obviously a step in the right direction. But we are beginning to witness the emergence of pressure groups of laymen who no longer are satisfied to trust the collective wisdom of the professionals to supervise our environment. The task is to restore trust in our ability to tackle comprehensive problems comprehensively.

Our aims must be comprehensive.
Our building competent.
But priorities must be fixed by men, not by machines.

I have said both too much and too little. I have tried to place the problem in its global or overall setting and therefore courted and, I am afraid, not avoided the dangers of superficiality. But I have made it clear, I think, where I stand.

I honestly cannot see how the BSES can achieve what it set out to achieve as long as the principal institutions concerned with building oppose it. It would become a bone of contention instead of a unifying influence.

And we very much need a unifying influence. I am all for a society of this kind, but the name should be something like the Society for the Built Environment. And it should not be the property of any institution. I cannot see the architects flocking to a meeting at the Civils or the engineers coming to the RIBA.

The venue could be changed from time to time, meetings could be arranged also in other cities. It should, of course, be supported by all those institutions who are now sulking – no disrespect intended – and it should collaborate with or absorb the Junior Liaison Organization and perhaps other groups who have the same aim. And the governing body, or at least the body that takes the initiative, should not consist of a representative from each of the sponsoring institutions or anything of that kind. It is not their job to represent anything except common sense. To run the show we should have people who understand the problems, who are convinced of the need for collaboration and have the enthusiasm, drive and tact to further the aims of the society. (The last is inserted to leave me out.)

And finally I suggest that the matter should be taken to the Presidents' Committee for the Urban Environment to initiate the formation of such a reformed society. This was Alex Gordon's suggestion, and it is obviously a sensible one, as you would expect. I hope the present sponsors would generously agree to that.[*]

It remains to thank my hosts for affording me the liberty to express my views. If I should have caused offence I regret it – but I can only say what I think is right. If I am not right, then I can only ask you to forgive me. If I should have been able to convince you that my views are sound, you will be generous enough to act on them.

But I cannot help thinking of Orwell's words in the recently discovered foreword to *Animal Farm*: 'Liberty means the right to tell people what they do not want to hear.'

To which my secretary cynically added: 'Stupidity is expecting that they will listen.'

---

[*] Alex Gordon (1917–1999), architect, was president of the Royal Institute of British Architects in 1971. He was the author of 'Long Life, Loose Fit, Low Energy', a paper presented at the RIBA conference in 1972, two years before the major world oil crisis (Maxwell Hutchinson, *The Guardian*, 19 July 1999).

Institution of Structural Engineers Gold Medal Speech

This address was given by Ove on receiving the 12th Gold Medal of the Institution, on 11 October 1973.

The Institution of Structural Engineers Gold Medal. Inscription reads 'Awarded to Ove Nyquist Arup for his contributions to structural engineering through his rare ability to influence the thoughts of his colleagues, engineers and architects alike in fundamental matters of form, function and structure'.

First of all I want to thank the President and Council and all of you for honouring me in this way. I am naturally very pleased, and I don't think this statement needs supporting evidence or argument. I was also very surprised, at least in the sense that I didn't expect it. Whether I think I *deserve* it is yet another question, and one to which I am not prepared to give a straight answer – sometimes I do and sometimes I don't.

In your very generous citation you honour me for my rare ability to influence the thoughts of my colleagues. If you say so, I suppose I must have influenced them – it is not for me to judge. It must obviously be left to those who have been so influenced to bear witness; which presumably they have done – and that it is a good influence is obvious from the whole context, so that is very gratifying. In fact it is quite marvellous what you say, I couldn't ask for more. But – I ask myself – what does this influence all amount to?

Perhaps that is a naughty question to ask, and perhaps I am fundamentally naughty, although I try to conceal it. But obviously everyone must put his own valuation on whatever praise or blame comes his way, so as not to get swollen-headed or unnecessarily dejected. As I have said before, to be fooled by praise or praised by fools profits no one. And it could be said that all the things I have spent my life trying to say and do and teach are simple, commonplace, and obvious, things that every moderately sensible person would know. For instance:

> that design and construction are interdependent and must be adjusted to one another

> that simplicity of design makes economic and aesthetic sense

that two parallel brick walls covered with a reinforced concrete slab don't provide a good shelter against blast

that when we build we don't want a good structure, but a good house

that when many cooks make a dish, they had better agree amongst themselves about the recipe

that to start thinking about the cost of what you are designing after you have designed it, is a bit late

that it is a waste of time to base exact calculations on rough assumptions, or a strong building on weak foundations, or in general to pursue the means without defining the ends.

All that, and more – it hardly seems to merit a Gold Medal, exactly. At least, if it does, it isn't because it is particularly clever. It must be because it needed saying just the same.

And as for influence – my persuasive powers may have worked with my colleagues, and with my collaborators especially. But I don't always seem to have made much headway with government departments or with official bodies. During the war, for instance, I remember I struggled hard to save steel for the war effort, and to knock some sense into official shelter policy – with scant success.

So you see, it isn't just a matter of what you say. It also depends on whom you say it to and when. You have to be fortunate enough to find people who will listen to you, so that concerted action can result. Ideas are powerful: that's why totalitarian states are afraid of them. But it's a delayed action.

They take time to sink in, and still more time to produce practical results – and the latter depends on other people.

Mind you, I am not trying to argue that I don't deserve the medal. It would be very sad if my rare ability to influence others persuaded you to take it back again. It may be that my ideas are not explosive, that they are very simple; they are just common sense.

But it is unfortunately also true that most of the mistakes made by engineers – and I suppose it applies to other people too – are elementary, are in fact due to lack of common sense. It is not so much that the involved calculations go wrong. It is more often that the structural system to which they are applied is basically unstable, or acts as a mechanism. Or that some forces are simply forgotten. Or that people think and draw in two dimensions, forgetting the third which may contain some awkward forces. Or they forget that the design has to be built, and must therefore be possible and preferably not too difficult to build and should be stable during all stages of the construction. Or that they put things in the wrong place altogether, because the whole purpose of what they are doing is barely considered.

I could tell you many frightening stories of failures of common sense. There was one glaring and almost incredible case. I know I shouldn't tell you about it, because it casts a not too favourable light on the *Journal of the Institution of Structural Engineers*. But it was in 1929, and the *Journal* now is not what it was then, it has improved beyond all measure, and what happened then certainly couldn't happen now. So perhaps I may be forgiven.

An article by a past President of the Institution appeared in the *Journal* under the heading: 'Notes on a failure due to subsidence under tidal pressures'. He had been called in to apportion blame in a case where a retaining wall or wharf had collapsed as soon as the backfilling was placed. The wall was L-shaped, some 20 ft. high, with counterforts about every 10 ft., each supported on two, almost vertical, piles. There was absolutely nothing there that would prevent the wall from being pushed forward by the filling, one could see that at a glance by looking at the cross-section. No anchors, no raking piles. And isn't it remarkable that in those days a design like that could be adopted, the contractor could build it without protest, and a learned and respected engineer could undertake completely unnecessary measurements of minute vertical and horizontal movements of the mud in front of the wall under the influence of the tides, and his report could be published in an engineering journal, without anybody raising an eyebrow so far as I know? So I piped up. I sent an article to the *Journal* gently pointing out the facts of life – only to be told that it was controversial and couldn't be published under the umbrella of the editor. I could only be allowed to send in a private letter, which could go in at the back of the journal on my own responsibility. So that's what I did and waited for the explosion. And I never heard another word about it.

That was long ago, and times have changed. But wasn't Ronan Point a similar case?* Isn't it clear as daylight that when you have an end wall, which is not tied back, supporting a portion of the building, and when an explosion takes place behind it, then what must happen is exactly what did happen? The important difference is, of course, that a backfilling is bound to exert a pressure, whereas explosions are not bound to take place, and were in any case not officially anticipated in the regulations. So perhaps the remedy is official anticipation; in other words more regulations. Or perhaps what is needed is the kind of common sense that would reject a structure which only needed a hard push to come tumbling down. And if once it is generally accepted that designs may be successfully produced simply by applying a host of detailed regulations, common sense does tend to get left out.

So perhaps after all it is useful to repeat obvious things again and again. When I was young and innocent I would have hesitated to do so – but now that I am old and cynical, I have learned better; and so I fully intend to continue to utter platitudes for the rest of my life.

And that, surely must be the perfect lead-in to allow me to trot out again some of my old hobby horses. To say again, for instance, that a structure exists for a purpose and as part of an entity that also has its purpose; and that the efficiency of a structure can only be judged in the light of these various purposes great and small. To insist again on the need to integrate the work of the various disciplines in the building industry, in order to achieve greater efficiency, and greater artistic control. All right – old hat it may be; but the hat still fits. The plain facts are that architecture will die if it is not efficient; and that we *need* an environment where we can feel at home – which is what architecture stands for. Such facts are no less true now that we are undertaking tasks of ever-increasing size and complexity, with ever more complex technical resources at our command. And when I say that design should aim at a practical fulfilment of purpose, this is the purpose I have in mind.

But it is not the purpose that is forced upon us. For totally integrated comprehensive architecture will result in efficiency of execution, but will also require much effort and dedicated involvement on the part of the directing team. And the onslaught of mechanization and standardization, the compulsion to minimize human efforts, to reduce cost at whatever cost, all this may spell – I am afraid – the end of design as an art. And of course many people realize now that our economic thinking is faulty, that the cost in human happiness is too high, that we are frantically busy building on sinking foundations. We can afford, if need be, a lowering of material standards. What we can't afford is to lose our humanity.

But there is no agreement on what we can do about it; the radical measures required for reversing the trend seem impossible to realize. Perhaps I can put it this way: that unless we cultivate an art of the impossible, we may well be doomed.

This is a gloomy note to end on, I am afraid.

But receiving a Gold Medal should be, not an impediment, but an encouragement to speak one's mind. It is in my mind that the time ahead is going to call for common sense to a quite uncommon degree.

Finally, I thank you again for my Gold Medal. I am aware that to get a Gold Medal one also has to be lucky. One must firstly have collaborators who follow up ideas with actions and one must live long enough for such actions to bear fruit. I have been lucky in both respects. One of my partners, a very distinguished member of your institution, happens to have been with me for 30 years this very day, and I honestly don't know what the firm or I would have done without him. I think you can guess his name.

I conclude therefore by thanking my partners and collaborators who should really be sharing my medal with me and also last but not least, my wife, who *will* share the medal with me.

---

* Ronan Point was a 22-storey tower block in Newham, east London, completed on 11 March 1968, and was part of the wave of tower blocks built in the 1960s as cheap, affordable prefabricated housing. It suffered a partial collapse on 16 May 1968, when a gas explosion demolished a load-bearing wall, causing the collapse of one entire corner of the building. Four people were killed in the incident, and seventeen were injured. See Matthys Levy and Mario Salvadori, *Why Buildings Fall Down*, new edn (W.W. Norton & Co., New York, 1994).

Co-Operation between Architects and Allied Professions

This article was published in the Arup Journal, *2 June 1975.*

I am invited to write a short piece (600–800 words) on 'The Theory and Effective Practice of Co-operation between Architects and Allied Professions'. Not just a quart, but a couple of cubic metres into a pint bottle! A tough proposition! But I'll try.

First the Theory.

It is a fact, that any building or construction nowadays must be preceded by a design or a number of designs, if you like – what I call a Total Design – which is the key to what it is intended to build and how it is going to be built.

It is also a fact that such a Total Design can rarely be produced by one man. It requires the collaboration of several people who have been trained to deal with particular aspects of this total design – a spatial arrangement, structure, services and so on. But if every specialist produced the perfect solution to his particular problem, these part designs would simply not fit together to produce a successful whole. And of course, it is the whole we want. In fact, we want more and more things, as many as we can get for our money. And we want to satisfy not only the client, but also the people using or having to live with the building or bridge, or whatever it is. We want it to harmonise with the environment and we want to ensure that there are no destructive or anti-social side effects.

That this calls for close integration of the part designs and close collaboration between all the people who should or who do influence the design is obvious, and is all the theory that is needed, as far as I can see.

This consideration of every aspect of the design and fitting the bits together to produce the best possible total solution is the real art of designing. And as in all art, there is more to it than meets the eye. It is not only a question of meeting all the different requirements in the fullest possible way at the least cost, it depends also on the simplicity or elegance of the solution, the felicity of design which has the power to inspire those who comprehend it, and which is the reward the designers hope for. It can rarely be produced without taking great pains and it cannot be defined or measured.

How to ensure that every design gets the care and attention needed to produce a thing of quality is, I suppose, the question covered by the second part of the title: 'the effective practice of co-operation between planners, architects etc.' That is a much more difficult question to deal with because there is obviously no general rule and none that by itself would guarantee the desired result. There is even no generally accepted criteria which can decide whether it has been achieved or approached in a particular case. But whereas abundant lip service has been paid for years and years to the need for such co-operation in all its forms (in fact the energy spent in moving all those thousands of lips for the last 40 years must have contributed to our present energy crisis), the progress in 'effective practice' has been disappointing.

The reasons for this are manifold and well known. The different professional institutions have nursed their separateness for too long to be able to change their attitude in a few years. Educational establishments have concentrated on turning out specialists, thereby fostering a narrow outlook. The whole organisation of the building industry has its roots in the past and cannot adapt itself so quickly to the vastly changed social and technical climate of today. It is fragmented, full of vested interests, of rivalries between professions and trades, about status, money, responsibility and influence. It clings to outworn practices and is governed by partly irrational legal restrictions. There is also the traditional chasm between design and execution and the stranglehold of the costing system leading to the costing of non-existing designs as if quality and integration did not matter. This is not the whole picture, of course, but it is things like that which make it difficult to create the conditions where collaboration can take place between those technicians who really understand the business of building and who are eager to get on with the job of finding the right answers i.e. the right designs at the right price.

But what then is 'the effective practice of co-operation' and how can it be brought about?

My short answer is that you learn co-operation by practising it. You will then learn to understand the other fellow's point of view and the value of his contribution and you will learn to see your own work as part of a whole, which will gradually tend to make your collaboration more effective. But of course, it depends on the quality of the people in the team, and especially on the leaders inside each of the disciplines represented. If they have the necessary enthusiasm and will to produce a work of quality, half the battle is won.

Talking or writing about collaboration and integration is not nearly as effective as we have seen. But that does not mean that it is useless – on the contrary – it is a necessary preparation. But also here it depends on the quality of the talk. The tendency is for talking to be done by those who are good at talking. But it is much more important that it is done by those that know how to build well, and who understand the need for integration. Each job is in many ways unique, but designers can help each other by explaining how they have surmounted certain difficulties on their job, especially in the domain of integrating the various disciplines, including the method of construction or manufacture which has, or should have, a major influence on all designs where economy is of importance – which in varying degrees applies to all of them. And, even after 40 years of talking about collaboration and integration, it is still necessary to convince authorities, private clients and their legal and financial advisors that it will repay them handsomely to ensure that they have got the right design before they start to build and that this means that the advice of all those who have a significant contribution to make to the Total Design should be sought *before* the basic design decisions are taken. This means, at the very least, that they must have the opportunity to meet and harmonise their requirements on the basis of priorities established by the leaders of the team and the clients. This can be a long process but out of this melting pot a purified design should emerge which will more than repay the effort expended.

It is a sad fact that most of the people who are not designers but have the power to get things built, do not understand this. They think that designing is a routine matter. It can be reduced to that and that is what is the trouble with our environment.

The Building Centre

This lecture was given at the Building Centre, London, on 18 May 1978.

Origins

The Building Centre came into being because a number of public spirited people concerned with building in some way or other felt that something like that was needed to take advantage of the many new materials and inventions which had come on the market lately, and they decided to *do* something about it. They were not so very clear about what exactly was needed and how to finance the venture, but in the typical British way they started on a small scale with something obviously useful, a samples room at the Architectural Association perhaps, roped in like-minded people who gave of their time and money, and off they were. Where to – that could be and was discussed on the way, as the nature of the country dictated.

That this developed into the present Building Centre is a tribute to the devotion and tenacity of the founders. But that is not what I want to dwell on tonight. Instead I will try to tackle the problem from the other end: why do we need a Building Centre? What is it for, and what should it provide, ideally speaking, if money were no problem?

My point of view will be that of a designer who is trying to find the best possible solution to design problems occurring in buildings, and I am suggesting that to help designers in this task should be the main aim of the Building Centre.

Total Design

This is not such a one-sided view as it may seem to be. For it can be argued – as I have done for 40 years – that what I call the Total Design is the key to what is built. If the design is right, and, if it is executed as intended, then the job will be right. And the aim of the designer of buildings or parts of buildings, and that of the Building Industry as a whole, as well as that of the general public, must of course be to get the best possible buildings at the right cost, which as I have argued, means ensuring that the design is right. The execution must be right as well, of course, but that is another matter; the design must be tackled first.

The word design can mean so many things, however, and it is necessary to emphasize that here I am talking about the Total Design, by which I understand the sum of *all* the design decisions made by many people with different functions and which collectively define the finished job. The decisions may be recorded in specifications, on drawings or sketches, in by-laws and regulations, or it may be contained in the client's brief, or consist of verbal instructions by clients or foremen or others; the test is whether the decision affects what is being built or constructed.

The Total Design for a building embraces a great many part-designs, for foundations, windows, lifts or what not, and each of these may have smaller parts – 'and so ad infinitum'. And the building itself may be a part of a group of buildings; a university, a town, a district or country.

It will be readily seen that there is practically no limit to the number of Total Designs which could be made for an artefact consisting of parts which can be varied and combined in an almost infinite number of ways – good, bad or indifferent. But how do we know which is which? How do we recognize the 'goodness' of a building, or of any human artefact, for that matter? Which of all the possible designs is the best one?

Quantity

A Quantity Surveyor can't help us, for he can only sum up the quantities and transform them into costs, but he will miss what is most important – what we may call the quality of the building. But quality – what is it?

We come up against the fact that quality can't be measured. We may recognize quality when we see it, but we can't define it. And the worst is, that it means something different to different people. 'One man's meat is another man's poison' as they say.

But it would be wrong to conclude from this that quality only exists in the eye of the beholder. When it comes to works of art we have plenty of 'Quality Surveyors' – critics, historians, practising artists, or students of art, who are very willing to tell us what is good and what is bad, and they would strongly deny that they only spoke for themselves. They consider themselves as experts on particular art form, at least inside a cultural frame of reference.

It is true that they often disagree. There are factions and fashions in the world of art. But inside each of these factions or fashions it is possible to distinguish works of character and quality from what is just immature rubbish, more or less. And unless an artist has this veneration for art, and believes in the mission of the artist, he is unlikely to produce anything outstanding. The highest accolade which can be bestowed on a work of art is to call it timeless art. But how timeless? If humanity perishes – 'timeless art' has no meaning.

When we come to Building the situation is somewhat different, for a building is more than a work of art. It has work of its own to do, it should satisfy a great many different requirements, which might, with some contrivance, be summarized under the headings: commodity, firmness and delight. Unfortunately they often clash with each other and money is mostly short.

We therefore have to fix our priorities to make a judgement and these priorities are bound to vary for instance according to whether we judge the building as users, owners or just onlookers.

The quality of a building thus appears as a conglomeration of different qualities which, however, cannot be added up to produce a sum which would be an index of the total quality, for they have no common denominator. Some qualities, like stability, are essential up to a point and useless thereafter – others are marginally desirable, some make for comfort, some for beauty and some for economy – it is a question of what you want most.

The functional and what we might call the engineering qualities of rival schemes can, to some extent, be measured and compared. It may take some time before their true worth is revealed, however. In contrast, we are immediately aware of the visual aspects of a scheme as represented by perspectives or models, and it is on this basis that its place in the architectural hierarchy is determined. This can often be very misleading.

Many people suffer through having to live or work in architectural masterpieces and many highly praised designs in architectural competitions couldn't be built as depicted or would fall down if they were built.

In line with this, it is nearly always the architect who is blamed if a building project happens to displease, or praised if it pleases, for whatever reason. This is often unjust – but on the whole it makes sense, for it is the architectural direction which determines what we get – the technique is only the means of getting it.

Any good design must strive both to create internal harmony between its parts and outward harmony with its surroundings. As the Total Design is not often the creation of one man, as the public is led to believe by the media, but is affected by the design decisions of numerous people largely motivated by their own aims, this internal and external harmony or integration can only be achieved if the designers themselves work in harmony.

Choosing

Designing is choosing: the materials, the structure, the spatial layout, the services, all of it. Without choice there can be no perfection – perfection is choosing rightly all the time. But we don't invent everything from scratch. More and more designing is becoming the judicious assembling of pre-manufactured parts. The right parts, assembled the right way.

The choosing must therefore be guided by a vision of the whole. If this vision is accepted by the whole design team, and has the enthusiastic backing of the clients, then there is the best possible chance of a happy ending. Unfortunately this does not happen too often.

To choose the right materials and parts, we must, of course, also know that they exist, where they can be got, their properties and price, so that we can compare them and choose those that best serve our purpose. If I may quote from an address which I gave to the British Society for the Advancement of Sciences during the war in January 1942 '… a wealth of new knowledge, new materials, new processes has so widened the field of possibilities, that it cannot be adequately surveyed by a single mind … and the usual problem arises how to create the organisation, the "composite mind" so to speak, which can achieve a well-balanced synthesis from the wealth of available detail. This is, I suppose, one of the central problems of our time.'

My answer was at that time, briefly:

1) One is to have the planning carried out by a team of experts whose combined knowledge covers a substantial part of the relevant technical information.
2) Another is to have all the technical information which may have a bearing on the problem checked up, classified, standardised and made easily available.

If this was needed then, it is ten times as much needed now, and what the Building Centre is trying to do is really to help with the second requirement, that of knowing which materials and resources are available. They are doing a very useful job in that line, but there is still a considerable gap between what the sponsors would have liked to do and what they in the nature of things can do.

The user

The user would like the exhibition to include anything which could be useful to him. For obvious reasons it would be impossible to include everything being manufactured or imported for use in Building so a selection must be made to reduce it to a manageable dimension. But on what basis? The present policy of allotting space to those that pay for it may be unavoidable, but is obviously unsatisfactory. What could replace it? Selection according to quality? We have already discussed the difficulties inherent in that. Besides, cost is so important that we cannot make quality the over-riding condition. The exhibition is also meant for housewives and 'do it yourself'-ers, who have every right to decide what they want their kitchen to look like, but who do not necessarily care for the opinion of well-wishing quality surveyors. And think of the consequences. The cry of 'Why weren't we included?' The very idea of selection bristles with difficulties.

But there are two ways of selling:

1) By producing goods which are good, durable and yet cheap – which are easy to sell.
2) Or, to rely on advertising, packaging and salesmanship to seduce people to buy.

It would be a good idea to favour the first kind – but they are not always easy to distinguish – there are many grades between the two. But that there ought to be some kind of selection cannot be gainsaid, also because the whole purpose of the Building Centre was to further *better* building. I am afraid this is a matter I will have to leave to the management to solve – it calls for tact and diplomacy, which is not my country, but it could become easier as the prestige of the Building Centre grows, as I am sure it will.

If space is scarce and sought after, it might be possible to impose certain restrictions and conditions.

But there is another need which is still more important, and also more difficult. The Building Centre provides information mainly by referring to the trade literature of the exhibiting firms. This naturally praises their wares, more or less truthfully, but doesn't say anything about the snags, except perhaps in a few cases of truth in advertising.

But it's the snags we are interested in. We want to know how long the thing will last, what can go wrong, what are the maintenance costs, how does it compare with a rival article? These things the Building Centre cannot disclose – it would upset its customers. And if one turns to the various research stations we have the same trouble. They will issue a report of their research to the firm that pays for it, and the firm will use its discretion about what to publish. The law of libel is probably too strict. If you tell a truth which damages somebody's economic interest, truth is no excuse – if I am not mistaken.

It somehow reminds me of an Old German couplet which I was taught when, as a child, I went to school in Hamburg and which in my childish innocence I embraced with enthusiasm. It was this:

Wer die Wahrheit kennet
und saget sie nicht,
der ist für wahr
ein erbärmlicher Wicht.

As there may be some of you who don't understand German, I will attempt a translation:

He who knowest the truth and doesn't
   speak out,
He is indeed a contemptible lout!

The last word should have been 'knave' – but what rhymes with knave? A more up-to-date version might be:

He who knowest the truth,
Had better forget it,
Lest otherwise,
He should live to regret it.

So what can be done about that?

The Building Centre wants to be a force for good; but it must pay for itself, it must be solvent to exist, as it gets no grant from the Government.

The solution has been to run the Centre on strictly commercial lines, and with the profit it makes it endows a trust which hands out money to socially useful activities. This is probably an excellent policy – for it is difficult to mix business with charity. But I do think they should not forget their primary business of giving the public an overall view of what industry and commerce can do for Building, by making their exhibition selective and yet inclusive and their information a model of truth in advertising. It is a formidable task and I know it is what the present leaders would want to do. Ought it to have Government consideration, particularly at this time when Agreement activities are under review?

The Engineer Looks Back

This article was written for the Architectural Review, *vol. 166, issue 993, November 1979, pp. 315–21.*

To be asked, at very short notice, to write an article on the architecture of the '30s – presumably from an engineering aspect – is a tough assignment. The subject is vast, there is no time to sort out and consult the large amount of stored up evidence to jolt the memory and check its accuracy. All I can do is to write down some memories about what the '30s meant to me. I speak as an outsider – a double outsider, in fact – a foreigner among the British and an engineer among architects. It is axiomatic, of course, that a foreigner can never hope to understand the British, nor an engineer architecture. But otherwise, being an outsider has its advantages. And I was, of course, not the only foreigner in the game, for the 'Modern Movement' in Britain was at that time essentially a foreign import. It was by definition international, being steered by the prophets of the movement organised in CIAM, with branches in the countries which were sufficiently awake to receive the message. Britain was considered rather backward in this respect, but with the help of a few disciples who had worshipped at the shrine of the masters a propaganda centre, the MARS Group, was established. According to some undated 'Regulations' of the Modern Architectural Research Group I found in a MARS file, the objects of the group were:

1) The [founding of an?] Association of Architects Engineers and Allied Technicians and other persons for the purpose of furthering an architecture to serve the needs of Society.
2) To co-operate in furthering and supporting the aims of the National Groups organised in other countries who are associated in the International Congresses for Modern Architecture.

Those who were also members of CIAM were automatically honorary members and did not have to pay a subscription. Obviously they were the elite. This was modified later, but the pecking order tended to be defined by closeness to the source. I became a member of the group shortly after it was formed. Being a foreigner and an engineer was no obstacle but I was, of course, supposed to agree with the objects of the Group and be prepared to participate 'effectively' (!) in the realisation of its programme. Which I did, and was – but with some reservations.

To explain these reservations I would have first to say a few words about my own situation. If this article ends up dealing more with me than with architectural history it is not because I wish it so – it is simply because that is all I am competent to deal with, and even then it is probably unavoidable that some hindsight will creep into the story. I had studied philosophy for three or four years at Copenhagen University during the First World War, and had then embarked on a five-year study of engineering, because philosophy could not solve the riddles of the universe or the conundrum of the human predicament. Truth evades us, but we can make things, and if what we make is good, we feel good, that, in short, was my argument, and I knew I could become a good engineer – I was not sure about becoming a good architect or artist, and being a second-rate one didn't appeal to me.

Towards the end of my studies I specialised in reinforced concrete because this exciting new material obviously had a potential which was still waiting to be exploited. And in the beginning of 1922 I was lucky to be employed by a Danish firm (Christiani & Nielsen) specialising in reinforced concrete design and construction, a combination which was essential if the potentiality of this material was to be tested in practice. That the designer must know not only the qualities of his materials and the way they are made, but also how they can be built into the job was something I was soon to learn, if I did not already know it. At that time the concrete was made on the job – 'cast in situ' was the expression – and could be given any desirable shape, so here was something for the imagination to work on. I was first sent to their Hamburg office, and then transferred to London in 1923. When we reached the '30s I had had nearly 10 years' experience in reinforced concrete design and construction, mainly in marine work, bridges and industrial structures, I was chief designer in the firm's London office and had contributed to the technical press – especially a series of articles on the design of jetties. So my credentials as 'concrete specialist' were in order.

But my interest in architecture had received little nourishment. I got an introduction to visit Mies van der Rohe in Berlin in 1921, and in 1922 and 1923 in Hamburg I subscribed to progressive papers such as *Neue Rundschau* and Wasmuth's *Monatshefte*,[*] the latter dealing exclusively with modern architecture, visited the 'Munchener Kammerspiele[†] which had moved to Hamburg to escape the reactionary atmosphere in Munich (Adolf Hitler!) and attended most of the 'Uhrauffhrüngen' [premières] of the plays of Ernst Toller, Fritz von Unruh and other modern authors and experienced the intellectual turmoil of the post-war period coupled with the fantastic inflation – the currency was stabilised shortly after I left at the rate of one 'goldmark' to 1,000,000,000,000 papermark – worth about one shilling.

In London I had to adjust to a completely different intellectual climate – it was like stepping 50 years back in time. There were plenty of things going on in England, of course, but I was a foreigner with but a poor command of the language, and I did not happen to land in a circle where social, aesthetic or moral problems were being discussed. At that time England was even more than now split into social layers which mostly communicated with their own kind. As an engineer, I never met any architects. A year or two after I arrived in England I was happily married, lived in a studio in Battersea, cycled to the office and at lunchtime went to Battersea Park for picnic lunches with my wife. We listened to Bertrand Russell and Bernard Shaw and went to the Gate Theatre, went for walks in the countryside and punted on the Thames – all on £5 a week to begin with. And we heard Hitler on the crystal set and saw the post-war problems merging into pre-war problems.

I had plenty to do and gradually got interested and absorbed in my work and had no plans to start a new firm or anything of that sort. But I often felt frustrated, for only 10 per cent of the schemes I produced were built, and not the best ones at that.

The resistance against any kind of new idea at all was great, the bureaucratic obstructions and imbecilities were difficult to combat, and worst of all I could not complete my jobs as I wanted to because of the overriding necessity of beating our competitors on price – that was the whole idea

---

[*] The *Neue Rundschau* was a German literary magazine founded in 1890. *Wasmuth Monatshefte*, a German magazine for architecture, first appeared in 1914 and was discontinued in 1942. It consisted of long essays and generous illustrations covering modern architecture in its various movements between the First and Second World Wars. The focus was on buildings and architects in German-speaking countries, but international developments were also presented.

[†] The Munich Kammerspiele was founded in 1911 and featured German-language theatre classics and contemporary drama.

of the game and nothing, certainly no aesthetics or dreams of 'delight' were allowed to interfere with that – they weren't even appreciated. It is not the same now, but in the sphere of private industry it was certainly the case, then.

Then in the early '30s various things happened – I am not quite sure about the chronological order: I met someone who introduced me to the Architectural Association, which I joined. I was aware that concrete was increasingly being used for building and tried to interest my firm in it. Then I was approached by Godfrey Samuel on behalf of Tecton and asked whether our firm was interested in quoting for 'Highpoint'. I was, but my firm wasn't. I wrote to the head office in Copenhagen, but they were not interested. They were not builders, they had no joinery shops or plumbers, they were making exciting new concrete structures all over the world, why should they bother with some such fiddly work? Very understandable. But by chance I was at that time approached by Kiers – Lotz & Kier at that time – who wanted to move their head office to London from Stoke-on-Trent and offered me the job of chief designer and a directorship. I agreed on condition that they would quote keenly for the work of Tecton and other modern architects. Not without serious misgivings, for it was certainly a come-down as far as structural excitement was concerned. The structural problems presented by building seemed trivial compared with what civil engineering had to offer. Admittedly I underrated the capacity of architects to complicate the structure! But I needed in any case to cultivate the architectural 'dimension' for my own satisfaction to improve the quality of my work and I did not give up civil engineering altogether, although the move diminished my chance of getting that kind of work.

I had already helped Tecton to build the gorilla house at the Zoo while still at Christiani & Nielsen. To the consternation of the foreman the whole firm of Tecton came to help 'stirring' the wet concrete to get a feel of the material. After joining Kiers I worked with Tecton on the Penguin Pond and on Highpoint. Lubetkin was delighted when I suggested leaving out the columns and most of the beams and allowing the walls to take over the work of columns and lintels. This was both simpler to do and neater and was in line with what I had been doing for industrial structures, coal bunkers and silos. I had realised earlier that the reinforced concrete slab was a much underrated structural member. It was always considered as a panel which had to be supported by beams or columns at the edges, whereas in fact it was very strong in its own plane and able to resist forces in that plane. Used as a wall it could take vertical loads and span over openings. Because of the simplicity of the formwork I considered the slab to be the natural element for reinforced concrete. This view had already been put forward by [Robert] Maillart, but I had never heard of him. It also influenced Tecton's design for the Penguin Pool at the Zoo. Another advantage of designing the structure as a simple box was that it would make it possible to rationalise the formwork, using the same set of wall forms for the whole building by inventing a way of lifting the forms up from bottom to top in a series of steps three to each floor. Nowadays one would only use one lift per floor, but at that time one was not allowed to concrete more than 3ft 6in at a time to ensure proper tamping of the concrete. Another of those completely unnecessary restrictions!

That the design must include designing or specifying the way of building was one of the useful lessons I learned at C & N, a lesson which I have tried to preach to all and sundry with severely limited success.

That what we may call sculptural simplicity mostly favours constructional simplicity is, however, not the only reason for pursuing it. For me simplicity has always been an aim in its own right, presumably because it is allied to clarity and architectural quality. But neither sculptural nor constructional simplicity can be identified with structural simplicity. The visual simplicity is often deceptive; it can conceal a pretty contorted structure resulting in high stresses and an unhealthy concentration of steel reinforcements at critical points. The internal stresses produced by outer forces and temperature movements may revolt against being constrained by an artificially imposed spatial straitjacket. And it was very difficult to get unusual, so-called 'special' structures which did not conform to LCC [London County Council] regulations passed by the authorities. These regulations only covered the normal orthogonal grid and if Highpoint had not been situated in Hornsey, which was outside the LCC area, it could never have been built in that form.

Unfortunately most of my designs were of that special kind so I had a running battle with authorities and didn't always win. To my surprise the Highpoint structure was later hailed as a great innovation, largely through Lubetkin's flair for publicity, and he bestowed on me the name of 'doctor' – a name by which I am still known to some people. It did not help that later I sent a notice to *The Architects' Journal* promising a reward of £500 – or was it £50? – to anyone who could prove that I was a doctor.

Anyhow, through Lubetkin's help I acquired a kind of reputation among modern architects.

It was not far from being hinted that I had practically invented reinforced concrete. Which shows on what flimsy ground reputations are built.

As I mentioned before, Lubetkin welcomed my proposal to do away with columns and beams, and then, typically, as I was to discover, proceeded to make it almost impossible for me to do so. I had started my first lesson in architecture! It is well known that the aims of the dyed-in-the-wool architect are not always the same as the ditto engineer. There is obviously something wrong with the dyes; they clash. They must be harmonised. It is easy to demonstrate the nature of these clashes in a simple case, like Highpoint, and it may be useful to do so, even if this kind of construction is now obsolete.

That the block of flats had to be put on columns *à la* Corbusier was a purely architectural device. It would be difficult to pretend that it is useful in this case, it would be much simpler to start the whole apparatus for lifting the formwork at ground level. And as the vertical forces are taken to the ground through the outer walls, it would have been simpler, if there had to be columns, to place them in the line of the external wall instead of pushing them inwards to a position which pleased the eye rather than the physical facts. Transferring the whole weight of the building horizontally creates considerable moments, necessitating crossbeams which again have to be concealed, etc. This causes a fair amount of trouble and expense. But it could be done fairly easily, and the architects of course wanted it done, and when I visualised the building without this and other architectural 'gimmicks' – an expression which engineers often apply to architectural expression – I could easily see that they were right. The same applies to the small balconies on the end elevation. They are not really made for use or easy construction, they are ornaments, 'gimmicky', but highly successful, in my opinion. Ornaments were supposed to be out, of course. They had to have a functional or economical excuse for their existence, and architects have developed a great flair for producing such excuses out of thin air for clients who would not take kindly to 'aesthetic' reasons. In this case the balconies could be fire escapes. Not a bad excuse, actually.

Matters get worse when we come to the large window openings in the living room of the larger flats. These cut away most of the wall on this side, leaving only wall strips on each side to take the vertical load. Coinciding with this opening there is a balcony cantilevered out from the floor slab with a heavy balustrade and no sidewalls to support it. The weight of the floor and balcony has to be transferred to the vertical wall strips by the panel wall under the window acting as a horizontal beam, which it can just do by thickening it and adding steel reinforcement. But then comes the final blow – this panel has to be cut away on one side to give way for the door to the balcony, so that it never reaches the supporting wall on this side. The floor is the only connection.

There is no satisfactory solution to this structural problem. However, reinforced concrete cast in situ is a very adaptable material. The structure forms one monolithic whole, where a stress or strain in any part can be felt in every other part. If one point is in danger of being overstressed, other parts can be persuaded to come to its rescue by suitable reinforcement. In this case the floor can be cross-reinforced to spread the shear and moment sideways over a wide area of floor and balcony, the remaining panel wall can be cantilevered from the column strip on the other side, etc. It's a muddy kind of structure, one doesn't know exactly how the stresses are distributed, but one can ensure that the structure is perfectly safe, although it probably would not comply with the regulations. Not at that time, anyhow.

All this could have been avoided if we had provided a narrow vertical wall support between the door opening and the window, but this would have interrupted the horizontal sweep of the view. Was it worth it? It's a moot point. I didn't like this kind of contorted structure. The architects didn't mind. They had got what they wanted, it couldn't be seen, nobody would know about it, it wasn't their money. Should the client have been consulted? He rarely is, in such cases. The architect takes it upon himself to act for the client. Which, it can be said, is what he is supposed to do. What does the client know about architecture? He might make the wrong decision. The engineer should not be asked; his job is to keep mum. He has an easy way out, of course. He can simply say that it can't be done, or that the architect must take the full responsibility. That would put an end to it. But it wouldn't be true. It can be done. It's safe enough. I certainly wouldn't like to take this line. And I honestly do not know what the answer should have been in this case. I can see the architect's point of view. If I had been the client I might well have agreed with him.

I have described this case in detail because it so simply highlights the kinds of problem which keep occurring in architect-engineer collaboration. In the work we did for Tecton there are many such cases, and it is the same with any 'strong' architect, who has a very definite opinion about where he wants to go. They are, in fact, the kind of architects

I like to work with, in spite of the extra effort required. I don't think much of those who say that I should decide on an appropriate structure for the job and they will fit their architecture to it, and I have met a few of those, especially in the early days of functionalism, when the functionally 'right' thing was supposed to produce the right architecture. It doesn't, it produces no architecture at all.

In those days I got quite a reputation for doing tricks with reinforced concrete. It was even assumed by some that I liked doing it. That was entirely wrong. Simplicity is what I have always been striving for. A tortuous structure is not an architectural asset – it is a flaw in the total architecture. It is a potentially weak point in the structure.

I owe a great debt to Lubetkin and Tecton. They taught me that architecture can only be produced by trying again and again until a satisfactory solution has been reached, and that the engineer, bent on creating logical, elegant and buildable structure, must realise that there are other more important aims which may take precedence, even at the cost of a distorted and more expensive structure. The architect, on the other hand, must realise that the engineer's aim is important and should not be jeopardised for a mere whim, and that there may be a case for a fresh look if it can't be achieved with the present arrangement. Engineers may complain that the architect is not willing to do this because it requires more effort and he is not really interested in the structure or even the cost as long as he gets what he wants. And the architect may complain that the engineer doesn't try hard enough to meet his requirements. Getting to know a group of architects concerned about the fundamentals of architecture and joining MARS meant much to me. It was like entering a new world, there was a complete change of atmosphere. Here was a group of people with a sense of mission, a common cause: to create a new architecture which would cast off the tyranny of 'Beaux-Arts' and all the old styles for all time and replace it with a new international style based on our new technology, which was capable of satisfying the needs and aspirations of mankind if used with reason and justice. Or words to that effect. The cause was never very clearly defined, but the enthusiasm was there, there were debates on social and technical problems, on ends and means, there were arguments and strife. In short, there was life. There was the feeling of 'Bruderschaft' which had received a message from on high and had a duty to convert the world, and there were individuals who followed their own line which was then adopted as approved 'modern' although it looked a bit odd in the context. What, for instance, had Corbusier and Frank Lloyd Wright in common?

I agreed with the need to sweep away old cobwebs and start afresh. 'Functionalism' to me meant that the buildings we build should fulfil their function – priority number one – and that materials should be used in accordance with their physical properties and the way they are manufactured and placed in the final fabric of the building. But I soon found that that was not the general opinion – or not the general practice at any rate. In most cases priority number one seemed to be that the building should look 'modern', like a building by Corb or Mies or some of the other masters.

I am tempted to quote from a report of 11 April 1935 sent by the MARS exhibition committee (Sise, McGrath, Drake) to the executive committee. Although it was fortunately rejected by the latter, it was a very typical interpretation of the 'Modern Style'. After some paragraphs about the exhibition, etc, there is one on 'General considerations':

> The attitude it is proposed to adopt is as follows: There exists throughout the world to-day a manner of building which 'orders the visible manifestation of a certain close relationship between structure and function'. This healthy situation – the life force of so many historical styles – has been brought about in our day by a deliberate and self-conscious application of the logic of modern constructional methods employing, for the most part, steel and reinforced concrete, to the solution of a purely objective analysis of modern needs.

and later on 'Morphology':

> It would seem that a style is born of the marriage of structural with functional forthrightness. The forms which result are found to be pleasing for their own sake and introduce into the mind of the designer certain considerations or principles which guide him in the realm of pure design after the needs of structure and function have been fulfilled. The stressing of these aspects for their own sake without prejudice to structure or function marks the period of maturity. The period of decadence has been defined as the time of stressing or distorting certain characteristics to a degree of perversity. In any case we are not here concerned with decadence. It must be suggested, however, that the beginning

of the period of maturity has been reached though there is undoubtedly a wealth of development ahead. These distinctions, however suspect they may be in some respects, are useful to us in forming categories of the various subjects to be described in the exhibition and for explaining those values which are beyond pure structure or pure functionalism.

The new style is then described under four headings:

1. Characteristics

1) Steel and reinforced concrete for structural members.
2) Glass, insulators and plastics as sheathing materials.
3) Frame construction with non-bearing walls as the norm.
4) Variations, using bearing or part-bearing walls.
5) Typical span-proportion of steel and reinforced concrete – the result of economic forces restricting the very wide structural possibilities of the material.'
6) The characteristic proportion-module which results and which lends to give a horizontal emphasis to the essential anatomy of the structure and which, if honestly expressed in the facades, gives a horizontal emphasis to the outside appearance of the building.
7) The possible wide openings of all kinds.
8) The cantilever.
9) The hung wall.
10) The resultant possibility of continuous horizontal windows.
11) The use of balconies, flat roofs and roof terraces.
12) Freedom of planning due to frame construction.
13) The use of 'pilotis'.
14) The standardisation of parts.
15) The frequent use and aesthetic validity of machinery as an integral part of the building.
16) Detail, gadgets, lighting fixtures etc, supplying decorative 'spots of emphasis'.
17) The use of sculpture in the round, mural painting and mural photographs for decoration.

2. Principles

1) Functionalism as a state of health – a discipline.
2) The wall as an enclosing shell – which derives from the non-bearing wall of frame construction.
3) The feeling of 'surface tension' which such a wall should have – achieved by keeping projections to a minimum and by placing glass as close to the face of the wall as possible.
4) 'Architecture as volume' as opposed to the conception of 'architecture as mass' which applies to most historical styles.
5) Clear articulation of form and function.
6) Maximum simplicity – the preservation of the bounding edges of large geometric forms.
7) Building to be light and effortless. Should almost have appearance of floating – of being poised, like a soap-bubble.
8) Classic repose – no dramatic effects of movement.
9) The flat roof – for lightness and to preserve clear geometric forms.
10) The principle of regularity. The aesthetic validity of standardisation. Use of the repeat of some structural proportion or standardised feature such as a window which can bind dissimilar elements together in the same way that the stressed tempo binds together contrapuntal music.
11) The use of new synthetic materials for their own sake and in general, the honest use of all suitable materials.
12) The avoidance of brick or anything giving an ashlar effect for wall surfacing as these give an effect of weight.
13) The scientific and sociological approach to all new problems.
14) The use of white and light tones both to add to the effect of weightlessness and to secure maximum of reflected light.

3. Negative principles

1) No conscious striving for symbolism of function.
2) Avoidance of axial symmetry which was an historic device for binding together dissimilar elements having no horizontal emphasis. It is seldom functionally

justifiable and in these days merely looks pretentious.
3) Avoidance of applied architectural ornament. Historically we must go through a period of discipline and let ornament grow naturally – probably out of gadgets – at the moment it is distasteful as it tends to give effect of weight and to break up surfaces of clean cut geometric volumes.
4) Avoidance of stressing any 'movement' in the design not honestly derived from the nature of the structure.

4. Considerations

1) Our central aesthetic credo: That the essential qualities of a work of art lie in the relationship of form to form and of colour to colour. From these the eye, and especially the trained eye, derives its pleasure and all emotion in art must be transmitted through these means.
2) Internationalism. Why the style is international, etc. etc.
3) The search for the 'norm'.
4) Avoidance of stressing any 'movement' in the design achieved by the spectator if he is to understand and enjoy the style.

Obviously there is much to baulk at in this summary. As I said before, I had my misgivings. If the study of philosophy had taught me anything, it was to distrust all ideologies, all all-embracing systems, all belief that human affairs can be explained or governed by logic alone. I did not know enough about architecture to express an opinion about architectural style – so on that theme I kept a low profile as the saying goes. As an engineer I was really a second-class citizen in this context, a fact which I fully accepted. I could be useful, a good midwife in assisting the birth of a new architectural creation, but I was not responsible for the architecture and what we were talking about was the birth of a new architecture. That I had my preference is another matter. I was enthusiastic about some modern buildings and some left me cold, and as time went on it seemed to me that the best got better and the bad got worse and more numerous.

In 1935 Lubetkin and Tecton (and I) won the first prize in a competition for 'working men's flats' sponsored by the Cement Marketing Co. and with the prize money Tecton and I with our wives went to France to see some of the work of Le Corbusier. The Pavillon Suisse was the first I saw, and it really made a deep impression on me. I also admired the Villa at Garches* – although I was not sure I would like to live in it, it was too cold and too public, one would have to be very careful about how to choose and place the furniture, it was an exhibition more than a home, and it obviously would not weather well; the steel was already beginning to rust and the concrete had lost its pristine whiteness. The Salvation Army home for old people did not appeal to me at all, but that may have been because of the foul air inside caused by malfunctioning air-conditioning – one of the much praised innovations. I was glad to get out. Back in London I worked with Wells Coates, [Ernő]Goldfinger, [Cyril] Mardall† (then called Sjøstrøm). Kaufmann‡ (who won an 'honourable mention' in the Cement Marketing competition), [Clive] Entwistle and others on a number of schemes – but it was all a labour of love – no building resulted. Some were published in some articles I wrote for *Architectural Design and Construction* about how to design reinforced concrete structures for buildings, which I hoped would teach architects some basic facts, and also to attract customers, of course. Others were published in *Boxframe Construction*, one of several publications I issued to all and sundry, the later ones dealing mostly with air-raid shelters, a chapter by itself which ought to be told one day as an example of how not to do things.

To MARS I contributed a number of papers and took part in the work of committees. I have counted up to 17 such committees over a certain period. My first paper made it clear that Modern Architectural 'Research' Group was a misnomer, for a dozen or so young architects working a few hours at weekends cannot do scientific research into soundproofing, thermal insulation, etc. without the necessary apparatus and technical expertise. But my proposal to establish architectural research instead met with the probably valid objection that a group of architectural personalities could never be expected to agree on what was the best architectural solution to a problem.

The CIAM Conferences provided a unique opportunity to meet interesting people from all over the world in beautiful surroundings, people who were devoted to architecture, many of them great artists and personalities in their own right, and who, therefore, had some difficulty in agreeing on very much, which led to stimulating discussions. But I did not think much of the manifestos issued at the end which tried to extract some general principles from the welter of discussions. Generality leads often to banality, but to see the work of other groups and have it explained and discussed was certainly useful.

I remember working very hard in a little restaurant in the mountains as a member of 'comité quatre' dealing with structure in architecture under Wells Coates' chairmanship, trying to produce a summary of our week's deliberations. A French engineer, whose name at the moment I have forgotten, but who worked for Corb and was a man of some importance insisted on pushing a super logical and categorical declaration to which Wells and I could not agree. We ended up with a completely banal document which was of no value at all and was never referred to later by anybody – in spite of, or perhaps because of – Wells' considerable skill in manipulating committees. A beautiful afternoon wasted, not for the first or last time.

The work on the MARS exhibition was not wasted, however. That was a really great achievement, I was the 'treasurer' at that time, a job nobody else wanted but which was thought to be suitable for an engineer. I was in fact extremely unsuited for that work, and had no control whatsoever over what Entwistle, Wells and the others spent on the various sections which they designed. They just ordered the general contractors to do this and change that, and we ended up with an enormous deficit and then went to industry begging to be baled out. But it was not enough; in the end the executive committee had to fork out – Max Fry made a great contribution, I remember. He was always one of the most enthusiastic. But that exhibition really made an impact. It showed the sunny side of modern architecture – but it was probably too good to be entirely true.

Another important contribution by MARS was the 'London Plan', but that came later. It was the work mainly of Arthur Korn and Felix Samuely. By that time I was so busy with my own 'shelter' war that I had no time to participate.

The shady side of the Modern Movement was for me represented by the previously quoted 'Modern Style' document. It appalled me, it wasn't functionalism at all, how could the various functions be justified in terms of function? But I must make it clear again that it was not the view of the MARS executive committee or most MARS members. It was more the followers, those who caught the fashion but didn't quite know what to do with it, who caused the quality to deteriorate. If we turn to another contemporary document, the booklet produced for the MARS Exhibition in 1938, we get quite a different picture. There is an extravagant foreword by Bernard Shaw and a very mature and sensible Introduction which actually attacks the idea of a new style. I should like to quote it in full, but here are a few sentences:

The architect who is committed, at the outset, to thinking in terms of a style – that is, of an idiom which is already crystallised and inflexible – is hopelessly shackled.

Modern architecture is not based on the crude assumption that whatever functions best is right. Such an assumption is in any case, meaningless. Architectural design cannot, except in the very simplest cases, be mathematically controlled; it is an affair of infinite adjustment, and unity can only be achieved by sure intuitive judgment on the part of the architect. Calculated structure – i.e. engineering – is only one component in the synthesis which we call Architecture.

This makes sense. But for me there was still something phoney about the whole business. It was a strange situation. Here was a group of people with a romantic attachment to science and technology, to new materials, steel, glass, lightness, air, elegance, speed and power – it was beautiful, it could solve all our problems, bring peace, justice and happiness. One would have thought that they were the scientists, engineers and manufacturers who knew what these materials and scientific methods could do for us, who understood their great potentialities, who were enamoured with the world they themselves had created. Not a bit of it. Engineers and scientists had no part in it. They were admired at a distance. The people who instigated the movement knew next to nothing about science or engineering construction; they were visionaries, artists, social reformers who had never calculated or constructed anything, and followers who were enraptured by the vision. To explain this one must, I think, go back to the time when architects ceased to be 'master builders'. I am not thinking of the Middle Ages, but to the time they ceased to know the nature of their materials and how they were used in building. Turning architecture into a genteel occupation concerned with styles, proportion, grandeur, poetry or what have you, and leaving building to builders, paved the way. But the real body-blow to 'master building' was delivered by the new materials and technology introduced by the industrial revolution. The reaction of architects

---

* A house designed by Le Corbusier for Michael Stein and his wife, Sara, in Garches, in the western suburbs of Paris, and built between 1926 and 1928.
† Of the architectural firm Yorke, Rosenberg and Mardall.
‡ This possibly refers to the English-born American architect Gordon Kaufmann (1888–1949), known for his work on the Hoover Dam.

to this development was the one natural for them – it enabled them to design differently, to make longer spans, to imitate forms and images used by engineers whose achievements were much admired, or by the new movements in the visual arts. I do not want to pontificate about architectural history – I may be wrong – my point is that they did not think it necessary to learn how to build differently, for them designing and building were two different domains. They are not. A design should show how to build so as to fulfil the purpose of building in the best way or to the greatest extent, and this cannot be done without knowing how to build.

It is as if there is a streak of dishonesty running through the architectural profession. They do not face facts, they fake facts.

This is a serious accusation and, of course, it cannot be applied generally, and leaves much out. But the tendency is there. I have been consulted by architects presenting finished designs, but who hadn't yet decided what materials to use – reinforced concrete, aluminium or plastic. And those who design in brick with concrete lintels, plaster the whole thing and paint it white to make it look like a building by Connell Ward & Lucas, and I could mention many more such examples.* I will not talk about the hiring of specialists who make attractive perspectives to confuse prospective clients, or those who enter competitions with striking designs or soaring arches or whatever which could not possibly be built in that form – it may still show, whether they are good architects.

And then there are the Archigram type of fancies – what are they for?† A look into the future? A better way of living? A possible way of building? None of these. I can enjoy Heath Robinson, etc. but Archigram isn't all that funny. But all this is comparatively harmless. It is when their lack of knowledge is allowed to penetrate into their buildings that the harm is done and their reputation is impaired. Perhaps they think it is enough to employ a quantity surveyor. I have nothing against quantity surveyors personally and in many cases they are the most useful members of the design team in the present circumstances. But as I have preached in lectures and articles for 40 years – I am convinced that the whole system as used only in the British Commonwealth is wrong. Costing should be an integral part of designing. It is no use finishing the detail drawings, compiling an absurdly detailed bill of quantities, serving the legal purpose of tying the contractor to an adjustable contract, pricing it without knowing what method of construction is to be used or what the local conditions are – and then finding that the cost is too high and that something must be chopped off. It's wasteful in every way. Costing must act as a check on designing. If something is wrong it is not cured by more costing but by better design. What we need is quality purveyors.

But the system is flourishing – presumably because clients have much more faith in people who are supposed to understand money matters. I know I am sticking my neck out – and may I say here that all I say is off my own bat – but I have done that for 40 years and there is a perfect way of dealing with this sort of thing. Cotton wool! Complete silence and smothering kindness. Engineers have been taught to deal with the forces of nature. You cannot defy the forces of nature, Therefore they have to face facts, and if they know their job, they do. In that respect they have their professional integrity, they are not tempted to cheat.

Architects are dealing with human beings. Human beings are unpredictable, fickle, but also easily bamboozled. But what's wrong with engineers is that they only deal with facts which can be weighed and measured, and simply ignore the others, the intangible, the dreams and visions, delight and despair – all the most important things, in fact. Of course, this again must be taken with more than a grain of salt – I am dealing with caricatures – but they reveal something of the characters of architects and engineers. What we need is a combination of the integrity of the engineer with the vision, sense of beauty and human understanding of the architect. A good architect, that is. Only a few can do the whole thing alone these days, unless it is a very simple job.

But even this may not be enough. Our technology has moved so fast that even engineers don't know how to build. They are specialists. We don't build in the old sense. What happens on the site is preordained, a large technical apparatus takes over. It's in the factories that things really happen and each branch of manufacture contains a world of technical expertise. The capital invested exercises a tyrannical compulsion, innovations cost time and money, inconvenient improvements are suppressed. Computers and machines take command, if used to make things easier instead of better.

Engineers will still be needed, if they toe the line. But will we need architects? My opinion is, that we need what architecture stands for, or should stand for, more than ever. Humanity must win the battle for control. But it will be difficult. Architects need to face the facts of our industrial society – which was in fact the theme of the modern movement. But not by just 'designing' according to their fancy, but by understanding how things are made in our age and in the relevant locality. Their 'design' must be a part of a 'total' design which takes in all the design decisions which are needed for the job. And it must take notice of the repercussions the design has in other spheres, it must be comprehensive, or must at least try to be.

I am on my old hobby horse, teamwork and all that. I am aware that I do not know how to cope with the complexities of the modern world and have nothing to contribute to design in present circumstances, although I may have an inkling of what design is about. When you think of how the enormously complicated and interwoven technical apparatus, allied with the power of high finance, functions according to its own inexorable laws, is there not a danger that it will end up controlling our life? And if we interfere, the complicated nature of the beast will require an enormous bureaucracy which will create havoc and destroy the efficiency of the system. Of course, the problem could be solved, but can we solve it? Are we good enough? But people are changing too. Some like excessive noise, 'happenings' in quick succession, speed, excitement. Some like to be told what to do, others are a law unto themselves. Some like to love, some like to hate. The ingredients in the human cauldron are too numerous to count. I only hope that we need not all become robots to fit in. Although – if that's what people like – why should I?

* Amyas Connell (1901–1980) was a New Zealand architect, influential in introducing the Modernist architectural style into Great Britain. With Basil Ward and Colin Lucas he established the Connell, Ward Lucas architectural practice in 1933. The private house at 66 Frognal Lane, built in 1938, is an important example of the International Style in London.
† Archigram was an avant-garde architectural group formed in the 1960s, based at the Architectural Association in London. It was Futurist in approach, drawing inspiration from technology, suggesting a new reality. Principal members included Peter Cook, Warren Chalk, Ron Herron, Dennis Crompton, Michael Webb and David Greene.

Thinking and Getting Things Done

The following article was published in The Ove Arup Partnership Newsletter *(an internal publication of Ove Arup and Partners) in April 1981, and is accompanied by an introduction from Ove.*

In March 1977 Edward de Bono[*] wrote to a number of people who had made their mark in industry or other practical fields suggesting that they should get together to discuss 'the type of thinking involved in getting things done'. In his view the case for practical thinking had always gone by default although it was the most important type of thinking for the running of society. This resulted in a long series of dinner – or after-dinner discussions at the Athenaeum and at his private apartment in Albany – to which I also was invited – although I had indicated to him that I did not believe that practical thinking was essentially different from other kinds of thinking and I could in any case not see the point of discussing this unless we first agreed on what things we wanted to get done, which would take a lot of doing.

The following is one of my contributions to these discussions which have continued throughout 1978, 1979 and 1980, but which, though very interesting in themselves, have not so far led to any tangible results. That this is now inflicted on readers of the Newsletter *is entirely Peter Hoggett's responsibility.*[†]

Action starts in the brain. Messages go out; we talk, write, move, push or pull, use tools, play games, or whatever.

The brain part of the action can vary from a quick and instinctive impulse to deeply laid plots, plans or designs, schemes for action. On the conscious level this is *thinking*.

The brain of a human being is 'programmed' to think along certain lines, inherited and added to from generation to generation and in the lifetime of the individual. Strange forces, emotions, casual and spiritual desires, logic, ethical concepts, ideas about good and evil – all these can act as motives for or as restraints on action.

So we can say that action involves thinking, and thinking, if actively pursued, is a kind of action.

The success of an action depends on many things:

1) A clear idea of the aim
2) Correct thinking based on correct and relevant data needed to prepare and choose or plan for action, which should take into account all the steps needed to implement it and all the consequences flowing from it
3) A strong will and tenacity in pursuing that aim
4) Ability to influence other people to collaborate and to support the plan – power, money, charisma, charm, tact, ability to present the case, to persuade and deal with people.

1) The first point is the most important and the most difficult one, for we are as a whole fairly good at doing things, but very bad at knowing what to do and collectively we obviously do many things which are completely mad from almost any point of view (wars, atomic bombs, sending sophisticated armaments to primitive people, polluting our own nest, etc.). The trouble is, that we do not agree on what we want, which leads to strife, which could if we don't watch out, lead to ultimate disaster. And secondly we cannot foresee the long-term effects of our actions; we live – relatively speaking – from hand to mouth.

It is obvious, therefore, that we are not just interested in action, which can be good or bad, but in what I may call 'beneficial' action. Beneficial to whom? That is where strife comes in. If I only want to benefit myself, I will have few allies … If I want to benefit my country – that's OK – but other countries might object. The fact is we need to have aims which benefit us without harming others, and preferably which also benefit others. This means that both our aims and our means and all the consequences of our actions must be judged from this standpoint.

2) The second point deals with the thinking required to implement our aim. It must of course be logical and must be based on correct data. But logical thinking alone will not be enough. The relevant data can never be assembled *in toto*, they stretch out indefinitely in all directions. As mentioned, we can only estimate the short-term result of our actions. And more important still, to decide *what* to do next invariably involves value judgements, ethical and aesthetic considerations, and an understanding of human aspirations and behaviours – all of which cannot be logically deduced. We need intuition, and what the Germans call Einfühlung, or what we – at the risk of sounding bombastic – may call love.

Art

When we for instance talk about design – industrial, structural, architectural, sculptural, etc. – we move into the realm of 'Art' at least as an important ingredient. And artistic creation – is that thinking? If so, it is a different kind, where the aim cannot be stated before it has been achieved, And 'Art' in the widest sense is needed in human affairs. But does it lead to action? It seems more likely to prevent or delay action – it is exclusively concerned with the quality of the end-result.

3) The third point is obvious, but will and tenacity presuppose a clear aim – and as we cannot achieve much be action alone, it will not be enough without point 4.

4) Point 4 deals with obtaining agreement on aims. Without that our aim will not be clear, and our will will falter.

We must however strike the right balance between thinking and action. A quick answer may be better than the perfect answer. Perfection takes time. Most designs could be improved, given time, but if time is not available, only a compromise is possible. Politics is the art of the possible!

The natural thinkers tend to strive for perfection, whereas the natural doers act quickly, relying on intuition, and they are the ones who often get most done. But that is not to say that we don't need better thinking. We need it very much. Hence my insistence on the central role of design in construction and industry. It is the key to everything we construct or produce, and it would pay us handsomely to pay more attention to this fact and allocate the time and resources to it which it deserves.

Method of attack

All this does not enable us to define the kind of action which gets things done. If we want to produce a report which will help people to improve their creative thinking we will have to be more specific. It might be possible to produce some useful hints about how to become a good cook, or a good swimmer, or how to organize a building team, or how to be a good chairman. But a general method of practical thinking is something which I,

* Edward de Bono (b.19 May 1933) is a Maltese consultant, inventor and author.
† Peter Hoggett was editor of *The Arup Newsletter*.

at least, am unable to imagine. *It may be worth trying to attack the problem from the other end, the doing end.*

Are there not people, or groups of people, who get things done? Would it be possible to identify them, and then study them? How do they do it, how are they motivated? Do we like their aims, do we like the means they employ, do we like what they achieve?

Recently at the Department of Industry I heard about a survey to find out what makes a good school. They couldn't define what they meant by a good school, but they proceeded on the basis that they all knew a good school when they saw one – an idea with which I have a great deal of sympathy. So they investigated a great many schools – two or three thousand I believe – and selected 50 of them which were deemed to be good. And from these 50 they selected the 10 best, and studied them closely. The result of their investigation can be expressed shortly:

Good schools have good heads!

I suspect, that if we made a similar study of places where things really happened, we would reach a similar result; that it is people that matter. It is the character of the leaders who instigate or inspire action which determines the kind of action we get, and the force with which it is pursued.

If that is true, what can we make of it? How can we find the best leaders and give them freedom to act? They cannot be selected by some democratic procedure. They have selected themselves; they have fought their way to leadership by overcoming obstacles; they are the tough ones. And they are not necessarily the best thinkers. The latter cannot easily be found either, for if they don't have the drive and ambition to push themselves forward they will be ignored.

Further, the very idea of leadership is under attack. We are all supposed to be equal now. Obviously the 'input' of each ought to be adapted to his talents – but the reward could perhaps be equal. But that would require a great change in human nature?

Institutions, organizations, government departments, hospitals, the laws of the country could undoubtedly all be improved, but they must have rules which treat human beings as numbers. And it is the clash between officialdom and individual initiative which produces frustration and lost opportunities.

Even round this table, are we all agreed what we want? The difficult question of what constitutes 'the good life' keeps cropping up.

It is not just efficiency we are after. Efficiency can be bought too dearly, it can easily be combined with inhumanity. Teamwork, smooth collaboration between many individuals is necessary in most cases, but it must be given freely – the discipline must not be based on fear and tyranny.

Good design

If we are talking about production, for instance of making British Industry more competitive, then we must first of all have good design – taking this word in its widest sense – then good management and good labour relations, and the latter will be very difficult to achieve unless we can make the work more interesting, and every member of the team can be made to identify with the result. They must feel that they are helping to create something worthwhile, which they can be proud of.

And if all this can be achieved it may turn out that they cannot compete with other concerns run on much more unscrupulous lines. And one can begin to query the whole basis of our industrial civilization. Is it on the right lines, with the chimera of a continuing rise in productivity and increase in material standards? Do we not produce too many unnecessary things when others lack the essentials? Have we got the right priorities?

And so we can go on. I think it is necessary in a democracy to have a public discussion of all these topics, but we cannot expect to reach a consensus of opinion for the response of each person does not depend so much on logic or reason as on what kind of person he is, his background and previous experience. People are different. It may be that too many are talking too much and doing too little.

But those who hold this view and say so very loudly are not necessarily doing much themselves. The comforts of inaction are just as great, and more real, than the comforts of unreason.

If 'people' are at the centre of all our achievements and all our troubles then the emphasis must be on *education* in all its forms. But who educates the educators?

What I Believe

This document is not dated. It is unclear whether it was ever published. The cover page has the reference 'no. 53. An article written in connection with Mary Spain's interview in March.'*

When I was quite small I was struck by the discrepancy between what people *said* they believed and what they obviously did believe. There were fairy tales which weren't meant to be believed, of course – but which nevertheless had a great emotional impact. But did people really believe in heaven or hell? Then they surely ought to act differently. The stork bringing babies and Father Christmas were obviously not to be believed, but religion, God creating the world in 7 days, the Trinity, the Holy Ghost, that meant something, but what? How could one create something out of nothing, and what was before that? Only grown-ups could understand that, I had to wait.

Living in a big town (Hamburg) I loved the country, especially the animals. I wanted to be a naturalist, an explorer, but most of all I wanted to find out how things worked, what was behind it all. It was a quest for Truth. Truth with a capital T. And parallel with that, there was this business of good and bad. To be truthful was good. But it was difficult to be good, to curb one's temper, to give others what one valued most. And the foundation of ethics – was it just God's will? I felt that if one could imagine that God was evil, I wouldn't like God, I would have my own ideas about what was good. But why? I had to find out.

I found Darwin's *Origins of Species* and *Descent of Man* in the school library (in my Danish boarding school). They had an enormous influence on me. The scientific approach, starting with no preconceived ideas, gradually building up the evidence, applying logic in the process. Science was the search for Truth. But on what was science founded? Even in mathematics you had to start with some dogmas or assumptions. That was where philosophy came in. What was Truth? There was no doubt in my mind, I had first to study philosophy.

---

* Attempts have been made to trace this reference without resolution.

At that time, at the turn of the century, the whole world looked different. One believed in science and enlightenment which would conquer want and evil. The first world war shattered much of that faith.

So for the next three or four years I studied philosophy at the University of Copenhagen. My idea was, that when I had found what was right, wrong, etc., I would proceed to live my life accordingly. Very logical and naïve and also quite conceited.

Needless to say, I did not find absolute Truth anywhere – you don't find that by studying philosophy or anything else. What I did get out of it was a conviction that absolute truth does not exist, it can't be defined, it cannot be understood by any mortal. It is an unending quest, or a figment of the imagination, like infinity of space or time – we can operate with it but it cannot explain the essence of existence, Kant's 'Ding an sich'. Science can do amazing things for us, but it is just a tool, it cannot explain 'God', whatever that means.

And ethics can't be founded on science or logic either. The many attempts to rationalise ethics have failed.

But we have got to live this life. We must know what we live for. A much advertised way to solve this problem is to have 'faith'. But there are so many faiths. My system revolted against having faith in something I couldn't believe in. Mysticism, at that time, did not appeal to me. Now, being completely mystified anyhow, I'm not so sure – anything may be possible, but nothing we can imagine is likely. And that is as far as I can get in the way of believing. All I can do, or rather try to do, is to live in the way that I feel right, without having the assurance that what I think is the only right way to think. And that is difficult enough.

So I quit philosophy and went over to civil engineering. I had to be involved in something. Something practical, creative, away from the study into contact with people. If I had been an artist with a compulsion to paint or compose or write I would have known what to do. In Copenhagen I had experienced the power of music. An Organ Symphony and Fugue by Bach played by a master it builds up, grows, comes together – and you are in heaven! Great Art is intrinsically good, no matter whether you can explain the workings of the universe or solve the social problems. But even on a lower plane whatever you create can give you satisfaction if you have the ability and the will to do it well. I remember at that time thinking about a joiner making tables. A table can be good or bad. It can be strong, durable, practical, well-proportioned, beautiful, etc., or it can lack some of these desirable qualities. A good table gives pride and satisfaction to the maker, his customers are delighted, he is respected by other people, he has friends. It is not the ultimate good, it doesn't solve anything but if you can't solve the metaphysical problems it may help to solve one's private problems to get involved. I was not so sure that I would make a good joiner, I was not sure either, that I had it in me to become a great architect – which I would have liked to be but I knew I could become an engineer and I also knew that this knowledge would come in very useful should I ever be inclined to study architecture as well. It was some such thoughts which led to my choice of engineering.

In the sphere of practical thinking, then, what I believe in is to be involved in what you do, to strive for quality. Otherwise work becomes a burden, when it could be a joy. But when it comes to building, what exactly is quality? That is the problem which is almost as complicated as solving the riddles of the universe. Quality must take into account our reasons for building. It is a composite quality we must seek, the best possible compromise between conflicting aims. We must never forget that we are building for people. And people are fickle and often don't know or don't agree about what they need and what they want.

Inevitably my propensity for 'philosophising' led me further. To know how to build is all very well, but to build what? Which people, what sort of life should we aim for? The way modern sophisticated technology is leading us seems disastrous. Megastructures, mass production, computers and the rest, sending sophisticated weapons to technically primitive people, stockpiling atomic bombs – it is sheer madness. We are the slaves of greed, of money and of the machines we have invented. It is degrading labour, destroying quality and humanity. What can we do to stop it? We are forgetting that people, or human relations, are the most important things in life. A sunny day can be spoiled by a hard word, human kindness, love, can change sorrow into joy. No theory, no ideology, no set of rules can deal with human complexity, human sensitivity or vulnerability. This is something I somehow know, perhaps this is the real truth. But to turn this truth into a precept for living is not easy. Yet this is the essential problem facing mankind. If we can't improve on what we do now, the outlook is grim. I am no expert. Reflection, even understanding, is no substitute for compassion. But you could say perhaps that I believe in trying.

This essay leaves out more than it contains. But it will have to do.

Index

Page numbers in **bold** refer to figures.

aesthetics
 considerations 37–40, 148, 212
 and the engineer 116–21
 modern 46
 pure 47, 52, 194
 standards 37, 39, 43
 see also art; delight
aims and means 11–14, 103, 161–8, 188, 216–18
 aims and values 89
air raid shelters 86–7
Ankobra Bridge, Western Ghana 76–80, **76**, **77**, **78**, **79**
Archigram 214
architects
 and builders **12**, 158–60
 co-operation with allied professions 200–1
 and engineers **12**, 58–63, 88–9, 158–60, 187–8
 human role of 169–73
 see also collaboration
Architects Copartnership (ACP) 193
architecture
 of the 1930s 206–15
 and art 99–107
 current 122–6
 from an engineer's viewpoint 147–50
 and structure 37–8, 42–52
art
 and architecture 38, 99–107, 123, 125, 138, 147, 154
 artistic climate 38
 artistic discipline 93, 105–6
 artistic values 188
 criticism 97, 117, 203
 defined 190, 212
 design as 121, 155, 170, 179, 199, 200, 217, 220
 and engineering 14, 113, 134, 155
 importance of 104
 and science 110, 111, 114
 timeless 35, 203, 220
 see also aesthetics
Arup, Ove
 background and career 10–11, 82–9, 133–46, 207
 images of **8**, **9**, **10**, **14**, **88**
 interviews 82–90, 108–15, 174–6
 Key Speech 11, 12, 161–8
 personal philosophy 83, 89–90, 219–20
 reminiscences 206–15
Arup and Arup Ltd. 86
Arup Associates 106
Arup, philosophy of 161–8

Banham, Reyner 149
Barzun, Jacques 146
Bauhaus 10, 13, 102, 126, 136
beauty 39, 43, 46, 203, 214, 215
 inherent beauty 47
 truth and beauty 83
Black Volta Bridge, Ghana 80–1, **80**, **81**
Bono, Edward de 216

Bossom Lecture, 1970 **12**, 151–60
Brett, Lionel 195
bridges, design of 70–81
 see also individual bridges
Broadcasting House, Copenhagen 23
Brynmawr Rubber Factory 193, **193**
builders, and architects and engineers 158–60
building
 building a better world 172–3
 practice of 27–33
 quality in 91–5, 203–4
 what to build 145
Building Centre, London 202–5
Building Services Engineering Society 182
built environment, the **12**, 182–96

café and shelter, Canvey Island 191, **191**
Candela Outeriño, Félix 63, 86
Centre Pompidou, Paris 11
Chermayeff, Serge 48
Christiani and Nielsen 10, 84–5, 191, 207, 208
CIAM (Congrès Internationaux d'Architecture Moderne) 86, 206, 212–13
civil engineers
 education of 53–7, 60
 role of 29, 32, 59, 130, 149, 155, 166, 172–3, 174
Clacton Pier, model of spiral tower 191–2, **192**
Clapeyron, Emile 23
Coates, Wells 11, 86, 212, 213
Coignet, François 64
collaboration
 and artistic wholeness 159, 162, 187
 between architects and engineers 14, 20, 26, 38, 41, 43, 60–1, 68, 101, 103, 149, 209
 with clients 62, 180
 between engineers and contractors 30, 32, 41, 139, 159
 multidisciplinary 92, 107, 173
 with Ove Arup 11, 86, 102, 111, 113–14
 requirements for successful 43, 59, 61, 185–6, 201
 between specialists 33, 59
 see also Total Architecture; Total Design
College of Physicians, London 103
commodity 34, 35–6, 37, 42, 43, 105, 140, 178–9, 180
composite mind concept 13, 19, 105, 155–7, 204
Connell Ward & Lucas 214
contractors
 collaboration with engineers 30, 32, 41, 139, 159
 and consulting 137–8
 and designers 134–6
 difficulties surrounding 44, 85, 86, 93, 101, 106, 135, 143, 159
 nominating 32–3, 41, 43, 63
 package deals 105, 106, 142, 176, 159, 196
 role of 29, 33, 43, 58, 62, 63, 84, 88, 92, 142, 144, 155, 174, 175

Le Corbusier 10, 11, 38, 40, 49, 86, 126, 136, 137n, 150, 191, 209–12
costing 159, 180–1, 201, 214
costs 23, 35–6, 42, 43, 140, 178–9
Coventry Cathedral **9**, 11, **11**, 47, 68–70, 223
creative design 54, 57, 93, 119, 143, 160, 190
creativity
 in engineers 54, 57, 120, 134, 185
 importance of 38, 90, 114, 158

Darwin, Charles 83, 109, 219
Davies, R.L. 62
De Architectura (Vitruvius) 12, 35n, 147
delight 35–43, 93, 140, 156, 180
Descent of Man, The (Darwin) 83, 219
design
 deficiencies in 142
 defined 152, 177–8
 design-construction gap 158–9
 the design team 194–6
 efficiency in 121, 124, 163, 165, 181, 199
 good practice 119–20, 153–4, 179–80, 180, 189–90, 218
 requirements for integrated 143–5
 see also bridges, design of; creative design; holistic design; Total Design
Dischinger, Dr Franz 26
Donat, John 108–15
Donny-brook Garage, Dublin 33
Drake and Lasdun 48
Drew, Jane 193
Dunican, Peter 6, 7
Duxford 112
Dyckerhoff and Widmann 25

Eames, Charles Ormond 120
economic methods 129
economy of means 35, 37, 43, 156
education, of engineers 53–7, 60
efficiency
 cost-efficiency 178, 181, 189
 in design 121, 124, 163, 165, 181, 199
 formula for measuring 35, 140, 178
 functional 86, 92, 143
 soulless 8, 110, 140, 159, 218
elegance 37, 69, 97–8, 104, 190, 200, 210, 213
Elements of Architecture (Wotton) 34–5
engineering
 advances in 127–9
 and art 14, 113, 134, 155
 and philosophy 10–11
 system engineering 145–6, 171, 189
 value engineering 145–6, 171, 189
engineering structures 154–5
engineers
 and aesthetics 116–21
 and architects **12**, 58–63, 88–9, 158–60, 187–8
 and architecture 147–50
 and builders 158–60
 creativity in 54, 57, 120, 134, 185
 education of 53–7
 production engineers 195
 relationships with architects 88–9

see also civil engineers; collaboration; production engineers; structural engineers; system engineering; value engineering
enthusiasm
  for collaboration 102, 156–7, 166, 167, 180, 196, 201
  importance of 106, 126, 154, 155, 156, 179
  for innovations 10, 39, 61, 126, 136, 149
  unity and 166, 165, 168
Entwistle, Clive 48–9, 212–13
equality of opportunity 167–8
excellence
  all-round 96, 180
  criteria for 145
  formula for 35–6, 178–9
  kinds of 92
  pursuit of 90, 112, 153–4, 162, 171
  standards of 94
  see also quality

Finsbury Health Centre, London 11, 86, 191n
firmness 35, 36, 37, 42, 97, 156, 203
Fisher Cassie, Professor William 54
Freyssinet, Eugène 65, 138
Fry, Maxwell 11, 45, 46, 86, 102, 213
function 37, 51–2, 59, 92, 148, 154, 172, 172–3, 211
functionalism 39–40, 52, 101, 102, 126, 130, 210–11, 213

God 219, 220
Goethe, Johann Wolfgang von 71
Goldfinger, Ernö 11, 98, 212
Gordon, Alex 196
Gropius, Walter 13, 86, 102, 126
Guggenheim Museum, New York 192

Hallfield Estate, Paddington, London 48
Handbuch des Eisenbetonbau (Dischinger) 25
harmony 71, 144, 162, 203–4
Hein, Piet 179, 190
Highpoint flats, Highgate, London 11, 86, 89, 102, 109, 192–3, **193**, 208–9
Hobbs, Ronald 7
holistic design 7, 162, 179, 180, 181, 188
  see also Total Architecture; Total Design
human role of architects 169–73
humanitarianism 162–3

imagination 14, 54, 55, 57, 58, 93, 94, 134, 154, 171, 172, 178
ingenuity 10, 93, 154, 178
innovation 7, 11, 39, 89, 126, 140–1
Institution of Civil Engineers 117n, 118, 130, 182
Institution of Structural Engineers 182, 197–9, **197**
Intentions in Architecture (Norberg-Schulz) 147
intuition 10, 14, 47, 54, 58, 93, 134, 154, 157, 178, 213, 217
intuitive design 59, 67, 71, 118, 155
invention 10, 54, 55, 93, 154, 178

Jenkins, Ronald 6, 7, 23

Kant, Immanuel 7, 83, 134, 189, 220
Kaufmann, [Gordon] 212
Kennedy, Senator Robert F. 145
Key Speech, The 11, 12, 161–8
Kier, J.L. 10, 86, 192, 208
Kingsgate Bridge, Durham 11, 81, **81**, **88**, 89, 113
Korn, Arthur 102, 213
Kresge Auditorium, Massachusetts Institute of Technology 47

Lake Shore Apartments, Chicago 47, 48
Lamé, Gabriel 23
Lasdun, Denys 87, 103
London Zoo, Penguin Pool **10**, 11, 109, 191, 208
Lota 120
Love, A.E.H. 23
Lubetkin, Berthold 11, 86, 87n, 89, 102, 192–4, 208–10, 212

Maillart, Robert 61, 64, 99, 208
Maitland Lecture, 1968 133–46
Manasseh, Leonard 98
Mardall, Cyril 11, 212
MARS (Modern Architectural Research group) 10, 45n, 86, 88n, 102, 136, 206–7, 210, 212, 213
Martin, Leslie 111
mass production 139–41
means *see* aims and means
membrane theory 23, 26, 30
Mendelsohn, Eric 191
Mies van der Rohe, Ludwig 46, 47, 48, 104, 207, 210
Modern Movement 7, 46, 98n, 101, 102, 126, 131, 136, 145, 149, 153, 155, 181, 191, 193n, 206, 213, 215
Monier, Joseph 64
Morandi, Riccardo 99
motivation 185–6

Nervi, Pier Luigi 63, 86, 99, 101
Norberg-Schulz, Christian 147

On the Origin of Species (Darwin) 83, 219
Ove Arup & Partners 11

Pavillon Suisse, Paris 10, 136, 212
Perth Narrows Bridge, Australia 72–4, **72**, **73**
Petersen, Robert Storm 177
philosophy 10, 11, 14, 83, 85, 108, 109, 112, 117–19, 130, 143, 147, 149, 161, 165–6, 207, 212, 219–20
planning
  large-scale 129, 142, 145, 157
  modular 31, 32, 105
  town 89, 92, 112, 145, 155
Pompidou Centre, Paris 11
prefabrication 9, 20, 30, 31–2, 44, 153
production engineers 59, 62, 195

quality
  aesthetic quality 43, 68

architectural quality 38, 43, 61, 86, 120–1
  and education 256
  in building 91–5, 203–4
  in design 155–7, 181
  importance of 159–60, 162
  and judging 59, 71
  and leadership 61
  of staff 163, 165–6, 201
  striving for 86, 112, 123, 140, 156, 158, 178, 190, 220
  see also excellence
quantity surveyors 136, 137, 142–3, 158–9, 175–6, 183, 203

Read, John 108
religion 89, 90, 109, 112, 153, 162, 186, 219
repetition 31, 51, 74, 101, 141
Richards, J.M. 48
Ronan Point, Newham, London 198
Royal Charters 142, 176, 184

Saarinen, Eero 47
safety and cost 36–7
Samuely, Felix 102, 213
school construction 31, 32
science
  and art 110, 111, 114
shelters, designs for 86–7
Sise, Hazen 102, 210
Smith, Donald 96–7
specialization 12–13, 54, 131, 141–2, 149, 150, 188–9
Spence, Sir Basil 11, 47
spiritual needs 114, 117, 123, 189, 216
spiritual quality 152, 153, 155, 156
stability 22, 36, 42, 43, 50, 51
staff, quality of 163, 165–6, 201
Steinberg, Saul 47
Store Street bus terminus, Dublin 26
structural engineers
  role 20, 43, 60, 130, 131, 149
  world of 133–46
structure
  and architecture 42–4, 45–9, 50–2, 154–5
  style 35, 45, 70, 102, 123–4, 148–9, 210–13
Sydney Opera House 9, 11, 89, 113, 119, 193–4, **194**
system engineering 145–6, 171, 189

Tay Bridge, Scotland 74–6, **74**, **75**
teamwork 95, 126, 142–3, 155–7, 215
  see also Total Architecture; Total Design
Tecton 11, 86, 102, 109, 191, 192–3, 208, 209, 210, 212
Theory and Design of Cylindrical Shell Structures (Jenkins) 23
Torroja y Miret, Eduardo 61
Total Architecture 103n, 106, 107, 142, 146, 155–56, 162, 163, 167, 180, 183, 210
Total Design 7, 11, 13, 14, 103, 105, 111, 112, 124–5, 130–1, 140, 143, 152, 153, 171, 178, 180–1, 190, 200–4, 215
Truth 83, 90, 134, 207, 219–20

unity
  architectural 33, 41, 48, 70-1, 131, 213
  and enthusiasm 163, 165, 168
unobtrusiveness 51-2
Utzon, Jørn 11, 113, 114, 193-4

Value
  and culture 117
  and delight 26, 42, 140
value engineering 145-6, 171, 189
value for money 58, 87, 140, 160, 175, 188
value judgements 117, 153, 217
values
  artistic 35, 100, 121, 123-4, 188
  immeasurable 36, 140, 143, 146, 160, 180, 181
  personal 89, 152, 157, 158, 162
Vitruvius 12, 35n, 147

water tower project (unspecified location) 192, **192**
Wilkinson, Ellen 87
Wood, Geoffrey 6
Wotton, Henry 12, 34-5
Wright, Frank Lloyd 46, 102, 192, 210

Yorke, Rosenberg & Mardall 11, 213n

Picture Credits

All images ©Arup, except the following:

Introduction: © Times Newspapers Ltd (p.11), © ICE Publishing (p.12 top), © The Building Services Engineering Society at the Institution of Civil Engineers (p.13).

Permissions for Texts

'Shell Construction'. *Architectural Design*, vol.17, no.11 (November 1947), pp.290-93.
'The Practice of Building'. Lecture given at the South African Concrete Association, 1954. Reprinted with permission of the Cement and Concrete Institute.
'Structural Honesty'. *Irish Architect and Contractor*, vol.4, no.9 (1954), pp.25-30. Pomeroy Press (formerly Fleet Publications).
'Modern Architecture: The Structural Fallacy'. *The Listener*, vol.54, no.1375 (7 July 1955), pp.12-15. Gale Cengage Learning (formerly a BBC publication).
'The Architect and the Engineer'. *ICE Proceedings*, vol.13 (August 1959), pp.499-533. Reprinted with permission of ICE Publishing.
'An Account of Progress in Reinforced Concrete Design'. *Financial Times Survey* (13 November 1961). Reprinted with the permission of Financial Times Ltd.
'Coventry Cathedral: How the Plan Took Shape'. *The Times* supplement (25 May 1962).
'The Design of Bridges'. Part I, *The Arup Newsletter*, no.21 (February 1964), pp.43-53; Part II, *The Arup Newsletter*, no.22 (April 1964), pp.73-80; reprinted in *Arup Journal* (March 2009), pp.4-13.
'Art and Architecture'. *RIBA Journal*, vol.73, no.8 (August 1966), pp.350-59. Reprinted with permission of *RIBA Journal*.
'Builder Extraordinary'. *Builder Extraordinary: Ove Arup*. Directed by John Read. BBC Productions. 52 mins.
'Aesthetics and the Engineer'. *The Surveyor and Municipal Engineer* (3 December 1966), pp.13-15. Reprinted with permission of *Surveyor*.
'Advances in Engineering'. *Financial Times* (11 July 1967), p.19.
'Teams for Total Design'. *The Times* (15 July 1968), supplement on 'Civil Engineers', p.8.
'The World of the Structural Engineer'. Lecture given to the Institution of Structural Engineers at the Queen Elizabeth Concert Hall, London, 14 November 1968. Reprinted with permission of the Institution of Structural Engineers.
'Architects, Engineers and Builders'. Alfred Bossom Lecture, 11 March 1970. Published in the *Journal of the Royal Society of Arts*, vol.118 (June 1970), pp.390-401. Reprinted with permission of the Royal Society of Arts.
'I Am Not a Prophet'. *Contract Journal*, vol.237, no.4761 (29 October 1970), pp.961-2. Formerly Reed Business Information, UK.
'The Architect's Human Role'. *RIBA Journal*, vol.77 (November 1970), pp.524-6.
'Future Problems Facing the Designer'. Royal Society discussion meeting, 'Building Technology in the 1980s'. Paper no.5 (4 November 1971). Permission granted by the Royal Society.
'Institution of Structural Engineers Gold Medal Speech'. 11 October 1973. Reprinted with permission of the Institution of Civil Engineers.
'Co-Operation between Architects and Allied Professions'. Originally published in *Built Environment Quarterly*, vol.1, no.1 (1975). Reprinted with permission of Alexandrine Press (www.alexandrinepress.co.uk). Also published in the *Arup Journal*, vol.10, no.2 (June 1975), p.2.
'The Engineer Looks Back'. *Architectural Review*, vol.166, no.993 (November 1979), pp.315-21. Reprinted with permission of *Architectural Review*.
'Thinking and Getting Things Done'. *Ove Arup Partnership Newsletter*, no.124 (April 1981), pp.1-2.

Acknowledgements

Making a book is like making a building. A large team of people have collaborated with me. I am most grateful for all the generous help and enthusiastic support that I have received from those who got the idea. I should like to express my sincere thanks to Amy Lewis, who has patiently assisted with research and with carefully cataloguing all the material, and whose enthusiasm and warm humour have always kept the project moving forward. My thanks to Denis Kirtley, who designed the draft book, which was instrumental in gathering escape velocity. Gavin Davies arranged the first exciting trip to the archive. Andrew Riley and his staff at the Cambridge Archive made us welcome, and Head Conservator Sarah Lewery assisted us in photographing the works. Stephanie Emmitt, Stuart Nutton and Marlys Bridge in Arup's Information and Library Services tracked down permissions and citations for these historic documents. Thanks to David Brown for sharing insight into his work with Ove, and to Tom Graham, Daniel Imade and Justin Perks for their work on the images, and to Martin Hall for his illustrations in 'Shell Construction'. Thanks to Andrew Sedgwick, who gave considered guidance and encouragement throughout, and to Alan Belfield for his support. Andrew Hansen, Ali Gitlow, Matthew Taylor and the team at Prestel provided the digital transcription and copy-editing. Thanks to Stephen Barrett and Fraser Muggeridge at Fraser Muggeridge studio for making the design – like all design can be – an enjoyable collaboration. I am grateful to Derek Sugden for his recollections of Ove, which brought to life the printed word.

My thanks to Caroline Cole, her family and the Ove Arup Foundation for their consent and authorisation to reproduce this work. All proceeds from the sale of the book go to the independent charity the Ove Arup Foundation, whose mission is to stimulate and educate those working in the built environment (www.ovearupfoundation.org).

© Prestel Verlag
Munich · London · New York, 2012.

© For the text by Sir Ove Arup, Nigel Tonks and Derek Sugden

All rights reserved. No part of this book may be reproduced, stored in a retrieval system or transmitted, in any form or by any means, electronic or mechanic, including photocopying, recording or otherwise without express written permission from the publisher.

Prestel, a member of Verlagsgruppe Random House GmbH

Prestel Verlag
Neumarkter Str.28
81673 Munich
Tel. +49 (0)89 4136-0
Fax. +49 (0)89 4136-2335
www.prestel.de

Prestel Publishing Ltd.
4 Bloomsbury Place
London WC1A 2QA
Tel. +44 (0)20 7323-5004
Fax. +44 (0)20 7637-8004
www.prestel.com

Prestel Publishing
900 Broadway, Suite 603
New York, NY 10003
Tel. +1 (212) 995-2720
Fax. +1 (212) 995-2733
www.prestel.com

Library of Congress Control Number: 2012942092

British Library Cataloguing-in-Publication Data: a catalogue record for this book is available from the British Library.

The Deutsche Nationalbibiothek holds a record of this publication in the Deutsche Nationalbibliografie; detailed bibliographical data can be found under: www.dnb.d-nb.de

Prestel books are available worldwide. Please contact your nearest bookseller or one of the above addresses for information concerning your local distributor.

Editorial direction: Ali Gitlow
Editorial assistance: Francesca Dunnett, Supriya Malik
Production: Friederike Schirge
Design: Fraser Muggeridge studio

Origination:
Reproline Mediateam, Munich
Printing and binding:
TBB, a.s., Banská Bystrica
Printed in Slovakia

Verlagsgruppe Random House
FSC-DEU-0100
The FSC-certified paper Munken Lynx has been supplied by Arctic Paper

ISBN: 978-3-7913-4731-8